Shadows of the Slave

This book is a transnational and comparative study examining the processes that led to the memorialization of slavery and the Atlantic slave trade in the second half of the twentieth century. Araujo explores numerous kinds of initiatives such as monuments, memorials, and museums as well as heritage sites. By connecting different projects developed in various countries and urban centers in Europe, Africa, and the Americas during the last two decades, the author retraces the various stages of the Atlantic slave trade and slavery including the enslavement in Africa, the confinement in slave depots, the Middle Passage, the arrival in the Americas, the daily routines of forced labor, until the fight for emancipation and the abolition of slavery. Relying on a multitude of examples from the United States, Brazil, and the Caribbean, the book discusses how different groups and social actors have competed to occupy the public arena by associating the slave past with other human atrocities, especially the Holocaust. Araujo explores how the populations of African descent, white elites, and national governments, very often pursuing particular political agendas, appropriated the slave past by fighting either to make it visible or to conceal it in the public space of former slave societies.

Ana Lucia Araujo is a Professor in the Department of History at Howard University, Washington, DC. She is the author or editor of six books, including *Public Memory of Slavery: Victims and Perpetrators in the South Atlantic* and *Politics of Memory: Making Slavery Visible in the Public Space*.

Routledge Studies in Cultural History

1 **The Politics of Information in Early Modern Europe**
Edited by Brendan Dooley and Sabrina Baron

2 **The Insanity of Place/The Place of Insanity**
Essays on the History of Psychiatry
Andrew Scull

3 **Film, History, and Cultural Citizenship**
Sites of Production
Edited by Tina Mai Chen and David S. Churchill

4 **Genre and Cinema**
Ireland and Transnationalism
Edited by Brian McIlroy

5 **Histories of Postmodernism**
Edited by Mark Bevir, Jill Hargis, and Sara Rushing

6 **Africa After Modernism**
Transitions in Literature, Media, and Philosophy
Michael Janis

7 **Rethinking Race, Politics, and Poetics**
C.L.R. James' Critique of Modernity
Brett St Louis

8 **Making British Culture**
English Readers and the Scottish Enlightenment, 1740–1830
David Allan

9 **Empires and Boundaries**
Rethinking Race, Class, and Gender in Colonial Settings
Edited by Harald Fischer-Tiné and Susanne Gehrmann

10 **Tobacco in Russian History and Culture**
From the Seventeenth Century to the Present
Edited by Matthew P. Romaniello and Tricia Starks

11 **History of Islam in German Thought**
From Leibniz to Nietzsche
Ian Almond

12 **Israeli-Palestinian Conflict in the Francophone World**
Edited by Nathalie Debrauwere-Miller

13 **History of Participatory Media**
Politics and Publics, 1750–2000
Edited by Anders Ekström Solveig Jülich, Frans Lundgren, and Per Wisselgren

14 **Living in the City**
Urban Institutions in the Low Countries, 1200–2010
Leo Lucassen and Wim Willems

15 **Historical Disasters in Context**
Science, Religion, and Politics
Edited by Andrea Janku, Gerrit J. Schenk, and Franz Mauelshagen

16 **Migration, Ethnicity, and Mental Health**
International Perspectives, 1840–2010
Edited by Angela McCarthy and Catharine Coleborne

17 **Politics of Memory**
Making Slavery Visible in the Public Space
Edited by Ana Lucia Araujo

18 **Neutrality in Twentieth-Century Europe**
Intersections of Science, Culture, and Politics after the First World War
Edited by Rebecka Lettevall, Geert Somsen, and Sven Widmalm

19 **Americans Experience Russia**
Encountering the Enigma, 1917 to the Present
Edited by Choi Chatterjee and Beth Holmgren

20 **A Social History of Disability in the Middle Ages**
Cultural Considerations of Physical Impairment
Irina Metzler

21 **Race, Science, and the Nation**
Reconstructing the Ancient Past in Britain, France and Germany
Chris Manias

22 **Identity, Aesthetics, and Sound in the Fin de Siècle**
Redesigning Perception
Dariusz Gafijczuk

23 **Disease and Crime**
A History of Social Pathologies and the New Politics of Health
Edited by Robert Peckham

24 **Critical Perspectives on Colonialism**
Writing the Empire from Below
Edited by Fiona Paisley and Kirsty Reid

25 **Old World Empires**
Cultures of Power and Governance in Eurasia
Ilhan Niaz

26 **The Afterlife of Used Things**
Recycling in the Long Eighteenth Century
Edited by Ariane Fennetaux, Amélie Junqua, and Sophie Vasset

27 **Holocaust Consciousness in Contemporary Britain**
Andy Pearce

28 **The Invention of Race**
Scientific and Popular Representations
Edited by Nicolas Bancel, Thomas David, and Dominic Thomas

29 **Indigenous Networks**
Mobility, Connections and Exchange
Edited by Jane Carey and Jane Lydon

30 **Shadows of the Slave Past**
Memory, Heritage, and Slavery
Ana Lucia Araujo

Shadows of the Slave Past
Memory, Heritage, and Slavery

Ana Lucia Araujo

Taylor & Francis Group
NEW YORK AND LONDON

First published 2014
by Routledge
711 Third Avenue, New York, NY 10017

and by Routledge
2 Park Square, Milton Park, Abingdon, Oxfordshire OX14 4RN

First issued in paperback 2016

Routledge is an imprint of the Taylor & Francis Group, an informa business

© 2014 Taylor & Francis

The right of Ana Lucia Araujo to be identified as author of this work has been asserted in accordance with sections 77 and 78 of the Copyright, Designs and Patents Act 1988.

All rights reserved. No part of this book may be reprinted or reproduced or utilised in any form or by any electronic, mechanical, or other means, now known or hereafter invented, including photocopying and recording, or in any information storage or retrieval system, without permission in writing from the publishers.

Trademark Notice: Product or corporate names may be trademarks or registered trademarks, and are used only for identification and explanation without intent to infringe.

Library of Congress Cataloging-in-Publication Data
Araujo, Ana Lucia.
  Shadows of the slave past : memory, heritage, and slavery / Ana Lucia Araujo.
    pages cm. — (Routledge studies in cultural history ; 30)
  Includes bibliographical references and index.
  1. Slavery—History. 2. Slave trade—History. 3. Slavery—Atlantic Ocean Region—History. 4. Slave trade—Atlantic Ocean Region—History. 5. Collective memory. I. Title.
  HT867.A73 2014
  306.3'6209—dc23
  2014005750

ISBN: 978-1-138-20072-2 (pbk)
ISBN: 978-0-415-85392-7 (hbk)

Typeset in Sabon
by Apex CoVantage, LLC

For Alain

Contents

List of Figures   xi
Acknowledgments   xv

Introduction   1

1 Tales of Enslavement   15

2 Sites of Deportation   45

3 Places of Disembarkation   76

4 Invisible Sites of Slave Labor   113

5 Great Emancipators   146

6 Iconic Rebels   179

Conclusion   211

Bibliography   216
Index   241

Figures

1.1 *Slavers Revenging Their Losses* (Livingstone and Waller, 1874: facing p. 56). 17
1.2 *Gang of Captives Met at Mbame's on Their Way to Tette* (Livingstone and Livingstone, 1893: 376). 17
1.3 *Trône du roi Glele* (postcard, author's personal collection). 20
1.4 *Hey, white man. One day I will drink from your skull!* (Herzog, 1987/2000). 21
1.5 *Armed Women with the King at Their Head Going to War* (Dalzel, 1793: facing p. 54). 22
1.6 Square Ayidjoso, Abomey, Republic of Benin (photograph by Ana Lucia Araujo, 2005). 23
1.7 Amazon. Ouidah, Republic of Benin (sculpture by Cyprien Tokoudagba; photograph by Ana Lucia Araujo). 25
1.8 *A Son Going to Sell his Mother and His Father* (Taylor, 1820: fig. 24). 31
1.9 *Kidnapping* (Taylor, 1820: fig. 34). 34
1.10 *Esclaves conduits par des marchands* (1780: engraving by Nicolas Delaunay [1739–1792], after Jean-Michel Moreau le Jeune [1741–1814]). 39
1.11 *Nègres de traite en voyage* [Hugo, 1835, vol. 3, 265; drawing by Eugène-Ferdinand Buttura (1812–1852); engraving by Lalement]. 40
2.1 *Une habitation a Gorée (Maison d'Anna Colas)* (1839 lithograph by Adolphe d'Hastrel de Rivedoux). 57
2.2 House of Slaves, Gorée Island (picture by Robin Elaine Taylor, 2004). 58
2.3 Joseph N'Diaye at the House of Slaves (scene from the film *Return to Gorée*). 62
2.4 Schoolchildren visiting the House of Slaves (scene from the film *Return to Gorée*). 62

xii *Figures*

2.5 Drancy, les premiers gratte-ciel de la région parisienne (postcard, author's collection). 66
2.6 Memorial of Drancy Camp (Shelomo Selinger. Drancy, France; picture by Olivier Quéruel, 2011). 68
3.1 *Africans Thrown from Slave Ship* (*Liberator*, 1832). 78
3.2 Slave Ship (Museu AfroBrazil. São Paulo, São Paulo, Brazil; photograph by Nelson Kon, 2011). 83
3.3 *Vicissitudes* (Taylor [website]). 84
3.4 *Débarquement* (Disembarkation) (Rugendas, 1835: 4th issue, plate 2). 87
3.5 African Burial Ground National Monument (Ancestral Chamber's external wall; photograph by Ana Lucia Araujo, 2010). 96
3.6 Memorial of New Blacks (Rio de Janeiro, Brazil; photograph by Halley Pacheco de Oliveira, 2013). 101
3.7 Basement of Mercado Modelo (Salvador, Bahia, Brazil; photograph by Ana Lucia Araujo, 2009). 104
3.8 *Gate and Slave Market at Pernambuco* (drawing by Augustus Earle; engraving by Edward Finden; Graham, 1824: facing p. 107). 106
3.9 *Marché aux nègres* (Slave Market) (Rugendas, 1835: 4th issue, plate 3). 107
4.1 Church Nossa Senhora do Rosário dos Pretos (Our Lady of Rosary of Black Men), Salvador, Bahia, Brazil (photograph by Ana Lucia Araujo, 2009). 118
4.2 Church Nossa Senhora das Dores (Our Lady of Sorrows), Porto Alegre, Rio Grande do Sul, Brazil (photograph by Ana Lucia Araujo, 2011). 120
4.3 *Cristo na coluna* (Christ at the Column). Porto Alegre, Rio Grande do Sul, Brazil (photograph by Ana Lucia Araujo, 2013). 122
4.4 Tambour, Museu do Percurso do Negro (Black's Route Museum), Porto Alegre, Rio Grande do Sul, Brazil (photograph by Ana Lucia Araujo, 2013). 123
4.5 *Feitors corrigeant des nègres* (Overseers Correcting Negroes) (lithograph in Debret, 1834–1839: vol. 2, plate 25). 129
4.6 *L'éxecution de la punition du fouet* and *Nègres au tronco* (The Execution of the Whipping Sentence and Negroes in the Trunk) (lithograph in Debret, 1834–1839: vol. 2, plate 45). 130
4.7 *Punitions publiques sur la Place Ste Anne* (Public Punishments) (lithograph in Rugendas, 1835: plate 15). 131
4.8 Collection of Museu Júlio de Castilhos. Porto Alegre, Rio Grande do Sul, Brazil (photograph by Ana Lucia Araujo, 2009). 132

4.9	Section of Solar do Unhão's *senzala*, Salvador, Bahia (photograph by Ana Lucia Araujo, 2009).	137
4.10	Courtyard of Museu do Escravo. Belo Vale, Minas Gerais, Brazil (photograph by Glauco Umbelino, 2007).	140
5.1	*The First Reading of the Emancipation Proclamation before the Cabinet* (lithograph by Alexander Hay Ritchie, based on the painting by Francis Bicknell Carpenter, 1866).	150
5.2	*Reading the Emancipation Proclamation* (lithograph by J. W. Watte, based on a drawing by H. W. Herrick, 1864).	151
5.3	*Freedom's Memorial* (lithograph by Currier & Ives, c. 1876).	152
5.4	*Revista Illustrada*, July 9 (drawing by Angelo Agostini, 1888).	156
6.1	Monument to the Ghetto Heroes, Warsaw, Poland (2013. © User: Bosyantek/Wikimedia Commons/CC-BY-SA-3.0).	186
6.2	Gaspar Yanga, Yanga, Mexico (2008. Photograph © Erasmo Vazquez Lendechy/CC-BY-SA-3.0).	190
6.3	Monument to Benkos Bioho, San Basilio de Palenque, Colombia (2009. Photograph © User:Wehwalt/Wikimedia Commons/CC-BY-SA-3.0).	197
6.4	Bust Honoring José Leonardo Chirino, Macanillas, Venezuela (2010. Photograph © User: ArwinJ/Wikimedia Commons/CC-BY-SA-3.0).	201
6.5	Monument to Zumbi, Rio de Janeiro, Brazil (2013. Photograph © Halley Pacheco/CC-BY-SA-3.0).	204

Acknowledgments

Many people helped to give birth to this book. Between 2008 and 2011, the Provost Office of Howard University provided me with a generous two-year start-up grant and an additional summer grant that allowed me to conduct archival and fieldwork research and start writing this book. I am particularly grateful to Associate Provost Joseph Reidy and Budget Officer Rohington Tengra for their assistance in obtaining and administrating the grants. The Department of History and the Graduate School of Howard University provided me with three amazing research assistants and promising scholars who helped me during the various stages of the research to complete this book: Alhaji Conteh, Brett Fraser, and Erica Metcalfe. Dr. Edna G. Medford, Chair of the Department of History, was an enthusiastic interlocutor and gave me tremendous support. I am indebted to my Routledge editors, Laura Stearns and Max Novick, who believed in this project since its beginning and who greatly supported me during the long process of completing this book. I am also grateful to Stacy Noto and Jennifer Morrow for their assistance in completing all the stages needed to finalize the book manuscript.

David Lowenthal read the entire manuscript and provided criticism, comments, and detailed suggestions that contributed to improve the book overall. I am greatly indebted to him. My colleague Jeffrey Kerr-Ritchie also read the full manuscript. His comments were very useful to strengthen my argument in the various chapters. I also thank the anonymous reviewers for their comments, which also allowed me to improve the book project. I received insightful comments by various colleagues. Mariana P. Candido, Cristiane Smith, and Jonathan Wiesen read different chapters of the book, and their suggestions were much appreciated. Several colleagues and friends on three different continents helped me by patiently answering my numerous questions via e-mail or in person. I thank Diane Barnes, Hebe Mattos, Martha Abreu, Jean-Michel Mabeko Tali, J. Cameron Monroe, Suzanne Preston Blier, Laura Mann, João José Reis, Daryle Williams, Bryan McCann, Robert Slenes, Mariza de Carvalho Soares, Christina Sue, Marcus Carvalho, Celso T. Castilho, Joseph Adande, Jerome Handler, Maria Helena T. Machado, Raquel Pinheiro Loureiro, and Manuel Barcia. I am especially indebted to all the artists, photographers, and museum curators around the world who generously allowed me to use pictures of their works and museum exhibitions. Olivier Quéruel gave me permission to use his beautiful picture of the Memorial of Drancy Camp (France), and Robin Elaine Taylor allowed me to use her picture of the House of Slaves in Gorée Island (Senegal). I am grateful to Jason DeCaires Taylor, who allowed me to use his photograph of his amazing set of underwater sculptures *Vicissitudes* (Grenada) and Glauco Umbelino, who authorized me to use his photograph of Museu do Escravo in Belo Vale, Minas Gerais (Brazil). Halley Pacheco de Oliveira and Merced Guimarães (Instituto de Pesquisa Pretos Novos) also gave me permission to use the photograph of the Memorial of New Blacks in Rio de Janeiro (Brazil). Finally, I am indebted to Ana Lúcia Lopes, curator of the Museu AfroBrasil in São Paulo (Brazil), for allowing me to use Nelson Kon's photograph of the slave ship displayed in the museum. I also thank the Museu Júlio de Castilhos for granting permission for the use of the numerous pictures I took of its collections and exhibition in 2009.

Different versions of the chapters of this book were presented in several conferences, workshops, and seminars in the United States, Brazil, and the United Kingdom. I am indebted to Eduardo França Paiva who invited me to give a seminar at Universidade Federal de Minas Gerais in 2009. During my short time in Minas Gerais, I was not only able to discuss my research with an enthusiastic group of students but also to visit a number of slavery heritage sites. I am also grateful to Karl Monsma and Regina Xavier for the invitation to talk about this project at the University Federal do Rio Grande do Sul (Porto Alegre, Brazil) in 2011. The participants of the conference Slavery and its Aftermath in the Atlantic World: An International Symposium, held at the University of Illinois Chicago (Chicago, 2012); the CLACS Colloquium at New York University (New York, 2012); and the Workshop Utopian Archives (Norwich, UK, 2013) provided me with provoking comments. I thank Barbara Ransby (University of Illinois, Chicago), Sarah Sarzynski (Claremont McKenna College), and Ferdinand De Jong (University of East Anglia) for inviting me to present my work in these conferences. Chapter 2 was also presented in the Consultation on African-American Studies Outreach led by the Center for Advanced Holocaust Studies United States Holocaust Memorial Museum and Harvard University in 2012; my thanks go to Atina Grossman and Krista Hegburg for the invitation to participate in this event. In addition, I presented a section of Chapter 3 at the conference Dialogues on Historical Justice and Memory Network organized by the Institute for the Study of Human Rights at Columbia University (New York, 2013). Moreover, versions of the first and second chapters were presented in the annual conferences of the American Historical Association, African Studies Association, and Latin American Studies Association between 2011 and 2013. On these occasions, I received fruitful and generous comments from Martin Klein, Clifton Crais, and Robert Slenes.

The support of my parents was precious. They welcomed me in Porto Alegre and patiently accepted my absences during the time I was conducting research. I thank the support of colleagues and friends in Salvador, Minas Gerais, and Rio de Janeiro, especially my friend and colleague Lisa Earl Castillo, who was always a patient interlocutor. Also in Bahia, I thank the members of the Church of Our Lady of Rosary of Black Men and the staff of Museu da Cidade in Pelourinho. In Porto Alegre and London, the staff members of Museu Júlio de Castilhos and the Museum of London Docklands were extremely helpful as well. My lovely husband, Alain Bélanger, was my biggest supporter in achieving this project. Over the last 16 years, he has been my greatest interlocutor, following my work step by step and encouraging and supporting me with love and kindness, despite my absences. This book could not exist without him.

Introduction

After the end of the Second World War, the heritage of the Atlantic slave trade and slavery slowly started occupying the public spaces of former West African ports. Unlike Europe and the Americas, where the past use of former slave trade sites frequently remained concealed from the public gaze, the present-day local populations of former slave ports in West Africa, such as Cacheu, Saint-Louis, Cape Coast, Ouidah, and Badagry, are conscious of the slave trade activities undertaken in the coastal areas of these regions. Introduced by French and English colonial authorities and then continued by the governments of newly independent African countries, numerous initiatives attempted to preserve slavery heritage sites and buildings, including royal palaces, castles, and fortresses that until the early nineteenth century served as slave depots to export Africans to the Americas.

When various projects to commemorate the Atlantic slave trade and slavery emerged in the early 1990s, one of the major issues at stake was how to reveal the multiple dimensions of the slave experience. This task was not an easy one. In addition to the Atlantic slave trade that gradually started at the end of the fifteenth century, it was necessary to address the issue of the slave trade on African soil that provided captives for the internal African market and also the Muslim slave trade, which intensified in the eighteenth century and lasted until the end of the nineteenth century, providing slaves to the Middle East, North Africa, and Northeast Africa. Yet the various initiatives developed in West Africa only emphasized the Atlantic slave trade, which not only was the largest forced oceanic migration, estimated at about 12.5 million African individuals, but also involved Africa, Europe, and the Americas.[1] Therefore, the interpretation of existing slave trade heritage sites and the creation of monuments and memorials initiated by local governments, international agencies like UNESCO, and nongovernmental organizations were intended to show the Atlantic journeys of enslaved Africans and highlight the perspective of the victims who were captured, sold, and sent into slavery in the Americas. This is not to state that enslavement and the slave trade were always depicted and reenacted from the point of view of the victims but rather that enslaved men and women were placed at the center of the narratives presented in the public sphere.[2] As a result, in West

African countries like Senegal, Ghana, and Republic of Benin, newly built monuments, memorials, and museum exhibitions, as well as the ways in which heritage sites were interpreted for public audiences, tended to emphasize victimhood. However, as David Lowenthal demonstrates, this modern victimhood has not emerged with the memorialization of slavery but rather is indebted to the public memory of the Holocaust.[3] Moreover, especially in the West African context, it is a difficult task to "disentangle descendants of victims from those of victimizers."[4] Therefore, former West African slave ports became the playground for all sorts of experimentation projects aimed at commemorating slavery and the Atlantic slave trade. Still, these initiatives are often intended to develop cultural tourism and not necessarily to promote awareness and collective healing of the wounds of the slave past whose shadows remain present in several Atlantic societies. In addition, unlike the creators of public monuments and memorials honoring the victims of other human atrocities like the Holocaust, the various social actors involved in the debates and the projects aimed at developing public initiatives to commemorate the Atlantic slave trade in West Africa and Europe were not victims or witnesses of enslavement and deportation. Although the context of emergence of these projects differed from one another, in the two continents the creation of monuments, memorials, and museum exhibitions had to rely on imaginative evidence rather than on firsthand testimonies. Consequently, most of these enterprises combined the use of visual images of European travel accounts and slave narratives in order to portray the various stages of the Atlantic slave trade and represent the context of slave labor in the Americas. Yet, as I argue in this book, the use of these images still presents several challenges because these renderings largely rely on European interpretations that emerged with the British abolitionist movement during the late eighteenth and the early nineteenth centuries.

Most visible projects memorializing the Atlantic slave trade started in West Africa during the 1990s, but in the first decade of the twenty-first century, this wave was already widespread in Europe, especially in England, and in the Americas, particularly in the Caribbean, and then in the United States, where a very few public sites timidly highlight the country's slave past. Already in 1989, Nobel Prize winner Toni Morrison declared, in a famous interview, that considering the absence of historical markers in the public space to remember slavery, her book *Beloved* (1987) was a site of the memory of slavery:

> There is no place you or I can go, to think about or not think about, to summon the presences of, or recollect the absences of slaves . . . There is no suitable memorial, or plaque, or wreath, or wall, or park, or skyscraper lobby. There's no 300-foot tower, there's no small bench by the road. There is not even a tree scored, an initial that I can visit or you can visit in Charleston or Savannah or New York or Providence or better still on the banks of the Mississippi. And because such a place doesn't exist . . . the book had to.[5]

Despite the overall lack of public official markers memorializing slavery in the public spaces of the United States and Brazil, starting in the 1990s, a small number of monuments, memorials, and museum exhibitions were gradually unveiled. In these two countries, this interest in the Atlantic slave past was favored because of the new context that emerged with the end of the Cold War, which benefited the assertion of national identities and collective identities of historically oppressed groups. Moreover, the 500th anniversary of the arrival of Columbus in the Americas sparked the discussion of the crucial role of the Atlantic slave trade in the construction of the American continent. Additionally, in a nation like Brazil, the end of the Cold War was intertwined with the end of the military dictatorship that ruled the country from 1964 to 1985. With the conclusion of the military regime, Afro-Brazilian activism resurfaced in the public space, demanding affirmative actions and calling for the official recognition of the role played by black historical actors in the construction of the nation. This dynamic climate was accompanied by international initiatives, especially The Slave Route Project launched by UNESCO in 1994. Although the impact of the project was not very visible in the United States and Brazil, its influence was clear in West Africa and the Caribbean, with the development of cultural tourism projects highlighting the Atlantic slave trade as well as the creation of monuments, memorials, museum exhibitions, festivals, and academic conferences. During this period, among the first projects highlighting the US slave past was the traveling exhibit *Back of the Big House: The Architecture of Plantation Slavery*, based on a companion book carrying the same title.[6] After being shown in Baton Rouge (Louisiana), Knoxville (Tennessee), Columbia (South Carolina), and Fayetteville (Arkansas), the exhibit was opened to the public at the Library of Congress (Washington, DC) on December 16, 1995. Still, following protests by African American and white members of the library's staff who felt offended, the exhibit was closed just some hours after its opening. For some individuals, the exhibit's focus on slave quarters somewhat justified the institution; for others, showcasing the architecture of slave cabins highlighted the submissive dimension of slave labor. At this point, the national capital was not ready to address its slave past in one of its most iconic buildings. After the incident, the exhibit was reopened in the Martin Luther King Jr. Library and then traveled to other US cities, including Easton (Maryland), Huntsville (Texas), and Richmond (Virginia), where it was well received.[7] Although the controversy surrounding the exhibition was a local incident associated with the particular context of the US national capital, where African Americans compose more than 50 percent of the population, the episode reveals the challenges to representing slavery in the public sphere, in a country whose legacy of this painful past is still so visibly present. In this context, it was easier to remove the problem from the public sight than to face the sensitive issue of slavery and promote a public debate on how slavery should be represented.

Despite the controversies, other initiatives slowly emerged around the United States but very often far from Washington, DC. Contrasting this lack of recognition are former British slave ports like Bristol and Liverpool that since the 1990s have been pioneers in publicly acknowledging their involvement in the Atlantic slave trade, through the development of exhibitions and heritage trails highlighting areas of the city and the public buildings associated with the trade.[8] In the next decade, the creation of monuments, memorials, exhibits, and especially the unveiling of the International Slavery Museum, was sped up in 2007 by the commemoration activities of the bicentennial of the British abolition of the slave trade.[9] These numerous ventures also derived from the necessity to respond to the demands of the British populations of African descent. Likewise, but at slower pace, slavery also started gaining public attention in France during the commemoration activities of the 150th anniversary of the second abolition of slavery in the French colonies in 1998. Nevertheless, as Charles Forsdick notes, these first French initiatives were not intended to memorialize slavery and highlight past wrongs but rather to emphasize the process of abolition, very often celebrating white emancipators like Victor Schoelcher.[10] Over time, these celebratory national narratives were highly contested by some scholars and the leaders of various French communities of African descent. Eventually, the French government had to respond to the demands of these social actors by publicly recognizing that slavery was a crucial chapter of its national history encompassing not only the French Caribbean but also continental France. On May 2001, the French Parliament passed Law number 2001–434 (the Taubira Law) that recognized slavery and the slave trade as crimes against humanity. The passing of the law did not put an end to the public debate regarding France's slave past, and social unrest resurfaced in 2005, eventually leading to the creation of the Committee for the Memory of Slavery and the establishment of May 10 as an official national day of commemoration of the abolition of slavery in Metropolitan France.[11]

Notwithstanding their modest economic means in comparison to the United States, several Caribbean countries initiated projects in recent decades to develop public initiatives commemorating the Atlantic slave trade. These projects gained visibility especially during the 1960s during the Cold War and on the eve of the independence of several of these countries. Most initiatives inspired by the anticolonial movements, were fueled by the action of organized groups supported by local governments seeking to assert their position vis-à-vis the former colonial powers and US influence in the region. As a result, several monuments in countries like Haiti, Barbados, Jamaica, and Cuba highlighted the enslaved and freed individuals who fought against slavery. Eventually, since the 1990s, following the orientation of UNESCO's Slave Route Project, new projects commemorating slavery and the Atlantic slave trade were developed in Latin American and Caribbean countries, including Guyana and Venezuela.[12]

As in the United States, the memorialization of slavery in Brazil faced several challenges. During the 1960s, African cultural heritage gained importance in certain Brazilian states, especially in Bahia and Rio de Janeiro, although this trend was limited by the military dictatorship that took control of the country in 1964.[13] Restricted to particular regions and occasions, especially in religious festivals and during the period of Carnival, the celebration of African roots was not combined with the construction of public monuments, memorials, and museums honoring the victims of the Atlantic slave trade.[14] After the end of the dictatorship in 1985 and the gradual reemergence of the black movement, the first public monuments honoring Zumbi (the leader of Palmares Quilombo, the country's largest and longest-lasting runaway slave community) were unveiled in various Brazilian cities. Starting in the 1990s, following the international interest in issues regarding slavery and responding to the actions of Afro-Brazilian organized groups, Brazil eventually began addressing its slave past in the public sphere.

Unlike Britain, the commemoration in 2008 of the bicentennial of the US abolition of the slave trade was rather discreet. This situation changed with the election of Barack Obama as president of the United States. Hence, the country's slave past finally started gaining greater visibility in the public sphere. During his presidential campaign, in a speech delivered in a public meeting in Berlin, Barack Obama referred to his Kenyan grandfather as an heir of European colonization in Africa: "my father grew up herding goats in Kenya. His father—my grandfather—was a cook, a domestic servant to the British."[15] In another speech, he also evoked the slave ancestry of his wife Michelle Obama, whose great-grandfather, born in 1850, was enslaved in a rice plantation in South Carolina until the Civil War: "I am married to a black American who carries within her the blood of slaves and slave owners."[16] Despite not addressing the present conditions of racial and social exclusion of the African American population, Obama evoked slavery to recall the multiracial background of his family, an issue that four years later was again underscored with the publication of a book retracing the origins of Michelle Obama's enslaved and white ancestors.[17]

Obama's election in 2008 had a major impact in promoting the history of US slavery and African American history. The same year of his election, the US Capitol building gained a new Visitor Center, including a large new exhibition room. Named Emancipation Hall, the new structure is intended to finally recognize the contribution of African Americans to the building of the United States. Since 2008, three statues honoring Sojourner Truth, Rosa Parks, and Frederick Douglass were placed in the Capitol. Moreover, as the first black US president, Obama's election transcended the national level, giving hope to the peoples of African descent worldwide. Nevertheless, over the past four years, the possibility of creating a slavery museum in the United States in the National Mall in Washington, DC, is still far from being accomplished due to a lack of financial and political support. Some social actors still believe that displaying images of slavery in public spaces might have a negative impact on African Americans' self-esteem, whereas other individuals consider slavery an issue of the past that should not be highlighted in the National Mall, close to other memorials and monuments that celebrate the nation.

Though there has been reluctance in highlighting the US slave past in the public space, the commemoration of the leaders of the Civil Rights Movement has been more positively received. In 2011, a memorial paying homage to Martin Luther King Jr. was eventually unveiled in West Potomac Park, in Washington DC. The installation resulted from a resolution that was passed in the Senate and the House of Representatives in 1996 and signed by President Bill Clinton in 1998. Placed on the shore of the Tidal Basin, across from the Thomas Jefferson Memorial, the memorial is also located some steps from the Franklin Delano Roosevelt Memorial and about a third of a mile from the Lincoln Memorial, where Martin Luther King Jr. delivered his famous speech, "I Have a Dream," in 1963. In addition, in February 2012, the construction of the National Museum of African American History began in the National Mall, marking the long process that is gradually recognizing the importance of black history in the US national narrative. Although not exclusively dedicated to slavery, the new institution, scheduled to be opened in 2015, will highlight the history of the Atlantic slave trade and slavery not only in the United States but also in other countries of the Americas.

Until recently, some European nations like Spain and Portugal clearly avoided publicly acknowledging their involvement in the Atlantic slave trade, even though the marks of their slave past are identifiable in some permanent museum exhibitions and heritage sites across the two countries. Portugal, which along with Brazil, was one of the countries that transported more than 5 million Africans to the Brazilian ports, the largest number in the continent, has not developed public memorials to acknowledge its participation in the Atlantic slave trade. Indeed, in recent years, the country seemed to be working in the opposite direction. In 2009, the government of Portugal, with the support of several institutions, including the University of Coimbra, launched a contest to choose "The Seven Portuguese Wonders in the World," which included the Elmina Castle in Ghana, a slave trade depot, the Cidade Velha of Ribeira Grande on Santiago Island, Cape Verde, as well as Luanda and Mozambique islands. By referring to these colonial and slave trade sites as "wonders," the contest totally ignored the importance of these sites in the Atlantic slave trade. This was highly contested by some academics in Portugal but especially by scholars based in France and the United States, who wrote a petition denouncing the contest. Despite the controversy, the discussion of the legacies of slavery in Portugal and consequently of colonization remains far behind other countries.[18] In contrast with Portugal, on February 17, 2010, Spain's Comisión de Igualdad (Equality Commission) agreed to approve two laws: the "Project of law regarding the recognition of the Spanish black community" and the "Project of law about the memory of slavery, recognition, and support of black, African, and African descent communities of Spain."[19] The text of the two laws proposed to pay homage to the millions of individuals who fought to abolish slavery in the world, to officially recognize the black population of Spain, to fight racism and xenophobia, and to erect a monument in the memory of the victims of slavery.[20]

Much like Portugal, the issue of the slave past has been hardly addressed in West Central African former slave ports and former Portuguese colonies such as Luanda, Benguela, Loango, and Cabinda. Yet, unlike Ghana, Senegal, and Benin in West Africa, because of the particular context of the long colonial rule and the civil wars that ravaged the region, very few public endeavors underscored the Atlantic slave trade in the territory. In recent years, no new public monuments or memorials paying homage to the victims of the slave trade were unveiled in the region except for the Museu Nacional da Escravatura (National Museum of Slavery). Created in 1977 by the National Institute of Cultural Heritage, this small museum housed in a chapel situated 15 miles from Luanda was reopened in 1997 as part of the wave of the initiatives developed by UNESCO's Slave Route Project. Although it was Africa's largest slave port during the Atlantic slave trade, Luanda, unlike Elmina, Cape Coast, Ouidah, and Gorée Island, is not among the main tourist destinations in West Africa and West Central Africa.[21]

This book is a transnational and comparative study examining the processes that led to the memorialization of slavery and the Atlantic slave trade in the second half of the twentieth century. I explore numerous kinds of initiatives such as monuments, memorials, and museums, as well as heritage sites. By connecting projects developed in various countries and urban centers in Europe, Africa, and the Americas during the last two decades, I retrace the different stages of the Atlantic slave trade and slavery including the enslavement in Africa, the process of confinement in slave depots, the Middle Passage, the arrival in the Americas, the daily life of forced labor, and the fight for emancipation and the abolition of slavery. Relying on a variety of examples from the United States, Brazil, and the Caribbean, I discuss how groups and social actors have competed to occupy the public arena by associating the slave past with other human atrocities, especially the Holocaust. I look at how populations of African descent, white elites, and national governments, very often implementing particular political agendas, appropriated the slave past by fighting to make it visible in the public space of former slave societies—or conceal it.

Although the collective memory of slavery embraces nondiscursive forms, this book focuses on how different groups and social actors, engaged in asserting a particular identity of descendants of enslaved Africans, appropriate the slave past. I argue that once this past is appropriated, these groups, fighting to occupy the public space, invest it with a multitude of visual images as well as oral and written narratives from different time periods and places.[22] In dialogue with the works of Rosalind Shaw and Michael Rothberg, in this book memory is conceived not as a unilineal process but rather as a multidirectional and dynamic activity, involving different places and times.[23]

My analysis shows that the past of slavery and the Atlantic slave trade is characterized by gaps and interruptions. Even though this traumatic past has been silenced and concealed, lasting recent years it has been reinterpreted and recycled, gradually reemerging in the public sphere in the form of physical markers, like monuments, memorials, museums, and heritage sites, which are intended to be permanent.[24] Yet this aspired permanent position is in contradiction with the identity dimension of public memory carried out by individuals and groups who address not past events but their present aspirations. The analysis of several ventures commemorating slavery and the Atlantic slave trade reveal three different categories of initiatives. In the first category are the slave trade heritage sites. In Laurajane Smith's work, heritage, like memory, is conceived not only as something belonging to the past but also as an engaging process that gives meaning to things in the present. I show that the idea of authenticity that derives from what Smith calls "authorized heritage discourse" is not always emphasized in the promotion and interpretation of slave trade heritage sites.[25] Consequently, a heritage site is rather a place that, according to hegemonic discourses, is officially recognized locally and internationally as having had a significant role during the period of the Atlantic slave trade and slavery.[26] Yet this category also encompasses sites that are not yet formally acknowledged and promoted as heritage sites, as well as contested sites whose roles played in the Atlantic slave trade have been questioned in public debates led by historians and archaeologists. The second category of projects discussed in this book includes monuments and memorials constructed by the initiative of local groups or commissioned by national governments. This kind of venture clearly conveys the competition of varied and sometimes opposed visions regarding the slave past. Whereas white elite groups tend to promote the commemoration of Great Emancipators, although sometimes receiving the support of populations of African descent, black organizations and governments of countries whose populations are predominantly black tend to sponsor public projects celebrating freedom fighters. The third type of initiative explored in this book includes the few museum and museum exhibitions representing slavery and the Atlantic slave trade. In some countries like the United States and the United Kingdom, the development of this kind of project is rather associated with the discipline of public history. With the advice of scholars and museum professionals, these initiatives are intended to convey, update, and redress a national (and usually official) discourse about the slave past. Yet modest museums and poorly conceived exhibitions in countries like Brazil barely evoke slavery and usually prevail by portraying it as a benevolent institution. Overall, by examining these memorialization projects that are intended to engage with the painful and traumatic slave past, this book shows that, because dissenting positions regarding this past prevail among the several social actors that lead these initiatives, most of these ventures are not successful in presenting the complex and multidimensional history of slavery and the Atlantic slave trade. Once one group succeeds in making its own particular perspective on the slave trade and slavery visible in the public space, the perspectives of other groups are excluded. This dynamic hinders the emergence of possible initiatives that could more effectively address and perhaps contribute to healing the wounds of the past. It also indicates how the legacies of slavery, including racism and racial inequalities, remain significant problems in former slave societies.

Although during the last ten years several scholars have examined the debates that led to the memorialization of slavery in different contexts, most of these works have focused on West Africa, England, and the French Caribbean.[27] Among the very few books that focused on the United States, most studies examined slavery from the public history perspective but have not addressed the problem of public memory, namely, how particular social actors and groups engaged with the process of memorializing the Atlantic slave trade and slavery.[28] Moreover, despite its crucial role as a slave society in the Americas, none of these scholarly works addressed the memorialization in Brazil. Perhaps the only exception is Marcus Wood's recent book *Black Milk: Imagining Slavery in the Visual Cultures of Brazil and America*. Yet, except for one chapter, the main focus of this work is on the nineteenth-century visual cultures in both countries. In addition to not engaging with Brazilian primary and secondary sources, Wood's examination of the Brazilian case presents a number of inaccuracies, making his analysis problematic.[29]

This book is divided into six chapters. Chapter 1, "Tales of Enslavement," discusses how visual and written accounts from the eighteenth and nineteenth centuries depict the process of enslavement on African soil during the Atlantic slave trade. Through the comparison of visual images and written narratives representing enslavement in Africa produced by European and West African historical actors, I examine the various depictions of enslaver West African elites and intermediaries, as well as slave merchants and enslaved individuals. Mainly intended to disseminate British abolitionist propaganda, these renderings are characterized by two main features. First, by eliminating warfare and emphasizing individual abductions led by Europeans and not by Africans, these images underscore African victimhood. Second, whereas these visual and written representations show the processes of enslavement in West Africa, they exclude West Central Africa, a region that provided the great majority of captives to the Atlantic slave trade but where the British presence was not significant. I argue that the impact of these portrayals is still present in the way the history of enslavement is conveyed today in public initiatives, including monuments and museum exhibitions, by revealing the difficulties in representing a sensitive past whose legacies remain alive in former slave societies. I show that by failing to provide a complex portrait of African and European interactions, these recycled images, which were originally intended to promote British abolitionist ideas, are now aimed at responding to the demands of present-day black audiences. Consequently, they continue to place the populations of African descent in a position of absolute submission, denying them any kind of agency.

Chapter 2, "Sites of Deportation," examines the second stage of the Atlantic slave trade, when Africans were confined in slave depots before their deportation to the Americas. I discuss how the deportation of Africans is memorialized in heritage sites located in former West African slave ports, including present-day Senegal, Ghana, and Republic of Benin. I look at how the public memory of the Atlantic slave trade is constantly associated with representations of the Holocaust by the social actors who visit West African heritage sites of deportation. Relying on Michael Rothberg's idea of multidirectional memory, the chapter discusses the former slave port of Gorée Island (Senegal) and its controversial *Maison des esclaves* (House of Slaves) by exploring the recent twinning initiative connecting the island and the Drancy concentration camp, the most important of French Holocaust heritage sites. Through the analysis of these various examples, I show how official initiatives or individual social actors have consistently established fruitful and sometimes intriguing dialogues between these sites and the heritage sites of the Holocaust, including Dachau, Buchenwald, Auschwitz, and Drancy. Such constructed relations can be understood as the expression of a context of memories in competition inasmuch as they possibly mitigate the particularities of each of these atrocities. However, in times when the victims and witnesses of the horrors of slavery are silenced, the constant references to the Holocaust in public discourses about the Atlantic slave trade can also be understood as a way to legitimize the memorialization of slavery, which is far from being recognized in the public landscape of former slave ports. Yet, although these slave trade sites were successful in obtaining international and official recognition, they are paradoxically based on imagined accounts and not on historical evidence.

In the third chapter, "Places of Disembarkation," I look at how the experiences of deportation from Africa, the Middle Passage, and the arrival in the Americas were memorialized in museum exhibitions and heritage sites in Brazil and the United States. I argue that sites of the disembarkation of enslaved Africans remained concealed in the urban areas of the former slave trade ports of Rio de Janeiro, Salvador, Recife, Jamestown, New York, and Charleston. This context started to change only in the early 1990s, a period of great transformations both in Brazil, with the end of the military dictatorship, and in the United States, with the end of the Cold War. As the two countries opened themselves to global exchanges, black activists could finally occupy the public arena to assert their identities and to address the wrongs of the past. In Brazil, to face the invisibility of actual heritage sites where slaves were disembarked, the local population created stories that allow the reenacting of the painful past of the Atlantic slave trade, a phenomenon I call memory replacement. But both in Brazil and the United States, unexpected events have led to the discovery of slave wharfs and slave cemeteries, forcing public authorities to officially acknowledge and create permanent markers to commemorate the slave past of cities like Rio de Janeiro and New York City. Gradually, black social actors, usually supported by scholars who provide their expertise to the study of the newly uncovered wharfs and burial grounds, are forcing the governments of Brazil and the United States to officially recognize the Atlantic slave trade as a central element of an uncomfortable chapter in the histories of the two countries.

Chapter 4, "Invisible Sites of Slave Labor," explores the places where enslaved men and women performed their work activities. I examine how slavery is incorporated or neglected in the public space in the United States and Brazil. In the United States, the public presentation of slavery heritage sites very often omits slaves' daily lives to emphasize the lifestyles of slave owners. In Brazil, heritage sites and museum exhibitions focus on slave labor rather highlighting the victimization and physical punishments of slave individuals. These two approaches divert the various audiences from the crucial role of slave labor in the construction of these two countries, either by concealing its existence or by denying agency to enslaved individuals who labored at these sites. In Brazil, even though enslaved workers constructed most public and private buildings, their contributions are rarely officially acknowledged. By excluding any references to slave daily life and African heritage, most initiatives presenting slavery in Brazil portray enslaved individuals as passive victims and rather endeavor to mask the country's slave past. Unlike Brazil, over the last ten years, the contribution of enslaved African American men and women is officially acknowledged in most public projects developed in the United States, especially in Washington, DC. This new visibility can be associated with two main factors. Historical and contemporary slavery is gaining growing attention in the works of scholars and international organizations like UNESCO. More importantly, the election of Barack Obama as the first black president of the United States in 2008 and the fact that First Lady Michelle Obama's ancestors were enslaved are elements that have contributed to giving more visibility to African American historical actors, including enslaved men and women. The chapter concludes that acknowledging the contributions of Afro-Brazilians and African Americans to the construction of Brazil and the United States is still a problematic task because the slave past and its legacies of racism and social inequalities are still very much present in these two societies.

Chapter 5, "Great Emancipators," focuses on the various public initiatives commemorating the Emancipation Proclamation in the United States and the abolition of slavery in Brazil, comparing the representations of the two main white emancipators in the two countries: Abraham Lincoln (1809–1865) and Princess Isabel Cristina of Bragança and Bourbon (1846–1921). I show that monuments and museum exhibitions not only celebrate Lincoln and Isabel as the great Redeemers but also exclude enslaved, freed, and free black social actors from these public representations. I also emphasize that in both

Brazil and the United States, when enslaved men and women are presented along with Lincoln and Isabel, they occupy positions of submission and gratitude. In addition, the chapter sheds light on the political debates that led to the construction of public monuments honoring Isabel and Lincoln and how governments of the two countries instrumentalized the image of the two emancipators to obtain support from local black populations. I close the chapter by discussing how the paternalistic vision of the Brazilian abolition of slavery as a gift from the great Redeemer was constructed and how over the years this conception was gradually deconstructed and made barely visible in the public sphere.

Chapter 6 "Iconic Rebels," shows how old representations of slaves as passive victims were progressively replaced by a new image of slaves as rebels, fighters, and maroons. I argue that this new trend follows a transformation that is much like the various manifestations visible in the public memory of the Holocaust, which since the end of the Second World War started featuring a growing number of monuments paying homage to men and women who organized resistance movements in the ghettos and Nazi camps. Moreover, the emergence of slave rebels in public memory is associated with three changes that occurred during the second half of the twentieth century: first, the transnational movements for civil rights led by populations of African descent in Europe, Africa, and the Americas; second, the independence and the creation of new nations, especially in the Caribbean, whose new national identities were closely connected to the image of freedom fighters; third, the growing number of scholarly studies focusing on slave resistance and agency. I look at public representations of loyal and submissive slaves in both Brazil and the United States by giving particular attention to the representations of Nanny, Uncle Tom, *Pai* João, and Slave Isaura. I explain how the images of these enslaved men and women were gradually replaced by the images of enslaved and freed black fighters. Starting in the 1960s, several monuments and activities commemorating slave rebels or maroons were created in different countries of Latin America and the Caribbean. Yet the memorialization of maroons as symbols of the struggle against oppression was not always intended to empower the populations of African descent but also served to reinforce the political agendas of governments who were seeking to assert their political, economic, and cultural independence vis-à-vis the former European colonial powers and the United States. Finally, the chapter examines the memorialization of Zumbi. It shows how Zumbi, today represented as a national hero in Brazil, became the exemplary slave rebel in the Americas.

The book concludes by discussing the connections among the ways that the Atlantic slave trade and slavery were, and continue to be, represented in the public space. I emphasize the similitudes and differences between these representations in the various former slave societies of the Americas. I explain how slavery and the Atlantic slave trade moved from a state of concealment to be eventually highlighted in the public space, but at the same time I insist on how this new visibility is still challenging, and its results rather hinder a full assessment of this traumatic past.

Before concluding this introduction, it is important to underscore that as in any other study focusing on a process still in development, the picture I offer in this book is imperfect and that many gaps remain to be filled in by other scholars who will be able to work in several other regions. As a historian writing transnational and comparative history, I had to make numerous choices. For example, it would be impossible to cover all countries affected by the Atlantic slave trade in a single book. As a result, most of the examples I chose to study come from Brazil and the United States, two central former slave societies of the Americas, where I had the opportunity to live and conduct research for several years. Brazil imported more than 5 million enslaved Africans during the Atlantic slave trade, the largest number of the Americas. United States imported not even 10 percent of the number of Africans brought by force to Brazil. Still, because of all the wounds left by slavery and racial segregation in the wealthiest country of the Americas, African Americans remain the most politically powerful group of the African diaspora. Thus, despite all obstacles, the study of memorialization of slavery in the United States is crucial because it still orients the ways in which slavery and the Atlantic slave trade are commemorated not only in the Americas but also in other parts of the Atlantic world. Finally, I would like to add two technical notes. Most images illustrating this book are mine. Other images are in the public domain, or their authors granted me permission to use them in this book. Except otherwise indicated, all translations from Portuguese, French, and Spanish are mine. Because of a lack of space, most of the time I do not provide the quotes in the original languages.

NOTES

1. Eltis et al., *The Transatlantic Slave Trade Database: Voyages* (website).
2. See Eltis and Richardson, 2010: 257, map 170, 305.
3. Lowenthal, 2009: 905.
4. Lowenthal, 2009: 905. See also Araujo, 2010a.
5. Interview with Toni Morrison, *The World*, 1989. See Morrison, 1987.
6. See Vlach, 1993.
7. Rhodes, 1997: 12. On the controversy, see also Célius, 1998: 260.
8. On Bristol, see Chivallon, 2001: 347–363; Dresser, 2009: 223–246.
9. Many works on the British public memory of slavery were published in recent years. Among them, see Wallace, 2006; Rice, 2010; Smith, Cubitt, Fouseki, and Wilson, 2011.
10. Forsdick, 2012: 279–297. See also Schmidt, 2012: 106–123: Hourcade, 2012: 124–140.
11. See Chivallon, 2009: 83–97; Reinhardt, 2006: Chivallon, 2012: Chap. 1.
12. See Reinhardt, 2006: Chap. 2.
13. See Araujo, 2010a: especially Chap. 5.
14. See Araujo, 2010b: 131–167.
15. Obama, 2008; *Barack Obama, Change We Need*, 2008.

16. Obama, 2009: 238.
17. Swarns, 2012.
18. The website of the contest no longer exists and was replaced by another contest to elect the best beaches of Portugal. However, the petition prepared by several scholars denouncing the omission and signed by hundreds of individuals was published. See "Carta Aberta, Open Letter, Lettre Ouverte," 2009: xiii–xvii. Among the few academic works addressing the legacies of slavery in Portugal is Araújo and Maeso, 2012: 151–166. However, this chapter refers to Europe as a whole and frequently fails to address the issue of the public memory of slavery in Portugal.
19. "Proposición no de Ley relativa al reconocimiento de la comunidad negra española . . .," 2009; "Proposición no de Ley sobre memoria de la esclavitud, . . .," 2009.
20. "Boletín Oficial de las Cortes Generales, . . .," 2010: no. 343, 6.
21. West Africa is the region down to present-day Gabon that comprises Senegambia (present-day Senegal, The Gambia, and Guinea-Bissau: Guinea, Sierra Leone Windward Coast (present-day Liberia and Côte d'Ivoire: Gold Coast (modern Ghana: the Bight of Benin (present-day Togo, Benin, and western Nigeria: and the Bight of Biafra (present-day Cameroon, Equatorial Guinea, and northern Gabon, in addition to Bimbia Island, São Tomé, Príncipe and Bioko Islands. West Central Africa covers the region from Cap Lopez (in modern Gabon) to the southern end of Africa, including the modern countries of Gabon, Republic of Congo, Democratic Republic of Congo, and Angola. See Eltis and Richardson, 2010: 257, map 170, 305.
22. On collective memory and memory social frameworks, see Halbwachs's pioneer works: Halbwachs, 1925. For a distinction between collective memory and historical memory, see Halbwachs, 1950: Chap. 2. About collective memory in the context of nation-states, see Connerton, 1989.
23. See Shaw, 2002: 15; Rothberg, 2010: 11.
24. On the nondiscursive forms of remembering the past, see Connerton, 1989: Chap. 3.
25. Smith, 2006: 1; 4.
26. See Smith, 2006: 11.
27. Reinhardt, 2008; Chivallon, 2012; Holsey, 2008; Wallace, 2010; Wood, 2010; Rice, 2010.
28. See Eichstedt, and Smalls, 2002; Oliver and Horton, 2006.
29. Wood, 2013.

1 Tales of Enslavement

Visual images and written narratives from the eighteenth and nineteenth centuries represented the enslavement of men, women, and children who were captured on West African soil to be exported during the period of the Atlantic slave trade. These representations have been widely disseminated, transformed, recycled, and transferred to other contemporary media, including novels, television series, films, monuments, memorials, and museum exhibitions. Through the comparison of these accounts, I discuss the various ways enslaver West African elites and intermediaries, as well as slave merchants and enslaved individuals, are represented in two forms of narratives: those emphasizing the enslavement through kidnapping and those describing enslavement through warfare. I show that although warfare was the main form of obtaining captives, written narratives and visual representations emphasize random abductions, concealing the complex dynamics that provoked enslavement in the African continent. Produced both by European travelers and traders, as well as by former enslaved persons during the eighteenth and nineteenth centuries, these visual depictions were mainly intended to disseminate British abolitionist propaganda. They are characterized by two main features. First, by eliminating warfare and emphasizing individual abductions led by Europeans and not by Africans, these portrayals emphasized African victimhood. Second, whereas these visual and written representations show the processes of enslavement in West Africa, they exclude West Central Africa, a region that provided the great majority of captives to the Atlantic slave trade but where the British presence was not significant. Indeed, most surviving images that show enslavement in West Central Africa portray the Muslim slave trade and date to after the end of the Atlantic slave trade. How in the last 20 years were these depictions of enslavement appropriated and reinterpreted in public initiatives such as monuments, memorials, museums exhibitions, and films? What new meanings did these visual and written representations receive according to the several contexts, actors, and political struggles involved in the various initiatives commemorating slavery and the Atlantic slave trade, which emerged in the second half of the twentieth century? Despite the changing contexts, social actors, and political struggles involved in the various initiatives commemorating slavery and the Atlantic slave trade developed in the second half of the twentieth century, these images of British abolitionist propaganda continue to be disseminated with the purpose of including the history of the Atlantic slave trade in official national narratives. Without being challenged, however, these representations continue to position enslaved Africans and the populations of African descent in a position of mere commodities.

WARFARE

Prior to the eighteenth century, very few visual images and written narratives represented slave raids in the African continent. Although some of these renderings are not based on direct observation, during the eighteenth and nineteenth centuries, slave narratives and European travel accounts extensively represented episodes of enslavement in West Africa. However, even though the large majority of enslaved individuals sent to the Americas were captured in West Central Africa coastal and hinterland areas, most existing written accounts do not describe the process of enslavement in this vast and important region.

Toward the end of the nineteenth century, with the ban of the Atlantic slave trade to the Americas and as part of the broader enterprise of colonial propaganda, European travelogues contain an increasing number of visual images portraying enslavement in Africa. These narratives were used to report and denounce Muslim slave raids, even though during the European colonial rule in several regions of Africa, the forced labor imposed by colonizers was very similar to slave labor. Thus, most images of enslavement produced in the second half of the nineteenth century indeed represented the Muslim slave trade. Today these renderings are commonly employed to represent the Atlantic slave trade in exhibitions, websites, book covers, textbooks, and films. For example, in the third chapter of the documentary *Prince Among Slaves,* the narrator states that the Atlantic slave trade was "the largest forced migration in human history draining away some 12 million people in four hundred years."[1] However, the narration is accompanied by a slide show presenting the engravings *Slavers Revenging their Losses* (1866) (Figure 1.1) and *Gang of Captives Met at Mbame's on Their Way to Tette* (1861) (Figure 1.2), which indeed portray the slave trade in East Africa.[2] Although not accurate, the use of these illustrations of slave caravans led by Muslim slave traders acts as a substitute in the absence of images portraying the capture of slaves during the Atlantic slave trade.

Africanist historians have explained that enslavement and slavery were always characterized by violence deployed in various manners, especially through warfare but also through slave raids, banditry, and kidnapping.[3]

Figure 1.1 Slavers Revenging Their Losses (Livingstone and Waller, 1874: facing p. 56).

Figure 1.2 Gang of Captives Met at Mbame's on Their Way to Tette (Livingstone and Livingstone, 1893: 376).

In addition, enslavement could be the result of religious and judicial punishments, including the crimes of theft, adultery, robbery, and homicide.[4] Yet, scholars also agree that, at least in the large slave-trading kingdoms and empires of West Africa, including the Asante Empire, the Kingdom of Dahomey, and the Oyo Empire, interstate wars were the main way of capturing prisoners for the Atlantic slave trade markets.[5] Even though warfare was the main form of acquiring captives, various kinds of visual images and written narratives describe the transition from freedom to slavery as the result of hazardous kidnapping.

West African historical actors narrated the wars that affected their home countries by describing the process of enslavement from the points of view of enslaver rulers and enslaved victims. In West Africa, ruling elites left important visual records narrating the wars they waged against other states. One of the most enlightening visual accounts of war and enslavement can be found in the unique bas-reliefs displayed on the walls of the royal palaces of Abomey, the former capital city of the Kingdom of Dahomey, in the present-day Republic of Benin. The several palaces are eighteenth-century earthen structures with thatch roofs that represent ten generations of kings, including Gezo (r. 1818–1858) and Glele (r. 1858–1889).[6] In addition to depicting the animals that symbolize the various kings, the bas-reliefs display images of warriors fighting and cutting off the heads of their enemies. Produced by artisans in the service of the kings, these images are corroborated by the extensive correspondence exchanged between the Dahomean and Portuguese rulers from the middle of the eighteenth to the early nineteenth century, describing in detail the wars waged by the Kingdom of Dahomey against other neighboring states.[7] For example, whereas one bas-relief on the façade of King Glele's palace shows a Dahomean warrior pointing a shooting gun at another warrior holding a bow, others show Daghessou, a mythical figure with an animal head and horns and human body, holding a rifle and other kinds of weapons. On the façade of King Gezo's palace, Fon women warriors of Dahomey's army, or Amazons as they were called by the Europeans, are carrying war prisoners on their backs. A bas-relief displayed on King Glele's palace presents an Amazon torturing a Ketu warrior, whose stomach "is being split and filled with earth."[8] Additional bas-reliefs represent horses transporting the head of the chief of a neighboring kingdom. In Dahomean tradition, decapitating vanquished enemies was practiced not only during the wars but also during the Annual Customs, the sacrificial ceremonies to celebrate military victories and honor the kings.[9] In 1727, the English sea captain and slave merchant William Snelgrave witnessed the Dahomean army returning from a battle and carrying the heads of dead prisoners as trophies of war.[10] Indeed, British and Luso-Brazilian slave merchants like Snelgrave and Francisco Félix de Souza praised the benefits of the Atlantic slave trade by justifying that they were saving captives from being killed in the sacrificial ceremonies and giving West African societies the opportunity to dispose of undesirable individuals.[11]

Regardless of the apparent shock of contemporary observers, impaling and displaying heads on pikes were not unusual practices in European societies. As recently as the French Revolution (1789–1799), monarchs and noblemen were decapitated, and their picked heads were publicly displayed.

This practice was depicted in numerous paintings and engravings that show French revolutionaries parading in the streets of Paris carrying impaled heads on pikes.[12] Moreover, during the eighteenth and nineteenth centuries, Portuguese and British colonizers decapitated slaves and freedmen who led revolts in the United States and Brazil. In 1798, the leaders of the Conspiracy of the Tailors were hanged and quartered, and their heads were displayed at Praça da Piedade in Salvador, Bahia.[13] In 1832, following the bloody repression of the Baptist War in Jamaica, some of the slaves convicted "were to be decapitated after execution and their heads to be displayed on poles."[14] The decapitation of enemies was also practiced in other regions of West Africa. In a letter sent to the Prince Regent Dom João Carlos de Bragança of Portugal, Adandozan (r. 1797–1818), King of Dahomey, warned the Portuguese ruler of the hostilities suffered by the Portuguese in other neighboring ports by mentioning that the King of Badagry "used the head of a White as a *couco de beber agoa* (calabash for drinking water)."[15] Beheading is also evoked in the *Narrative of the Most Remarkable Particulars in the Life of James Albert Ukawsaw Gronniosaw, an African Prince, as Related by Himself*. This book was published in 1770 as part of a series of works, written by Afro-British authors, that became very popular among a British audience who by the time were becoming progressively more supportive of the abolition of the Atlantic slave trade. In this narrative, Gronniosaw explains that after being led to the Gold Coast by a slave merchant, the local ruler believed he was a spy. Thus, he was brought to the king's palace where he expected to be beheaded: "The morning I was to die, I was washed and all my gold-ornaments made bright and shining, and then carried to the palace where the King was to behead me himself (as is the custom of the place)."[16] Even though Gronniosaw escaped decapitation, the episode indicates that the practice of beheading enemies also existed in the Gold Coast. But in popular memory, the spectacle of displaying heads on pikes as war trophies for the decoration of royal palaces is usually associated with the Kingdom of Dahomey. European travelers who had visited Abomey since the early eighteenth century, including Bulfinch Kamb, William Snelgrave, Robert Norris, Richard Burton, and Frederick Forbes, reported the purchase of heads by the various Dahomean kings. In addition, they also described how human skulls tiled some rooms of the Abomey palaces.[17] Human skulls were also employed to mount the throne of Dahomean rulers, including the throne of King Glele, which image was circulated in postcards based on photographs taken by French colonial authorities (Figure 1.3). Moreover, renderings of Dahomey's beheaded vanquished enemies survive to this day. In a scene from the film *Cobra Verde* by Werner Herzog, heads impaled on pikes are displayed in the courtyards of the Abomey palaces.[18] The film also shows the floor of the apartment of King Adandozan's palace covered with human skulls. Then in another scene, the king receives the Brazilian slave merchant Francisco Félix de Souza, made prisoner, in the royal palace's courtyard,

Figure 1.3 Trône du roi Glele (postcard, author's personal collection).

Figure 1.4 Hey, white man. One day I will drink from your skull! (Herzog, 1987/2000).

which is also fully decorated with human skulls. During a ceremony, the king threatens the slave trader (Figure 1.4): "I'll thatch my roof with the skulls of my enemies [...]. Hey, white man. One day I will drink from your skull. This [calabash] was the king of the Mahis."[19]

Notwithstanding the uniqueness of Dahomean images, British military, travelers, slave merchants, and other officers produced the most popular visual depictions of warfare in West Africa. Most of them had not witnessed the events they portrayed, but their sketches were later transformed into engravings and disseminated among larger audiences. In one account, Captain Ringard describes the invasion of the Kingdom of Hueda by the Dahomean army.[20] According to him, the locals reported being captured by the Fon, who sold the best individuals and left the others to die.[21] In addition, after a visit to Savi, the ancient capital of the Kingdom of Hueda situated close to Ouidah, Ringard was led to the beach. There he met the merchants and captains of the French Compagnie des Indes, who told him that in the last 15 days very few captives were available, leading him to conclude that the war was hindering the slave trade in the region. Like Ringard, Archibald Dalzel (1740–1811), a British traveler and governor of the Gold Coast who visited Dahomey, also narrates in detail the conquest of Hueda by the Dahomeans. He notes how in 1727 King Agaja (r. 1708–1740) led his troops to conquer the Kingdom of Hueda, gaining access to Ouidah by providing a vibrant description of the Dahomean army: "The rear he composed of a great number of women, armed like soldiers, having their proper officers, and furnished like regular troops, with drums, colours, and umbrellas, making at a distance a very formidable appearance."[22] The text is illustrated by the line engraving *Armed Women, with the King at Their Head Going to War* (Figure 1.5). The image is based on the account provided by the slave trader Robert Norris (d. 1791), the author of *Memoirs of the Reign of Bossa Ahadee, King of Dahomy* (1789), which was incorporated in the 1793 edition of *The History of Dahomy*.[23] The army is moving, and some of its male members carry huge flags and umbrellas, whereas others play big drums. The Amazons, wearing head cloths and tunics leaving their breasts naked, are holding big rifles and small cross-shoulder cloth bags to carry ammunition. The rendering highlights King Agaja, who is leading the group. Holding a big sword, he is wearing a long tunic and a large European hat, distinguishing himself from the other warriors.[24] This exuberant image conveying Dahomey's militaristic vocation has probably inspired

Figure 1.5 Armed Women with the King at Their Head Going to War (Dalzel, 1793: facing p. 54).

written accounts and visual representations produced later. Isaac Taylor (1759–1829), a British engraver and writer, relied on various travelogues to write his youth-oriented book, *Scenes of Africa, for the Amusement and Instruction of Little Tarry-At-Home Travellers*. Published in 1820, when the British slave trade had already been abolished, Taylor's account was part of the propaganda against the Atlantic slave trade that continued to be practiced by other nations after 1807. Taylor provides an account of the role of Dahomey's Amazons played in military campaigns, similar to Dalzel's report: "Of these women several hundreds are regularly trained to arms; have female commanders, appointed by the king, and parade with drums and standards; going through their evolutions with great accuracy. Sometimes, on particular occasions, the king puts himself at the head of these women, and goes to war."[25] More recently, the film *Cobra Verde* also offers a carnivalized depiction of these processions. In one scene, the king and his subjects, holding rifles and huge umbrellas, sing and dance during a parade in the courtyard of the Abomey palaces.[26]

Still today visitors to Abomey can see how warfare was memorialized in the old Kingdom of Dahomey. In the Square Ayidjoso, located in the interior of the Lycée Houffon, close to the royal palaces, there is a monument consisting of an enormous pile of granite stones (Figure 1.6) dating from

Figure 1.6 Square Ayidjoso, Abomey, Republic of Benin (photograph by Ana Lucia Araujo, 2005).

the period of the Atlantic slave trade. The British officer Frederick Forbes probably referred to this monument in his travel account; according to him, it commemorated the conquest of Anagoo.[27] He explains why Dahomean soldiers and the prisoners captured during the battle carried the stones from the land of the vanquished enemy: "the Anagoos had a tradition, which they steadily believed, that when their enemies removed stones the country would fall. The Dahomans conquered them, and fulfilled the prophecy by causing the whole army, each (soldier and camp follower) to carry a large stone. Nearly all are granite in different stages of formation."[28]

Another local oral tradition states that the monument was created during the reign of King Gezo to commemorate a victory in a campaign against the Mahi Kingdom. The monument was intended to show the difficulties met by the Dahomean army. On that occasion, the neighboring peoples resisted and retreated into the mountains, from where they threw stones against the Dahomean soldiers. In this more likely version of the oral tradition, following the end of the campaign, each prisoner and Dahomean warrior were forced to carry from Savalou to Abomey a stone intended to build a monument reconstituting the symbolic image of the mountains. A less likely version for the origin of the monument states that a Mahi chief was buried under the stones. Another one explains that the pile of stones served as a shrine where the prisoners of war would pray to forget their origins and avoid the temptation of returning to their homeland.[29] Finally, a different version asserts that the stones were used to count the captives who arrived in Abomey, constituting evidence of the great number of captives who were sacrificed or sent into slavery in the Americas.[30] Regardless of the actual explanation for the origin of the monument, the pile of granite stones is a figurative representation of warfare in the Kingdom of Dahomey that reminds locals and visitors about how Dahomean rulers obtained prisoners to be sold in the Atlantic slave trade.

In the contemporary Republic of Benin, several monuments of Ouidah's Slaves' Route, unveiled during the festival *Ouidah 92: Retrouvailles Afriques-Amériques*, reveal representations of the Amazons along with Vodun deities.[31] Even though the statues displayed along the route were primarily intended to commemorate the victims of the Atlantic slave trade and not the enslavers, among the dozens of monuments at least two statues model Amazons of Dahomey's army (Figure 1.7), emphasizing how warfare was central for the production of slaves. Crucial figures in the Dahomean wars, the Amazons are represented with their traditional horns, which are icons of power associated with animals such as the antelope and the buffalo. As in existing nineteenth-century engravings and photographs, these women warriors are proudly holding rifles, which were provided by European traders in exchange for captives. This monument shows that, despite the Western-oriented attempts to memorialize the victims of the Atlantic slave trade, in countries like Benin the militaristic-enslaving character of the Kingdom of Dahomey is not the object of public guilt. On the contrary, the

Figure 1.7 Amazon. Ouidah, Republic of Benin (sculpture by Cyprien Tokoudagba; photograph by Ana Lucia Araujo).

promotion of heritage sites like the Abomey palaces and the construction of new monuments paying homage to the voduns of the kings of Dahomey and the Amazons indicate that, despite the official public discourses, the kingdom's slaving past is a source of pride rather than public shame.

Museum exhibitions in Europe and the Americas rarely detail the processes through which African men and women were captured and enslaved. On August 23, 2007, to commemorate the bicentennial of the British abolition of slave trade and to mark the UNESCO Slavery Remembrance Day, the International Slavery Museum was opened in Liverpool. The museum's mission is not only to present the history of the Atlantic slave trade and slavery but also to raise awareness about modern slavery and racism.[32] Despite the term "international," the museum engages in a project to develop a more inclusive narrative of British history that recognizes the contributions of the populations of color in the construction of the British empire. Though British-centered and mainly North Atlantic region-focused, the exhibitions of the International Slavery Museum include some explanation about mechanisms of the Atlantic slave trade and how Africans were enslaved in many African areas. Its various sections are chronologically organized. After the first gallery introduces the contribution of particular regions of West Africa to global culture, the second gallery "Enslavement and the Middle Passage," reveals, through screening projections and several instruments like shackles and chain, how Africans were captured, sold, and sent to North America. The texts in the panels displayed in the gallery, as well as the at the museum website, explain that although Europeans participated in slave raids, most of the time they bought captives from African and Afro-European traders who acted as intermediaries. Additionally, the texts displayed emphasize that most Africans were captured through wars and sometimes were kidnapped, even though debt and judicial punishment could also lead to enslavement. To illustrate these ideas from an African point of view, the gallery also presents the transcriptions and audio clips from a letter from Egboyoung Offeong, an African intermediary, and Olaudah Equiano. But by excessively focusing on West Africa, a region where the British had an important presence during the period of the Atlantic slave trade, and on the British colonies in the Americas, the museum fails to explain the processes of enslavement in West Central Africa, the most important slave-exporting region, dominated by the Luso-Brazilian slave merchants.

A similar approach is found in the permanent gallery *London, Sugar, and Slavery: Revealing Our City's Untold History*, in the Museum of London Docklands. The gallery comprises a section dedicated to the Transatlantic Slave Trade. Opened on November 10, 2007 as part of the commemorations of the bicentennial of the British abolition of the slave trade, the exhibit presents London's involvement in the Atlantic slave trade. The museum is located at the West India Docks in a former 1802 sugar warehouse that was used to store goods from the Caribbean plantations. Although the museum's building is part of the material heritage of the Atlantic slave trade, between the 1990s until its opening in 2007, its publicity materials did not mention the slave trade but rather highlighted the architectural value of the warehouses and praised it as one of the "great monuments of European

Commercial Power."³³ As the bicentennial approached, the mercantile and maritime discourse of the museum was slowly modified to incorporate the presentation of the Atlantic slave trade. Since 2007, the huge new gallery displays accounts, film, music, paintings, maps, interactive displays containing illustrations and text, as well as 140 objects explaining the history of the trade and London's role in it. One panel shows the engraving *Slave Trade* (1791) by J.R. Smith after the homonymous painting by George Moorland (1763–1804) rendering an African shore where two European merchants are quarreling over an African man whom they probably just bought and are attempting to embark on slave ships in the background. The text accompanying the image explains that by the late seventeenth century, the Royal Africa Company controlled British slave trade activities on the west coast of Africa. The panel notes that Europeans purchased captives "from the interior and assembled them for sale at the coast." However, it also adds that the British slave trade relied on African collaborators who "also organized workers to maintain the company forts and 'canoe-men' to carry people and supplies from shore to ship. [. . .] As the trade became more profitable it fostered a new African 'elite' in the coastal areas and contributed to destructive divisions in African society."³⁴ As in the International Slavery Museum, in *London, Sugar, and Slavery*, the context of enslavement is not emphasized. Together, texts, images, and artifacts underline the contrast between an idealized image of Africa that precedes the contact with the Europeans and the disorganized context that emerges after their arrival. By privileging a British-centered narrative, these simplified representations do not engage the discussion about the crucial role of war to produce captives for the Atlantic slave trade. Because these museums and exhibitions were designed to commemorate the bicentennial of the abolition of the slave trade, they are not successful in providing a complex portrait of the diversity of African societies and the various kinds of interactions developed with Europeans. Indeed, these initiatives attempted to respond to the long existing demands for the recognition of organized black groups and to include slavery and black history in the country's official narrative. Nevertheless, addressing sensitive issues was and still is a difficult task. This problem became clearly visible in the numerous public debates that eventually culminated with Prime Minister Tony Blair's expressing his sorrow for the role Britain played during the Atlantic slave trade in 2006. In short, portraying slavery in British museum exhibitions and acknowledging the role of Britain in the development of the Atlantic slave trade was a step forward, but the populations of African descent in Britain and its former colonies in the Caribbean and Africa remain discriminated against and largely excluded.³⁵

In the United States, small exhibitions have briefly highlighted the process of enslavement in Africa in order to explain US slave life. The African Burial Ground Visitor Center is the museum component of the African Burial Ground memorial, opened in February 2010. The museum portrays the particular experiences of Africans who lived and died New York City. Even though the collections of the African Burial Ground Visitor Center are very modest in comparison to those of the International Slavery Museum and the Museum of London Docklands, a section explains the development of the Atlantic slave trade. The gallery exposes a large map of Africa, a second map of the triangular trade, and a big glass display presenting various kinds of West African artifacts. A second glass display, titled "Slave Traders Used Metal and Beads to Enslave African People," presents a cord with glass beads and three *manillas*, which Europeans used as currency to purchase enslaved people. The text states: "Europeans and Africans bartered with metal bands called manilas and beads like these. They were only two of the items used in a centuries-long trade that also included firearms, gunpowder, gold, palm oil, salt, textiles, and more." Attempting to provide an African perspective on the Atlantic slave trade, this part of the exhibition avoids presenting images of explicit violence or descriptive panels underscoring the various methods used by Africans and Europeans to supply and acquire slaves. Overall, the Atlantic slave trade is presented as a commercial enterprise that involved the exchange of human beings for particular kinds of commodities. But this static presentation eliminates the violence involved in the process of enslavement by presenting African men and women as passive victims who were stolen, bought, and then sold overseas.

KIDNAPPING

Most African-born enslaved individuals who wrote narratives reported their enslavement as being the result of isolated kidnappings, even though sometimes their autobiographies inscribe such abductions in the warfare context.[36] The analysis of slave narratives and European travelogues describing these kidnapping episodes raises a number of questions. Why do so many written and visual representations tend to conceal warfare and emphasize individual kidnapping as a significant form of acquiring African captives? Is war erased because most of these enslaved men were abducted when they were children? Did the trauma of being captured through violent methods provoke a sort of amnesia? Is emphasis on kidnapping related to the main purpose of most of these accounts, namely British abolitionist propaganda? How is the passive role of Africans in abduction narratives associated or dissociated from the image of these enslaved African men who were able to free themselves? While attempting to answer these questions, it is clear that, although eliminating from their accounts any clear references to war or slave raids by, in turn, accentuating individual kidnappings, the abduction narratives of Equiano and Cugoano were appropriated in accounts by European writers, who often neglected the broad context of warfare. Moreover, these abduction narratives became models for numerous fictional tales that emerged in the nineteenth and twentieth centuries.

Starting in the sixteenth century, European travelers described the growing insecurity associated with the slave trade in the Gambia region. In the *Tratado Breve dos Rios de Guiné do Capo Verde*, the Cap Verdean merchant André Alvares d'Almada narrates the intensive slave trade activity in the Gambia River and how the local population took protective measures from slave raids.[37] As Walter Hawthorne notes when he examines the slave trade in the Upper Guinea Coast, "coastal communities found themselves forced to engage with slave purchasers" in order "to avoid becoming their victims."[38] Descriptions of the general environment of insecurity persisted in the eighteenth century. Europeans who traveled to the Guinea coast witnessed how local chiefs and ruling men experienced the vulnerability associated with the Atlantic slave trade. According to d'Almada, robbery and kidnapping were current practices in the region, forcing local chiefs to carry firearms on a regular basis. In addition, engaging in slave trading activities was a means to avoid being enslaved: "each knows it is their Villanies and Robberies upon one another that enables them to carry on a Slave-trade with Europeans; and as Strength fluctuates, it is not unfrequent for him who sells you Slaves today, to be a few days hence sold himself at some neighbouring Town."[39]

Kidnapping resulting from warfare was also part of the daily life in the hinterlands of Bight of Benin and the Bight of Biafra.[40] James H. Sweet explores the history of Domingos Álvares, a West African healer from the Mahi country (north of the modern Republic of Benin). Captured between 1728 and 1732 by the Dahomean army, he was brought to the coast and sold into slavery in Brazil.[41] In 1739, Broteer Furro (later Venture Smith) was victim of a slave raid. In an account published in the late eighteenth century, he describes his enslavement in detail: "Then they came to us in the reeds, and the very first salute I had from them was a violent blow on the head with the fore part of a gun, and at the same time a grasp round the neck. I then had a rope put about my neck, as had all the women in the thicket with me [. . .]. In this condition we were all led to the camp."[42] He was brought to the Gold Coast, sold into slavery in Anomabu (contemporary Ghana), and then sent to the United States.

Other West African men lived similar experiences of enslavement. Mahommah Gardo Baquaqua, who was born in Djougou (north of the contemporary Republic of Benin), was captured, sold, and sent into slavery to Pernambuco (Brazil). In his biography published in the middle of the nineteenth century, he underscores the internal conflicts that led to war in his kingdom: "The kings are continually quarreling, which quarrels lead to war. [. . .] When a king dies, there is no regular successor, but a great many rivals for the kingdom spring up, and he who can achieve his object by power and strength, becomes the succeeding king, thus war settles the question. [. . .] Slavery is also another fruitful source of war, the prisoners being sold for slaves."[43] Baquaqua's account confirms that among royal families, during the period of succession, it was not uncommon to sell members of opponent factions into slavery. By the end of the eighteenth century, in the Kingdom of Dahomey, Agontimé, one of the wives of King Agonglo (r. 1789–1797) and *kpojito* (the queen mother) of King Gezo, was sold into slavery and sent to the Americas, possibly to Brazil. Her enslavement was associated with the dispute to the Dahomey throne that led King Adandozan to power and resulted in the punishment of all his opponents.[44] Despite the lack of archival evidence, Agontimé became a legendary figure in Brazil as the woman who allegedly introduced the Vodun of Dahomey in the country and founded the Candomblé temple Casa das Minas in Maranhão.

In his *Interesting Narrative*, Olaudah Equiano describes his early life in Igboland, in contemporary southeastern Nigeria. He mentions that when adults were absent and children remained outside to play, one child was usually chosen "to get up a tree to look out for any assailant, or kidnapper."[45] Equiano recounts in detail his abduction, which occurred despite the villagers' constant surveillance. According to him, he was enslaved in 1753, when he was still a young boy of possibly seven or eight years old: "One day, when all our people were gone out to their works as usual, and only I and my dear sister were left to mind the house, two men and a woman got over our walls, and in a moment seized us both; and, without giving us time to cry out, or make resistance, they stopped our mouths, tied our hands, and ran off with us into the nearest wood."[46]

A similar abduction narrative underscoring the surprise element is provided by Quobna Ottobah Cugoano in his *Thoughts and Sentiments on the Evil and Wicked Traffic of the Slavery and Commerce of the Human Species,* published in 1787. Born by 1757 in Agimaque or Ajumako, a Fante village of the Gold Coast region (present-day Ghana), Cugoano was kidnapped in 1770, when he was about 13 years old. In his account, he shows he was aware of the dangers of enslavement and relates how he was abducted in the woods and sent to the coast to be sold into slavery: "we went into the woods as usual; but we had not been above two hours before our troubles began, when several great ruffians came upon us suddenly. [. . .] Some of us attempted in vain to run away, but pistols and cutlasses were soon introduced, threatening, that if we offered to stir we should lie dead on the spot."[47]

Similarly to Equiano's narrative, Baquaqua chronicles his enslavement as the result of the treacherous behavior of a group of fake admirers, who conducted him to the house of a king of a neighboring village and encouraged him to drink a large amount of an alcoholic beverage. The following morning after the binge drinking, he realized he had been betrayed and sold into slavery. However, in an earlier account of 1847, Baquaqua tells he was "taken captive when a child, while playing at some distance from his mother's door." Then later, in another account, he stated he was kidnapped "while playing truant from school."[48] As Baquaqua's story indicates, the idea of enslavement as the result of betrayal is not uncommon in slave narratives, travelogues, oral tradition, and historical records.

In the book *Scenes of Africa,* in a section titled "A Son Going to Sell his Mother and His Father," focusing on the Gambia region, Taylor explains how West Africans were kidnapped by their own relatives to be sold into slavery:

> As soon as a European vessel heaves into view, neighbours of all sorts begin quarrelling, and the strongest seize the weaker ones, and run with them down to the shore, to barter them for as much as they can gain of that fiery poison. Sometimes parents sell their children; but the prize seems more important when a strong man can seize one or both his parents, and thus obtain a larger portion of brandy. As soon as he receives it, he begins drinking; his appetite is inflamed by all he takes, and he usually lies in a state of stupid drunkenness as long as any of the vile liquor remains.[49]

The engraving (Figure 1.8) accompanying the text shows a man (the son) dragging to the beach a man and woman (the parents), attached at their wrists. As a result, Taylor describes enslavement as a process of chaotic abductions, leading the reader to conclude that the Atlantic slave trade mainly involved the selling of persons of the same families and kin groups.

Figure 1.8 *A Son Going to Sell his Mother and His Father* (Taylor, 1820: fig. 24).

Nonetheless, he does not diminish the role of Europeans in the trade by emphasizing how the Atlantic slave trade and the introduction of goods such as alcohol had a disrupting effect in the Gambia region. Because his book was addressed mainly to the British youth, he warns his young readers about the importance of the duty of memory and the necessity of fighting the Atlantic slave trade in order to avoid its continuation in the future: "the English have made many laws against this trade in flesh and bones; but their power cannot reach every where; and it is right we should remember what once it was, and would be again, if not watched and resisted."[50] At the same time, Taylor's discourse contributes to underscore and propagate the idea of the British humanitarian role in the abolition of the slave trade, even though slavery continued in the British colonies in the Americas until its abolition in 1834, and the slave trade to Cuba and Brazil persisted until the middle of the nineteenth century.

Kidnapping was not uncommon in political decentralized societies, but it was never the main form of enslavement in the large slave-trading states, where producing a large number of captives would be impossible through individual abductions. Likewise, selling the members of the same family was not a significant way to provide enough captives for the Atlantic slave trade. However, oral tradition reports cases of family betrayal. In the early nineteenth century a Nupe man from Bidda (contemporary Nigeria), named Gouye, was sold by his family and sent into slavery to Rio de Janeiro, where he was baptized Sabino. After purchasing his freedom, Sabino took the last name of his master, Vieyra, and returned to the Bight of Benin, settling in Ouidah with other former slave returnees. In the early 1990s, one of his descendants explained that Sabino's brothers had sold him to the slave merchants, probably because of a dispute related to the family's inheritance.[51] Still, a younger female member of the family narrated the enslavement of her ancestor in a very different way, which was relatively similar to the account found in Baquaqua's autobiography. By stating that Gouye was not an ordinary person but the son of a West African chief, she explained how her ancestor was misled by his Brazilian friends, omitting any mention of a family dispute: "[h]e came with his white horse to see the Brazilian ships that arrived at the coast, they became friends with him, and very gently they made him enter in the ship and the ship departed very gently and he left."[52] Although keeping with the idea of a kidnapping, this member of the Vieyra family embellished the story of her ancestor by suppressing all traces of violence.[53] This kind of replacement, as explained by Primo Levi when examining similar processes among Holocaust survivors, "may begin in full awareness, with an invented scenario, mendacious, restored, but less painful than the real one; they repeat the description to others but also to themselves, and the distinction between true and false progressively loses its contours."[54] In short, if at the private level these embellished narratives allow the descendants of slaves to cope with the inherited trauma of enslavement, when these accounts are disseminated in the public sphere, they are rather intended to cover the role of those who benefited from the Atlantic slave trade and whose descendants very often still occupy positions of political and economic power in West African societies.

Similar motifs of a young man enticed by slave merchants can also be found in slave narratives. In his *Narrative*, Gronniosaw relates how he was enslaved in Bornu (modern Nigeria) when he was about 15 years old. When he became a young man and started exhibiting physical and emotional disturbances, his parents agreed to send him to the Gold Coast with a merchant of ivory, who in his own words "expressed vast concern for me, and said, if my parents would part with me for a little while, and let him take me home with him, it would be of more service to me than any thing they could do for me."[55] Omitting any references to slave ships, the merchant attracted him by saying he would "see houses with wings to them walk upon the water, and should also see the white folks;"[56] After a long trip by land, once Gronniosaw arrived in the Gold Coast, he ended up being sold into slavery to a captain of a Dutch slave ship.

Selling relatives into slavery resulted from the combination of internal family conflicts and the general disorder caused by the Atlantic slave trade. For example, the death of the head of the family usually provoked rivalries. On these occasions, as in the disputes for the throne in royal families, quarrels related to the division of assets or disagreements about who would become the next chief of the family could easily result in selling family members considered to be undesirable or perceived as competitors to known slave merchants. Moreover, during periods of war, hunger, and drought, individuals would sell themselves into slavery. Families who were in debt had often no other alternative than selling or giving away the children they were not able to feed.

In another section of *Scenes of Africa*, titled "Kidnapping," Taylor focuses on the Guinea region. After providing a sensationalistic portrayal of the Kingdom of Dahomey, the author notes how the slave merchants and local intermediaries obtained enslaved individuals "which they sell for iron, cloths, [. . .] and especially for brandy."[57] Although mentioning several methods of enslavement, including individual kidnappings and punishment for alleged crimes committed by local individuals, Taylor eventually adds that war was also an important means to obtain prisoners to be sold into slavery:

> All manner of tricks are put in practice, to get the poor creatures condemned for crimes real or pretended; and many a time war is declared only to get prisoners. But when they do not procure enough by such means, a chief sends out his subjects into some neighbouring district: they lie in wait near a village during the day, and catch any stragglers;

but at night they come and set fire to their huts in several places; when the poor creatures run out in terror and confusion, then the soldiers seize upon all they can catch, and hurry then to the seaside, to sell them. And sometimes Europeans will thus steal them.[58]

Underscoring several forms of enslavement, the image illustrating Taylor's text (Figure 1.9) shows a village in flames during a slave raid as two white men dressed in European fashion hunt an African woman and her child. Here the inconsistency between text and image exemplifies the way collective memory of enslavement was constructed over time. Even though Dahomean rulers waged wars and organized raids aimed at producing slaves, by depicting two white men hunting individuals in the hinterland of the Bight of Benin, Taylor helps to reinforce the idea that Europeans commonly captured people during the period of the Atlantic slave trade in that region. This imagery of abolitionist propaganda survived in the next decades and still today is regularly conveyed in movies and film documentaries that have represented slave raids in West Africa's hinterland. For example, Steven Spielberg's film *Amistad* (1997) explores the famous case of the schooner *La Amistad*, which was sailing to Havana and transporting newly purchased Africans. After the eruption of a slave revolt on board, the US Navy eventually captured the schooner. Once in the United States, Sengbe Pieh (Djimon Hounsou), the young Mende man who led the rebellion, remembered his enslavement when he was asked by his lawyer Roger Sherman Baldwin (Matthew McConaughey) to explain

Figure 1.9 Kidnapping (Taylor, 1820: fig. 34).

how he has arrived in the United States. Then a flashback scene shows Sengbe in his village, when four African men suddenly appeared from the bushes. The men easily caught him in a net and led him to the coast. As in the travel accounts of the eighteenth and nineteenth centuries, Spielberg does not provide any element to help the audience understand the internal and external conditions that led to the enslavement of West African men and women. Instead, he reinforces the traditional narrative of hazardous kidnappings. However, in other films like the documentary *Middle Passage* (1999) by Martinican filmmaker Guy Deslauriers, the process of enslavement is depicted in more detail. A dramatic scene shows how the Dahomean army under King Agaja raided the villages of neighboring states during the dry season in the night by setting fire to the huts and kidnapping men, women, and children to be sold into slavery.[59] Similarly, the documentary film, *Prince Among Slaves,* shows the enslavement of Abdul-Rahman, a Muslim prince who was sent by his father, the king of Futa Jallon, into a battle to protect his domains. After winning the battle, the prince and his men were ambushed by a group of natives, armed men with firearms. Yet no details about the abductors are provided, except that they are visibly black. Made captive, Abdul-Rahman was brought to the coast in a slave coffle and sold into slavery to English merchants. As in the eighteenth- and nineteenth-century narratives and visual images, the context of the enslavement remains obscure.

Enslavement in West Africa is also portrayed in the fictionalized abolitionist account *Slavery Illustrated: In the Histories of Zangara and Maquama, Two Negros Stolen from Africa and Sold into Slavery Related by Themselves* (1849). The account tells the story of two Africans who were enslaved and sent to the Americas. Despite admitting that the memories of his early years in the African continent had faded, Zangara explains that it "could not exist on earth a happier society than ours then was. We all lived harmoniously together, having no disputes that I ever heard of."[60] Still, this blissful vision of his homeland changed in his adulthood. Already married and with three children, the young man participated with his father in a trading expedition that led them to the coast, "the place to which the White Men came."[61] On this occasion, he became aware of the Atlantic slave trade for the first time. In his first encounter with white Europeans, he was impressed by the importance of guns and luxury products in the trade with African natives: "I found the white men very different from what I had anticipated, being so covered with clothing, that there was hardly any knowing, except by their faces, whether they were black or white. They had a great variety of articles to dispose of, such as I had never seen; the use of many of which I could not comprehend."[62] In addition, he also provides an account of the participation of African intermediaries in the slave trade: "A Negro, who could speak both their language and ours, told them who we were, and bargained for us with them. It was now that I first saw a gun, heard its report, and witnessed its effects, and I was indeed truly astonished. A watch and a looking-glass greatly excited my wonder. They were, however, things of too much value for our purchasing."[63] Following this quick encounter with Europeans during which he witnessed how white merchants and local intermediaries developed the slave trade business, Zangara's peaceful life in his village was totally transformed. On their return, his father encouraged the villagers to prepare themselves for self-defense, including the use of spears, knives, and clubs. Some three weeks after the first encounter with the whites in the coast, white kidnappers attacked his village:

> I was awakened by a dreadful noise, which I knew at once was caused by the guns of the white men, for I had never heard any other noise at all like it. This was accompanied by continued shouting and screaming. I instantly jumped up, seized my spear and my knife, and telling Quahama to attend to the little ones, I rushed out of the house. The uproar and confusion were horrible, but I had no time to attend to small matters. Half the village was in flames! The roaring and flashing of the guns, with the shouts of the men, and the screams of the women, were truly appalling. I turned towards my father's house; two ruffian white men were dragging him, bleeding, away.[64]

Although Zangara's portrayal of the slave raid is similar to other slave narratives, the uniqueness of his account is that despite the long distance of his village from the coast, European men were in position to raid his community.

Kidnapping episodes are also present in legendary accounts of prominent African figures who were sold and sent into slavery to the Americas. For example, according to the oral tradition, Otampê Ojarorô and Obokô Mixôbiwo were twin princesses of the Kingdom of Ketu who founded the Candomblé temple Alaketu in Salvador (Brazil). Like Equiano and Cugoano, they were abducted together by Dahomean soldiers when they were only nine years old.[65] Similar stories of brothers and sisters kidnapped in the hinterland of the Bight of Benin were retold several times in novels and films as well. In the novel *Um defeito de cor* by Brazilian author Ana Maria Gonçalves, the protagonist Kehinde, an eight-year-old girl, narrates how she and her twin sister were abducted in Savalou by the soldiers of the Dahomean army, who brought them to Ouidah where they were sold and sent into slavery to Bahia in Brazil.[66] In the novel *Someone Knows My Name* by Canadian novelist Lawrence Hill, the protagonist and narrator is Aminata, a Muslim girl of eleven years of age from Futa Jallon.[67] The novel stresses the insecure climate that dominated this area of West Africa. Aminata was raised with stories "of men in other villages being stolen by invading warriors or even sold by their own people."[68] She also mentions that "others talked of the mysterious *toubabu*, the white men, whom none of us had ever seen."[69] As in other slave narratives, while Aminata, her mother, and an enslaved man were returning to their village during the night, they were ambushed by "four men with massive arms and powerful legs."[70] According to the narrator, the abductors had faces similar to hers but "no facial carvings," leading her to conclude that they came from another village.[71] Notwithstanding her father's attempt to escape the kidnappers and rescue her, the whole village was burned, its inhabitants were made captives, and they walked in coffles for days until arriving at the coast, where they were sold and sent to the Americas.

In other novels, however, the kidnapping narrative is slightly different. The presence of white men is introduced in order to clearly identify the Europeans as the perpetrators and West African natives as the victims. In the Pulitzer Prize–winning novel *Roots* (1976) by Alex Haley, a passage featuring a white man who ambushes and attacks with a club the protagonist Kunta Kinte became one of the iconic narratives of enslavement: "he heard the sharp crack of a twig, followed quickly by the squawk of a parrot overhead. [. . .] In a blur, rushing at him, he saw a white face, a club upraised, heard heavy footfalls behind him. *Toubob!*"[72] Likewise, in the television series adaptation of the novel, West African slavers, closely supervised by a *toubob*, a white North American man, penetrated the bushes. Then they caught the main character Kunta Kinte by surprise and abducted him, despite his strong resistance.

Haley's narrative of enslavement contains some iconic elements found not only in novels and films but also in visual images. In West Africa, the region featured in all these accounts, there were few isolated episodes of Europeans abducting men and women in the Bight of Biafra, including the case of the princes Little Ephraim Robin John and Ancona Robin Robin John. In 1767, the princes were made captives by English slave merchants in Old Calabar during a slave trade transaction and then sent into slavery in the Americas.[73] Isaac Parker, an English shipkeeper, also described his participation in a slave raid in the interior of Old Calabar, but he was rather an observer, whereas the local slave trader Dick Ebro led the initiative.[74] Despite these examples, it was unlikely or at least uncommon for North Americans and British to lead raids in the hinterland or coastal areas of West Africa and The Gambia, where Juffureh, the place where Kunta Kinte's village was allegedly situated. Indeed in these regions, most captives were obtained as "byproducts of civil war."[75] Yet this configuration was different in the hinterland and the coastal areas of West Central Africa, where Luso-Brazilian individuals actively participated in slave raids until the middle of the nineteenth century.[76] But if individual kidnappings were not the main form of supplying slaves, why did Haley choose to depict Kunta Kinte's enslavement as the result of a kidnapping led by a white North American, instead of a warfare raid?

Perhaps this choice was based on possible oral accounts transmitted by Haley's ancestors in which the traumatic context of warfare was erased and only the idea of kidnapping survived. More probably, the choice of placing the white man as the leading individual in the kidnapping is also related to the work of historical memory that relies not on actual facts of the past but rather on the present struggles of social groups that fight to assert their identities. In the context of the Civil Rights Movement, the opposition between whites and blacks was predictable because this antagonism was closely connected to the contemporary experience lived by African American men and women whose ancestors were enslaved Africans. Dismissing West African warfare and interstates conflicts was a means to avoid creating division among African Americans who faced daily racial segregation and violence.

Images and narratives depicting the capture of Africans provide elements to understanding how the Atlantic slave trade is remembered not only in the Atlantic world but also in the regions among which these visual and written accounts were disseminated. Matching the context of war and political conflicts involving the presence of European traders and intermediaries, the idea of kidnapping successfully conveys the general atmosphere of incertitude that characterized the era of the Atlantic slave trade.[77] As Rosalind Shaw points out, the trauma of the Atlantic slave trade also "includes the vast hinterland of violence and terror among those who remained on the African side of the Atlantic and were never taken as slaves, but who lived for centuries with both the anticipation and the consequences of warfare, raiding, and other means of enslavement that the Atlantic trade engendered and multiplied."[78] Therefore the figure of the white man that haunted the daily life of many African men and women during the eighteenth and nineteenth centuries symbolizes not only those who mainly benefited from slavery at the other side of the Atlantic Ocean but also African rulers and intermediaries.[79]

After being captured in the coastal areas or in the hinterland of West Africa, enslaved men and women were transported to the coast to be sold. Several visual illustrations and written accounts also depict slave coffles led by white merchants. One of the first renderings of a slave coffle (Figure 1.10) appeared in the definitive edition of *Histoire philosophique et politique des établissements et du commerce des Européens dans les deux Indes* (1780).[80] This book is the first global history of European colonization and until the French Revolution was considered one of the most important philosophical works of the eighteenth century. Its various tomes contain a total of nine engravings representing the main themes examined in the book. The engraving *Esclaves conduits par des marchands* (Slaves Led by Slave Merchants) illustrating the frontispiece of the third tome is a theatrical representation of a slave coffle in the West Indies. In the early nineteenth century, the original image was retaken and modified in the engraving *Nègres de traite en*

Figure 1.10 Esclaves conduits par des marchands (1780: engraving by Nicolas Delaunay [1739–1792], after Jean-Michel Moreau le Jeune [1741–1814]).

Figure 1.11 Nègres de traite en voyage [Hugo, 1835, vol. 3, 265; drawing by Eugène-Ferdinand Buttura (1812–1852); engraving by Lalement].

voyage (Negroes of Trade in Travel) (Figure 1.11), published in the account *France Pittoresque ou description pittoresque, topographique et statistique des départements et colonies de la France*.[81] The reproduction, modified to represent the enslavement of Africans in the region of Senegal, depicts the Muslim slave trade. The image accompanies a section of the book on Muslim slave merchants described as "active and intelligent for the trade, but liars, misleading, and robbers."[82] The author also explains that "[t]he trade of negroes, which was formerly the main branch of their trade, decreased a lot, since the English, after having filled their colonies with slaves, who they could need for one half-century, persuaded the peoples to whom they gave up their exhausted and depopulated colonies, to renounce to this infamous trade."[83] If the text only mentions the British abolition of the Atlantic slave trade, the three European slave merchants and part of the slave coffle depicted in the original engraving were suppressed in order to successfully convey the representation of the Muslim slave trade. Thus, *Nègres de traite en voyage* is an example of how images of slavery were adapted and transformed to represent the slave trade in many areas of the world. The manipulation to suppress the presence of European merchants was related to the British necessity of emphasizing on the one hand its benign role in the abolition of the Atlantic slave trade and on the other hand the nocuous presence of Muslim merchants who continued trading in slaves within the African continent. These transformations allowed publishers to adapt existing images to the new needs of European audiences. As a result, the construction of this image, allegedly representing the slave trade in Africa, is based on what Georges Didi-Huberman calls *montage*, an editing process that results from the selection, addition, and suppression of various elements.[84] As a composite unity, this kind of image depends on the art of memory because it reconstructs the past according to the needs that the prevailing groups have in the present moment. However, as any recycled object, this type of visual representation is formed by numerous layers, establishing a set of relations to different times and spaces, allowing viewers to follow the changing meanings attributed to slavery and the Atlantic slave trade.[85]

ABDUCTION NARRATIVES

The analysis of eighteenth- and nineteenth-century pictorial images and written accounts representing the enslavement of men, women, and children in West Africa during the period of the Atlantic slave trade reveals a certain form of continuity. Except for the accounts provided by the Dahomean rulers, most written, visual, and oral narratives tend not to emphasize warfare, even though it was the most important means to supply captives for the Atlantic slave trade. Whereas European travelogues and narratives written by former enslaved men from West Africa mention the context of warfare and instability that plagued this region of the African continent in the eighteenth and nineteenth centuries, very often the most common form of enslavement described is individual abduction. In addition to these abduction narratives, even if some of these written histories indicate that West African warriors, merchants, and other intermediaries were deeply involved in enslaving individuals, travel account illustrations systematically represent slavers and slave merchants as white men. This twist can be associated with three elements. First, the images published in most travelogues were produced by individuals who did not witness the events depicted and were rather influenced by British abolitionist ideas. Consequently, by portraying scenes of enslavement in this manner, these artists and engravers were trying to call attention to the harmful role played by Europeans in Africa. Second, because these images were printed in black and white, the only way to identify enslavers and enslaved was by distinguishing the color of their skin. Therefore, in these renderings African enslavers become white as a result of a technical need on the one hand and on the other hand as a metaphor that evokes the impact of the European presence in Africa. Third, even though the events portrayed occurred in West Africa, the creators of these images may have been influenced by reports and stories of enslavement in West Central Africa, a region where Luso-Brazilian individuals were deeply involved in capturing individuals until the end of the Atlantic slave trade.

The impact of these images is still present in the way the history of enslavement is represented today in public initiatives. If the role played by African slaver elites is sometimes highlighted in monuments recently built in West Africa, most movies and television series continually convey images relying on ideas provided by European travelogues, essentially exhibiting white European and North American men abducting individuals in the coastal areas or the interior of the African continent. This vision is also suggested in recent museum exhibitions or in the few existing museums that have dedicated particular sections to explain, through images, texts, and artifacts, the history of African societies and the contexts that led to the enslavement of millions of individuals. In most showcases, the context of enslavement is not explained in detail. Oftentimes, there is a clear contrast between the idyllic representation of African societies before the contact with the Europeans and a chaotic image that emerges after their arrival. These renderings reveal the difficulties in representing a sensitive past, whose scars remain present in all former slave societies. By failing to provide a complex portrait of African and European interactions, the recycled images that were originally intended to promote British abolitionist ideas are now aimed at responding to the demands of present-day black audiences. As a result, they continue to place the populations of African descent in a position of absolute victimhood, denying them any kind of agency.

NOTES

1. *Prince Among Slaves*, 2007 (DVD).
2. On the use of images of the slave trade to East Africa to represent the Atlantic slave trade, see Handler and Steiner, 2006: 52–54.
3. See Lovejoy, 2000: 4; Thornton, 1998: 99.
4. Lovejoy, 2000: 4.
5. See Sweet, 2011: Chap. 2. See also Araujo, 2012: 1–19.
6. Piqué and Rainer, 1999: 42. Today the palaces house the collections of the Musée historique d'Abomey (Historical Museum of Abomey).
7. Araujo, 2012: 1–19. The entire correspondence between Dahomean and Portuguese rulers was recently translated and published in Portuguese. See Parés, 2013: 295–395.
8. Piqué and Rainer, 1999: 70.
9. Law, 1989: 413.
10. Law, 1989: 402.
11. See Snelgrave, 1734: 160–161. On Francisco Félix de Souza, see Araujo, 2010a: 323. On William Snelgrave, see Sassi, 2006: 96–97.
12. See the painting *Boissy d'Anglas salue la tête du Député Féraud à la Convention Nationale, 20 mai 1795* (1830) by Jean-Auguste Tellier and the engravings *C'est ainsi qu'on se venge des traîtres* (1789), illustrating Bernard René

Jourdan de Launay's (1740–1789) beheading, and *Le Marquis de Launay gouverneur de la Bastille, Foulon [. . .]* (1789), representing the decapitated head of Joseph François Foulon (1715–1789).
13. See Araujo, 2010a: 261.
14. Craton, 1982: 314.
15. Instituto Histórico e Geográfico Brasileiro: Lata 137, Pasta 62, Doc. 1, ff. 6v, 7, n.d. See Araujo, 2012: 405.
16. Gronniosaw, 1770: 8.
17. Law, 1989: 403–405.
18. Chapter 19, "Abomey, House of the Kings," in *Cobra Verde*, directed by Werner Herzog (2000, DVD).
19. Herzog, 2000: Chap. 20.
20. "Relation de la Guerre de Juda par le S[ieu]r Ringard Capitaine du Navire le Mars de Nantes." The account was fully transcribed and published by Law, 1988: 321–338.
21. "ils firent main basse sur eux, & en vendirent les meilleurs, laissant impotoyablement perir les autres." Law, 1988: 326.
22. Dalzel, 2005: 55.
23. Norris, 1789. On Robert Norris, see Law, 1989: 219–235.
24. During the eighteenth century, European luxury products, including hats and various kinds of cloths like silk, were largely exchanged with Dahomean rulers, see Araujo, 2012.
25. Taylor, 1820: 62.
26. Herzog, 2000: Chap. 19.
27. Here the term is probably a reference to the communities of the north of the Mahi country. See Law, 1997: 214.
28. Forbes, 1851: vol. 1, 85. Many thanks to J. Cameron Monroe for calling my attention to this extract.
29. This information is available in the official tourist folder of the city of Abomey: "Visitez Abomey, Bénin: capitale historique de l'un des plus puissants royaumes d'Afrique" (Abomey, 2010). See also Lao, 2008.
30. I first heard this version from Professor Joseph Adande (Université d'Abomey-Calavi) during a visit to Ayidjosso (Abomey) in 2005, which he still confirms today.
31. The festival *Ouidah 92* was indeed held in February 1993. On the festival, see Araujo, 2010a: Chap. 4.
32. On the objectives of the International Slavery Museum, see Benjamin, 2012: 178.
33. Wemyss, 2009: 42.
34. Panel of the exhibition *London, Sugar, and Slavery: Revealing Our City's Untold History*, Museum of London Docklands, London, UK.
35. On the debates generated by the intervention of these organized groups, in both Liverpool and Bristol, see Chivallon, 2001; Dresser, 2009: Wallace, 2006: Chap. 1.
36. On the warfare in Africa during the period of the Atlantic slave trade, see Thornton, 1998: Chap. 4.
37. The account was written in 1594 and published for the first time in 1733. See d'Almada, 1841: 29–34.
38. Hawthorne, 2010: 64.
39. Atkins, 1735: 151.
40. See Curtin, 1997.
41. Sweet, 2011: 26–27.
42. Smith, 1798: 6.
43. Lovejoy and Law, 2003: 121. For a comparison of the slave narratives by Venture Smith, Olaudah Equiano, Mahommah Gardo Baquaqua, and Muhammad Kaba Saghanughu, see Lovejoy, 2011: 91–107.

44. On Agontimé's legend, see Araujo, 2011: 45–68. On Agontimé as the person who introduced Dahomey Vodun into Brazil, see Verger, 1952: 19–24; Parés, 2013: 91–115.
45. Equiano and Carretta, 2003: 47.
46. Equiano and Carretta, 2003: 47.
47. Cugoano, 1999: 12–13. For the original edition, see Cugoano, 1791.
48. See Lovejoy and Law, 2002: 137n, 151.
49. Taylor, 1820: 45.
50. Taylor, 1820: 46.
51. Papa Joãozinho in an interview to Milton Guran, 1999: 78.
52. Jacqueline Abul (born Vieyra), interviewed jointly with Renée Sadeler (born Vieyra), Cotonou, Republic of Benin, June 25, 2005.
53. See Araujo, 2010a: Chap. 7.
54. Levi, 1989: 27.
55. Gronniosaw, 1770: 4–5.
56. Gronniosaw, 1770: 5.
57. Taylor, 1820: 62.
58. Taylor, 1820: 62.
59. For a critique of the representations of the Middle Passage in *Amistad* and *The Middle Passage*, see Eckstein, 2008: 72–84.
60. *Slavery Illustrated...*, 1849: 2–3.
61. *Slavery Illustrated...*, 1849: 6.
62. *Slavery Illustrated...*, 1849: 6.
63. *Slavery Illustrated...*, 1849: 6.
64. *Slavery Illustrated...*, 1849: 7.
65. See Silveira, 2003: 345; On the narrative of the foundation myth provided by the *ialorixá* Olga de Alaketu, see Lima 1984: 11–28.
66. See Gonçalves, 2006.
67. See Hill, 2007a. The book was originally published in Canada as *The Book of Negroes* (Hill, 2007b).
68. Hill, 2007a: 13.
69. Hill, 2007a: 13.
70. Hill, 2007a: 23–24.
71. Hill, 2007a: 24.
72. Haley, 2007: 192.
73. See Sparks, 2004: 20–21.
74. See Thomas, 1997: 364.
75. See Lovejoy, 2000: 54.
76. See Candido, 2010: Chap. 5.
77. About European intermediaries and the case of Portuguese *lançados* in the Upper Guinea Coast, see Mark, 2002: Chap. 1.
78. Shaw, 2002: 32.
79. See Hawthorne, 2010: 64.
80. The book was first published in France in 1770, then reedited in 1774. See Raynal, 1780. See also Colin-Thébaudeau, 2005: 110.
81. Hugo, 1835: vol. 3, 265.
82. Hugo, 1835: 266.
83. Hugo, 1835: 266.
84. Didi-Huberman, 2009.
85. About the idea of image as a set of relations to time, see Didi-Huberman, 2009: 175.

2 Sites of Deportation

Former large slave ports, such as Badagry and Lagos in Nigeria, Luanda and Benguela in Angola, and Bunce Island in Sierra Leone, have not been successful in attracting international authorities or thousands of tourists from the African diaspora. The reason for this neglect is hard to determine, but in the cases of Sierra Leone and Angola, the political instability that followed their independence, leading to dictatorships and civil wars, played a crucial role in preventing the emergence of initiatives to publicly highlight the major role of their local ports in the Atlantic slave trade. Whereas in Sierra Leone, the memories of slavery were rather confined to the private sphere, in Angola they were intertwined with the memory of forced labor imposed during Portuguese colonial rule.[1]

After exploring the memorialization of enslavement in Africa, this chapter discusses how the deportation of Africans is memorialized and reenacted in slave trade heritage sites located on the West African coastline, especially in present-day Ghana, Republic of Benin, and Senegal. Although scholars have questioned the very possibility of accurately depicting the various stages of dehumanization associated with the Atlantic slave trade and other human tragedies, the chapter looks at how the public memory of the Atlantic slave trade is constantly associated with representations of the Holocaust by political authorities and other social actors who visit heritage sites of deportation in West Africa. My analysis relies on Michael Rothberg's idea of multidirectional memory as "the dynamic transfers that take place between diverse places and times during the act of remembrance."[2] I argue that in Ghana, slave trade sites became iconic not only because of their use as slave depots during the Atlantic slave trade but also because of structural elements, especially gates that, much as in Holocaust heritage sites, work as symbolical features connecting the worlds of the living and the dead. For example, I show that in Republic of Benin, where the only surviving slave fort is two miles from the coast, the lack of visible symbols representing the deportation of Africans was replaced with a newly built Gate of No Return. The chapter also discusses the former slave port of Gorée Island (Senegal) and its controversial *Maison des esclaves* (House of Slaves). Even though I have examined this case in my previous book, here I explore the recent twinning initiative connecting the island and the Drancy concentration camp, the most important of French Holocaust heritage sites.[3] By looking at these various examples, this chapter reveals how the presentation and interpretation of slave trade sites of deportation have established fruitful and sometimes intriguing dialogues with the public memorialization of the Holocaust. The study of these related initiatives shows the persistent difficulties in officially inscribing the memory of the Atlantic slave trade in the public space.

SLAVE DEPOTS

The first Atlantic slave trade heritage sites were constructed as early as the beginning of the fifteenth century. Yet the discussion about the challenges of representing the tragedy and the trauma of the various stages of the slave trade in the public space emerged only in the aftermath of the Second World War. At a time when European rule in Africa was dramatically shaken and when the horrors of the Holocaust were gradually unveiled, both Africans and peoples of African descent in Europe and the Americas were reminded about the atrocities of the Atlantic slave trade and colonization. Consequently, although the Atlantic slave trade ended in the 1860s, most slave trade heritage sites, such as the slave castles and European fortresses created along the coast of West Africa, were restored and opened to public visitation after 1945, coinciding with the unveiling of the main Holocaust sites. However, most monuments and memorials of slavery and the Holocaust were created in the early 1990s. This is not a coincidence. Although the Atlantic slave trade and the Holocaust are two very different phenomena, the processes of memorialization of these two atrocities gained importance at the same time during the period following the end of the Cold War, and they sometimes carried similar features.

Following the end of the Second World War, when the massive crimes committed in Nazi camps were revealed and disseminated through photographs and written narratives by Holocaust survivors, scholars intensively debated the relevancy and the prospects of representing situations involving extreme human suffering. The questions about how to render the Holocaust in words and images were similar to the issues associated with memorializing the Atlantic slave trade and slavery in the public space.[4] Whereas some scholars consider fiction an adequate means to portray atrocities, other scholars and Holocaust survivors opposed fictional representations by underscoring the ethical problems that it posed. Theodor Adorno, for example, maintains that eyewitness accounts are the most powerful instruments to accurately convey the horrors of the experiences in the concentration camps during that genocidal period.[5] But historians like Christopher R. Browning underscore the problems related to the use of testimonies, especially when "the emotional desire to believe has been allowed to eclipse the critical approach that should apply to any historical source."⁶ Despite these debates, since 1945 multiple forms of fictionalization of the Holocaust, including novels, plays, films, and television series, continue to appear every year, even though their success among various audiences was and still is closely related to the ability of its authors to incorporate true stories or elements of eyewitnesses' testimonies. During this period, these testimonies greatly inspired the development of initiatives memorializing the Holocaust in the public space. However, unlike the survivors of the Holocaust, the witnesses of the Atlantic slave trade were no longer alive to provide accounts of their traumatic experiences. Though the memories of the atrocities committed during the era of the Atlantic slave trade and slavery were transmitted to descendants of slaves and slavers and survived among some particular families and groups, these memories remained private and hardly appeared in the public sphere. Consequently, the public interpretation of West African heritage sites of deportation is not based on direct testimonies of descendants of slaves. Instead, like the depictions of enslavement on African soil discussed in the first chapter, they rely on European travel accounts and slave narratives. Moreover, very often these interpretations are based on reenactments that depend on the performing ability of local actors, such as tourist guides and curators, whose aim is targeting international audiences.

In West Africa, the main heritage sites of the Atlantic slave trade were fortresses and slave castles used as slave depots. After being captured and displaced, captives were kept in these places for several weeks before being deported to the Americas. Some of these sites have existed since the fifteenth century. However, the first initiatives aiming at preserving these buildings can be traced to the 1940s and became more intense during the period of the decolonization of Africa. Although, the inhabitants of coastal areas of West Africa were used to the presence of the castles and slave depots, only the largest and better conserved buildings became renowned heritage sites and attracted international visitors. Starting in the 1960s, the House of Slaves (Gorée Island), the Cape Coast and Elmina castles (Ghana), and Ouidah (Republic of Benin) were among the most important slave trade destinations for political and religious authorities as well as for international tourists. The prominence and popularity of these West African sites—regions highlighted in European travel accounts—contrasted with the lack of initiatives promoting the departure ports for the majority of captives where they left to the Americas, like Lagos in present-day Nigeria, Bunce Island in Sierra Leone, and Luanda and Benguela in modern Angola.

The development and promotion of the Atlantic slave trade sites were launched by their addition to the national heritage lists in the various countries and later helped by their inclusion in the UNESCO World Heritage List. Because of its numerous slave castles from where Africans were deported to the Americas, Ghana became a crucial player not only in the process of memorializing the Atlantic slave trade in the public space but also in the promotion of African diaspora tourism.[7] In 1972, the government of Ghana added 22 old fortresses and castles to its National Heritage List, which remained under the protection of the law and under the authority of the Ghana Museums and Monuments Board.[8] Among these sites is the Elmina Castle. Built by the Portuguese in 1482, it is the first European trading post established in West Africa. In 1637, the Dutch seized the castle, transforming it into an important slave trading post until 1814, when the Anglo-Dutch Treaty (Convention of London) abolished the Dutch slave trade. Eventually, in 1872 the British took control of the castle. When the Gold Coast won independence in 1957, waves of African Americans, including prestigious visitors such as Malcolm X and Maya Angelou, traveled or moved to the new independent Ghana. W. E. B. Du Bois moved to Ghana in 1961 and lived there until his death in 1967.

In 1974, the Cape Coast Castle Museum, housed in the castle, opened to the public. In 1979, UNESCO approved the inclusion of Elmina and Cape Coast castles on the World Heritage List, along with another ten castles in the regions of Volta, Accra, and its environs.[9] In 1994, the Cape Coast Castle Museum permanent exhibition, *Crossroads of a People, Crossroads of Trade,* was reconfigured with the help of numerous consultants from Ghana and the United States. The exhibition examines the history of the country, encompassing the period of the Atlantic slave trade, and includes panels with texts, maps, engravings, and photographs, in addition to a station that evokes the Middle Passage with reproductions of the holds of slave ships. It was only in 1997 that a museum was opened in the Elmina Castle. As in the Cape Coast Cast Museum, its modest exhibition titled *Images of Elmina Across Centuries* is constituted mainly of panels containing texts and images and focuses on local history.

Notwithstanding these initiatives, the most popular feature of Cape Coast Castle is the guided tour of its dungeons, the condemned cell, and the so-called Door of No Return. Unlike the experience of visiting static exhibits, by touring these parts of the site with a guide, visitors can experience the confinement atmosphere in which African captives were maintained for long weeks after being captured and brought in caravans from the hinterland to the Atlantic coastline.[10] Over time, if the dungeons and cells became powerful icons of the brutal conditions in which Africans were kept before embarkation to the Americas, the Door of No Return was transformed into a symbolic element of the deportation of Africans to the New World, whose symbolism was also reproduced in other West African heritage sites.

In the middle of the 1980s, Elmina Castle received some international attention as one of the main locations where Herzog's film *Cobra Verde* was shot. Since the 1990s, during the government of Jerry Rawlings, Elmina and Cape Coast castles received prestigious visitors, including former US presidents Bill Clinton and George W. Bush, along with

Michäelle Jean, then General Governor of Canada.[11] Moreover, in 1999, the story of Ghana's slave castles became known to a larger US audience through the television series *Wonders of the African World*, presented by African American scholar Henry Louis Gates. In the episode called "The Slave Kingdoms," Gates visited the Elmina Castle. Arriving in the castle, he notes that in Elmina the memory of slavery is always lurking. According to him, "even a pretty little harbor town like Elmina is dominated by a slave castle and for us a slave castle is like Auschwitz."[12] This statement is reinforced in another scene of the documentary, when the Ghanaian guide who leads visitors through the Elmina dungeons asserts that half of the slaves kept there would die of malaria or yellow fever because of the poor hygiene conditions. Despite the comparison, the documentary does not discuss any possible similarities between a slave depot, where enslaved Africans were gathered under horrible conditions to be exported to the Americas, and a Nazi killing camp. The lack of explanation could lead to the assumption that the goal of the Atlantic slave trade was to exterminate prisoners of war and other individuals enslaved for various reasons. Although death was present during the whole process of enslavement, the Middle Passage, and the arrival in the Americas, enslaved individuals were valuable commodities not only to the local intermediaries but also to the European merchants. Therefore, stating that the Atlantic slave trade was intended to kill particular groups of Africans just as the Holocaust was designed to exterminate Jews and other groups (Roma, homosexuals, and opponents of the Nazi regime) is misunderstanding the complexity of an enterprise whose nature was primarily economic. Although numerous enslaved men and women were placed in noisome, small dungeons before being shipped to the Americas, death was a consequence of a lack of knowledge about sanitary conditions and not a final solution, unlike what activists and scholars like Elizabeth Kowaleski Wallace seem to suggest when they freely use the term "African Holocaust."[13] Also, in another scene of the documentary, the guide adds an anachronistic explanation about the slave trade by declaring that Africans sold other Africans to the Europeans. The guide's discourse is reinforced during the documentary as Gates repeats several times that Africans sold their "own people," dismissing the fact that the idea of Africans and peoples of African descent being "one people" gradually emerged as a consequence of the Atlantic slave trade late in the nineteenth century. Indeed, the groups involved in the trade were individuals living in different lands, belonging to different states and societies, with different ethnic origins and religions, and speaking different languages. In other words, they could hardly be identified as "one people." In addition, the guide also adds: "It was the Africans who did the raiding and selling of Africans to the Europeans. No European ever went into the hinterland to raid for slaves. It was the Africans who did it."[14] Although this statement can be applied to the Gold Coast, as discussed in Chapter 1, Portuguese were deeply involved in raids in West

Central Africa.¹⁵ Following this scene, some tour participants tell Gates they were surprised and angry to learn the extent of the African involvement in the Atlantic slave trade. As a result, the visit to Elmina's dungeons presented in the episode "The Slave Kingdoms" of *Wonders of the African World* shows disappointed and moved African American visitors, whose journeys to Ghana are primarily intended to reconnect with their ancestors who were deported to the Americas. Moreover, as Gates states in the first Elmina's scenes of the episode, African Americans feel happy to be in Africa because they are among blacks. Thus, in a first moment, there is a sentiment that they share the same heritage with Ghanaians of various origins. It is this assumed common pan-African heritage that led the guide and Gates to use the term "Africans" as one people to refer to the local rulers and intermediaries who actively participated in the Atlantic slave trade.¹⁶

In July 2009, first African American US President Barack Obama and his family visited the Cape Coast Castle in Ghana. On this occasion, Obama gave a special interview to CNN anchor Anderson Cooper. While they were walking in the castle's courtyard, Cooper asks the president how he felt about visiting the site. Obama responds: "I am reminded of the same feeling I've got when I went to Buchenwald with Elie Wiesel, you know [. . .] as the walls can speak, and you try to project yourself into these incredibly harrowing moments that people go through."¹⁷ The president's observation refers to a comment made by Wiesel when they visited Buchenwald together on June 5, 2009. While they toured the Nazi camp and saw the area surrounding the site, Wiesel asked himself "if these trees could talk," thus evoking the vision that the beautiful landscape was a silent witness to the atrocities committed there. By associating the experience of enslaved Africans with the experience lived by the Jews who were sent to Buchenwald to perform forced labor and eventually to be killed, Obama highlights two main issues. First, despite the absence of living eyewitnesses to the Atlantic slave trade and slavery, the memories of these atrocities are imprinted forever in the sites where these crimes were committed. Second, by remembering his visit to Buchenwald with Holocaust survivor Elie Wiesel, Obama underscores how the experience of visiting these sites of memory become even more powerful in the company of the eyewitness victims. But with Obama and Cooper, there was no local guide interpreting the castle as there was during Gates' tour of Elmina. After crossing Cape Coast Castle's Door of No Return, Cooper asks Obama whether the slave experience was something that should be talked about and remembered and whether it should be present in everyday life. The president answers:

> I think that the experience of slavery is like the experience of the Holocaust, I think it is one of those things you don't forget about. I think that it is important that the way we think about it, the way it is taught is not one in which there is simply a victim and a victimizer

and that's the end of the story. I think that the way it has to be taught about, the reason it is relevant it's because whether it is ... what is happening in Darfur or what is happening in the Congo or what is happening in too many places around the world, and the capacity of cruelty still exists, the capacity for discrimination still exists, the capacity to think about people who are different not only on the basis of race but on the basis of religion or the basis of sexual orientation or gender.[18]

When Obama associates slavery and the Holocaust, he emphasizes that the main legacy of slavery is discrimination in general, even though at the same time he cleverly omits specific examples. By stating that the simple opposition between victim and victimizer should be avoided, the president seems to suggest that during the Atlantic slave trade there were African victims and African perpetrators. Although he cleverly establishes a relation between the slave past and the conflicts occurring today in Congo and Darfur, which are the result of centuries of slave trade and decades of European colonial rule, the president does not explain what possible similarities existed between the genocides in Congo and Darfur and the Holocaust and what elements in common these genocides could possibly have with the enslavement of Africans. In short, Obama avoids engaging in the discussion of the present legacies of slavery in the Americas in general and in the United States in particular.

Gates and Obama were not the first African Americans to establish a connection between slavery and the Holocaust. In 1949, following previous visits to Poland and to Nazi Germany, W. E. B. Du Bois visited the Warsaw Ghetto, an experience that transformed his vision of the issue of color line.[19] The city was in ruins, and most of its population had been killed during the war. In his 1952 article "The Negro and the Warsaw Ghetto," Du Bois explains the way this visit impacted his understanding of the problems of racism and prejudice. The article addresses issues similar to those raised by Obama, almost 60 years later, by emphasizing that the result of the visits to Poland and to the Warsaw Ghetto was a "much clearer understanding of the Jewish problem in the world as it was a real and more complete understanding of the Negro problem. In the first place, the problem of slavery, emancipation, and caste in the United States was no longer in my mind a separate and unique thing as I had so long conceived it."[20] As Michael Rothberg notes, the connection between the segregation of African Americans and the Jewish issue was heavily influenced by the context of the Cold War and increasing anti-Communist persecutions, of which both Jewish and African Americans activists such as Du Bois were victims. In this new context, Communism "provided one of the discursive spheres, both in the United States and elsewhere, in which the articulation of genocide and colonialism" could be developed.[21] Still, over the ensuing decades these connections continue to influence the ways in which the

Holocaust and slavery in the Americas are memorialized in Africa, Europe, and the Americas.

Every year, thousands of visitors from around the world, especially African Americans and Afro-Caribbeans, visit Elmina and Cape Coast castles to pay homage and to commemorate the memory of their ancestors.[22] In the entrance of the courtyard of Elmina Castle, next to the door of a condemned dungeon, a marble plaque reads: "In everlasting memory of the anguish of our ancestors may those who died rest in peace, may those who return find their roots, may humanity never again perpetrate such injustice against humanity. We the living vow to uphold this," evoking the idea of mourning and return. Since 1998, in order to encourage the dialogue about the African diaspora, August 1, the date of the emancipation of slaves in the British colonies, is officially celebrated in Ghana.[23] To mark the first celebration of Emancipation Day, the skeletons of two Africans enslaved in Jamaica and the United States, whose origins were retraced and associated with the Gold Coast, were brought back to Ghana. In a public ceremony, the remains were introduced through the Door of the No Return. On this occasion, the Cape Coast Castle's door was renamed Door of Return, and a plaque with the new name was added to the external side of the door. Hence, the focus was no longer the memorialization of the deportation of Africans from the Gold Coast but rather the celebration of the return of the members of the diaspora from the Americas and the Caribbean, who now contribute to a growing tourism industry in the country.

Although the Door of No Return of Elmina Castle is rather discrete and its access to the sea is not clearly visible, the visit to its dark, humid, and moldy dungeons where enslaved men, women, and children were kept confined, sometimes for several months in atrocious conditions, is shocking and moving, even to the visitors who were well prepared for the visit. Unlike a museum exhibition, the visit to the dungeons offers a unique perspective of the atrocities experienced by enslaved men and women before being sent to the Americas. In addition to touring and taking pictures of the dungeons, African American visitors post the videos of their visits on YouTube, to which they give the titles "Cape Coast Holocaust Dungeons" or "Elmina Holocaust Dungeons," showing that the association between the slave trade and the Holocaust, established by tour guides, is disseminated by tourists as well.

In Ghana, as in other slave trade heritage sites in West Africa, tour guides often provide accounts of the Atlantic slave trade to satisfy broad audiences, in particular African diaspora tourists. As Elizabeth MacGonagle explained, what is usually emphasized is "the suffering of Africans at the hands of Europeans."[24] Unlike the guide of Gates's documentary, in general there are few mentions of African participation in the slave trade enterprise. These simplified narratives respond to the specific demands of tourism consumption, preventing the emergence of conflicts not only among the local communities that today still include descendants of enslaved individuals but also among international visitors, most of them members of the African diaspora along with a smaller number of nonblack individuals from Europe and the Americas.[25]

Although heritage sites like Elmina Castle continue to attract thousands of visitors each year, tourists' presence around the castles contrasts with the poor living conditions of Elmina's population, leading locals to say that "Americans come here to cry but they don't leave their money behind."[26] In Elmina, as in other coastal cities of West Africa, several obstacles prevent tourism development, including what local administration calls harassment of tourists. According to a 2003 report released by Elmina town, the harassment of tourists "typically takes the form of young boys inventing stories to invite sympathy of the tourist and subsequently pestering them for addresses, money and other valuables. In some cases tourist's wallets and bags are snatched."[27] Moreover, the intervention of police authorities has not been able to stop the harassment of tourists. These observations, formulated by the local administrative authorities, show a deep contradiction. Whereas the town aims to develop cultural tourism based on the denunciation of human atrocities of the past, slavery tourism is totally dissociated from the difficult living conditions of deprived local communities who underwent the effects of the Atlantic slave trade for centuries. Despite the popular African diaspora discourses promoting the unification of the populations of African descent, a deep cleavage between wealthy black tourists, who among others have the means to travel overseas, and the impoverished local population is clearly visible. Indeed, Obama observed this division when asked by Anderson Cooper how he felt returning to Africa:

> I know African Americans who come to Africa, are profoundly moved, but also realize, how American they are when they're here, and you know, recognize they could never live here, and that is part of the African American experience, you are in some ways, you are connected to this distant land, but on the other hand you are about as American as it gets, in some ways African Americans are more fundamentally rooted in the American experience because they don't have a recent immigrant experience to draw on, it is an unique African American culture that has existed in North America for hundreds of years long before we actually founded the nation.[28]

By avoiding questioning how Ghanaians receive African Americans, President Obama suggests that today African American travels to Africa are rather temporary journeys that do not put their deeply anchored national identities in question.

The linkages between the memorialization of the Atlantic slave trade and the Holocaust are also visible in more recent and commercial initiatives led by prominent African Americans who visited the Nazi camps. Following Adorno's recommendation that no other representation of atrocities could replace eyewitnesses' accounts, in January 2006, Oprah Winfrey and Holocaust survivor Elie Wiesel paid a visit to the Auschwitz death camp complex. On May 24, 2006, the Oprah Winfrey Show aired a 60-minute episode documenting the visit. The show presented Oprah and Wiesel touring Auschwitz I concentration camp, Auschwitz II (Birkenau) killing center, and the Auschwitz III forced labor camp, totally covered with snow. Footage of their detailed visit, including the barracks, the crematorium, the prison, the gas chambers, and the various displays of the Auschwitz-Birkenau State Museum State, was alternated with pictures and footage showing the death camp during the Second World War and extracts of Wiesel's book *Night*.[29] While they visited the various parts of the death camp complex, Oprah interviewed Wiesel, who movingly recalled the atrocities he experienced and witnessed in the death camp. During the interview, Oprah does not evoke any similarity between the Holocaust and the Atlantic slave trade and slavery, but Wiesel offers an enlightening description of what it was like to perform forced labor in a Nazi camp. Unlike plantation slaves, in the Nazi camps, failure to perform the work would provoke not recurrent physical punishment but rather a death sentence: "When they order you something, you had to run. A slave runs. And we were the exemplary slaves, therefore you had to run."[30] Wiesel's statement rejoins Christopher R. Browning's description of the Starachowice labor camp by underscoring how labor was a "Jewish strategy of survival."[31] Although the Atlantic slave trade is not mentioned, Wiesel's description of slave labor in a Nazi camp contradicts the main element of the popular association with the Holocaust. Like enslaved Africans kept in the dungeons to be exported to the Americas, Jews who performed slave labor were not supposed to be killed immediately.

Other West African slave trade heritage sites have also attracted African American and Afro-Caribbean tourists. Ouidah was the second most important slave port after Luanda. Starting in the early seventeenth century, France, England, and Portugal established fortified factories in Ouidah, but only the Portuguese fort of São João Batista, built in 1721, survived the end of the Atlantic slave trade. The building, which today houses Le Musée d'histoire de Ouidah (The Ouidah Museum of History), is smaller than any Ghana's slave castle and located more than two miles from the Ouidah's coastline.[32] Also, unlike Elmina or Cape Coast castles, the museum is not intended to tell the story or recreate the experience of the victims of the Atlantic slave trade.[33] The museum's exhibition offers little explanation about how the building was used. Instead the focus is on the history of Ouidah, its involvement in the Atlantic slave trade, and the connections between Dahomey and Brazil.

In 1992, on the eve of the festival Ouidah 92 celebrating African religions and Benin's connections with the African diaspora in the Americas, Benin's President Nicéphore Soglo, one of the most enthusiastic supporters of a new Marshall Plan for Africa, pronounced various speeches addressed to international audiences in which he compared the Atlantic slave trade to the Holocaust.[34] In a speech given on July 13, 1992, during the 28th Summit of OUA (Organization of African Unity), he reminds his peers about the necessity of discussing in the public arena the impacts of the Atlantic slave trade and the colonization, in the view of attracting international tourists, by stating: "Elie Wiesel wrote somewhere that the perpetrator always kills twice, the second time, through forgetting. The black peoples, from here and elsewhere, for their survival and their renaissance do not have the right to forget."[35] Indeed, Soglo was referring to a passage of the preface of *La Nuit*, the original French version of *Night* published in 1958, in which Wiesel states that: "For the survivor who chooses to testify, it is clear: his duty is to bear witness for the dead and for the living. He has no right to deprive future generations of a past that belongs to our collective memory. To forget would be not only dangerous but offensive; to forget the dead would be akin to killing them a second time."[36] Following this speech, Soglo used this quote once again in November 1992, in his call to the "black peoples," in which he made a public invitation to the festival *Ouidah 92*, published in the local newspapers.[37] In the festival's opening speech, Soglo did not quote Wiesel. Instead, he quoted his own speech pronounced at the unveiling of the Ouidah's Portuguese fort (The Ouidah Museum of History) some months earlier by stating: "No Dahomean, no Beninese, no Africain, no African American, no man of culture can fail to be deeply moved at discovering one of the high points of the Black Holocaust."[38] At this point, Soglo was publicly positioning Ouidah's name in the competition for the most important sites of memory of the Atlantic slave trade, but because this title was not sufficient, he seems to reinforce the position of the former slave port by comparing it to a site of the Holocaust. As part of this enterprise, he invites the descendants of slaves from the Americas, in particular from the United States, to develop an "active solidarity," which was indeed intended to attract them to visit Benin as tourists. As part of this context, a Slaves' Route, starting at Ouidah's downtown and ending on the beach, was opened in 1993, as part of the activities of the Vodun festival *Ouidah 92*. To mark the route, dozens of monuments and memorials created by several Beninese artists were placed along the route. However, the idea at the heart of this initiative was not new. A report commissioned by UNESCO in 1984, aimed to establish an international center for the study and research about the slave trade and the black diaspora in The Ouidah Museum of History. In this report, UNESCO recommended to highlight Ouidah's crucial role in the Atlantic slave trade, including giving the city the title of "museum city."[39] Relying on work developed in collaboration with Beninese and French scholars, including Pierre Verger (1902–1996), the report proposed the museum's exhibition be expanded in order to help the discovery of the city's slave past. In a clear, and perhaps the first, attempt to initiate a process of memorialization of the Atlantic slave trade in Ouidah's public space, the creation of a route evoking the path taken by the enslaved before their embarkment to the Americas was recommended. For this purpose, the document recommended the installation of several markers all over the city to explain these various stations. Among the places to be highlighted were the Zoungbodji site, which allegedly was the location where the enslaved were branded with red-hot irons; the place of the "captains' tree," where the enslaved "would abandon their spirits" before their departure; the site where the enslaved were embarked on canoes to cross the lagoon; and a site situated at the end of the path towards the beach, where the enslaved were allegedly locked up before their embarkation. To underscore the importance of this last place, keeping the site's "authenticity and emotional power" was proposed.[40] Finally, the report also suggested marking the numerous Vodun temples spread all over the city and opening the residences of former Brazilian slave returnees and Luso-Brazilian slave merchants, "which are themselves small museums," to public visitation, in particular the home of Brazilian slave trader Francisco Félix de Souza (1754–1849). However, UNESCO did not follow up on any of these recommendations. Until 1991, Benin had been under a military dictatorship. As a result, it was unlikely that government authorities would wish not only to highlight the country's slave past but also to develop any initiative to promote Vodun religion. Only in 1991, after the end of the dictatorship ended and when democratic elections took place, did the country's slave past become an important topic of public debate, leading to the creation of the Slaves' Route.[41]

In 1995, a new imposing Gate of No Return was unveiled on Ouidah's beach, at the end of the Slaves' Route. The memorial is an enormous door opening to the sea, aiming to commemorate the victims of the Atlantic slave trade. Traditionally, doors and gates depicting a hole are considered as female symbols associated with both fertility and an opening to another world. In monuments commemorating the Atlantic slave trade, the doors or gates are usually located in former slave ports from where the enslaved were sent the Americas. In these monuments and memorials, the continent is usually depicted by the figure of the mother, symbolizing the transition between two worlds, between life and death. In Ouidah's Gate of No Return, a slave ship is represented exactly in the middle of the entablature atop the four columns of the gate. Two converging lines of naked captives walk in the same position in the direction of the slave ship, representing the last stage of dehumanization before the beginning of the Middle Passage. At the other side of the monument facing the sea, two sculptures depict the Egunguns, symbolizing the spirits of the ancestors and evoking the dead, the thousands of captives who did not survive deportation to the Americas. Here, the lack of heritage sites with doors opening to the sea (like those existing in Ghana's slave trade heritage sites) marking the deportation of Africans from Ouidah, was compensated by the creation of newly constructed memorials and monuments.

FROM GORÉE TO DRANCY

Senegal was the first West African country to promote its slave trade heritage sites. In 1944, the French colonial administration listed Gorée Island as an historical site, and in 1951, some measures to safeguard the island were undertaken. During the 1960s, the House of Slaves started acquiring international notoriety. Among its visitors were political and religious authorities and African American tourists for whom West African slave heritage sites replaced the absence of sites of remembrance of slavery in the United States.[42] Despite this popularity, the name "House of Slaves" is a more recent creation. In 1839, a lithograph titled *Une habitation a Gorée (Maison d'Anna Colas)* (Figure 2.1), by the French artist and engraver Adolphe d'Hastrel de Rivedoux (1805–1875), represents the building today known as the House of Slaves. The title of the engraving suggests that the owner of the house was not a European slave merchant but a *signare* named Anna Colas. *Signares* were Afro-European and free African women slave traders, well-known during the eighteenth and the

Figure 2.1 Une habitation a Gorée (Maison d'Anna Colas) (1839 lithograph by Adolphe d'Hastrel de Rivedoux).

nineteenth centuries in the region of Gorée and Saint-Louis.[43] Nevertheless, as in other West African initiatives promoting slave trade heritage sites, the public interpretation of the House of Slaves never underscored the role of these in-between women. Addressing this issue would require not only discussing the role of local men and women in the development of the Atlantic slave trade but also explaining internal enslavement and therefore the existence of slave ownership by indigenous families.[44] By 1951, a guide of the island, written by the French historian Raymond Mauny (1912–1994) and published in French, is probably the first written work referring to the building as the House of Slaves.[45]

Although a modest building in comparison to other slave trade heritage sites found on the West African coastline, the Houses of Slaves (Figure 2.2) gained reputation due to the narrative developed by its curator Boubacar Joseph N'Diaye (1922–2009). A veteran of the French army during the Second World War, N'Diaye became the curator of the House of Slaves, a position he occupied until his death in 2009.[46] In his guided tours, he moved international visitors by explaining how the two-story house was used as a slave depot.[47] In his performances describing the house, the curator used to state that the house could lodge about 200 slaves, who remained in the

Figure 2.2   House of Slaves, Gorée Island (picture by Robin Elaine Taylor, 2004).

dungeons for two to three months before embarking to the Americas. In one of the moving parts of the tour, he explained that each small cell accommodated between 15 and 20 enchained men and women, by holding a set of chains and shackles. During the 1990s, N'Diaye's narrative was officially incorporated into the building, when "plastic signs were put over the doors, labeling each room by the classification it held."[48] By this same period, African American Professor Dwain Pruitt published a series of letters titled "Across the Globe" in the newspaper *Herald-Journal*, reporting on his visit to several "Third World" countries, including Senegal. In an article recalling his visit to Gorée Island, Pruitt helps to disseminate N'Diaye's invented estimates by repeating that "Gorée served as the final West African port of departure for approximately 12 million African slaves, possibly including my ancestors."[49] After describing in detail N'Diaye's office as containing "remnants of the slave trade like chains, rifles and old shipping manifests," he explains that the walls were covered with photos of prominent visitors to Gorée, including then chairman of the Democratic Party Ron Brown, the actor Danny Glover, and Pope John Paul II.[50] In addition, according to Pruitt, there were also "passages of poetry written by the curator. One particular poem caught my eye: "Gorée, Dachau . . . what long road remains before we become human beings?"[51] Unique to Gorée, this kind of explicit written reference to the Holocaust is not only the result of N'Diaye's particular vision of the Atlantic slave trade but also of his own agenda to promote the site.[52]

The pictures and texts displayed in N'Diaye's office are intended to confirm the importance of the House of Slaves. Whereas the portraits of international personalities speak for themselves, the poem written by the curator attempts to legitimize the site by establishing an association with the Dachau Nazi concentration camp located in the suburb of Munich. From 1933 to 1945, 200,000 individuals were imprisoned in Dachau, and 41,500 of them died.

Like Elmina and Cape Coast, the House of Slaves has its Door of No Return opening out to the sea. According to N'Diaye's narrative, the captives were embarked through the door on slave ships sailing to the Americas, even though the rocks outside the door indicate that it would be difficult for any boat to embark captives in this location. The curator also stated that 10 million and 15 million enslaved Africans passed through the House of Slaves before leaving for the Americas.[53] These numbers greatly differ not only from Philip Curtin's initial census establishing how many enslaved Africans crossed the Atlantic Ocean during the Atlantic slave trade but also from the most recent estimates of 12,521,000.[54] Still today, despite the latest estimates provided by *The Trans-Atlantic Slave Trade Database: Voyages* indicating that, between 1514 and 1866, the slave exports from Gorée Island numbered 33,562, the House of Slaves continues to occupy the position of an important site of memory of the Atlantic slave trade, attracting 200,000 tourists every year.[55]

Indeed, the discourses of the various actors involved in the memorialization of the House of Slaves are rather marked by present political issues than by concerns with historical accuracy.[56]

Over the years, N'Diaye continued describing the tragedy of the Atlantic slave trade by employing the word "holocaust." On October 20 and 21, 1991, N'Dyaie toured the United States. In a lecture titled "The First Storyteller of the Slave House in Gorée Island" at the Rackham Memorial Auditorium and the Wayne County Community in Detroit, Michigan, he stated: "Torture, humiliation and total separation of African families fostered the Industrial Revolution. No other human holocaust matches the Atlantic slave trade where 30–50 million people died during transport to Europe and the Americas."[57] According to him, the death rate during the Middle Passage was three to five times higher than the total number of Africans deported from Africa during the Atlantic slave trade.

During the 1990s, when a growing interest in the memory and the heritage of slavery emerged in West Africa, historians like Philip Curtin publicly manifested their disagreement regarding the narrative that insisted on Gorée as an important slave port and the House of Slaves as a slave depot.[58] During the discussion, the association with the Holocaust emerged once again, when scholars labeled Curtin's criticism as similar to Holocaust negationism. In the following years, the debate also became visible in French circles, especially in 1996, when the journalist Emmanuel de Roux published a short article in the newspaper *Le Monde,* challenging N'Diaye's account of the House of Slaves, extending the debate to Senegalese newspapers as well.[59]

Over the years, the great visibility of the House of Slaves as a site of memory overshadowed important initiatives developed on Gorée Island, especially the Musée Historique du Sénégal à Gorée (Historical Museum of Senegal on Gorée), which is the institution in charge of presenting the history of the Atlantic slave trade on Gorée Island and conveying the various dimensions of the history of Senegambia and French West Africa.[60] Instituted in 1954 as the Musée de l'Afrique Occidentale (Museum of French West Africa), the museum was established, almost ten years prior to the House of Slaves, in a house owned by a *signare* in the nineteenth century.

In spite of the controversies regarding Gorée's House of Slaves, recent works of scholars examining the public memory of the Atlantic slave trade in Senegal continue to repeat N'Dyae's estimates, which are higher than the volume of slave imports for all of the Americas.[61] Even on the official website of UNESCO's World Heritage List, the text describing the house is a transcription of N'Diyae's account:

> A small house contained between 150 and 200 slaves, who had to wait for very long periods—up to three months—before being carried away on board ship. Their departure to the Americas also depended on

the buyers, and family separation was total. There were special cells where children were stored and in these the mortality rate was obviously the highest in the house. The young girls were separated from the women because they were more expensive. All the houses situated on the edge of Gorée—even the actual presbytery—were former slave houses. [...] This sloping corridor is today known as the gate of 'the trip from which no one returned,' because once the slaves left through this gate leading into the sea, it was their farewell to Africa. Just outside this gate, there was a wharf of palm wood, which served as a loading dock, and some of the slaves obviously awaited the loading to try to escape by plunging into the sea. They could not go far as they were either shot by the guards or devoured by the sharks, attracted because the sick and injured were thrown into the sea.[62]

Many public figures—like James Brown, Jimmy Cliff, US President Jimmy Carter, Nelson Mandela, Pope John Paul II, Bill Clinton, George W. Bush, Danielle Miterrand, and Brazilian President Luiz Inácio Lula da Silva—visited the House of Slaves under great media coverage. In 2012, French President François Hollande, in his first African tour, visited Gorée Island as well. During an interview held at the House of Slaves, Hollande stated that he "celebrated the memory, the remembrance of all these men, women, and children who departed from here to be slaves in the Americas and the Caribbean."[63] Curiously, as Hollande pronounced these words, two Senegalese women dressed as *signares* observed the interview in the background, by showing that, despite the call to memorialize the victims of the trade, in Gorée daily life, the women who served as intermediaries during the slave trade are those who continued to be celebrated. Hollande's statements were widely commented on in the social media, where historians criticized the French president for endorsing "Gorée's legend."[64]

In the initial scenes of the documentary movie *Youssou N'Dour: Return to Gorée*, the Senegalese singer and composer Youssou N'Dour traveled to Gorée Island before starting his trip to the United States to follow the slave roots of jazz music.[65] On Gorée, N'Dour visited the House of Slaves to explain to N'Diaye his project of retrace the slave roots of jazz and other music styles and to reconnect his own work with the black diaspora music. In one scene, N'Diaye plays the role of the wise old man who gives the singer his permission and benediction to continue his journey on the other side of the Atlantic Ocean, by saying: "I am satisfied with your position and your project because you don't do it just for yourself, but for the whole of Africa and the Diaspora. Be proud and worthy of what you do and you'll succeed because the whole of Africa is praying for you. You are young and plenty of energy. So continue, you are on the right track."[66] After providing this advice, in the next scene N'Diaye guides Senegalese school children on a tour of the House of Slaves. He explains that they were on a pilgrimage to an African sanctuary that witnessed humiliation

62 *Shadows of the Slave Past*

and suffering (Figure 2.3 and Figure 2.4). Following the sequence, N'Dyaie continues underscoring the importance of the site: "Because the misery and the number of deaths caused by the black slave trade are beyond anything imaginable, Gorée was the most important slave-transiting place in

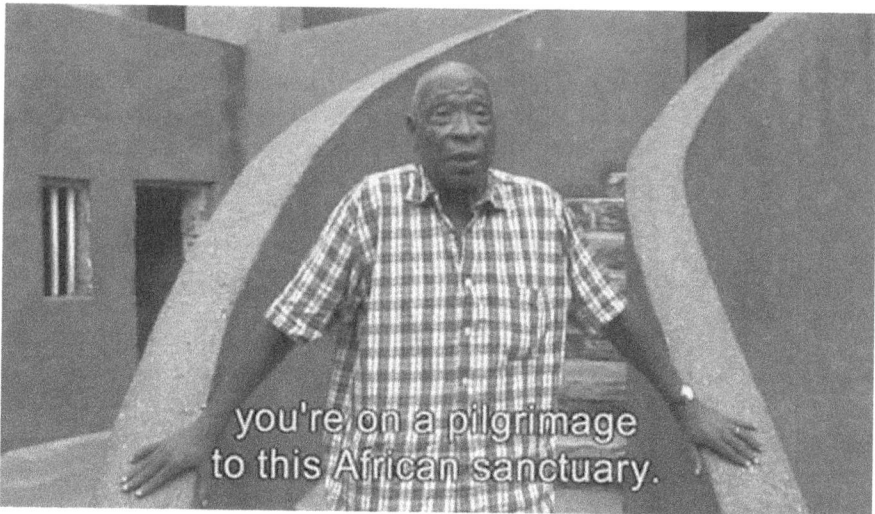

Figure 2.3   Joseph N'Diaye at the House of Slaves (scene from the film *Return to Gorée*).

Figure 2.4   Schoolchildren visiting the House of Slaves (scene from the film *Return to Gorée*).

Western Africa. The number in this house fluctuated between 150 and 200 human beings, men, women and children."[67] The content of the curator's discourse is consistent with his performance for international audiences and was not modified for the local student audience. As Paulla Ebron explains, the word "pilgrimage" is often employed by West African tourist guides to characterize these journeys of return and healing, especially when the groups are composed of African Americans.[68] Ibrahima Seck also notes that it is not uncommon to meet schoolchildren and teachers from distant regions of Senegal traveling to Gorée, in what he calls "pedagogical obligation with whiff of pilgrimage" or "dust tourism" based on moving performances that do not highlight the regions where African captives were captured and that conceal the internal complexities of the Atlantic slave trade in African soil.[69]

At the end of the musical documentary film, N'Dour and several musicians, including the four African American singers of the ensemble Harmony Harmoneers, return to Gorée Island to perform the movie's closing concert. Once on Gorée, the group visited the House of Slaves, where N'Diaye explains once again the role of the building during the Atlantic slave trade and led them to the Door of No Return. This time, in addition to repeating the usual narrative that moved the African American visitors, he also underscores that the door was a very important site of memory not only because the enslaved left Africa through that exact place but also because, according to him, it was from that door that Pope John Paul II asked apologies to Africa for the Atlantic slave trade: "It is from this door that opens to the sea, that we call the door of the travel of no return, that the slaves said goodbye to Africa. It is then from this door of no return that we had the privilege to receive the Pope in 92, it is then from this door that the Pope asked apologies to Africa."[70] Even though the Pope's apologies were expressed during a speech at the Church of Saint Charles Borromée on Gorée Island, he effectively visited the House of Slaves and its Door of No Return in February 1992, as stated by N'Diaye.[71] Thus, drawing on the visits of international personalities, the role of the House of Slaves as a site of memory and its popularity continues to grow. After the visits of Bill Clinton in 1998 and George W. Bush in 2003, on June 27, 2013, President Barack Obama visited Gorée Island and its House of Slaves as part of a tour including Senegal, South Africa, and Tanzania.[72] Unlike his visit to Cape Coast Castle, Obama made very quick and general remarks about his visit to the House of Slaves. This time, the president did not make any analogy with Holocaust camps. In a respectful statement, he emphasized how important it was to visit the site, recognizing the building as a place where Africans were kept before the Middle Passage:

> it's a very powerful moment whenever I can travel with my family, but especially for Michelle and Malia and my mother-in-law to be able to come here and to fully appreciate the magnitude of the slave trade, to

get a sense in a very intimate way of the incredible inhumanity and hardship that people faced before they made the Middle Passage and that crossing. And I think more than anything what it reminds us of is that we have to remain vigilant when it comes to the defense of people's human rights—because I'm a firm believer that humanity is fundamentally good, but it's only good when good people stand up for what's right.[73]

The international media closely followed Obama's visit to Senegal, and although the debate on the controversy of the House of Slaves quickly emerged in various newspapers, most articles repeated the official and inaccurate account corroborated by UNESCO, according to which millions of Africans were kept in the House of Slaves and were embarked from there to the Americas. On that occasion, when interrogated by a journalist about the controversy surrounding the House of Slaves, its new curator Eloi Coly, who was N'Diaye's assistant until his death in 2009, "reacted violently to the suggestion that the house's history may be trumped up, saying those who question it are akin to Holocaust deniers."[74] In addition to comparing historians of slavery with Holocaust deniers, he also made an analogy between the House of Slaves and a Nazi concentration camp by insisting, "There are people who deny that there were concentration camps [. . .] What it shows is a lack of respect for blacks, for the memory of our people."[75] By establishing a division between "us" (black people) and the others who question the constructed account of the House of Slaves, the curator shows that in any event the work of memory prevails over historical evidence.

In spite of the controversies, it is important to understand the several factors that allowed the House of Slaves to become and continue to be a successful slave trade heritage site. N'Diaye's contested account, today disseminated by the new curator of the House of Slaves, replaced the voice of the "drowned," those who, as defined by Primo Levi, died at the hands of the perpetrators and who, unlike the "saved," are no longer alive to testify.[76] As a result, even though N'Diaye and his ancestors were not enslaved, he played the role of the saved by providing a survival account. His constructed narrative was effective because it incorporated iconic elements of representations of slavery and the Atlantic slave trade, which have been the object of documentaries, films, and novels, a phenomenon that also appears in the testimonies of actual Holocaust victims.[77] Accurate or not, his performance and detailed narrative explaining how enslaved men, women, and children lived under confinement and how their deportation to the Americas was a path with no return not only successfully conveyed the experiences of the victims but were also incorporated into official descriptions such as the one provided by UNESCO. N'Diaye explored the house's space, containing several characteristics of a slave depot, including dungeons and a door opening to the sea, elements that, according to Theresa A. Singleton, incarnate the memory of the Atlantic slave trade.[78] By doing so, he was able to engage several kinds of audiences, making the visitors feel the experience of enslavement and deportation, a task that historians were not able to easily accomplish. But N'Diaye's narrative of enslavement, confinement, and deportation from Africa also carried his own political project, which corroborates the position of some West African elite groups who refuse to acknowledge the participation of their ancestors in the Atlantic slave trade. The victimhood narrative could be successful only by removing any sensitive and controversial aspects. Indeed, as I argued elsewhere when examining the case of Republic of Benin, in various West African countries, initiatives aiming at highlighting the heritage of the Atlantic slave trade usually omit two important aspects: the involvement of local actors in the Atlantic slave trade and indigenous slavery.[79] African-born individuals, like *signares,* who actively participated in the Atlantic slave trade are still today widely celebrated in Senegal's public space, including the Gorée Diaspora Festival and the Lantern Festival of Saint-Louis.[80] Also, as the works of archaeologists have demonstrated, private buildings like the House of Slaves' cells probably lodged slaves owned by local families and therefore better illustrate the dynamics of indigenous slavery than the Atlantic slave trade.[81] As a result, in order to move the audience, the narrative should depict Africans as victims and the Europeans as perpetrators, by avoiding any mention of local traders and other intermediaries.

If from the point of view of scholars who study public memory the actual site from which slaves were embarked is as important as the symbolic heritage site of the House of Slaves, such a replacement has important consequences both at the international and local levels. At the international level, the myth of the House of Slaves blurs the importance of the actual slave trade ports from which millions Africans were effectively deported. At the local level, the legend helps Senegal to keep attracting legions of tourists every year. In addition, the story associated with the site places the country in a privileged position regarding the various international initiatives aiming to highlight the role of the Atlantic slave trade in West Africa. More importantly, keeping the story of the House of Slaves alive contributes to place Senegal and its ruling classes, whose ancestors participated and benefited from the trade, in a victimized position by protecting those elites from any form of symbolical or financial demands for reparations.

The role of Gorée Island as a site of memory was recently expanded and its association with the Holocaust formalized. Since July 5, 2004, Gorée Island and the commune of Drancy in the northeast of Paris are twin towns, in a pioneer initiative associating a slave trade heritage site with the most important site of memory of the Holocaust in France. Drancy housed a Nazi concentration camp, which was established in a modern apartment complex named "Cité de la Muette" (The Silent City, Figure 2.5). Designed by the architects

66 *Shadows of the Slave Past*

Figure 2.5 Drancy, les premiers gratte-ciel de la région parisienne (postcard, author's collection).

Marcel Lods (1891–1978) and Eugène Beaudoin (1898–1983) and constructed between 1931 and 1934, the complex was composed of five towers of 15 floors each, and several other buildings of three and four floors, comprising a total of 1,200 apartments, in addition to courts, malls, and community services, including a school and a church.[82] In 1941 the Germans established an internment camp for foreign Jews in one of the buildings called "horseshoe" because of its U-shape. In 1942, Drancy was already transformed into a transit camp, and French officials ran the camp until mid-1943.[83] From there, about 65,000 European Jews, especially French, were sent to Nazi killing camps, mostly to Auschwitz-Birkenau. Of them, only 2,000 survived.[84]

Although the historical assessment of German's occupation and the Vichy years took long to emerge in France, the memorialization of the Second World War years started very discreetly after 1945 and was carried out primarily by war veterans. Following the end of the war, the high towers of Drancy's Silent City were used for various purposes. But by 1947 the horseshoe building returned to its old use as a low-income housing, and three commemorative plaques were added to its southern wing. The oldest plaque, unveiled in a period when the estimated number of persons deported from Drancy was higher, states: "In this place, that was a concentration camp from 1941 to 1944, 100,000 men, women, and children of Jewish religion or Jewish ancestry were interned by the Hitlerian occupant, then deported to the Nazi extermination camps where the immense majority was killed." Above it, another plaque displaying the British and the French flags was then added, stating: "In this place British soldiers captured by the German army were interned in May and June 1940, before sent into exile in the stalags and commandos of Nazi Germany. Remember!" Finally, on May 20, 1951, the Association des Combattants Prisonniers de Guerre de la Seine (Seine's Association of Soldiers Prisoners of War) placed a third plaque, paying homage to French soldiers, below the oldest one: "June 1940. Here was the Front-Stalag III, where the sufferings of dozens of thousands of French soldier prisoners of war started. From this place, they were led to several years of captivity in the Nazi Germany. Remember!" These discrete plaques did not alter the landscape of the old internment camp that, in the years following the war, continued to be a populated neighborhood. Only in the 1970s was the old internment camp of Drancy visibly transformed into an official site of memory. In 1976, the high towers that had had several functions after the war were demolished, and only the horseshoe building was preserved. That same year, the Mémorial national des déportés de France (National Memorial of France's Deportees), conceived by the Polish-French-Israeli sculptor Shelomo Selinger to pay homage to the victims deported from Drancy, was placed at the entrance of the former camp (Figure 2.6). Placed on an elevated platform, the memorial is constituted of three large granite sculptures titled "Gates of Hell," evoking the homonymous sculpture by French sculptor Auguste Rodin. The ensemble forms the Hebrew letter *Shin*, a name for God. Traditionally, this letter is written on a small parchment scroll, inserted in the *mezuzah*, a small case placed on the doorposts of Jewish homes. The central granite block represents ten human figures, which is the number of Jews needed for a *myniam*, or quorum for prayer.[85] At either side of the sculpture, two other massive blocks of granite symbolize a gate closing. On the first block, the following text is carved:

> On August 20, 1941, 5,000 Jews were arrested in Paris and gathered in this place, inaugurating the Drancy camp, antechamber of the killing camps. About 100,000 Jews, men, women, children, elderly, were interned here before their deportation, mostly to Auschwitz. Only 1518 returned. 256 were shot as hostages.

On the second granite block, the text carved, followed by a Hebrew translation, reads: "This monument witnesses the Jewish martyrs of France, victims of the Nazi barbarism. Passerby, meditate, and don't forget. Look and see if there is any pain like my pain (Lamentation 1: 12).

In 1988, the memorial was expanded to include a small museum. At the back of the memorial, two sets of seven stairs lead the visitor to a rail that ends at a train car, of the same kind used to deport prisoners from the neighboring Bobigny train station. The museum, housed in the train car,

Figure 2.6 Memorial of Drancy Camp (Shelomo Selinger. Drancy, France; picture by Olivier Quéruel, 2011).

essentially consists of panel displays with pictures, documents, and text explaining the history of the internment camp. Even though the train and the gates symbolize and evoke the most powerful symbols of the Holocaust, it was only in the 1990s that commemorative plaques acknowledging

French collaboration during the Nazi regime and expressing apologies were added to the memorial complex. In February 1993, a plaque unveiled by the Union des Étudiants Juifs de France (Union of Jewish Students of France) states: "Here, the French State of Vichy interned several thousands of Jews, gypsies, and strangers. Deported to the Nazi camps, almost all of them were killed there. We, the memory generation, will never forget."[86] Some months later, in July 1993, another plaque was added to the site; it states: "The French Republic pays homage to the victims of racist and antisemitic persecutions and crimes against humanity committed under the de facto authority called 'Government of the French State' (1940–1944). We will never forget."

Despite the importance of Drancy as a site of deportation and the growing visibility it has received in France, probably because of its location in the suburb of Paris, the site does not attract the numerous visitors and the same media attention of its twin town, Gorée Island and its House of Slaves. It was only in 2005 that the façades, the roofs, and the staircases of the Silent City were included in the French list of protected monuments and sites. As part of the twinning cities program, on May 23, 2006, a statue titled *Aux Esclaves* (To the Slaves), commemorating the victims of slavery, was dedicated in Drancy during a ceremony with the presence of Jean-Christophe Lagarde, Drancy's deputy mayor, Victorin Lurel, president of the Regional Council and deputy of Guadeloupe, and Augustin Senghor, Gorée's mayor. The statue is a replica of a sculpture displayed in the city of Baillif (Guadeloupe) in 1998. Another replica of the same statue was offered to the city of Gorée by the General Council of Guadeloupe and placed close to the House of Slaves. Drancy's replica was placed at the site of the swimming pool of Drancy's Nautical Stadium, some half a mile from the horseshoe building and unveiled on July 31, 2002. Conceived by the Guadeloupian brothers Jean Moisa and Christian Moisa, the sculpture represents an African man and an African woman placed on a pedestal depicting a huge tambour. Whereas the woman has her arms around the man's waist, the man is raising his arms and breaking the chains attaching his wrists, in a traditional position that can be found in many other statues celebrating emancipation unveiled in the Caribbean since the 1960s. Ultimately, the statue celebrates freedom from slavery on a Holocaust's heritage site of deportation.

Even though the twinning agreement between Gorée Island and Drancy can be perceived as a fruitful way to engage relations between two sites of deportation, placing a statue commemorating the Atlantic slave trade in France's major site of the deportation of Jews during the Second World War shows how the public memory of atrocities is constituted by various layers and can also be interpreted as an attempt to blur the country's involvement in the Holocaust. Indeed, the statue honoring the victims of slavery in Drancy was unveiled one year after the 2005 riots that originated in Clichy-sous-Bois, a suburb a few minutes away from Drancy, indicating how the memory of the Holocaust and the memory of slavery are multidirectional but, in this particular case, in competition.[87] Today, Drancy is not a rich town. The average household revenue of its population of about 66,000 inhabitants is no more than €29,000. Perhaps today Drancy's population can associate its difficult living conditions more with the history of the victims of the Atlantic slave trade and French colonization in Africa than with the destiny of the Holocaust victims. Indeed, one year after the establishment of a twinning agreement between Gorée and Drancy, the memories of slavery and the Holocaust were at the heart of intense political debates in France. Following the 2005 riots and the discussion of the article 4 of the Law 205–158 of February 23, 2005, which proposed to recognize the positive of role of French colonization in North Africa, a new controversy emerged around the then recently published book, *Les traites négrières: Essais d'histoire globale*, by French historian Pétré-Grenouilleau. In this award-wining book, the historian dedicated equal attention to the Muslim slave trade, the African internal slave trade, and the Atlantic slave trade. But the debate took different contours when on June 12, 2005 Pétré-Grenouilleau gave an interview to the *Journal of Dimanche,* in which he questioned the Taubira Law. According to him, the law established a connection between slavery and genocide, even though the exact term employed in the law is crime against humanity. By arguing that slavery and the Holocaust were two very different phenomena in the very moment that both atrocities were being discussed in the French public arena, the historian declared that there was no Richter scale for suffering and pointed out that the activists and intellectuals who were identifying themselves as descendants of slaves were indeed choosing among their ancestors. These statements led Claude Ribbe, an author of several books on the history of French West Indies and Guiana and member of an association called Collectif antillais-guyanais-réunionais (Collective of West Indians, Guianese, and Reunionese), to release an open letter accusing Pétré-Grenouilleau of revisionism and negationism.[88] By using these terms, Ribbe again clearly established a connection between slavery and the Holocaust.[89] In September 2005, the association filed suit against Pétré-Grenouilleau but, after months of discussion and public manifestations, withdrew the lawsuit in February 2006.

In the aftermath of the riots of 2005, France was finally engaging in a series of initiatives to publicly recognize its participation not only in the Atlantic slave trade but also in the Holocaust. On January 25, 2005, ten years after acknowledging France's responsibility in collaborating with the Nazi regime, President Jacques Chirac dedicated the Shoah Memorial in Paris. Conceived as a site of memory and research center, including a Wall of Names containing the names of 76,000 Jews who were deported from France, this new initiative was an expansion of the Memorial to the Unknown Jewish Martyr and the Center for Contemporary Jewish Documentation.

On September 21, 2012, French President François Hollande unveiled a new Holocaust Memorial in Drancy, sealing the process of recognition of French collaboration with the Nazi regime. Located just across from the horseshoe building, the new initiative was financed by the Foundation for the Memory of the Shoah. It consists of a five-story building of glass and concrete, housing conference rooms, a research center, and a permanent exhibition portraying the daily lives in the internment camp. According to Roger Diener, the architect who conceived the building, because of its transparent façade, "the external observer can see all the time, what is being done in the interior: the work of memory."[90]

INTRIGUING DIALOGUES

Only few deportation sites became important symbols of the Atlantic slave trade, despite the existence of numerous former slave ports and slave depots along the coasts of West Africa and West Central Africa. Some officially recognized slave trade heritage sites were effectively used as slave depots to keep captives confined before their tragic Atlantic journey. Nevertheless, authenticity is not the main requirement to make these sites successful in acquiring notoriety and in captivating national and international visitors. This chapter showed that in addition to the existence of dungeons and doors opening to the sea, the interpretation of these slave trade heritage sites is essential to giving them life. As the controversial case of the House of Slaves on Gorée Island and Juffureh village in The Gambia show, the success of a slave trade heritage site greatly relies on the storytelling ability of West African local actors who perform the roles of the witnesses who no longer exist. N'Diaye, a Senegalese, played a vital role in making the House of Slaves (and Gorée Island) an iconic slave trade heritage site, whereas in the case of Juffureh, it was Alex Haley, an outsider, who was able to convey the story that transformed the village into a slave trade heritage site. Nevertheless, unlike the House of Slaves and Juffureh, imposing sites like Elmina and Cape Coast are not associated with any public personalities such as N'Diaye or Haley, even though the performances of anonymous tour guides can very often fill in for this absence. This factor can explain why the visits by international personalities and the apologies for slavery and the Atlantic slave trade addressed by them while they were on Gorée Island were much more publicized than their visits to Elmina and Cape Coast.

The analysis of slave trade sites also demonstrates how official initiatives or individual social actors have consistently established connections between these sites and the heritage sites of the Holocaust, including Dachau, Buchenwald, Auschwitz, and Drancy. Such constructed relations can be understood as the expression of a context of memories in competition because they possibly mitigate the particularities of each of these atrocities. However, in times when the victims and witnesses of the horrors of slavery are no longer alive, the constant references to the Holocaust in public discourses about the Atlantic slave trade can also be understood as a way to legitimize the memorialization of slavery, which is still not fully recognized in the public space. Although these slave trade sites were successful in obtaining international and official recognition, they are paradoxically based on imagined accounts and not on historical evidence.

NOTES

1. See Shaw, 2010; Schenck and Candido, forthcoming.
2. See Rothberg, 2010: 11.
3. See Araujo, 2010a, Chap. 2.
4. On this discussion, see also, Wallace, 2006: 27.
5. See DeCoste and Schwartz, particularly Chap. 2. See also Douglas 2000: 16–36 and Rothberg, 1997: 45–81.
6. Browning, 2010: 8.
7. MacGonagle, 2006; Holsey, 2008.
8. Singleton, 1999: 154.
9. UNESCO, 1979.
10. See Warren and MacGonagle, 2012: 86.
11. See Bruner, 1996: 290–304; MacGonagle, 2010: 249–260; and Schramm, 2010.
12. See Appio, Gates, Godwin, and Colton, [1999] 2003: DVD.
13. Wallace, 2006: 27.
14. Appio, Gates, Godwin, and Colton, [1999] 2003.
15. Candido, 2010, and Candido, 2013.
16. Gates's television series was criticized by several scholars for different reasons. See the H-Africa list-serve, November 1999, http://h-net.msu.edu/cgi-bin/logbrowse.pl?trx=lx&sort=3&list=h-africa&month=9911&week=&user=&pw. See also Cancel, 2000: 1, 4, 6, 8, 10, 86–88; Greene, 2012: 146.
17. Obama interview, 2009.
18. Obama interview, 2009.
19. Rothberg, 2010: 116.
20. Du Bois, 1952: 14–15.
21. Rothberg, 2010: 118.
22. See Richards, 2008: 291–301; Hartman, 2008.
23. Holsey, 2008: 151.
24. MacGonagle, 2006: 252.
25. Holsey, 2008.
26. Hartman, 2008: 56.
27. "Elmina 2015 Strategy . . .," 2003.
28. Obama interview, 2009.
29. Wiesel's novel was translated from the Yiddish into French and published by Éditions de Minuit in 1958. See Wiesel, 2007: 23; Wiesel and Wiesel, 2006: xv.
30. Wiesel and Winfrey, 2006: DVD.
31. Browning, 2010: 154.
32. For more details on the organization of the exhibitions, see Araujo, 2010a: 135–137.

33. See Law, 2008: 11.
34. Despite its title, the festival was held in February 1992.
35. Soglo, 1992: 5.
36. Wiesel, 2007: 23; Wiesel and Wiesel, 2006: xv.
37. "Ouidah 92 . . .," 1992: 3.
38. "Ouidah 92 . . .," 1993.
39. See Haas, 1984: 11.
40. Haas, 1984: 16.
41. Over the years, there were numerous studies on this initiative. See, among others, Tall, 1995: 195–208; Rush, 1998; Bako-Arifari, 2000: 221–231; Ciarcia, 2008: 687–706; and Law, 2008: 11–27. I also extensively published on this issue; among others, see Araujo, 2010a: Chap. 4.
42. See *Les Guides Bleus*, 1958: 123; quoted in Hinchman, 2000: vol. 2, 318; Tillet, 2009: 125. See also Salamishah Tillet, 2013: 102. However, Tillet seems to adhere to the myth of the House of Slaves to which she refers as a "slave castle."
43. On *signares* of Saint-Louis and Gorée, see Wilson-Fall, 2011: 273–303; Jones, 2013: Chap. 1.
44. See Bellagamba, 2012: 35–53.
45. Several references to the "Maison des esclaves" appear in Mauny, 1951.
46. Ayad, 2001.
47. Several scholars described the visits by N'Diaye when he was still alive. See Ebron, 1999: 922. See the visit's video at "Visite virtuelle de l'île de Gorée," http://webworld.unesco.org/goree/fr/index.shtml.
48. See Hinchman, 2000: vol. 2, 320.
49. Pruitt, 1994: C1.
50. Pruitt, 1994: C3.
51. Pruitt, 1994: C3. In French, the original verse reads, "Gorée-Dachau quel long chemin nous reste à parcourir avant de devenir des hommes?."
52. See Warren and MacGonagle, 2012: 85.
53. French, 1998.
54. See Curtin, 1969; Eltis et al., *The Transatlantic Slave Trade Database: Voyages*.
55. See Eltis et al., *The Transatlantic Slave Trade Database: Voyages*. This volume is based only on the existing records found by the editors of the database. The estimates are usually 25 percent higher than the actual volume, which would increase the slave exports from Gorée to 40,000.
56. See Thiaw, 2010: 17.
57. Warfield, 1991: A-7.
58. The discussion occurred on the Internet, in the H-Slavery list, in the http://h-net.msu.edu/cgi-bin/logbrowse.pl?trx=vx&list=H-Slavery&month=9508&week=a&msg=cb0O4UuI%2bT0IeKSltZ5NlA&user=&pw=.
59. Roux, 1996. On the debates published in Dakar's newspapers, see Hinchman, 2000: vol. 2, 322–323; Bassène, 2011: vol. 2, 391–402.
60. See "Guide du Musée historique de l'A.O.F. . . .," 1955: and Bassène, 2011: vol. 2, 383.
61. Among the scholars who took for granted N'Diaye's estimates is Katchka, 2008: 4.
62. UNESCO, World Heritage List, Island of Gorée (website).
63. The interview is available on two websites: www.senenews.com/2012/10/13/interview-special-francois-hollande-depuis-lile-de-goree/ and www.nettali.net/article.php3?id_article=27350.
64. Among others, see Lugan, 2012.
65. Borgeaud, 2007: DVD.

66. See Borgeaud (2007), according to the film English subtitles. In the original French version, N'Dour says: "Je suis satisfait de ta position, je suis satisfait de ton projet, parce que tu fais pas le projet pour toi-même. Tu fais ça pour toute l'Afrique et la diaspora. Sois fier et sois digne de ce que tu fais et tu reussiras parce que non seulement moi mais toute l'Afrique prie pour toi actuellement, toute l'Afrique, tu es jeune, tu es plein d'élan, donc continue, tu es sur le bon chemin."
67. See *Youssou N'Dour: Return to Gorée,* according to the film English subtitles. In the original French version, N'Dour says: "Chers élèves, vous voici en pélerinage. En pélerinage à ce sanctuaire africain témoin de tant d'humilation et de souffrance parce que la somme de misère et des morts qui a été produite par la traite des noirs est au delà de tout ce qu'on peut imaginer. Gorée était le centre de transit le plus important de l'Ouest africain. L'effectif dans cette maison varie entre 150 et 200 être humains, hommes, femmes, enfants."
68. Ebron, 1999: 916.
69. Seck, 2007: 114.
70. Borgeaud, 2006. In the original French version, N'Dour says: "À partir de cette porte qui donne sur la mer, que nous appelons la porte du voyage sans retour que les esclaves disaient adieu à l'Afrique. Et donc c'est à partir de cette porte du sans retour que nous avons eu le privilege de recevoir le Pape en février 1992, c'est donc à partir de cette porte que le Pape a demandé pardon à l'Afrique." (website)
71. See Araujo, 2010a, 63.
72. For a discussion on the visits of Presidents Clinton and Bush to Gorée Island and the House of Slaves, see Araujo, 2010a: 63.
73. Whitaker, 2013.
74. See Pace, 2013.
75. Pace, 2013.
76. Levi, 1989.
77. See Browning, 2010: 11.
78. Singleton, 1999: 150–169.
79. See Araujo, 2010a.
80. On Gorée, see Hinchman, 2000: 38–53.
81. Thiaw, 2006.
82. Wiedmer, 1999: 58–59.
83. Winstone, 2010: 21–24.
84. Henri Rousso was among the first French historians to address the issue of the history and the memory of the Second World War in France; see Rousso, 1987, 2001. See also Mathy, 2011: 146. For a detailed assessment of the Parisian camps and the silence surrounding French collaboration with the Nazi regime, see Dreyfus and Gensburger, 2011.
85. See Wiedmer, 1999: 64–66.
86. In French: "Ici, l'État français de Vichy interna plusieurs milliers de juifs, tsiganes et étrangers. Déportés vers les camps nazis, presque tous y trouvèrent la mort. Nous, génération de la mémoire n'oublierons jamais."
87. Several books and articles engaged the discussion about the events of 2005 in France. Among the works recently published in English, see Tshimanga, Gondola, and Bloom, 2009); Keaton, Sharpley-Whiting, and Stovall, 2012; Stam and Shohat, 2012; and Chivallon, 2012. See also in French, Vergès, 2006; Cottias, 2007.
88. For more details on the Petré-Grenouilleau controversy see Araujo, 2010a: 78–79.

89. Moreover, later in the fall of 2005, Ribbe published *Le crime de Napoléon*, in which he defined the repression of the Haitian Revolution as a genocide comparable to the Holocaust (Ribbe, 2005). The book was translated into English as *Napoleon's Crimes: A Blueprint for Hitler* (2008). For a comment on the book, see also Mathy, 2011: 160–161.
90. Le Mémorial de la Shoah à Drancy. (website)

3 Places of Disembarkation

Having explored the representations of enslavement in Africa and the public interpretation of West African sites of deportation, this chapter examines how the Middle Passage and the sites of arrival of slaves in the Americas are memorialized in museum exhibitions and heritage sites, especially in Brazil and the United States. In museum exhibitions, although the experience of arrival in the Americas is not often highlighted, there were attempts in a number of institutions to depict the tragic Atlantic crossings by portraying and reconstituting the interiors of slave ships. These portrayals, often based on travel accounts of the eighteenth and nineteenth centuries, offer new and challenging elements and sometimes are contested by the local audiences who question the representations of Africans in the holds of slave ships as passive victims.

For many decades, the sites of arrival of enslaved Africans remained concealed in the public spaces of former Atlantic slave ports because most old port areas had become either abandoned, impoverished, or replaced with new construction. Nevertheless, over the last 20 years, a number of slave cemeteries and sites of disembarkation of Africans were uncovered in the United States and Brazil through archaeological research. In this chapter, I explore the historical and political dynamics that brought these spaces to light and led to their eventual recognition as sites of memory of the Atlantic slave trade. I also show that their recovery, conservation, and valorization in the public space, developed over the last 20 years, were the consequence of a broader transnational movement that resulted in similar initiatives in other areas of the Atlantic world. This movement was characterized by the rise of the public memory of slavery and by the intervention of various social actors who fought to have the heritage of their ancestors finally officially acknowledged.

Both in Brazil and in the United States, slave markets and slave cemeteries were part of the context of the disembarkation experience. Starting in the nineteenth century, these places were destroyed or remained neglected in the urban spaces. Nevertheless, forgetting and remembering these sites are two sides of the same process. In Brazil, the invisibility of former slave markets and ports of arrival of enslaved Africans has led to a phenomenon that I call memory replacement, by which the local population appropriates an existing building or site and assigns to it stories related to the Atlantic slave trade and slavery as if it was an actual heritage site, similarly to the phenomenon of the House of Slaves on Gorée Island. As a response to the absence of public and official initiatives shedding light on the actual sites of the Atlantic slave trade, social actors and groups create alternate sites of memory, taking in their own hands the process of heritagization that, for several reasons, has been denied to them by the official heritage institutions.

MIDDLE PASSAGES

Popular since the eighteenth century, images representing enslaved Africans during the Middle Passage were appropriated in various ways by the abolitionist movement. These renderings usually combine three elements. First, they illustrate the structure of the slave ship by showing its various views. Second, they highlight the presence of slaves in the interior of the slave ship, often represented as mere blackened silhouettes. Third, they focus on the corpses of enslaved individuals who were thrown into the water, after dying by disease or being killed in unsuccessful uprisings. Very often combined, these symbolic images were largely appropriated in museum exhibitions and monuments attempting to represent the Atlantic slave trade.

Perhaps the most iconic image of the Middle Passage is the plate *Description of a Slave Ship*, published in London in 1789. The plate consists of seven small figures depicting various views of the slave ship *Brooks*. Largely used in abolitionist propaganda, the image was made available in several formats, and in just the year it was released, more than 10,000 copies of it were printed.[1] In five of these views, enslaved Africans are objectified as stereotypical blackened silhouettes filling out the interior space of the ship. Successful in giving the viewer a sense of the inhuman conditions that characterized the Atlantic slave trade, over the years these depictions continue to disseminate the idea of Africans as mere commodities, unable to develop agency. Another popular representation of the Middle Passage is a woodcut usually identified by the title *Africans Thrown from Slave Ship* (Figure 3.1), published in the newspaper *The Liberator* in 1832, illustrating a short anonymous article titled "Extract of a Letter dated Rio de Janeiro." The text that accompanies this image of abolitionist propaganda asserts that the scene does not aim to represent the Middle Passage but rather an event that allegedly occurred on arrival at the port of Rio de Janeiro in Brazil.[2] Later versions of the same image were used to depict tragic episodes when slaves were thrown overboard during the Middle Passage, especially the *Zong* massacre, which occurred in 1781.[3] Over the nineteenth century, the image of enslaved African individuals thrown overboard was largely widespread, but probably the most important representation of the

Figure 3.1 Africans Thrown from Slave Ship (Liberator, 1832).

crimes committed during the Middle Passage is the *Slave Ship* (or *Slavers Overthrowing the Dead and Dying—Typho[o]n Coming On*), painted by William Turner (1789–1862) in 1840, when the British slave trade was outlawed and slavery was also abolished in the British colonies. Despite its small size, the romantic painting of the slave ship in agitated seawaters dramatically joining the unfriendly storm-raged sky became a powerful icon representing the extreme horrors of the Atlantic slave trade and the Middle Passage. Instead of conjuring enslaved men and women packed in the hold of the slave ship or being overthrown overboard by the slave merchants, the painting evokes only the bloody pieces of enslaved bodies being eaten by sharks in the ocean waters.

Because the slave ship became the most important icon of the Atlantic slave trade, its image was equated with the idea of the Middle Passage. Notwithstanding the lack of slavery museums in both the United States and Brazil, various replicas of the slave ship have been presented in exhibitions and museums focusing on some aspect of African American or Afro-Brazilian history as well as on maritime history, including the Museum of African American History (Detroit, Michigan), the National Museum of American History (Washington, DC), the Museu AfroBrasil (AfroBrazil Museum) (São Paulo, São Paulo), and the Museu Nático da Bahia (Nautical Museum of Bahia) (Salvador, Bahia).

In the United States, the most impressive and controversial representation of a slave ship was displayed in the then Museum of African American History in Detroit.[4] Created in 1965 by Charles H. Wright (1908–2002), a prominent African American physician, the museum was not the result of particular demands of Detroit African American groups. Instead, Wright was inspired by his visit to the Ryvangen Memorial Grove in Denmark, the largest memorial park that commemorates the Danish resistance fighters during the Second World War, including several victims of Nazi camps. By associating the victims of the Holocaust and the hardships experienced by African Americans under enslavement and Jim Crow, Wright decided to sponsor a similar initiative in the United States because at the time there was no museum focusing on black history in the country.

In April 1997, the museum was relocated to a huge new facility and became the largest museum of its kind in the world.[5] The company Ralph Appelbaum Associates was chosen to conceive the museum's main exhibition titled *Of the People: The African American Experience*. Despite the company's lack of expertise in designing exhibitions focusing on African American history, Ralph Appelbaum Associates had designed the exhibitions of the United States Holocaust Memorial Museum, opened to the public four years earlier in Washington, DC. As in several other exhibitions depicting the Atlantic slave trade, the central element of the new show was a replica of a slave ship, within which there were 40 life-size figures depicting enslaved Africans. Painted in gray, the plaster sculptures portraying male and female figures wore tunic-like cloths. They were sitting and lying together, wrists and heels attached to chains. A bridge above this setting allowed the visitors to observe this recreation of the hold of a slave ship.[6] The début of the exhibition generated controversial reactions among the members of the African American community because, among others, the company's designers took a highly controversial decision to create life-cast sculptures of enslaved Africans by employing Detroit African American students as models.[7] In addition, the representation of Africans in the exhibition was severely criticized by various audiences because on the one hand they were not sufficiently black, and on the other hand they looked too healthy to represent men and women who had experienced the horrors of the Middle Passage.[8] Two years after its opening, the original exhibit was dismantled. However, the plaster figures were preserved and recycled. Painted in dark brown, the sculptures were redistributed along different newly conceived sections depicting the various stages of the Atlantic slave trade. Among the new sections, a new slave ship was created, this time following a traditional representation, consisting of a dark room, in which the newly painted life-size plaster sculptures are lying packed on wood structures representing the hold of the vessel, similar to existing representations found in the Middle Passage Gallery of the William Wilberforce House Museum, in Hull, United Kingdom.

If the Middle Passage and the Atlantic slave trade are important components of the Charles H. Wright Museum of African American History in Detroit, they are peripheral elements in the Smithsonian National Museum of American History. Situated in the national capital of Washington DC, the museum aims to provide an official narrative of the "infinite richness and complexity of American history."[9] In the museum, the history of the Atlantic slave trade to the United States is included in an exhibition on maritime history titled *On the Water: Stories from Maritime America*, opened on May 19, 2009. The Middle Passage is represented in the first of the seven sections composing the show, titled "Living in the Atlantic World, 1450–1800." Although the exhibition release does not contain any reference to the Middle Passage, its website explores the Atlantic slave trade in more detail, highlighting that it was the "largest forced migration by sea in history."[10] In a very simplified narrative illustrated with few images, the website provides brief information on the horrible conditions of the Middle Passage, the slave factories on the West African coastline, and the usual slave sale posters, manila, and shackles. The website also displays some daily objects and religious artifacts of various natures from present-day Nigeria, Senegal, Angola, and Liberia. Like many other museums, the exhibit's narrative is focused on North America, totally dismissing the fact that most Africans were exported to Brazil and the Caribbean. In addition, the website presents images of the slave ship *Brooks*, extracts of Olaudah Equiano's slave narrative, and a number of images of kneeling slaves depicted in abolitionist coins. The presentation of the slave trade ends with a few renderings celebrating the British abolition of the slave trade in 1807 and of slavery in 1834, even though slavery ended in the United States only in 1865. Still, the most original element of the exhibition is an eighteenth-century slave ship presented in one of the exhibition cases.[11] The ship model includes several pairs of painted urethane figures representing enslaved men and women, crew members, and rats. Even though providing a detailed and accurate replication of the slave ship and the enslaved individuals, the focus on maritime history resulted in the neglect of the living experience of the Middle Passage in detriment to the description of the slave vessel. Therefore, the exhibition *On the Water: Stories from Maritime America* situates the experiences of thousands of victims of the Atlantic at the same level as the experiences of sailors, pirates, and other individuals who traveled or migrated to the United States by their own choice.

Brazil imported the largest number of enslaved Africans in the Americas but is far behind England and the United States in attempts to address the Atlantic slave trade in museum exhibitions. In Salvador, the black capital of the state of Bahia, the Middle Passage is depicted in the permanent exhibition of the Museu Náutico da Bahia. Facing the Bay of All Saints, the museum is housed in the Forte Santo Antônio da Barra, the first Brazilian fortress, in the Barra neighborhood, a popular beach among locals and tourists. The fortress is not only an important landmark during Bahia's carnival but also a mandatory stop in the various touristic circuits developed in the city. In one of the opening panels of the permanent exhibition, the popular eighteenth-century horizontal views of the slave ship are presented, followed by the text explaining that since the beginning of colonization, Salvador figured as a trading post of maritime trade. It also explains that the Brazilian economy was based on brazilwood, sugar, rum, and tobacco and that, in the late seventeenth century, gold and diamonds also became important. The panel goes on to state that all these goods were traded by the sea via the Bay of All Saints and adds that "at the ports of Salvador and Recife, slave ships unloaded *negros* brought from Africa by force, in the beginning as an open trade, and later as clandestine traffic."[12]

The text, as displayed, attempts to portray Salvador as a mere trading post by omitting its central role in the Atlantic slave trade. Showing the popular image of the slave ship that was historically employed to denounce the horrible conditions to which enslaved men and women were submitted during the Middle Passage, the panels refers to Africans as simple commodities, even though these were the same men and women who labored on the sugarcane and tobacco plantations. Nevertheless, more details are provided in a second panel titled "Tipos que compuseram a civilização brasileira" (Types Who Composed the Brazilian Civilization). The panel shows several faces of black, white, and native individuals that illustrated various plates of the travelogue *Voyage pittoresque et historique au Brésil* by the French artist and traveler Jean-Baptiste Debret (1768–1848), as well as a twentieth-century portrait of Maria dos Anjos, an Afro-Brazilian woman, by ethnographer and photographer Pierre Verger.[13] In addition, it reinforces the myth of the three races, describing three human groups (blacks, whites, and natives) that according to the country's official narrative composed Brazilian society. By placing Africans along with whites and natives, the display was successful in diluting the importance of the Atlantic slave trade in Bahia. But despite this vague narrative, next to this panel, another bilingual panel is titled "Cidade Mestiça," translated as Multiethnic City, even though the appropriate translation would be Mixed City. The title evoking the ideology of *mestiçagem* contradicts the accompanying text that clearly presents Salvador as a black city and as the largest Brazilian slave port. It explains that about 5 million *escravos* [slaves] were taken to Brazil between the sixteenth and nineteenth centuries. The panel also emphasizes that a large number of Africans died during the Middle Passage, even though the death toll fell by the early 1800s. Finally, it declares that "Salvador was Brazil's first and foremost slave port. This explains the massive African presence and influence in Bahia and their descendants' living contribution to a multiethnic city."[14] The panel's background includes nineteenth-century illustrations of travel accounts and photographs representing enslaved men and women, newspapers announcements leasing slaves, runaway slave advertisements, as well as another view of the hold of a slave ship. Across from the panel, a glass case displays a reproduction of a slave ship, showing the interior of the vessel, including coal stones and barrels, along with miniature figures signifying enslaved Africans and crew members. Overall, the representation of the Middle Passage in the Museu Náutico da Bahia follows the traditional conception that focuses on the slave ship rather than on the suffering experienced by enslaved men, women, and children who were transported by force to the Americas.

Unlike the Museu Náutico da Bahia, whose focus is on maritime history, the representation of the Middle Passage in the Museu AfroBrasil is centered on the African experience, an approach that is closely related to the museum's mission. Unveiled in 2004 in São Paulo, the museum was never intended to explore the history of slavery but rather to promote the history and the contribution of Africans and Afro-Brazilians to the Brazilian society.[15] In order to narrate Afro-Brazilian history, the museum's permanent exhibition presents a similar account to the one developed in the Charles H. Wright Museum of African American History in Detroit and the International Slavery Museum in Liverpool, divided in various stages, starting on the African continent and ending with the present-day contribution of Brazilian black population. In the section "African Migration," of the permanent exhibition, the Middle Passage is depicted by a powerful installation composed of a wood skeleton of a slave ship (Figure 3.2). Sources of light are placed along the wooden structure, and on the walls surrounding the slave ship, numerous panels contain artifacts, like chains and shackles, in addition to photographs, and illustrations of European travelogues representing scenes on the African continent and of slave life in Brazil, including a section of the classic and idealized lithograph *Nègres à fond de calle* (Negros in the Hold of a Slave Ship), by Johann Moritz Rugendas (1802–1858).[16] Despite these figurative portrayals, the installation questions the limits of representation. Speakers placed along the carcass of the empty slave ship bring to life the absent bodies of enslaved Africans by emitting the sound of the sea, music, conversations, and lamentations. As a result, the lively rendering of the Middle Passage provided by the Museu AfroBrasil is centered around the tragic experience lived by millions of enslaved Africans who were brought to Brazil.

Except for the reproductions of slave ships in various scales displayed in some museums and some dispersed plaques, no significant monuments or memorials ever paid homage to the many thousands of African, men, women and children killed during the Atlantic crossing and who were buried in the waters of the ocean. Moreover, the memory of young men

Figure 3.2 Slave Ship (Museu AfroBrazil. São Paulo, São Paulo, Brazil; photograph by Nelson Kon, 2011).

and women who perished in the sea was lost and as a result could not be transmitted to their descendants and preserved in the private sphere. If through historical data historians attempt to reconstruct the chains of this disrupted past, the experience of the Middle Passage is difficult if not impossible to represent. But in various instances, ordinary social actors are leading a creative process of memory replacement that fills out the gaps of the forgotten experiences of death during the Middle Passage. Very often this process of reinvention is linked to the actual experiences by particular visual elements that are potentiated through the use of the Internet and new social media like Facebook, Twitter, and Tumblr. One of the most recent and richest examples of the Middle Passage's memory replacement is the underwater set of sculptures *Vicissitudes* (Figure 3.3), created by sculptor Jason DeCaires Taylor.[17] Installed in the Molinere Underwater Sculpture Park in Grenada in 2007, the work is composed of 26 life-size cement sculptures representing male and female children placed in a circle holding hands and facing out. According to the sculptor, he chose his models among local children of various ethnicities who agreed to undergo the life-casting process. By 2012, probably because of the physical traits of the cement figures (almost 80 percent of Grenada's population is of African descent) and the effect of the coral reefs created on the artworks, a wave of entries displaying pictures of the sculptures and stating that Taylor's

84 *Shadows of the Slave Past*

Figure 3.3 *Vicissitudes* (Taylor [website]).

works represented African ancestors started appearing on various social media websites. Even though the underwater sculptures were not originally related to the representation of the Atlantic slave trade, in a process of memory replacement, individuals of African descent from around the world appropriated Taylor's work. His cement figures received new meanings and gave life to drowned enslaved individuals, who otherwise would have continued to be invisible and confined to the traditional small replicas of slave ships displayed in obscure rooms of maritime museums and exhibitions.

SITES OF ARRIVAL

Some of the largest slave ports in the Americas were situated in Brazil and the United States, although the volume of the Atlantic slave trade greatly varied in these two countries. According to the last estimates made available in the *Transatlantic Slave Trade Database: Voyages*, between 1601 and 1866, 252,653 enslaved Africans disembarked in the United States, whereas between 1501 and 1866, 5,099,816 slaves arrived in Brazilian ports. Journals kept by slave ship captains who described their Atlantic journeys often do not provide precise information about the disembarkation of enslaved Africans in ports of the Americas. However, more details can be found in various kinds of sources produced by enslaved Africans who wrote slave narratives and by European travelers who observed the arrival of slave ships in the Americas. Moreover, some of these European contemporary observers also produced visual representations showing the arrival of enslaved Africans in ports of the United States, the Caribbean, and Brazil, in addition to other rendered images of slave markets. Despite the existence of these written and visual testimonies attesting to the existence and the precise locations of these sites of arrival, as well as the narratives by descendants of enslaved men and women referring to these sites, most of them remained neglected in public memory.

Several Africans described in their slave narratives their disembarkation in the New World. The arrival of Broteer Furro (Venture Smith) in Barbados in 1739 was marked by the trauma of realizing that, of 260 captives transported with him in the ship, no more than 200 completed the crossing alive.[18] Although his account, written many years after his arrival in the Americas when he was a young boy, does not provide any details about what happened to the men and women who died during the Middle Passage, it is possible to imagine that, as in other slave voyages with high mortality levels, the bodies of enslaved individuals were either thrown overboard or removed from the ship and buried in a common grave not far from the place of disembarkation. In 1756, Equiano also landed in Barbados. He does not mention slave mortality during the Middle Passage but explains that when the merchants came to examine the captives, they were terrified with the fear of being eaten: "We thought by this we should be eaten by these ugly men, as they appeared to us; and, when soon after we were all put down under the deck again, there was much dread and trembling among us and nothing but bitter cries to be heard all the night from these apprehensions."[19] According to Equiano, there was so much unrest "that at last the white people got some old slaves from the land to pacify us."[20]

Over the eighteenth and nineteenth centuries, European travelers certainly witnessed the arrival of slave ships in slave ports—like Rio de Janeiro, Salvador, and Recife—in travelogues but rarely provide written and visual descriptions of the disembarkations of Africans in Brazil. As Daryle Williams observes, Jean-Baptiste Debret narrates in detail his arrival in Rio de Janeiro in March 1816, a view also rendered in a large watercolor depicting the Bay of Guanabara that later gave origin to a lithograph illustrating his *Voyage pittoresque et historique au Brésil*, but his text fails in acknowledging the presence of slave ships.[21] When describing the Valongo Wharf, Debret quickly explains, without mentioning the Atlantic slave trade, that in this quay "there were the shipyards and once the ships of the French East India Company."[22] Debret's omission does not indicate he was not a witness of the intense slave trade activity in the Bay of Guanabara between 1816 and 1831, the period of his sojourn in Brazil. Indeed, later in his travelogue, he clearly acknowledges the arrival of new Africans in Brazil in the very few years prior to its prohibition, stating that in 1828,

Brazil imported 430,601 enslaved Africans, then 23,315, during the six first months of 1829.[23]

Like Debret, other travelers do not explicitly mention the movement of slave ships or the disembarkation of Africans in Brazilian ports. In 1828, Reverend Robert Walsh (1772–1852) was appointed chaplain at the British Embassy in Brazil. After spending almost one year in the country, he published a travelogue containing numerous observations about Brazil's slave life, as part of the British efforts to abolish the slave trade in the country. Arriving in Rio de Janeiro, he rather describes the picturesque view of the Bay of Guanabara: "Nothing could exceed the beauty of the place in which we lay next morning, when light rendered objects distinct. On our left was a range of fantastic hills, receding behind each other; those in front rising into cones, and terminated by the great Sugar-loaf."[24] Walsh also notices the presence of numerous ships "of all nations, both of war and commerce; not crowded together, as in our contracted rivers, but spread over the wide expanse of waters, and dotting the surface in all directions."[25] However, he also describes the Bay of Guanabara as a "moving panorama of boats of all kinds, passing from one side of the water to the other. They were generally manned by negroes, whose only covering was a pair of drawers, and an old straw hat."[26] Perhaps the few hours anchored at the bay observing the presence of boats with black crews did not allow him to associate these small boats, which usually transported the slaves from the slave ship to the shore, with the slave trade activity.

British traveler Maria Graham (1875–1842) arrived in Brazil in September 1821. She was among the few European travelers who provided detailed observations about the disembarkation of Africans in Brazil. On November 22, 1821, she describes the arrival of Africans in Salvador, Bahia: "This very moment, there is a slave ship discharging her cargo, and the slaves are singing as they go ashore. They have left the ship, and they see they will be on the dry land; and so, at the command of their keeper, they are singing one of their country songs, in a strange land."[27] Graham expresses sympathy for the enslaved, by thinking they were not aware of what was still to come: "Poor wretches! could they foresee the slave-market, and the separations of friends and relations that will take place there, and the march up the country, and the labour of the mines, and the sugar-works, their singing would be a wailing cry."[28]

Rugendas describes the arrival of Africans in Rio de Janeiro in a passage of *Voyage dans le Brésil*. His account, written with the collaboration of Victor Huber, does not provide the point of view of Africans, but it rather aims to describe the general conditions of the Atlantic slave trade in Brazil. Rugendas mistakenly states that no regular quarantine was imposed on slave vessels that arrived in Brazil, but he mentions that sometimes the customs forced the slave ships to stay anchored in the harbor or the port.[29] Then "as soon as the merchant obtains the permission to disembark his slaves, they are put on the ground near the customs, and there they are put on the

Figure 3.4 *Débarquement* (Disembarkation) (Rugendas, 1835: 4th issue, plate 2).

records, after collecting the taxes established for entry."[30] The arrival of enslaved Africans on Rio de Janeiro's shores is also pictured in Rugendas's lithograph *Débarquement* (Disembarkation) (Figure 3.4). The image shows how newly arrived Africans were brought in canoes from the slave ships to the customs house and represents in detail the various individuals involved in the process, including the merchants and their black employees, guards, and government officials. Rugendas's newly arrived Africans are young men and male children, and despite the horrible conditions of the Middle Passage, as in his other idealized representations of black individuals, the naked slaves have strong and muscled bodies.

Mahommah Gardo Baquaqua, the only enslaved African brought to Brazil who wrote a narrative of his life under slavery, describes his disembarkation on Brazilian shores. He entered the country in 1845, during the period of the illegal trade. Like thousands of other Africans who arrived on Brazilian shores during this period, he faced particularly difficult conditions. His slave ship landed early in the morning in a clandestine slave port in the then province (now state) of Pernambuco. As Baquaqua explains, "the vessel played about during the day, without coming to anchor. All that day we neither ate or drank anything, and we were given to understand that we were to remain perfectly silent, and not make any out-cry, otherwise our lives were in danger."[31] To avoid being sighted in public, the merchants disembarked the slaves during the night, as he explains, "when 'night threw her sable mantle on the earth and sea,' the anchor dropped, and we were permitted to go on deck to be viewed and handled by our future masters, who had come aboard from the city. We landed a few miles from the city, at a farmer's house, which was used as a kind of slave market."[32] Despite the scarcity of narratives written by Africans brought to Brazil, oral tradition collected by historians Hebe Mattos and Ana Lugão Rios shows that the memory of arrival during the Atlantic slave trade and the period of the illegal trade remained present in the communities of descendants of enslaved individuals.[33] Still, these narratives remained restricted to the private sphere among the families of descendants of enslaved Africans. Today they are not highlighted in the sites that served as ports during the period of the illegal slave trade, all located in more remote areas and far from public view.

Although neglected in the public memory, the ports of the illegal slave trade remained present in Brazil's toponymy.[34] Among these sites is the Praia do Chega Nego (Beach where the Negro Arrives), near the present-day Armação Beach in Salvador, Bahia.[35] A one-story stone building, which allegedly served as a slave depot for newly arrived African captives, was located on the beach. Until recently, the stone house served as a restaurant and a nightclub, but the old construction was demolished to give place to the construction of a luxurious residential development. Because the stone house is located in a zone of the beach included in Brazil's National Heritage List, its walls were preserved in the recently built condominium.[36] However, as in other parts of Salvador, there is no plaque indicating any possible use of the old building as a slave depot for newly arrived Africans.

In Pernambuco, one of the most notorious beaches where Africans were illegally disembarked, is situated in the present-day municipality of Ipojuca, south of Recife, and is called Porto de Galinhas (Port of Chickens). The beach was distant from the capital of the province, but slave merchants took numerous precautions to avoid having their slave cargoes apprehended by local officials, even though the repression of the illegal slave trade in the region was very inefficient.[37] Sometimes, as Brazilian historian Marcus J.M. de Carvalho explains, the disembarkation was performed so quickly that slave merchants would leave behind important evidence of their illegal activity. For example, in 1844, a slave ship was abandoned on the beach, with "37 barrels of water, some pairs of shackles and the corpse of an enslaved African."[38] The reputation of illegal slave trade port is also visible in the recent work of popular memory widespread through touristic initiatives. According to one of these popular accounts popularized on tourist websites, the name of the beach is derived from the coded statement, "There is new chicken in the port," allegedly used by the slave merchants when a slave ship arrived at the beach. Another popular version explaining the name of the beach states that the slave ships carried chickens to hide the slave cargo. Indeed, both versions are unlikely, inasmuch as the writings of Gabriel Soares de Sousa identify the beach as Porto de Galinhas as early as in the sixteenth century.[39] Today Porto de Galinhas is one of the most important tourist destinations in Brazil. Very probably, the attempts by local social actors to explain the relation between the beach's name and the Atlantic slave trade is a response to the national and international initiatives (especially The Slave Route Project led by UNESCO) promoting the public memory of slavery that became visible in Brazil in the last few years. By associating the name of the beach with the illegal slave trade, these local actors also engage in a process of memory replacement that is intended to compensate for the absence of official projects acknowledging the role of Porto de Galinhas in the infamous commerce of human beings, even though here the beach was an actual slave port.

In 2013, a group of Brazilian historians commissioned by UNESCO produced an inventory of 100 sites of memory associated with the Atlantic slave trade and the history of enslaved Africans in Brazil, which includes Porto de Galinhas.[40] Even though this document circulated among scholars and activists, especially through the Internet, it is not clear whether this inventory will lead to the construction of monuments and markers acknowledging the existence of slave trade sites.

As in Brazil, several sites of arrival of enslaved Africans in the United States remain concealed in the public space as well. The US slave trade was prohibited in 1808, about four decades prior to the final banishment of the Brazilian slave trade in 1850. As Laird W. Bergad explains, by 1860, the United States had a population of "31 million people, of whom 3.9 million (13 percent) were enslaved."[41] In other words, the country had the largest slave population in the Americas, even though Brazil imported ten times more enslaved Africans than the United States. As the two largest slave societies of the Americas, along with Cuba, these two countries share a common history of slavery. Although scholars have emphasized the differences between the slave systems developed in each country, new studies have underlined their many common elements. In both nations, during the twentieth century, sites of disembarkation of enslaved Africans and the burial grounds were memorialized in similar ways.

Founded at the banks of the James River in 1607, even though Jamestown was not an important US slave port, its position as the first English settlement in the New World makes the site a central and controversial landmark, associated with the arrival of the first "20. and odd Negroes" at Point Comfort in August 1619.[42] Textbooks, film documentaries, and websites constantly emphasize the role of Jamestown as the founding site of the English presence in the Americas, but usually the uncomfortable aspects that marked this early settlement, especially the massacre of native populations and the beginning of the Atlantic slave trade, are much less emphasized. Over the centuries, the controversial image of Jamestown as the founding site of the English presence in the New World was preserved but often contested.

In 1807, the bicentennial of Jamestown was celebrated. More than 3,000 people, including students of the College of William and Mary, politicians, historians, and several dignitaries, attended the commemorative activities. The commemoration included processions, dinners, and balls. Fifty years later in 1857, huge commemorative initiatives marked the site's 250th anniversary, this time with about 8,000 people in attendance. In 1907, under President Theodore Roosevelt, the Jamestown Ter-Centennial Exposition marked the 300th anniversary of Jamestown. On this occasion, the Tercentenary Monument, a 103-foot obelisk honoring the British founders of Jamestown, was unveiled. Moreover, several special buildings were erected to house public exhibitions highlighting achievements in education, science, arts, and industry. Held during the apex of the Jim Crow era, the narrative of the Ter-Centennial Exposition included a Negro Building, conceived by African American architect William Sidney Pittman (1875–1958), and constructed by black workers.[43] The initiative was highly contested by some African American intellectuals like W. E. B. Du Bois, who saw it as the symbol of racial segregation. But although segregated, the building recognized the Africans as one of the three founding groups of the United States and was attended by 750,000 black and white visitors.[44] This acknowledgment was particularly visible through a series of innovative dioramas created by African American sculptor Meta Vaux Warrick Fuller (1877–1968).[45] In *Landing of First Twenty Slaves at Jamestown*, depicting the arrival of Africans in Virginia, for the first time African Americans were incorporated into the official narrative of American civilization.[46]

The 350th anniversary of Jamestown in 1957 was also greatly celebrated with the presence of national and international dignitaries. Several initiatives were developed, including the Jamestown Festival Park (today Jamestown Settlement). The park was located near the entrance of Jamestown Island and the Colonial Parkway connecting the Historic Triangle of Jamestown, Williamsburg, and Yorktown. At this occasion, the various activities failed to mention not only the arrival of Africans in Jamestown in 1619 but also the existence of slavery in the settlement.[47] However, after the James Fort was unearthed during an archaeological excavation in 1994, Jamestown acquired new importance as a heritage site. This new approach cannot be dissociated from the public debates that evolved with the 1992 commemoration activities of the 500th anniversary of the arrival of Columbus in the Americas and was also involved in the dialogue with the emergence of several international initiatives led by UNESCO, especially The Slave Route Project. On August 20, 1994, a special commemorative event marked the 375th anniversary of the disembarkation of the first Africans in Jamestown, including a "symbolic landing ceremony and a variety of programs to educate visitors about the history of African Americans and their impact on American culture."[48]

During the preparations for the commemoration activities of Jamestown's 400th anniversary in 2007, which coincided with the bicentennial of the abolition of the British slave trade, for the first time various initiatives clearly recognized the contribution of Africans and Native Americans to the formation of Jamestown. Although not officially presented as a site of arrival of enslaved Africans, the Jamestown Settlement was renewed. An inclusive narrative was visible in the new permanent exhibition, *Three Cultures, One Century, America's Story*, unveiled in October 2006. Composed of various galleries, the exhibit not only provides the traditional account about the English settlement in Virginia but also highlights the presence of Central Africans and Powhatan natives, through the display of objects and artifacts and the screening of a documentary film, *1607: A Nation Takes Root*.[49] Unlike the exhibitions depicting enslavement examined in the first chapter, *Three Cultures, One Century, America's Story* emphasizes West Central Africa as the region of origin of the first Africans who were brought to Virginia. But even though a West African dwelling is displayed, including renderings of African characters performing various daily activities, the exhibition fails to show the crucial role that enslaved Africans played in the development of Virginia.[50]

A similar process occurred in Charleston, South Carolina, where the largest number of enslaved Africans brought to the United States was disembarked during the period of the Atlantic slave trade. Unlike the ports of Salvador and Rio de Janeiro, which together imported more than 2 million enslaved Africans, Charleston imported about 150,000 slaves from Africa, about 40 percent of the total US slave imports. After the abolition of the Atlantic slave trade to the United States in 1808, the city continued to be an important point of the internal trade.[51] Also a tourist destination, Charleston's population, estimated at 122,000, is much smaller than the populations of Rio de Janeiro (about 6 million) and Salvador (approximately 2.6 million). As Blain Roberts and Ethan Kytle argue, in spite of its important role in the Atlantic slave trade to the United States, Charleston "had worked hard since the nineteenth century to avoid candid discussions of its slaveholding past."[52] Although since the middle of the nineteenth century, black protests contested existing monuments commemorating proslavery historical actors like John C. Calhoun (1782–1850), until the end of the 1980s, the recognition of the slave past in Charleston's public sphere continued to be a problem.[53] But as Simon Lewis points out, this difficulty in dealing with Charleston's slave past was not only due to the city's particular context but was also part of a "broader Atlantic amnesia."[54] However, during the 1990s, this configuration started to change. On the one hand, the international context following the end of the Cold War and the support provided by institutions like UNESCO favored public discussion about the Atlantic slave trade and slavery. On the other hand, the pressures of

African American local residents led Charleston to start addressing its slave past in the public sphere. Among the first issues raised was the creation of a monument paying homage to Denmark Vesey (1767–1822), a freedman who led the slave conspiracy of 1822 and who, over the following decades, was depicted in novels, television series, and film documentaries.[55] The various local actors struggled to arrive at an agreement about the creation of a monument honoring a rebel, considered a hero by African Americans and a criminal by many white locals.[56]

Regardless of these debates, until the 1990s, the Gadsden's Wharf, site of the arrival of Africans during the Atlantic slave trade, was not highlighted in Charleston's public space. Instead, a number of initiatives were developed on Sullivan's Island, where slaves and crew members were put into quarantine aboard ships or in pesthouses upon their landing in South Carolina.[57] In June 1997, the South Carolina State Senate passed a resolution to create a special marker at Fort Moultrie National Monument.[58] In 1999, following a decree of the South Carolina General Assembly, a first official initiative to commemorate the Atlantic slave trade was developed on Sullivan's Island. The project was supported by descendants of slaves and by descendants of slave owners, including Edward Ball, the author of the book *Slaves in the Family*, published in the previous year, which uncovered the history of his slaveholding family and the enslaved men and women they owned in several South Carolina plantations.[59] Consequently, the South Carolina Department of Archives and History, the Charleston Club of South Carolina, and the Avery Research Center erected a huge commemorative inscription stating that the island is "a place where . . . Africans were brought to this country under extreme conditions of human bondage and degradation. Tens of thousands of captives arrived on Sullivan's Island from the West African shores between 1700 and 1775." Additionally, the plaque emphasizes that the memorial "also serves as a reminder of a people who—despite injustice and intolerance—past and present, have retained the unique values, strengths and potential that flow from our West African culture which came to this nation through the middle passage."[60] Highlighting the role of the island during the Atlantic slave trade, the marker underscores the resilience of Africans and their descendants and recognizes the contribution of African cultures to the United States.

This acknowledgment was a first step to the development of other initiatives. After having deplored the absence of historical markers in the public space to remember slavery and the Atlantic slave trade in an interview in 1989, Toni Morrison launched a project to create bench memorials in various sites of memory of slavery and African American history around the United States and in other cities of the world that had been involved in the Atlantic slave trade.[61] On July 26, 2008, a "bench by the road" was made public on Sullivan's Island.[62] Unlike traditional monuments, the benches placed in various sites in the United States and also in French territories (Paris and Martinique) are memorials leading the passersby to stop and reflect about the significance of the sites of memory chosen as part of the project. Morrison conceived the benches as opened spaces where individuals on a search can sit, and "that search is for anyone, not just black people."[63] Attended by 300 people, in the presence of Toni Morrison and representatives of the National Park Service, the ceremony that unveiled the memorial placed at Fort Moultrie, on Sullivan's Island, had "African drums, for a service that included the pouring of libations and a daisy wreath cast into the water to remember their ancestors."[64] According to Morrison, "It's never too late to honor the dead [. . .] It's never too late to applaud the living who do them honor."[65] The plaque accompanying the monument reproduces an extract of Morrison's interview of 1989, in which she criticizes the absence of sites of remembrance to mourn the slaves. Moreover, it explains that this first bench pays homage to the "enslaved Africans who perished during the Middle Passage and those who arrived on Sullivan's Island, a major port of entry for Africans who entered the U.S. during the Transatlantic Slave Trade. Nearly half of all African Americans have ancestors who passed through Sullivan's Island."[66] By consequence, the bench memorial honors not only the enslaved men, women, and children forcibly brought to the Americas but also their descendants who until recently did not have any site to mourn their ancestors, contributing to the development of further projects. For example, on March 25, 2007, a ceremony commemorating the end of the British slave trade to North America was held close to Gadsden's Wharf.[67] Moreover, a project to create a huge International African American Museum in the wharf's area is in progress.[68]

On March 22, 2009, the exhibition *African Passages* opened in the Fort Moultrie National Monument on Sullivan's Island.[69] The exhibit featured artworks and artifacts associated with the Middle Passage and the telling of stories of Africans who passed through the island, including the case of Priscilla, an enslaved girl brought from Sierra Leone to Charleston in 1756 and was purchased by Edward Ball's family.[70] Gradually, over a decade, and despite the debates among local citizens who opposed highlighting Charleston's slave past, the public memory of the city as a site of arrival of enslaved Africans in the United States was established and consolidated. Also in 2010, ground was eventually broken to create a monument to Vesey on Hampton Park in Charleston.

UNEARTHING THE SLAVE PAST

In 1991, hundreds of bone remains of men, women, and children, either African-born or of African descent, were discovered during an excavation to construct a new federal building at 290 Broadway, in New York City. After protests led by African American activists, the work stopped. A report examining the history of the burial ground as well as the recovered remains and artifacts was assigned to scholars based at Howard University in Washington, DC.[71] Research concluded that the site was a former burial ground containing the remains of about 15,000 enslaved and free African individuals buried during the seventeenth and eighteenth centuries. Located in a port city that imported about 8,500 enslaved individuals, the New York African Burial Ground, as it became known in the following years, is the largest of its kind in the United States.

The discovery of the burial ground occurred in a context that favored the promotion of black history in New York City, in as much as in 1990 David Norman Dinkins, the city's first African American mayor, took office. His intervention was crucial to the development of the African Burial Ground. In a statement to the African American newspaper, the *New York Voice,* he affirmed that he felt fortunate that the site was unearthed during his tenure: "by exploring this burial ground, commemorating it, and reinterring the remains with the respect and dignity they deserve, we can go a long way toward righting an old wrong."[72] But the controversies among members of the federal government, politicians, scholars, and activists (identifying themselves as "descendants" of the men and women buried in the site), regarding the future of the site continued in the next years. This context shows how the public memory of slavery is shaped by the disputes of various social groups that attempt to occupy public space.

The unearthing of the burial ground brought to light the importance of slavery in New York City. Henceforth, the debates involved questions on how to make the city's slave past visible and to memorialize African American ancestors in the city's public space. In 1998, the General Service Administration (GSA) launched a design competition for the memorial that would occupy the site, and received 61 proposals. Then, by the end of September 2003, the Schomburg Center for Research in Black Culture organized a series of ceremonies that started at Howard University, where the bone remains were examined, and culminated on October 4, 2003, with the reinterment of 419 bone remains in the New York's financial district (290 Broadway), the same site where they were discovered. The event, attended by thousands of people, including various African American and international dignitaries, was a privileged stage to address the necessity of publicly recognizing the contribution of Africans and peoples of African descent to the making of the United States. Howard Dodson, then director of Schomburg Center, explained that "basically everything that is including life on earth came from mother Africa and in this country, this western Babylon, we built it on our backs and on our suffering."[73] Jonathan Blount, one of the founders of *Essence* magazine, used the image of "the bones that rose up through the concrete of time" to illustrate the idea of the past that reemerges in the present, emphasizing the existing debt toward the African Americans whose ancestors were enslaved in the United States.[74] During the ceremony, then Mayor Mike Bloomberg made a statement underscoring that the South Street Seaport that is a place "now filled with shops catering to tourists, had once been the site where slaves were auctioned."[75]

Since 2003, every October 4, commemorative ceremonies are held in the African Burial Ground to pay homage to the men, women, and children who were buried in the site. Also in 2003, the US Congress eventually appropriated funds for the construction of the memorial. But the debates regarding how these Africans and African Americans would be memorialized continued and became highly politicized along racial lines. Central in the debate led by African American activists was whether a memorial would be placed on top of the African Burial Ground. The National Park Service (NPS) and the GSA organized a series of public forums to discuss the final decision, but activists contested the initiative. Ollie McLean, representing the Committee of Descendants of the African Ancestral Burial Ground, maintained that no structures should be placed on the sacred site. Instead, she suggested to "take land from that parking garage across the street or take land from other surrounding areas [. . .] They could do that for our ancestors, because this has already been paid for by our ancestors."[76] Another member of the same committee, Eloise Dix, stated that she wanted the "control of the burial ground out of the hands of people who are not of African descent: 'I want to get the Europeans out !' [. . .] They have no rights to it!'"[77] Another controversial issue was the possible choice of white architects to design the memorial. One activist stated: "I do not believe that Caucasian-Jewish people would be so disrespectful to themselves as to have me design a memorial for them [. . .]."[78] Then the same activist established a relation between slavery and the Holocaust, asking "why should black people accept a white architect's proposals for a memorial of people who died during the African holocaust?"[79] These various statements illustrate how the African Burial Ground became a contested site of the memory of slavery. Its unearthing and interpretation were closely associated with race and identity issues that were related not directly to the historical past of the site but to the present total lack of visibility of the city's slave past in the public arena. Although not all the issues raised by African American activists were addressed, eventually, in June 2004, two Haitian American architects, Rodney Leon and Nicole Hollant-Denis (AARIS Architects), won the competition to design the memorial.

On February 27, 2006, President George W. Bush officially proclaimed the African Burial Ground a National Monument.[80] But once again the motivations behind Bush's designation were questioned by African American activists like Ollie McClean, who reminded people that in 2005, during the Hurricane Katrina, the federal government left African Americans abandoned: "I need to know how the government can spend millions to preserve our ancestors' bones, and not care about our ancestors' descendants."[81] The memorial was eventually dedicated on October 5, 2007.[82] Built with granite, the memorial is divided into two sections, the Circle of the Diaspora and the Ancestral Chamber. Through a ramp, the visitor is led to the interior of a circular wall on which various Akan symbols are depicted. In the interior of the court, a map of the Atlantic world evoking the Middle Passage is depicted on the ground. The Ancestral Chamber, built with Verde Fontaine green granite from the African continent, was placed next to the ancestral reinterment ground. The chamber, symbolizing the interior of a slave ship, was conceived as a place for contemplation and prayer. As in other monuments, memorials, and heritage sites of the Atlantic slave trade, the idea of return is evoked by a Sankofa symbol carved on the chamber's external wall and dedicated as follows (Figure 3.5): "For all those who were lost; For all those who were stolen; For all those who were left behind; For all those who were not forgotten." In the various official descriptions of the memorial, the symbol is translated as "learn from the past," but a more accurate translation is "go back to fetch it," referring to a proverb that states, "It is not a taboo to return and fetch it when you forget," evoking the links between spiritual and material world."[83] The choice of this emblem was not accidental. One of the coffins recovered by the archaeological excavation displayed a heart-shaped pictogram that, according to one expert, was an Akan symbol associated with present-day Akan mortuary practices. Although today this association is contested by some scholars, the Sankofa symbol became the memorial's central element.[84]

Figure 3.5 African Burial Ground National Monument (Ancestral Chamber's external wall; photograph by Ana Lucia Araujo, 2010).

In 2010, as part of the development and promotion of the site, a visitor center housing a permanent exhibition was created in the federal building adjacent to the memorial, with the goal of celebrating the African presence in New York City and disseminating the history of the most important archaeological project ever undertaken in the United States.[85] African American tourists, scholars, and members of the African diaspora are the most frequent visitors to the memorial. During the year, and especially in October, various ceremonies to honor the African ancestors are held in the memorial. But despite its location close to Wall Street in Lower Manhattan at the heart of New York City, the promotion of the African Burial Ground was affected by the events of September 11, 2001. The two towers of the World Trade Center, destroyed by the terrorist attacks that killed thousands of individuals, were located just over half a mile from the burial ground. This tragedy created another mass grave near the site and imprinted the collective memory of New York City's population with a more recent traumatic event. When visitors to the area, whether they are whites or African Americans, ask where the African Burial Ground is, they will often be directed toward Ground Zero, where the National September 11 Memorial and Museum, dedicated on September 11, 2011, is located today. In spite of these hindrances, the unearthing of the site brought to light the existence of slavery as a central institution in New York until its abolition in 1827. This chapter of US history, unknown for most part, was absent from the various official narratives presented in textbooks and museum exhibitions, where slavery was usually described as existing only in the US South.[86] The discovery also led to the development of several other ventures focusing on the existence of slavery in New York City. Among these initiatives was the exhibit *Slavery in New York* held in the New York Historical Society in 2005, which was followed by a series of other exhibitions problematizing slavery in the United States.[87]

Unlike New York City, whose slave past was a forgotten chapter of US history, slavery was a central element in Rio de Janeiro's daily life until the end of the nineteenth century. Until the middle of the eighteenth century, enslaved Africans who arrived in Rio de Janeiro disembarked in the wharf near the Largo do Paço, present-day Praça XV (Square XV), where several public buildings, including the Customs House and the Royal Palace, were located. From there, the newly arrived Africans were brought into the city to be sold in the dozens of shops located at Rua Direita (Right Street), present-day Rua 1 de Março (March 1). In 1758, it was determined that the slave market would be transferred to the Valongo neighborhood.[88] By 1774, enslaved Africans who arrived in Rio de Janeiro could also be disembarked in Valongo, located in the city's northeastern zone, near the waterfront of present-day intersection of the Avenues Barão de Tefé and Perimetral.[89] This change, which took several years to be totally effective, was intended to prevent the lines of naked enslaved Africans from entering the city; according to Rio de Janeiro's authorities they brought numerous diseases from Africa.[90]

Between 1758 and 1831, and especially after 1811 when the construction of the quay was completed, about 1 million Africans came ashore in the Valongo Wharf. But the area of disembarkation of Africans was gradually erased from the urban space after the slave trade was banned in 1831 and during the chaotic process of modernization and urbanization of the early twentieth century.

There were numerous descriptions of Valongo Wharf, but its exact location remained unknown for over a century. In 1843, the wharf underwent major works to receive the Empress Teresa Cristina, who arrived in Brazil that same year to marry the Brazilian Emperor Dom Pedro II. The site was then covered with granite blocks and renamed Cais da Imperatriz (Empress Wharf). As historian Jaime Rodrigues notes, the renewal works and the new name were intended to conceal the slave past of the site where so many Africans disembarked, replacing it with a celebratory memory of Brazilian monarchy.[91] In 1871, the old wharf was the site of the ceremony that inaugurated the Dom Pedro II Dock, the first one to be built in Brazil, designed by the Afro-Brazilian engineer and military André Rebouças (1838–1898) and then transformed into the Praça Municipal (Municipal Square), the first of Rio Janeiro's monumental squares. In the early 1900s, Mayor Francisco Pereira Passos (1836–1913) led a major urban reform in Rio de Janeiro. On this occasion, a landfill covered the wharf. Finally, the construction of the Avenue Barão de Tefé added another layer to the old structure of the Valongo Wharf. During the twentieth century, the old port zone of Rio de Janeiro, close to the city downtown area, remained nearly abandoned. Not only had the underprivileged black population who were resident in the port zone been totally neglected by the public authorities, but also the buildings and heritage sites located in the area were in an advanced state of decay.[92]

Similarly to what occurred in New York City in 1991, in 1996, an archaeological excavation on a private property at 36 Pedro Ernesto Street (former Cemitério Street) in the Gamboa neighborhood revealed a burial ground containing bone fragments of dozens of enslaved African men, women, and children. The site was identified as being the Cemitério dos Pretos Novos (Cemetery of New Blacks), a common grave where recently arrived Africans who died before being sold in the Valongo market were buried. Between 1824 and 1830, after continuous complaints from the residents and because of the official ban of Brazilian slave trade, the cemetery was closed. Scholars estimate that more than 6,000 newly arrived Africans were buried at the site.[93] But following this important and unprecedented discovery, the cemetery and the port area continued to be neglected for a long period. Unlike the African Burial Ground in New York City, the site was private property and not a federal building, and the Brazilian federal government had no authority on the site, whose preservation was in charge of the City Hall. Although the couple who owned the property where the cemetery was uncovered decided to embrace the cause of protecting the site with the great support of activists of Rio de Janeiro's black movement, they barely received any public or official assistance. In 2001, the Municipal Secretary of Culture organized a symposium to discuss these new archaeological findings and in 2002 proposed a number of initiatives to highlight the African heritage in the port area. Among the proposals was to establish several markers indicating the significant sites of memory associated with the African presence in the region. By this time, the site of the former cemetery was opened to public visitation, but as the lack of public support persisted, the couple gradually transformed their old home into a nongovernmental organization titled Instituto de Pesquisa e Memória Pretos Novos (New Blacks Institute of Research and Memory). This initiative coincided with the election of President Luiz Inácio Lula da Silva and the emergence of numerous official projects promoting Afro-Brazilian history around the country. The space of the institute was expanded with the creation of modest exhibitions and a small library.[94] Yet this situation drastically changed when in March 2011 drainage works started in the Rio de Janeiro port region, as part of the project Rio de Janeiro: Porto Maravilha (Rio de Janeiro: Wonderful Port), aimed at recuperating the city's old port in view of the 2014 FIFA World Cup and 2016 Olympic Games.[95] During the works, the ruins of Valongo Wharf were eventually rediscovered. The excavations also recovered numerous African artifacts, including ceramic pipes, cowries employed in religious practices, and buttons made of animal bones.

Following this second discovery, similarly to what occurred in New York City, black activists, scholars, and politicians intensively debated the project that would be developed on the wharf. If until recently Rio de Janeiro's authorities never expressed major interest in promoting the slavery heritage of the city's downtown area, there was now an urgent need to find an urban solution to a site associated with the forthcoming Olympic Games. The possibility of nominating the newly discovered site for inclusion in the UNESCO World Heritage List raised the interest of various companies and organizations as well. The initial project of Rio de Janeiro's City Hall was to create a huge memorial with portals that, according to black activists, would divert the attention from the archaeological site. Moreover, because the wharf is located just next to Morro da Providência, the first Brazilian *favela,* most of whose residents are Afro-Brazilians, black organizations were concerned about how an architectural intervention on the wharf would affect the neighboring community. Finally, black activists were successful in preventing the creation of a memorial structure that would compete with the archaeological site by keeping the simple original structure of the wharf.[96]

Through the municipal decree number 34.803 of November 29, 2011, a pioneer initiative was created, Circuito Histórico e Arqueológico da Celebração da Herança Africana (Historical and Archaeological Trail of African Heritage Celebration). The trail highlights several heritage buildings and sites of memory associated with the Atlantic slave trade and African presence in the port area of Rio de Janeiro. The tour starts at the Valongo Wharf, where plaques and maps indicate and explain the various relevant markers. The trail includes the Pedra do Sal (Salt Stone), a site where Africans and Afro-Brazilians dockers used to get together, which is considered the cradle of the Brazilian *samba*. The next marker is the Valongo's Garden and the Valongo's Hill (or Conceição's Hill), a place of sociability, where enslaved men and women performed different kinds of activities. Also included in the tour are the Largo do Depósito (Warehouse Square), today Praça dos Estivadores (Dockers' Square), where slave warehouses were located, as well as the Instituto dos Pretos Novos (New Blacks Institute), comprising the archaeological site of the Cemetery of New Blacks. Some of these sites were included in the city of Rio de Janeiro's heritage list since the 1980s and were then identified by small plaques. However, only after the unearthing of the Valongo Wharf and the announcement of discovery in the Brazilian and international media did the City Hall take clear measures to eventually promote the slave trade heritage sites of the Rio de Janeiro port area.

The public impact of the rediscovery of Valongo Wharf was visible in the reaction by Rio de Janeiro Mayor Eduardo Paes, who compared the site to the Roman ruins and promised that a memorial to exhibit the artifacts found in the site would be created in the Valongo's Garden.[97] During a seminar organized by the Fundação Cultural Palmares (Palmares Cultural Foundation) and UNESCO in August 2012, it was proposed to present the nomination of Valongo Wharf to the UNESCO World Heritage List. On this occasion, Elói Araujo, then President of Fundação Cultural Palmares, a public entity created in 1992 to promote Afro-Brazilian cultural heritage, reacted against those who opposed the proposal of inclusion of the Valongo Wharf in the UNESCO World Heritage List: "are they cynical, and want to forget that there was slave trade? Nobody denies the Holocaust or the dropping of the atomic bomb."[98] As expected, the discussion about the strategies to preserve the site became politically contentious. Politicians, real state companies, scholars, and black organizations quickly understood its tangible and symbolical importance; both locally and internationally, the wharf embodies the connections between Brazil, Africa, and the African diaspora. With different interests in play, each of these groups attempted to appropriate the site and orient the ways the history of the Atlantic slave trade would be exposed or concealed.

Gradually both the Valongo Wharf and the Cemetery of New Blacks are being incorporated into Rio de Janeiro's urban landscape and becoming part of the country's official national narrative that now recognizes the importance of the Atlantic slave trade and Brazil's crucial role in it. In 2012, the site of the Cemetery of New Blacks was transformed into a memorial (Figure 3.6). The main exhibition was reshaped, with the inclusion of explanatory panels with text and images reconstituting the history of the site, large photographs of Africans and Afro-Brazilians, and a huge panel wall with the names of enslaved individuals brought to Brazil. Moreover,

Figure 3.6 Memorial of New Blacks (Rio de Janeiro, Brazil; photograph by Halley Pacheco de Oliveira, 2013).

glass pyramids were set on the memorial's floor, allowing the visitors to see the archaeological findings discovered in the site. As a sacred site, the memorial's unveiling ceremony had the participation of Candomblé priests who paid homage to the African ancestors who died without ever receiving a decent burial ground. The community of Gamboa and different black organizations are slowly appropriating the Valongo area, organizing black heritage tours, public religious ceremonies, and spectacles of *capoeira* (an Afro-Brazilian martial art, combining dance and music). Regardless of this appropriation by the local actors, until January 2013, the artifacts uncovered during the archaeological excavation were still housed under precarious conditions in containers left behind in the port area archaeological site. The archaeologists of Museu Nacional were waiting the Rio de Janeiro City Hall to fulfill the promise to build a facility to keep the findings and to hire the professionals to start cleaning, identifying, and classifying the artifacts.[99] Moreover, the Valongo area remains negligible in relation to most other Rio de Janeiro's tourist sites, and even many locals are not aware of its historical importance. Its visitors are mainly Afro-Brazilians or international tourists with a particular interest in the history of African diaspora. In addition, because no memorial was constructed on the Valongo Wharf—only the ruins were preserved—the visit to the site acquires meaning only if oriented by the few Afro-Brazilian guides associated with local black organizations.

SLAVE MARKETS

After disembarking in the US and Brazilian ports, enslaved Africans were usually put into quarantine. Especially after 1808, when the Portuguese royal court moved to Brazil, upon the arrival of a slave ship in Rio de Janeiro's port, a physician would go on board to examine the captives. Ill enslaved individuals were sent into isolation for at minimum eight days on the Ilha de Bom Jesus (Bom Jesus Island); after 1810, they were transferred to the Lazareto, a facility located behind the Morro da Saúde (Health's Hill).[100] Once the slaves left the quarantine to be brought to the slave market in Valongo, they were registered, and the duties were paid.[101]

In Salvador, Bahia, the slave market was located in the Lower Town, facing the Bay of All Saints. Amédée François Frézier (1682–1773), a Savoyard military who had traveled to Chile, Peru, and Brazil between 1712 and 1714, described Salvador's slave market: "There are shops full of these poor unfortunates that are exposed all naked, and they bought them like animals and acquire upon them the same power, so that on minor discontent, they can kill them almost with impunity, or at least mistreat them as cruelly as they want."[102] Surprised by how blacks outnumbered whites in the then the capital of Brazil, Frézier underscores how the enslaved population was badly treated.

British traveler Thomas Lindley sojourned in Bahia in 1802, during a period when foreign merchants were not allowed to trade in Brazil. In his travelogue, he describes the recently arrived Africans who were displayed in the slave market: "The streets and squares of the city are thronged with groups of human beings, exposed for sale at the doors of the different merchants to whom they belong; five slave ships having arrived within the last three days."[103] Lindley states that one could fear that the arrival of so many Africans could provoke the same results that led to then ongoing rebellions in Saint-Domingue, even though according to him, the "negroes are cheerful and content."[104] In an entry of her travel journal dated October 20, 1821, Maria Graham also describes the port area of Salvador's Lower City as being the place where the slave market was located: "passing the arsenal gate, we went along the low street, and found it widen considerably at three quarters of a mile beyond: there are the markets, which seem to be admirably supplied, especially with fish. There also is the slave market, a sight I have not yet learned to see without shame and indignation."[105]

Later on, the wave of rebellions in Bahia between 1807 and 1835, led by West African–born individuals (mostly Hausa and Yoruba), would show that Lindely's concerns were not unfounded.[106] During an uprising that took place in Salvador on April 1, 1830, a group of enslaved men attacked three hardware stores and robbed 12 swords and 12 knives. They then took to Julião Street in the Lower Town and attacked the slave depots of Wenceslau Miguel de Almeida. There, they rescued 100 new Africans who were waiting to be sold, most of whom followed the rebels.[107] Despite abundant historical evidence and Salvador's large population of African descent (today estimated at 80 percent), there are no markers on the wharf of the Lower Town indicating where enslaved Africans were disembarked. Today, the wharf includes a modernized port and piers that harbor expensive boats, as well as elegant restaurants and luxurious condominiums with great views of the sea. The lack of spatial markers remembering the sites where Africans arrived in the city, combined with the recent rise of the public memory of slavery, has led to a process that I call memory replacement. According to a legend widespread among local residents and tourists, the basement of the present-day central market, known as Mercado Modelo, was a former slave market. Scholars also reproduce the story, propagated by many workers of the tourism industry and taxi drivers and disseminated through videos and pictures on the Internet. In his book *Blind Memory*, Marcus Wood erroneously describes Salvador's Mercado Modelo as "the world's biggest slave market" during the eighteenth century.[108] Actually, starting in 1763, Rio de Janeiro became Brazil's capital, not only surmounting Bahia in numbers of slave imports but also becoming the country's largest slave port. In fact, the present-day building of Mercado Modelo was not the actual central slave market, but rather one that was located in another site close to the current location. In 1969, a fire destroyed the early building. In 1971, the market moved to the present-day three-story building, constructed between 1843 and 1861 to function as the customs house, which had been abandoned and vacant since 1958.[109] In 1984, following a huge fire, the current building of Mercado Modelo was renovated, and the basement was discovered, rehabilitated, and opened to the public (Figure 3.7). Because the basement is located at the sea level and is often flooded, popular accounts state that the site was a slave depot where enslaved men and women were gathered together before being sold. Another version of the legend also maintains that the building was a slave prison, even though there was no prison specifically intended to enslaved individuals. To this day, local residents report that the laments of enslaved persons who were held in the basement can be heard during the night. Although the association between a customs building and a slave depot or market is logical, after 1831 the slave trade to Brazil was outlawed, and even though many thousands of enslaved Africans continued to enter the country until the early 1850s, they could not be disembarked in the Salvador's main port area and gathered in a public building in the Lower Town. The legend, another case of memory replacement, is a good example of how the local Afro-Brazilian population deals with the lack of visible and official markers indicating the existence of sites remembering the Atlantic slave trade in Salvador. A basement in a central market can certainly successfully

104 *Shadows of the Slave Past*

Figure 3.7 Basement of Mercado Modelo (Salvador, Bahia, Brazil; photograph by Ana Lucia Araujo, 2009).

resemble a dungeon, one of the most popular structures in slave trade sites like Cape Coast Castle in Ghana and the House of Slaves in Gorée Island. But in the case of Salvador, memory replacement is just partially related to the needs of the tourism industry. At Mercado Modelo, tourists can attend spectacles of *capoeira*, eat typical Afro-Brazilian dishes, and purchase various types of souvenirs, including black dolls of all sizes and kinds. Indeed, the local tourism industry focuses on a stereotypical Bahian black culture, not on slavery and the sufferings caused by the Atlantic slave trade. As a result, the story about the basement of Mercado Modelo is a marginal account in the whole narrative celebrating black culture. In this context, memory replacement becomes an effective way of addressing the lack of official initiatives publicly recognizing the sites where slaves were disembarked and kept before being sold. From this erasure, by relying on existing images and recollections, Afro-Bahians developed a new story. If they cannot reconstruct, they can at least imagine where these sites were located and what the experience of confinement was like for enslaved Africans in these slave depots.

In Recife, the main slave market was located in the Rua dos Judeus (Jews' Street), which later was renamed Rua da Cruz (Cross Street) and today is called Rua Bom Jesus (Bom Jesus Street).[110] Artist Zacharias Wagener (1614–1668), who sojourned in Brazil from 1634 to 1642 during the Dutch occupation of Pernambuco (1630–1654), rendered the slave market in a watercolor showing dozens of African men, women, and children, almost naked, exposed in various locations along the street. When Maria Graham arrived in Recife 1821, she was disgusted to see for the first time a slave market in one of the main streets of the city's downtown: "[w]e had hardly gone fifty paces into Recife, when we were absolutely sickened by the first sight of a slave-market. It was the first time either the boys or I had been in a slave-country."[111] Unlike other travelers, Graham emphasizes the difference between imagining slavery through pictures and the actual experience of the "staggering sight of a slave-market." She explains that the owners kept the new slaves closely shut up in the depots: "Yet about fifty young creatures, boys and girls, with all the appearance of disease and famine consequent upon scanty food and long confinement in unwholesome places, were sitting and lying about among the filthiest animals in the streets."[112] In addition, she also describes in her journal the presence of sick and hungry African men, women, and children in a Recife outdoor slave market. Her observations reflect not only her personal sentiment toward the horrible scenes of slavery but also the abolitionist views that existed among her British compatriots. Graham's text is illustrated with an aquatint titled *Gate and Slave Market at Pernambuco* (Figure 3.8), based on an oil painting by the British traveler and artist Augustus Earle (1793–1838), who also produced other scenes depicting slavery in Brazil. As in the written description, the image shows distressed enslaved men, women, and young children, almost naked, in the middle of a street. In full view of street vendors and passersby, merchants and guards force the slaves to move toward the interior. Years later, the Swiss artist Luis Schlappriz also rendered Rua da Cruz, where the old open air slave market was located, showing how, despite the end of the slave trade, enslaved workers still constituted the main workforce in the neighborhood.[113] Still, despite its crucial role during the period of the Atlantic slave trade, today Rua Bom Jesus (former Rua da Cruz) contains no any marker indicating the previous existence of a slave market.

Other European travelers extensively described, in words and images, the horrible conditions to which enslaved men, women, and children were subjected at Rio de Janeiro's Valongo slave market, while waiting to be sold. British clergyman Robert Walsh also mentions Valongo in his travel account *Notices of Brazil in 1828 and 1829*. He explains that after disembarking, most slaves were sold by gypsies, who served as local intermediaries in the

106 *Shadows of the Slave Past*

Figure 3.8 Gate and Slave Market at Pernambuco (drawing by Augustus Earle; engraving by Edward Finden; Graham, 1824: facing p. 107).

local market. According to Walsh: "Almost every house in this place is a large ware-room, where the slaves are deposited, and customers go to purchase. These ware-rooms stand at each side of the street, and the poor creatures are exposed for sale like any other commodity."[114] He notes that the warerooms were spacious and could accommodate 300 to 400 slaves of both sexes and various ages: "Round the room are benches on which the elder generally sit, and the middle is occupied by the younger, particularly females who squat on the ground stowed close together, with their hands and chins resting on their knees."[115] Walsh's description perfectly corresponds to the lithograph *Boutique de la Rue Val-Longo* by the French artist Jean-Baptiste Debret, published in his *Voyage pittoresque et historique au Brésil*. The engraving shows a large, neat depot where emaciated enslaved men, women, and children sit on benches or lie on the floor waiting to be sold under the supervision of a gypsy slave merchant. The horrendous scene depicted in the image corresponds to the written description accompanying the lithograph, in which the artist explains that the "auction room, most often silent, is still infected of castor oil escaping from the pores of these wrinkled walking skeletons, whose look, curious, shy, or sad, reminds you the interior of a menagerie."[116] Still, in spite of the horrible environment, he notes that sometimes the slaves waiting to be sold would sing and dance "turning on themselves and clapping their hands to mark the beat, a kind of dance quite similar to the savages in Brazil."[117] This reaction was certainly not the expression of joy but rather the only way to survive the trauma of the Middle Passage.

A lithograph titled *Marché aux nègres* (Negroes Market) (Figure 3.9) by Rugendas possibly reveals the back courtyard of a slave market, even though it is not possible to identify where this market was located. Gathered in small groups, African men, women, and children are sitting and lying on mats placed on the floor. The scene organization and the idealized, healthy-looking bodies of the characters in the image do not suggest the extent of the grueling conditions to which they were submitted during the Middle Passage. Indeed, the text explains that slaves did not seem unhappy, an idea that contradicts other travelers, probably because they were relieved after overcoming the horrible conditions of the Atlantic crossing: "we rarely listen them complain, even if we see them crouching around the fire, singing loud and monotonous chants accompanied by clapping. The only thing that seems to worry them is some impatience to know what will be eventually their fate."[118]

In his travel account, Rugendas also observes the unhealthy and inhuman conditions of Africans kept in the various shops of the Valongo slave

Figure 3.9 *Marché aux nègres* (Slave Market) (Rugendas, 1835: 4th issue, plate 3).

market. He describes the warerooms as cowsheds. According to him, the market "is a shocking and almost unbearable spectacle: all day these unfortunate, men, women, children, stay sit or lie close to the walls of these huge buildings, and mixed with each other; or, if the weather is good, we see them in the street."[119] The artist adds that the slaves looked even more horrible when they have not yet rested from the Middle Passage. Also, he documents how badly they smelled to the point that it was hard to stay in the neighborhood. Despite stating that men and women were naked and just wore a cloth around the hips, he suggests that they were well fed with "cassava flour, beans, and dried meat; and they are not in lack of refreshing fruits."[120]

GAPS OF MEMORY

This chapter explored how the Middle Passage and the experience of arrival of enslaved Africans in the New World are memorialized in museum exhibitions and heritage sites in Brazil and the United States. Despite the absence of museums especially dedicated to slavery in both countries, reconstitutions of the slave ship are the central elements in attempts to represent the atrocities that marked the deportation of Africans to the Americas during the Atlantic slave trade. Because of the unrepresentable nature of the experiences of extreme suffering, depicting the Middle Passage and the slave ship as its main icon continues to be highly contested. In the face of the numerous visual and written accounts of insurrections onboard slave ships, museum exhibitions clearly privilege representations of enslaved Africans as simple commodities, as purely victimized individuals.

The sites of disembarkation of enslaved Africans remained concealed in the urban areas of the former slave trade ports of Rio de Janeiro, Salvador, Recife, Jamestown, New York, and Charleston. This context started to change only with the commemorations of the arrival of Columbus in the Americas in 1992, eventually culminating in the launching of The Slave Route Project by UNESCO in 1994. The early 1990s was a period of change both in Brazil, with the end of the military dictatorship, and in the United States, with the end of the Cold War. Whereas the two countries opened themselves to global exchanges, black activists could finally occupy the public arena to assert their identities and to address the wrongs of the past. In Salvador, a city whose population has a large majority of individuals of African descent, a rich process of memory replacement took place to fill in the gaps left by the concealment of its slave trade past. To face the invisibility of actual heritage sites where slaves were disembarked, the local population created stories that allow reenacting the painful past of the Atlantic slave trade. However, this phenomenon is less visible in the United States, probably because its established Civil Rights Movement was much stronger and its actions led to the development of official initiatives in Northern and Southern port cities.

Eventually, both in Brazil and the United States, unexpected events have led to the discovery of slave wharfs and slave cemeteries, forcing public authorities to officially acknowledge and create permanent markers to commemorate the slave past of cities like Rio de Janeiro and New York City. Although the preservation and the promotion of these heritage sites face various political and economic obstacles, Brazilian and US black populations are appropriating these spaces and transforming them into sacred spaces and public shrines to mourn and celebrate their African ancestors. Gradually, black social actors, very often supported by scholars who provide their expertise to the study of the newly uncovered wharfs and burial grounds, are forcing the governments of Brazil and the United States to officially recognize the Atlantic slave trade as a central element of an uncomfortable chapter of the histories of the two countries.

NOTES

1. On the representation of *Brooks* and abolitionist propaganda see, Reddiker, 2007: Chap. 10. See also Finley, 2002: 94.
2. "Extract of a Letter dated Rio de Janeiro," 1832: 2.
3. See Handler and Steiner, 2006. On Zong, see Walvin, 2011.
4. See Charles H. Wright Museum of African American History (website).
5. In 1998, the museum was renamed Charles H. Wright Museum of African American History.
6. For a full description of the exhibition as it was unveiled in 1997, see Banner-Haley, 1999: 420–425.
7. For a discussion on the choice of Ralph Appelbaum Associates to design the exhibition, see Wood, 2013: 340–356.
8. Francis, 2009: 195.
9. Smithsonian National Museum of American History (website).
10. "Forced Crossings" (website). For the exhibition's press release, see "National Museum of American History's New Exhibition Goes 'On the Water,'" 2009.
11. For details about the design of the slave ship prototype see Office of the Exhibits Central (website).
12. Exhibition panel, Museu Náutico da Bahia, Salvador, Bahia, Brazil.
13. See Debret, 1834–1839. See also Verger, 1968: fig. 59, n/p.
14. Exhibition panel, "Cidade Mestiça," Museu Náutico da Bahia, Salvador, Bahia, Brazil.
15. See Cleveland, 2012: 197–212.
16. Rugendas, 1835. On this lithograph, see Slenes, 2006: 55–80; Slenes, 2002: 147–168.
17. See Taylor (website).
18. Smith, 1798: 13.
19. Equiano and Carretta, 2003: 60.
20. Equiano and Carretta, 2003: 60.
21. Debret, 1834–1839. See Williams, 2012: 703.
22. Debret, 1834–1839: vol. 2, 30.

23. Debret, 1834–1839: vol. 2, 76.
24. Walsh, 1830: vol. 1, 128–129.
25. Walsh, 1830: vol. 1, 130.
26. Walsh, 1830: vol. 1, 133.
27. Graham, 1824: 155.
28. Graham, 1824: 155.
29. Other European travelers rather underscored the severity of the inspection led by the Brazilian authorities. See Rodrigues, 2005: 285.
30. Rugendas, 1835: 4e. div., 1er cahier, 4e livraison, fl. 7.
31. Lovejoy and Law, 2003: 155.
32. Lovejoy and Law, 2003: 156.
33. See the film documentaries by the team of the LABHOI (Laboratório de História Oral e Imagem) of Universidade Federal Fluminense, Rio de Janeiro, Brazil, directed by Hebe Mattos and Martha Abreu: *Jongos, calangos e folias: Música negra, memória e poesia* and *Passados presentes: Memória negra no sul fluminense* (both 2011): DVD.
34. Mattoso, 1979: 68.
35. See Mattoso, 1979: 68.
36. Conjunto arquitetônico e paisagístico incluído nos trechos da avenida Otávio Mangabeira, compreendendo as praias do Chega Negro e Piatã, no Subdistrito de Itapoã, no. 26, processo 464-T-52, fol. 005/007, July 14, 1959, see Instituto do Patrimônio Histórico e Artístico Nacional, 2009: 14.
37. Carvalho, 2009: 136.
38. Carvalho, 2012: 233.
39. Sousa and Silva, 1945: 113.
40. Mattos, Abreu, and Guran, 2013: 22.
41. Bergad, 2007: 29.
42. See Heywood and Thornton, 2007: 23; Thornton, 1998: 421–434.
43. Wilson, 2004: 318–320.
44. Wilson, 2004: 320.
45. Brundage, 2003: 1373.
46. Brundage, 2003: 1368–1369.
47. Schnee, 2011: 41.
48. See "The Arrival, Jamestown 1619 . . .," 1994: B-1; "Jamestown to Commemorate 1619 Arrival of Africans," 1994: 4-B.
49. Jamestown Settlement, 2006a: 27.
50. See the booklet Jamestown Settlement, 2006b.
51. For the exact estimates, see Eltis and al., *The Transatlantic Slave Trade Database: Voyages* (website).
52. Roberts and Kytle, 2012: 640.
53. Roberts and Kytle, 2012: 654.
54. Lewis, 2009: 126.
55. Among these works is the novel by Martin Robinson Delany, *Blake; or, The Huts of America, A Novel* (1970: originally published serially in *The Anglo-African Magazine* in 1859, then in the *The Weekly Anglo-African* between 1861 and 1862, in the television series *Denmark Vesey's Rebellion* (1982) broadcast on PBS, and in the film *Brother Future* directed by Roy Campanella II, 1991.
56. Roberts and Kytle, 2012: 677.
57. Meggett, 1999: A1. On the pesthouses of Sullivan's Island, see McCandless, 2011: 231.
58. Heilprin, 1997: 1.
59. See Ball, 1998. On Ball's work, see Campbell, 2006: 408–409.
60. Plaque on Sullivan's Island, Charleston, South Carolina, United States.

Places of Disembarkation 111

61. Interview with Toni Morrison, *The World*, 1989. Erika Doss calls sites associated with slavery, lynching, and racism, "sites of shame." See Doss, 2010: 302–303.
62. Morgan, 2010: 3. See Toni Morrison Society (website).
63. Lee, 2008: E1.
64. Lee, 2008: E1.
65. Lee, 2008: E1.
66. Plaque, "Bench by the Road," Sullivan's Island, Charleston, South Carolina, United States.
67. Lewis, 2009: 128.
68. International African American Museum (website).
69. Smith, 2009.
70. Ball interviewed her descendants. See Ball, 1998: 212.
71. See Blakey and Rankin-Hill, 2009: vol. 1; Perry, Howson, and Bianco, 2009: vol. 2; and Medford, 2009: vol. 3.
72. "Mayor Announces Acceleration of Construction . . .," 1992: 3.
73. Sengstacke, 2003: 1.
74. Sengstacke, 2003: 1.
75. "Remains of Colonial Era Slaves Buried," 2003: 5.
76. Carrillo, 2004b: 4.
77. Carrillo, 2004b: 4.
78. Carrillo, 2004a: 1.
79. Carrillo, 2004a: 1.
80. See "Establishment of the African Burial Ground National Monument: A Proclamation by the President of the United States of America" (website).
81. Moorer, 2006: 4.
82. Barker, 2007: 1.
83. Seeman, 2010: 109.
84. See Seeman, 2010: 101–122.
85. See African Burial Ground, National Monument, New York (website). See also Kardux, 2009: 165–180.
86. See Berlin and Harris, 2005: 23–33; Wilson, 2005: 58–61.
87. On the exhibition, see Hulser, 2012: 232–251.
88. See Rodrigues, 2005: 298–299; Honorato, 2011: 68–69.
89. Honorato, 2011: 147–174; Tavares, 2012: 82.
90. Honorato, 2008: 70–73.
91. Rodrigues, 2005: 298.
92. See Cicalo, 2010; Cicalo, forthcoming.
93. On the cemetery of Pretos Novos, see Portal Arqueológico dos Pretos Novos (website).
94. Saillant and Simonard, 2012: 223–225.
95. See Rio de Janeiro: Porto Maravilha (website).
96. Among these organizations are the Fundação Cultural Palmares (Palmares Cultural Foundation), the Conselho Estadual do Negro (National Black Council), the Coordenadoria Especial da Política de Promoção da Igualdade Racial (Special Coordination for the Promotion of Racial Equality Policy), and the Conselho Municipal de Defesa dos Direitos do Negro (Town Council in Defense of Black Rights).
97. Daflon, 2011,
98. Costa, 2012.
99. Candida, 2013.
100. See Honorato, 2011; Tavares, 2012: 54 n36; 82–90.
101. Honorato, 2011: Pereira, 2007: 75.
102. Frézier, 1716: vol. 2, 533.

103. Lindley, 1805: 176.
104. Lindley, 1805: 176.
105. See Graham, 1824: 137.
106. See Prince, 1972; Rodrigues, 1935: 75; and Reis, 1993: 67.
107. See Rodrigues, 1935: 83–84, and Reis, 1993: 66.
108. Wood, 2000: 292.
109. The information on the dates of construction can vary. See Azevedo, 1985.
110. It was named Jews' Street (Rua dos Judeus) in 1635, during the Dutch occupation of Pernambuco. Several Jewish merchants were active in the area. Brazil's first synagogue was established in the same street, and its building is still preserved.
111. Graham, 1824: 105.
112. Graham, 1824: 105.
113. The lithographs were published in Schlappriz and Carls, 1860.
114. Walsh, 1830: vol. 2, 323.
115. Walsh, 1830: vol. 2, 325.
116. Debret, 1834–1839: vol. 2, plate 23.
117. Debret, 1834–1839: vol. 2, plate 23.
118. Rugendas, 1835: 4e div., 1er cahier, 4e livraison, fl. 7.
119. Rugendas, 1835: 4e div., 1er cahier, 4e livraison, fl. 7.
120. Rugendas, 1835: 4e div., 1er cahier, 4e livraison, fl. 7.

4   Invisible Sites of Slave Labor

Although written narratives, visual images, and other primary sources document slavery in plantations and urban settings, the large majority of the sites where slave labor was performed and where enslaved men, women, and children were physically punished and sexually abused are not highlighted in the public space of the United States and Brazil. In the United States, some of these heritage sites are preserved and listed either as national monuments or as National Historic Landmarks, even though they are not always open for visitation. In the many sites where visitors are allowed, especially former plantations and public buildings, most public tours do not feature—and fail to mention—the work performed by enslaved men, women, and children. In plantation sites in Louisiana, South Carolina, Georgia, and Virginia, most of the time the focus relies on the wealth and sophisticated lives of its owners, and it is not uncommon that the work performed by the enslaved is acknowledged only in segregated tours.[1] Unlike the United States, Brazil does not have a plantation tourism industry. Various building structures of former sugar and coffee plantations in the northeast and southeast regions of the country, as well as southern cattle farms and jerked beef factories with their big houses and slave quarters, remain abandoned. Among those that are conserved, several were sold by their former owners and today remain in private hands, transformed into hotels as part of rural tourism initiatives.

How is slavery incorporated or neglected in the public space in the United States and Brazil? Although in the United States, written narratives have emphasized the hard working and living conditions of the enslaved population, the presentation of most important and visible slavery heritage sites frequently omits slaves' daily lives to emphasize the lifestyles of slave owners. In Brazil, despite the lack of slave narratives as a literary genre and the incipient plantation tourism industry, heritage sites and museum exhibitions focus on slave labor by highlighting the victimization and physical punishments of slave individuals. I argue that, although distinct, these two approaches divert the various audiences from the crucial role of slave labor in the construction of these two countries, either by concealing its existence or by denying agency to enslaved individuals.

Even though the goal of this chapter is not to provide an inventory of existing heritage sites and sites of memory of slave labor, a task that has been developed in some studies focusing on the United States but that is not yet available in the case of Brazil, it is possible, by comparing some heritage sites and museum exhibitions, to better grasp the similar and contrasting elements that characterize the memorialization of slavery in both countries.

DOUGLASS IN THE WYE HOUSE

One of the largest and most famous US slavery heritage sites is the Wye House and plantation, located at the Bruffs Island Road (Copperville, Talbot County, Maryland), whose main building was listed as a national historical landmark on October 5, 1970. The plantation became well-known because abolitionist and scholar Frederick Douglass (1818–1895) was enslaved in the site when he was still a child. At the time, the property was owned by Edward Lloyd V (1779–1834), or Colonel Lloyd, as Douglass called him. Lloyd was a famous US politician. During his life, he was a Democratic-Republican delegate to the General Assembly, a senator, and the governor of Maryland from 1819 to 1826. Moreover, he was a very wealthy planter and large slave owner.

In *Narrative of the Life of Frederick Douglass, An American Slave,* Douglass describes the Wye House plantation in great detail: "The principal products raised upon it were tobacco, corn, and wheat. [. . .] Colonel Lloyd kept from three to four hundred slaves on his home plantation, and owned a large number more on the neighboring farms belonging to him [. . .].[2] His description emphasizes Lloyd's great wealth as owning hundreds of slaves. The state was not a simple plantation but rather a complex of farms, where activities such as shoemaking, mending, blacksmithing, cartwrighting, coopering, weaving, and grain-grinding were performed by the slaves, who, according to him, had "a business-like aspect very unlike the neighboring farms."[3] Not without a sense of humor, in several passages of his *Narrative*, Douglass uses anecdotes to illustrate how rich Lloyd was. According to him, Lloyd kept about 15 house servants and was said to own a 1,000 slaves, to the point that he "did not know them when he saw them; nor did all the slaves of the out-farms know him."[4] To illustrate this, Douglass explains that one day Lloyd was riding along and met a black man and asked him: "'Well, boy, whom do you belong to?' 'To Colonel Lloyd,' replied the slave. 'Well, does the colonel treat you well?' 'No, sir,' was the ready reply. 'What, does he work you too hard?' 'Yea, sir.' 'Well, don't he give you enough to eat?' 'Yes, sir, he gives me enough, such as it is.'"[5] The enslaved man did not realize he had just had a conversation with his own master, and after the conversation, Lloyd verified where the slave belonged. About three weeks later, the slave was informed by his overseer that "for having found fault with his master, he was now to be sold to a Georgia trader. He was immediately chained and handcuffed; and thus, without a moment's warning, he was snatched away, and forever sundered, from his family and friends, by a hand more unrelenting than death."[6]

Even though underscoring the brutality with which Colonel Lloyd treated his slaves, Douglass also explains how the slaves were impressed by their owner's wealth, whose main symbol was the Wye House. Enslaved men and women who worked in the fields considered it a great privilege to be selected to do work in the great house.[7] But according to Douglass, Lloyd's slaves incorporated their owner's ideology, showing pride of belonging to the most prosperous planter in the region to the point of fighting among themselves to decide who was the richest master: "When Colonel Lloyd's slaves met the slaves of Jacob Jepson, they seldom parted without a quarrel about their masters; Colonel Lloyd's slaves contending that he was the richest, and Mr. Jepson's slaves that he was the smartest, and most of a man."[8] Douglass then adds that these disputes "would almost always end in a fight between the parties [. . .]. They seemed to think that the greatness of their masters was transferable to themselves."[9] However, albeit recognizing the wealth of the Wye House plantation complex, characterized by its luxurious great house, and noting how the enslaved workers were impressed by their master's opulence, to Douglass the plantation he left when he was about eight years old was a symbol of great pain and sorrow: "If any one wishes to be impressed with the soul-killing effects of slavery, let him go to Colonel Lloyd's plantation."[10]

In 1877, Douglass returned to the region where he was first enslaved to visit his former owner, Captain Auld, in his sickbed. Years later, attorney and former congressman for the Republican Party John L. Thomas (1835–1893) invited the abolitionist for a tour in the Chesapeake Bay.[11] On June 12, 1881, along with Thomas, Peter Thompson, and Samuel E. Chamberlaine, Douglass visited the Wye House plantation.[12] In his autobiography *Life and Times* (1881), he explains that on their arrival in the Wye House plantation, Edward Lloyd VII (1825–1907) was absent, but his son Charles Howard Lloyd (1857–1929), the great grandson of the infamous Colonel Lloyd, warmly received the group and invited them to visit the site. In his narrative, Douglass expresses his emotion in returning to the Wye House plantation: "That I was deeply moved, and greatly affected by it, can be easily imagined. Here I was being welcomed and escorted by the great grandson of Colonel Edward Lloyd—a gentleman I had known well 56 years before, and whose forms and features were as vividly depicted on my memory as if I had seen him but yesterday."[13] Although not referring to the emotions the site evoked on him, it is clear that Douglass was affected by painful memories of the period he spent there as a slave child. He stresses that the place was still very similar to what it was in the period of slavery: "it was so little changed from what it was when I left it, and from what I have elsewhere described it. Very little was missing except the squads of little black children which were once seen in all directions, and the great number of slaves on its fields."[14] During his visit to the Wye House plantation, Douglass also stopped at the Lloyd's cemetery, where he saw the tombs of various generations of the family. This particular part of the visit was memorialized in words and in a wood engraving illustrating *Life and Times*. Yet, unlike his earlier account, his description of the visit to the plantation omits any references to the atrocities he witnessed as a child in this slavery heritage site. Instead, the narrative emphasizes his deep emotional attachment to the Lloyd family. In addition, it is curious that Douglass does not mention having requested to visit a slave burial ground that may have been located not far from the Lloyd's cemetery, whose existence he was certainly aware of.[15] But considering the general tone of his narrative of the visit to the plantation and his cordial contacts with the Lloyds on that occasion, it is more likely that Douglass avoided placing the family in an uncomfortable position during a period when slavery was ended but its deep scars were still very fresh.

Today, almost two hundred years after Douglass lived in the Wye House plantation, the property is still owned by the Lloyd family. The state is very well preserved, even though today it occupies 1,300 acres instead of 42,000 acres. In 2006, the Wye House plantation started receiving increasing attention, when archaeology graduate students from University of Maryland conducted fieldwork in the site and started releasing new information about this historical slavery site. Among others, several findings confirmed the information provided by Douglass in his narrative. One of the buildings discovered was a big two-story slave quarter, which according to archaeologists was the largest to have been excavated in Maryland.[16] In 1993, the late Mary D. Tilghman (1919–2012) inherited the Wye House plantation from her great aunt Elizabeth Lloyd Schiller and moved with her husband to the property.[17] Today, her son, Richard Tilghman, and his family live in the Wye House.

In 2006, the late Mary D. Tilghman explained that she "opens her farm to her black neighbors, who, out of politeness, do not call it 'a plantation.'"[18] Harriette Lowery is one of those neighbors, whose family history is closely connected to the Wye House. She is also deeply involved in the projects to preserve African American heritage in Talbot County (Maryland), both as a member of the advisory board of the Frederick Douglass Historical Society and as cochair of Frederick Douglass Day, which since 2011 is celebrated at the Chesapeake Bay Maritime Museum (CBMM) in St. Michaels. According to her, Wlilliam Demby, the enslaved man whose murder by the overseer Austin Gore at the Wye House plantation was narrated by Douglass in his *Narrative*, is her ancestor.[19] However, Lowery stresses that people do not want to "conjure up bad memories on both sides."[20] But the reasons why the descendants of victims and the descendants of the perpetrators wish to keep the Wye House's heritage of slave labor, physical punishment, and death concealed from public scrutiny are different as well. For the descendants of the enslaved, the past unearthed with the excavations awoke painful memories. During the archaeological work in the Wye House, Lowery was moved by the discovery of the various artifacts related to the presence of enslaved population in the plantation. Moreover, as a descendant of individuals who worked as slaves in the site, these objects connect her and the population of Unionville to the heritage of their ancestors, about whom they knew very little: "It was amazing to me that they had a necklace or earring. And there was one particular bowl [. . .] it reminded me of a bowl my mother had [. . .] It's comforting to me to know at least there were some peaceful times."[21] Although recognizing the recovery of the Lloyd family's slave-owning past was necessary, the late Mary D. Tilghman was uncomfortable regarding the issue: "neither do I think my ancestors, who practiced an evil practice, were wicked people."[22] Still, even with this uneasiness, except for some short interviews published in local newspapers, the results of the archaeological fieldwork and the inscription of the Wye House plantation as a national heritage site have not encouraged the descendants of the Lloyds to publicly discuss this sensitive part of their family's history. Even though the excavations brought to light the Wye House's important position in the US slave past, the site remains closed to the public and is not promoted as part of the country's public memory of slavery. Because the descendants of slaves continue to not have free access to the places where their ancestors performed forced labor and where they were buried, the process of "symbolic excavation," which Derek H. Alderman and Rachel M. Campbell defined as the "resurrection of difficult and long suppressed (and repressed) historical narratives can only happen through memory work, the active construction and representation of the past," is far from being achieved.[23] Consequently, unlike Elie Wiesel who visited Buchenwald and Auschwitz with prominent figures like Obama and Oprah, if Frederick Douglass were alive, he would not be able to freely guide contemporary citizens through the Wye House plantation because the site continues to be closed to public visitors. As a site of terror, where enslaved men and women were submitted to atrocious working conditions, physical punishment, sexual abuse, and murder, the fragmented narrative that emerges from the Wye House remains in the private sphere and is still controlled by the descendants of the perpetrators.

SLAVE LABOR AND PUBLIC BUILDINGS

In the United States and especially in Brazil, slave labor was employed in urban settings. In both countries, enslaved individuals constructed many public buildings of the seventeenth, eighteenth, and nineteenth centuries. For example, the Church of Our Lady of Rosary of Black Men in Salvador (Figure 4.1), Bahia, is a heritage site that dates back to the period of

Figure 4.1 Church Nossa Senhora do Rosário dos Pretos (Our Lady of Rosary of Black Men), Salvador, Bahia, Brazil (photograph by Ana Lucia Araujo, 2009).

slavery. The church is situated in the historic center of a neighborhood that is also called Pelourinho (whipping post) because in its main square, public floggings were inflicted on all criminals, most of them enslaved individuals. Following the Malê revolt of 1835, the largest slave uprising in Brazil, the post was removed from the square, but the name Pelourinho was preserved.[24] The church is the head office of the Catholic lay brotherhood of Nossa Senhora do Rosário dos Homens Pretos (Our Lady of Rosary of Black Men), created in 1685.[25] The construction of the church building, which started in 1704 and continued during the eighteenth century, was financed with the donations provided by the members of the brotherhood, all black individuals, either free, freed, or enslaved. In 1938, the church and its collections were added to the National Heritage List of the then SPHAN (Serviço do Patrimônio Histórico e Artístico Nacional), National Historical and Artistic Heritage Service, present-day IPHAN (Instituto do Patrimônio Histórico e Artístico Nacional; National Historical and Artistic Heritage Institute).[26] Such an action was the result of broader heritage policies developed since the early 1930s and especially during the Estado Novo regime, a dictatorship led by President Getúlio Vargas from 1937 to 1945.[27] The plaque displayed at the church's main entrance indicates, both in Portuguese and English, that the building's construction started in 1704 and continued during the eighteenth century by the brotherhood of Our Lady of the Rosary of Black Men, one of the first black brotherhoods created in Brazil. Although emphasizing that the church was constructed by the brotherhood, the plaque does not refer to the slave status of the individuals who performed the work during their spare hours, which in part explains why the church took so long to be finished. This lack of information can be explained by the fact that Brazilian visitors and the residents of Salvador take for granted the slave status of most of the workers who built the church. But the English translation is clearly aimed at an international tourist audience, who would not necessarily be familiar with the history of the brotherhood and the importance of slavery as an institution in Brazil. This omission certainly concurs with the lack of official markers referring to Salvador's slave past in its historic center. In spite of its inclusion in UNESCO World Heritage List, Pelourinho's buildings are in a growing state of decay. Its Afro-Brazilian traditional residents are left unassisted. In addition, a large number of children occupy the streets requesting tourists to give them money and food. Even though Bahian connections with Africa are largely celebrated and commodified in Pelourinho, African heritage is not explained but rather taken for granted in initiatives associated with *capoeira* and carnival, highlighting drumming, dancing, and colorful parades. In this context, the existence of slavery is not emphasized because Bahian tourism authorities do not have any interest in promoting this unpleasant aspect of the city's past.[28]

In Porto Alegre, Rio Grande do Sul, the Church Nossa Senhora das Dores (Our Lady of Sorrows) is also a site of memory of slave labor (Figure 4.2). The construction of the building by enslaved and freed workers started in 1807, and its presbytery was unveiled in 1813. The church was completed only in 1901, when the two towers were eventually finished. Since the nineteenth century, a popular legend has associated the church's history with the horrors of the Rio Grande do Sul's slave system.[29] According to one version of the legend, a slave master named Domingos José Lopes sent his slave Josino to work in the church's construction. While Josino was working in the building, some bricks disappeared, and he was accused of robbery, arrested, and executed. The enslaved man, who claimed innocence, put a curse on the building causing the construction to be delayed for years. But another version of the legend tells that a young white man proposed marriage to a young woman, who accepted the offer only if the betrothed groom gave her the diamond necklace of Our Lady of Sorrows, displayed in the church's altar. The groom stole the necklace, but when the robbery was discovered, an enslaved bricklayer who worked on the site was accused, convicted of the crime, and sentenced to hang in the gallows. Before being hanged, the enslaved man put a curse on the church, and as a result the construction work was delayed for almost a century.

As in the early nineteenth century in Rio Grande do Sul, the death penalty was not always imposed even on enslaved individuals who committed murder, and it was not applicable to individuals who practiced robbery. The

Figure 4.2 Church Nossa Senhora das Dores (Our Lady of Sorrows), Porto Alegre, Rio Grande do Sul, Brazil (photograph by Ana Lucia Araujo, 2011).

legend can be explained by the amalgamation of two important elements.[30] First, the use of slave labor in the church's construction; second, the church's location across from the Porto Alegre's *pelourinho*, the official whipping post, where individuals convicted of crimes were tied and publicly whipped. Erected in 1810, when the town was formally established, the whipping post remained in use until 1833.[31] By 1830, when French traveler, diplomat, and naturalist Arsène Isabelle (1807–1888) visited Porto Alegre, he witnessed public floggings inflicted at this site:

> Every day, from seven to eight in the morning, you can attend a bloody drama in Porto Alegre. At the beach, at the side of the arsenal, in front of a Church, ahead of the instrument of torture of a divine legislator, you will see a column rising above a mass of masonry, and at its foot, a shapeless mass, certainly something belonging to the animal kingdom, but you can not rank it among the bipeds and bimanes . . . It's a negro! A negro sentenced to two hundred, five hundred, a thousand or six thousand lashes! [. . .] the unfortunate has only mutilated limbs that one hardly recognizes as the bloody shreds of his withered skin.[32]

Even though the whipping post was removed from the public space, as in Salvador's historic center, the memory of these floggings is present in one of the sculptures displayed in the church (Figure 4.3). The sculpture portrays a bleeding Christ attached to a column, a very common motive in Christian art that depicts the fourth station of the Passion of Christ. Brought from Portugal in 1871, when slavery was still very alive in Brazil, and placed in the church located across from the site where enslaved men and women were once flogged, the statue acquires a renewed meaning, evoking the slave workers who constructed the building. Moreover, in the church's street, there was also the Praça da Forca (Gallows Square), present-day Brigadeiro Sampaio Square, situated close to the banks of the Guaíba River, where individuals sentenced to death were hanged. Thus, even though slavery was part of the daily life for the local residents who attended the church, there was probably guiltiness associated with the fact that the very individuals who helped to construct the temple could be publicly whipped and hanged some meters away from the sacred building.

Notwithstanding the legend, the construction of the church was indeed belated by several reasons, including the lack of funds and the disturbances caused by the Farroupilha Revolution (1835–1845), a civil war that threatened to separate Rio Grande do Sul from the rest of Brazil. Yet in the collective memory, because of its location and the use of slave labor, the delay in the church's construction remained associated with slavery and the violence with which enslaved individuals were punished during the nineteenth century.

Like the church of Our Lady of Rosary of Black Men in Salvador, since 1938 the church of Our Lady of Sorrows in Porto Alegre was added to Brazil's National Heritage List.[33] In 2010, the IPHAN launched project

Figure 4.3 Cristo na coluna (Christ at the Column). Porto Alegre, Rio Grande do Sul, Brazil (photograph by Ana Lucia Araujo, 2013).

Monumenta, including a particular initiative named Museu do Percurso do Negro (Black's Route Museum), which established various markers related to the history of slavery and the black presence in Porto Alegre, including the church of Our Lady of Sorrows, which today is officially recognized as a site of memory of slavery. In the texts and videos displayed on the church's website, the use of slave labor is also clearly acknowledged.³⁴ In addition, as part of the same project, a sculpture representing a huge tambour was placed at Brigadeiro Sampaio Square to mark the site of the old Gallows Square where enslaved men and women were hanged (Figure 4.4).

Figure 4.4 Tambour, Museu do Percurso do Negro (Black's Route Museum), Porto Alegre, Rio Grande do Sul, Brazil (photograph by Ana Lucia Araujo, 2013).

Because slavery in Brazil was widespread all over the country and existed until 1888, the use of enslaved workers to construct public buildings was never a surprise and did not generate important public debates. Consequently, despite some isolated proposals, projects officially recognizing the use of the slave workforce in the construction of particular buildings still remain scarce.

Unlike Brazil, when the use of slave labor to construct important public buildings was publicized in the United States, there were strong public reactions. However, there was no reason for surprise because, exactly as in Brazil, oral histories and written documents referred to the work of enslaved African Americans in the construction of public edifices in Washington, DC during the late eighteenth and early nineteenth centuries, including iconic buildings like the Capitol and the White House.[35] In 2000, the existence of pay stubs was brought to public attention, indicating that enslaved carpenters, masons, roofers, brick makers, bricklayers, painters, and other workers helped to construct the original Capitol building between 1795 and its occupation in 1800. Indeed, "[r]enting slaves was a common practice in the Potomac region and elsewhere," as it was in many Brazilian regions.[36] Following the "discovery" of these documents, a long process aiming at recognizing the work of these enslaved African Americans was started. In May 2005, a Slave Labor Task Force Working Group, chaired by African American Representative John Lewis (Democratic, Georgia), was created to examine the role of enslaved men in the construction of the US Capitol and make recommendations to the Congress on how to acknowledge the efforts of these workers.[37]

Regardless of the important role of enslaved African Americans who built the Capitol, until 2013, Dr. Martin Luther King Jr. was the only African American man to be represented inside the Capitol. On January 16, 1986, his bronze bust was added to the National Statuary Hall Collection, to celebrate his 57th anniversary.[38] Still, if the size of the sculpture reveals the importance of the leaders honored, unlike the other dozens of US leaders, Dr. King is not depicted in a full-body large statue. In 2008, the new Capitol Visitor Center, a three-story structure constructed underneath the East Plaza, was made public. The new building, aimed at providing the millions of tourists who visit the Capitol every year with several amenities, was also intended to present a more diverse narrative of US history. A huge Emancipation Hall was created to honor "the contribution of enslaved African Americans in the construction of the United States Capitol and the long struggle against slavery."[39] The project was intended to include African American leading figures among the 100 sculptures of white men displayed in the Capitol's building. Moreover, the so-called Emancipation Hall also exhibits several large nineteenth- and twentieth-century full-body statues of Native American leaders.

On April 28, 2009, a bust honoring former enslaved woman and abolitionist Sojourner Truth (1797–1883), created by Black Canadian sculptor

Artis Lane, was unveiled in the Emancipation Hall. Truth's bust was placed in a corner on the right side of the enormous plaster model for the bronze Statue of Freedom that decorates the top of the Capitol's dome, whereas the bust of humanitarian Raoul Wallenberg (1919–1947), who rescued thousands of Jews in Hungary during the Nazi occupation, was placed on the left side of the statue, intentionally establishing a dialogue between the fight against slavery and the resistance against the Nazi regime.[40] The unveiling ceremony, that took place about three months after Obama took office, had a particular new tone as First Lady Michelle Obama addressed the crowd by stating: "I hope that Sojourner Truth would be proud to see me, a descendant of slaves, serving as the First Lady of the United States of America."[41] As the First Lady's statement suggests, the new bust, like other initiatives that emerged during the first term of President Obama, marked a turning point in the public discussion of the US slave past. However, both Wallenberg's and Truth's busts pass unnoticed by most visitors. Indeed, black and white visitors are rather attracted by the huge Statue of Freedom, and it is common to see them taking pictures in front of the big statue, while usually ignoring the two small busts.[42]

On June 16, 2010, the US Congress dedicated two plaques at the new Capitol Visitors Center, eventually acknowledging the work performed by enslaved men in the construction of the building. One plaque reads: "This original exterior wall was constructed between 1803 and 1807 of sandstone quarried by laborers, including enslaved African Americans who were an important part of the workforce that built the United States Capitol." On February 28, 2012, during Black History Month, a large stone marker was installed in the Capitol Visitors Center. The marker is composed of a granite base containing a block of sandstone, which was part of the East Front, and includes a plaque that reads: "this sandstone was originally part of the United States Capitol's east front, constructed in 1824–1826. It was quarried by laborers, including enslaved African Americans, and commemorates their important role in building the Capitol." In the ceremony that unveiled the marker, Democratic Leader Nancy Pelosi stated:

> For too long, the sacrifice of men and women who built this temple of democracy were [sic] overlooked; their toil forgotten; their story ignored or denied, and their voices silenced in the pages of history. Yet today, we join together to strive to right this wrong of our past, to honor the sacrifice of these laborers, to lay down a marker of gratitude and respect for those who built the walls of the Capitol. In doing so, we remember and honor not only the slaves who completed the construction, but their ancestors brought to our shores against their will. We remember and honor their children and grandchildren who struggled for emancipation and endured the 'fiery trial' of the Civil War. We celebrate the generations who returned to this ground as free

people. The stone we unveil today is a memorial to the tragedy and sin of slavery.[43]

Regardless of Pelosi's moving discourse paying homage to enslaved Africans and their descendants, similar to what happened to Truth's bust, the marker was placed in a hidden corner next to one of the ticket desks, remaining unnoticed to most visitors. As a result, the narrative honoring the slave workers who built the Capitol remains peripheral. Although the official printed guides, pamphlets, and especially the introductory film screened to all visitors who tour the Capitol clearly acknowledge that the majority of the workers who labored in the construction of the various buildings were enslaved men, this aspect remains diluted during the visit of the free Emancipation Hall. When arriving in this area of the building, visitors remain dispersed, and their gazes are not directed to the Truth's bust and the sandstone marker. Furthermore, during the official tours that lead the visitors inside the building, slavery is mentioned one or two times, if at all. Despite this neglect, very recently two other statues paying homage to African Americans were added to the Capitol. On February 27, 2013, a statue paying homage to civil rights activist Rosa Parks (1913–2005) was unveiled at the National Statuary Hall Collection.[44] After the National Congress authorized the statue's commission in 2009, the work was assigned to the sculptor Eugene E. Daub. The full-body bronze sculpture lying on a granite pedestal represents Parks sitting in a rock-like structure with the same clothes she was wearing when she was arrested in Montgomery (Alabama) in 1955 for refusing to give her seat to a white passenger. Parks' sculpture is among the few statues of a woman displayed in the Capitol. More importantly, it is the first full-length statue depicting an African American person, commissioned by the Congress to enter the Capitol.[45]

Some months later, on June 19, 2013, a long awaited full-length statue of former slave and abolitionist Frederick Douglass was eventually unveiled in the Emancipation Hall.[46] The bronze sculpture measures about 7 feet in height. Conceived by the sculptor Steven Weitzman, it was a gift from the District of Columbia. The statue was placed in a visible location close to a column to the right of the plaster model for the Statue of Freedom. Yet, unlike the bust of Sojourner Truth dedicated by First Lady Michelle Obama and the statue of Rosa Parks dedicated by President Obama, Douglass's statue was unveiled by House Speaker John Boehner (Republican, Ohio), Senate Majority Leader Harry Reid (Democrat, Nevada), Senate Republican Leader Mitch McConnell (Republican, Kentucky), and House Democratic Leader Nancy Pelosi (Democrat, California). On this occasion, Obama and his family were on an official tour in Europe, including Berlin. Indeed, on the very same day Douglass's statue was unveiled, the First Lady and her two daughters Malia Obama and Sasha Obama, were visiting the Memorial to the Murdered Jews of Europe in Berlin.[47] During the visit of the 2,711 concrete steles composing the memorial, the First Family was impressed that Germans had such a memorial in the center of the city.[48] Perhaps Michelle Obama asked herself why her country does not have any impressive memorial in its national capital to honor those men, women, and children who were deported to the United States during the era of the Atlantic slave trade.

More recently, Mark Auslander recovered evidence that between 1847 and 1855, slave workers were also employed in the construction of the Smithsonian building, today known as the Smithsonian Castle, located at the National Mall. Moreover, according to Auslander, by 1850 most men who labored in the Seneca quarry, which provided the stones to construct the Smithsonian building, were enslaved men, information that confirms the oral accounts transmitted to generations of African Americans who still live in the region, even though until recently these stories were neither recognized, nor were the archival sources investigated.[49] Although the initiatives to memorialize the contribution of enslaved African Americans to the construction of the Capitol and other buildings in Washington, DC, are certainly important, there are still several challenges to making this recognition effective and visible.

WORK AND PUNISHMENT

Contrasting with the United States, Brazil never developed any national project to collect the testimonies of former enslaved individuals. Men and women who performed slave labor in Brazilian rural and urban areas left very few written accounts describing their work and living conditions, the only exception being Mahommah Gardo Baquaqua. Unlike Douglass, who was born on US soil, Baquaqua was born in West Africa. Soon after his arrival in Pernambuco, he was put to work. In his narrative, he describes his grueling working conditions: "At the time of this man's purchasing me, he was building a house, and had to fetch building stone from across the river, a considerable distance, and I was compelled to carry them that were so heavy it took three men to raise them upon my head [. . .]."[50] In spite of trying to please his master, Baquaqua soon understood that these attempts would not change his situation. To endure his new life, like his slave mates, he started drinking alcohol, then ran away, but was "soon caught, tied and carried back."[51] But like other enslaved individuals born in Africa, Baquaqua resisted his fate. Sent to sell bread in the city, as many urban slaves did at the time, he took part of the money earned to buy alcohol but was discovered by his master, who severely whipped him. Following this event, he attempted to kill himself by drowning in a river but was rescued by a group of individuals in a boat. Once again, he was brought back home and severely beaten by his master, who then sold him to another man living in Rio de Janeiro. Baquaqua's new master was equally cruel. According to him, he treated a slave girl, bought at the same time as himself, with "shocking barbarity."⁵² Certainly the working and living conditions on the Pernambuco plantations were horrendous, and, unlike as Gilberto Freyre suggested, the relations between masters and slaves were far from harmonious.⁵³ Indeed, from the north to the south of Brazil, most heritage sites and museum exhibitions depicting slave labor highlight physical punishments. These representations contradict the traditional image of Brazilian slavery as more humane in comparison to the cruel slave system in the United States, at the same time emphasizing a victimizing image of the enslaved population.

Few visual images of nineteenth-century European travelogues portrayed physical punishments, but the existing ones were widely disseminated, helping to shape the collective and public memory of slavery in Brazil. Among the most popular images of physical punishments are two lithographs (Figures 4.5 and 4.6) illustrating Debret's *Voyage pittoresque et historique au Brésil* and one lithograph (Figure 4.7) of *Voyage pittoresque dans le Brésil* by Rugendas. Since the nineteenth century, these images have been displayed in museums, book covers, posters, documentary films, and soap operas.⁵⁴ Debret's visual representations certainly contain several accurate elements, but his renderings featuring physical punishments contributed to conveying an image of enslaved men and women that excessively focuses on victimhood and victimization. The Museu Júlio de Castilhos in Porto Alegre, for example, is one of the few museums in a Brazilian state capital that has two rooms dedicated to slavery. The rooms contain panels and glass cases displaying images of slavery and punishment, as well as torture artifacts from the museum's collection that were used by slave owners in Rio Grande do Sul during the period of slavery. One of the panels (Figure 4.8) combines two Debret's lithographs depicting physical punishments. The first image is a section of a lithograph showing two enslaved men and one enslaved woman in the streets of Rio de Janeiro. The three of them are barefoot, and each one is wearing a very heavy iron necklace called *gargalheira*. Also, a long chain is attached to the iron necklace of one enslaved man, who is carrying a barrel on his head. Enslaved individuals who attempted to run away were forced to wear *gargalheiras* that prevented them from attempting to escape again, and slaves who were convicted of crimes very often had to wear these necklaces for a number of months.⁵⁵ The other image displayed in the same panel shows a partial view of the lithograph *L'éxecution de la punition du fouet* (The Execution of the Whipping Sentence) (Figure 4.6), representing a barefoot enslaved man, with naked buttocks, attached to a *pelourinho*, being whipped by another enslaved man. On the left, a group of enslaved men, attached by the wrists and neck, are watching the scene, probably waiting their turn to be whipped. In the text of his travel account, Debret explains that this type of punishment was inflicted on slaves who committed any kind of infraction, including flights, robbery, and "injuries received as a

Figure 4.5 *Feitors corrigeant des nègres* (Overseers Correcting Negroes) (lithograph in Debret, 1834–1839: vol. 2, plate 25).

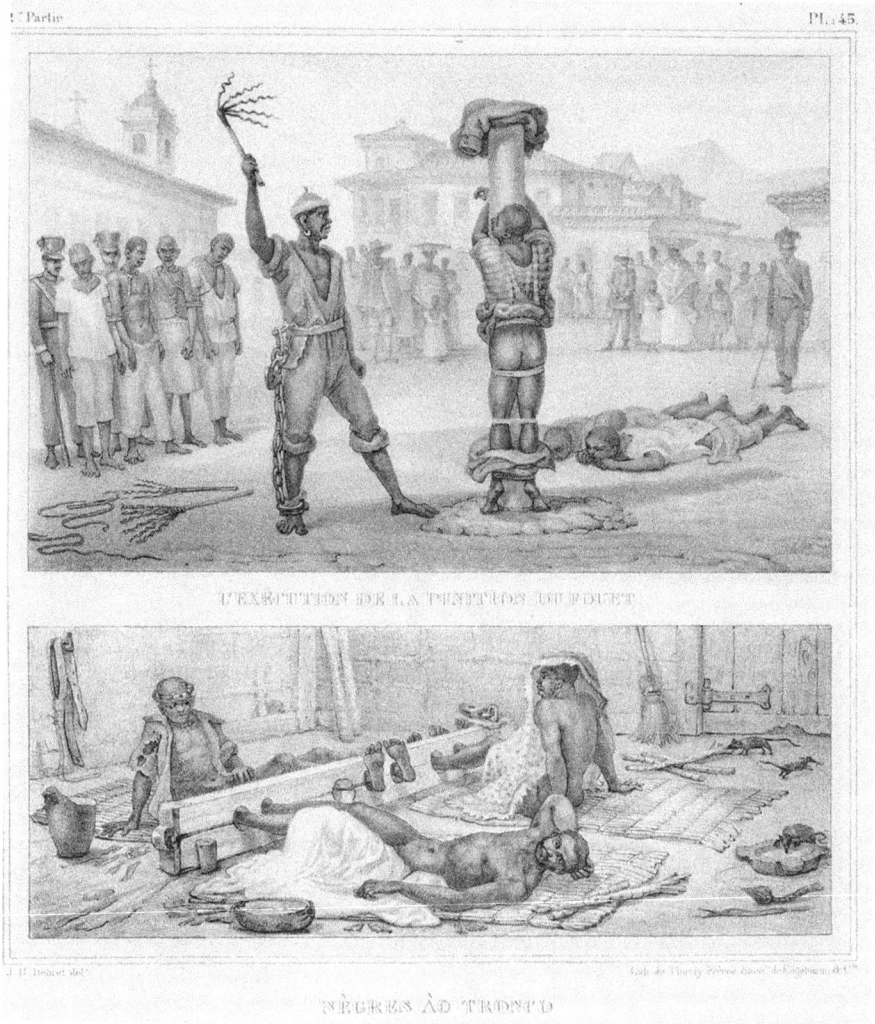

Figure 4.6 L'éxecution de la punition du fouet and Nègres au tronco (The Execution of the Whipping Sentence and Negroes in the Trunk) (lithograph in Debret, 1834–1839: vol. 2, plate 45).

result of a quarrel."[56] Two texts explain the images and the artifacts of the glass display. The first is titled "Gargalheira" and reads:

> It served to identify slaves who tried to escape, calling attention to the fact that they should be kept under surveillance. The ring is closed around the neck preventing them from lying down without hurting themselves, forcing the slave to drag the iron ball and chain around

Figure 4.7 Punitions publiques sur la Place Ste Anne (Public Punishments) (lithograph in Rugendas, 1835: plate 15).

his neck. Its weight, exceeding 10 kilograms, could cause injury in the column. The irons twisted over the head hindered flight through the woods, because became caught in the branches of the trees. In overnight camps these instruments dispensed of the need to watch the slave. Tired, poorly fed, even trying to escape, the slave did not go too far . . .

Even with the detailed description provided in the first text, the second one does not explain the second image depicting the slave man attached to the *pelourinho* and being whipped but rather refers to another instrument of torture, called *tronco* (trunk), depicted in the lower section of the same Debret's plate, which is not displayed in the museum. According to the text, the *tronco* was made of wood or iron and kept the slave attached by the ankles and wrists "keeping him in the same position for hours or days." Moreover, without any detailed explanation, the text jumps more than one century by mentioning that the *tronco* inspired the creation of a torture instrument called *pau-de-arara* used in Brazil during the military dictatorship

Figure 4.8 Collection of Museu Júlio de Castilhos. Porto Alegre, Rio Grande do Sul, Brazil (photograph by Ana Lucia Araujo, 2009).

(1964–1985), even though the instrument similar to the *pau-de-arara* is not represented in the panel but rather in another of Debret's lithographs, *Feitors corrigeant des nègres* (Overseers Correcting Negroes) (Figure 4.5), which is not displayed in the museum. At the bottom part of the panel, a glass display shows iron *gargalheiras* (iron necklaces) that are part of the museum's collection, which artifacts were donated by the heirs of Rio Grande do Sul's slaveholders. Still, the confusing combination leads the visitor to associate the image representing the nineteenth-century iron necklace and the real artifact. Furthermore, these objects and images inform the visitor about the cruelty of slavery, which was a crucial institution in Rio Grande do Sul and not only in the more well-known Brazilian states, such as Bahia and Rio de Janeiro. Nevertheless, as Myrian Sepúlveda dos Santos points out, the persistence in depicting physical punishment inflicted on enslaved men and women reduces the image of Afro-Brazilians to victimized individuals by failing to indicate their ability to resist slavery and their crucial role in the construction of the Brazilian nation, ultimately creating an image of the Brazilian black population that only contributes to undermine their self-esteem.[57]

Yet this emphasis on victimization is not limited to Museu Júlio de Castilhos. In some slavery heritage sites of Rio Grande do Sul, like the *charqueadas* (jerked beef factories) that have been restored and transformed into hotels, the emphasis on physical punishments is constantly present. These privately owned initiatives, run by local families who very often were not the heirs of the original owners of these states, do not aim to focus on the slave past of the region and are still perceived as part of rural tourism. These sites were adapted to receive visitors who can tour the property, stay for one or two nights, celebrate marriages and anniversaries, and visit the buildings of the former slave quarters. As expected, most sites are organized to emphasize the wealth of their owners and the luxury of their "European" lifestyles; slave labor is rarely mentioned.

In Rio Grande do Sul, about six miles from Pelotas, the Charqueada São João, one of the most important jerked beef factories in the region, is still preserved. By 1814, the population of what would become the town of São Francisco de Paula (present-day Pelotas) was constituted of 2,419 inhabitants, of whom 51 percent were enslaved and fewer than 30 percent were whites.[58] The property was built in 1807 and 1810 by its first owner, Antônio José Gonçalves Chaves, a Portuguese man. In 1820, French naturalist Auguste Saint-Hilaire sojourned in the Charqueada São João. In his travelogue, he observes that, unlike in the *estâncias* (ranches), in the *charqueadas* "the negroes are treated with rudeness."[59] Saint-Hilaire also notes that Chaves "only speaks with his slaves with exaggerated severity, in which he is imitated by his wife; the slaves seem to fear their owners."[60] Moreover, the French naturalist explains that this harsh treatment was extended to the enslaved children:

> There is always in the living room a small negro of 10 to 12 years of age, whose job is calling the others slaves, serving water, and providing

small domestic services. I do not know a more unfortunate creature than this child. He never sits, never smiles, and never plays! He sadly spends his life against the wall and is often mistreated by the owner's children. When sleepiness comes at night, and there is nobody in the room, he drops to his knees to sleep. This house is not the only one who uses this ruthless system: it is frequent in others.[61]

Like other rural estates of the same kind, the Charqueada São João is a private property used for tourism purposes. In 1952, it was bought by Rafael Dias Mazza and his wife Nóris Moreira Mazza. In 2000, after the passing of Nóris Moreira Mazza, the property was opened to public visitation. But the popularity of the site dramatically increased when the property was used to film the television miniseries *A casa das sete mulheres* (The House of the Seven Women), directed by Jayme Monjardim and aired in 2003 by the Brazilian television network, Rede Globo. The series was based on Letícia Wierzchowski's homonymous historical novel set in the period of the Farroupilha Revolution.[62] To film the series, some elements of the *charqueada*'s original main house were transformed, including the color of its walls, doors, and windows, in order to give to it an antique appearance. Every year, the property welcomes about 500 visitors per month.[63] In addition to visiting the site, tourists can also take a 60-minute boat tour along the Stream Pelotas, allowing them to see from the boat the various mansions that border the stream. During the tour, the architecture of the various mansions is emphasized, especially the property Estância da Graça, where the film *Concerto campestre* (Country Concert) was shot.[64] Still, the tour guide does not feature enslaved men and women who lived and worked on these properties.

According to the Charqueada São João's website, the state "is one of the most beautiful places of Rio Grande do Sul."[65] The website also highlights the beauty of the statues decorating the property's courtyards, which were brought from Portugal. Except for the rooms where the owner family resides, visitors can tour the 13 rooms of the main house, including the *Sala dos Tropeiros* (Room of Drovers), the internal courtyard, the drovers' dining room, a hallway, another dining room, an office, the master bedroom, an additional bedroom that hosted the French naturalist Saint-Hilaire in 1820, and a bathroom. The *Sala dos Tropeiros* and the internal courtyards are available to host dinners, lunches, marriages, anniversaries, and tea parties. In this room, where people eat and drink during the various receptions, are displayed a variety of objects, including artifacts, photographs, nineteenth-century lithographs, drawings, and tableware. On one of the walls hang numerous iron instruments, such as shackles and chains used to punish slaves.[66] Like the objects and artifacts on view in the other rooms, there are no panels or captions explaining their use. Additionally, tourists can also see the original slave quarters and the places where enslaved men and women were beaten, whipped, and tortured. Although during the visit of the slave quarters, the hard working conditions and physical punishments imposed on slaves are quickly presented, the word "slave" is never mentioned on the *charqueada*'s website. Like the approach found in the *Sala dos Tropeiros*, the website mixes the horrors of slavery with elements attesting to the rich lifestyle of the *charqueada*'s owners. For example, one picture posted on the website features a fig tree situated next to a whipping post, which is omitted in the picture, with the slave quarters visible in the background. Then, an intriguing caption states that "the slave quarters, the cave, the centennial fig trees, and pergolas are wonderful places among the rich vegetation."[67] In other words, slave labor is treated as one element among many other beautiful characteristics of a site described as an idyllic place. Indeed, despite some mentions of the use of slave labor during the visit to the property, the main element to attract tourists to the Charqueada São João is not the uncomfortable history of slavery and its heritage but rather its role in the Rede Globo miniseries.

Another important property situated on the banks of the Stream Pelotas is the Charqueada Santa Rita, located about six miles from the city of Pelotas. Constructed in 1826 by Inácio Rodrigues Barcellos, the site and its mansion are well preserved. During the twentieth century, the property changed hands three times. In the 1960s, the state was sold to Geraldo Mazza; in 1988, the Cunningham family purchased the property and in 2000 sold it to the Clark family. In 2005, a *pousada* (hotel) with six rooms was installed in two additional buildings. Visitors to the site, including several Brazilian television celebrities and the former President Luiz Inácio Lula da Silva, can enjoy the pool and engage in different kinds of activities, including biking, canoeing, kayaking, birdwatching, and fishing. In the old *saladeiro*, the place where the slaves salted the jerked beef, there is now a ballroom with access to the gardens with the capacity to accommodate up to 150 people. Rich individuals can have their marriages, graduation parties, receptions, and other festivities in the very place where enslaved men performed one of the hardest and unhealthiest tasks in a jerked beef factory. Even though the presence of slaves is mentioned three times on the *charqueada*'s website, the text and images do not describe the work performed by the enslaved workers. More importantly, when referring to the architecture of the main house, the text curiously states that the horseshoe format of the house's plan containing an internal courtyard was intended to protect the main house from slave rebellions, leaving the visitor with no explanation about the reasons that would lead slaves to organize rebellions in such a picturesque and peaceful place.[68] In addition, since 2004, the Charqueada Santa Rita houses the Museu do Charque (Jerked Beef Museum), maintained by the Fundação Museu do Charque (Jerked Beef Foundation, a private institution created in 1995), and transformed into the Associação Museu do Charque (Jerked Beef Association) in 1999. The museum is essentially composed of panels explaining the formation of the jerked beef industry and the various stages of jerked beef's production. Yet the museum's webpage not only fails to mention slavery and the enslaved workers who produced the jerked beef but also omits that jerked beef production was intended to feed the enslaved population of Brazil and the Caribbean.[69] Also, even though the museum's promotional CD-ROM, produced in 2002, explains the production of jerked beef, it does not provide any dates establishing the connection between jerked beef production and slave labor:

> Cattle were driven from paddock to paddock up to the killing hose on the edge of the water to be slaughtered. In the court it was skinned and quartered while still alive. The pieces were transported to the sheds where bones were removed, jerked [. . .], salted, and stacked in the form of blankets. After the beef went to the poles and when dried by the sun, they were again covered with leather, stacked and loaded at the ports of the properties.[70]

By using the passive voice and never stating that enslaved workers performed all the work, the text narrated in the CD-ROM contributes to separate slavery from the narrative of jerked beef production. Indeed, as Eichstedt and Small explain in their analysis of Southern plantation museums in the United States, the use of the passive voice is an efficient discursive strategy that allows the owners and guides of various initiatives to conceal the crucial role of slave labor on these heritage sites.[71]

Heritage sites and museum exhibitions in Salvador (Bahia) also conceal or misrepresent the work performed by enslaved men and women. Salvador, the state capital with the largest proportion of population of African descent in Brazil, is promoted by Bahian tourism authorities as the "capital of joy." When walking around its historic center, tourists are welcomed with the slogan *"sorria você está na Bahia"* ("smile, you are in Bahia"), a refrain that has also been successfully appropriated by street vendors and street children who beg for money. In addition to the Church of Our Lady of Rosary of Black Men, several other heritage buildings are associated with the region's history of slave labor, including the Solar do Unhão, a former sugar mill set on the waterfront of the Bay of All Saints. The site comprises several buildings, including a church, some of them dating back to the seventeenth century. In 1943, the site and some of its buildings were added to the National Heritage List by the IPHAN.[72] Since 1966, the various buildings house the Museu de Arte Moderna da Bahia (Bahia Modern Art Museum). In the basement of the main three-story building are a pier and a *senzala* (slave quarters), with direct access to the sea (Figure 4.9), which is fully preserved. Between 1967 and 2007, a touristic restaurant occupied it, even though there are no markers indicating that the restaurant was originally a *senzala*. There, in the same location where enslaved men and women used to live, white and black tourists from Brazil and abroad could eat "typical" Bahian food and be served by waitresses dressed like *baianas* (black women street vendors), while attending demonstrations of *capoeira* and other stereotyped performances of Afro-Brazilian dance.[73] In 2007, the restaurant was closed. The *senzala* was transformed into an art gallery, and a new café was opened in the pier's adjacent area. Although tourists and local visitors

Figure 4.9 Section of Solar do Unhão's *senzala*, Salvador, Bahia (photograph by Ana Lucia Araujo, 2009).

still can associate the place with a *senzala*, there was no effort to add any marker with information about the past uses of the place. Very probably not to disturb the "beauty" of the site, the government of the state of Bahia prefers not to draw attention to this unpleasant aspect of the architectural complex.

If the use of slave labor is not acknowledged in most Brazilian heritage sites, it is possible to divide museums, small and large, that depict slavery into two categories. First, there are the ones that tend to represent slavery only by underscoring physical punishments, whereas the second lean toward presenting slavery within the broad framework of labor, concealing the atrocious living and working conditions of the enslaved men and women. In the first category are the Museu da Cidade (City's Museum) in Salvador Bahia, the Museu do Escravo (Slave's Museum) in Belo Vale, Minas Gerais, and the Museu Júlio de Castilhos in Porto Alegre (discussed previously); the Museu de Artes e Ofícios (Museum of Arts and Crafts) in Belo Horizonte, Minas Gerais, fits into the second category.

The Museu da Cidade is situated in Salvador's historic center (Pelourinho), not far from the Church of Our Lady of Rosary of Black Men. The neighborhood, composed of numerous buildings, which are included in the UNESCO World Heritage List, attracts millions of Brazilian and international tourists every year. The museum is housed in a very visible three-story colonial building, just next to the building housing the Fundação Casa de Jorge

Amado (Jorge Amado's House Foundation) that honors one of the most famous Brazilian writers whose novels depict Bahian daily life. The museum presents slavery in glass displays containing miniature fabric dolls depicting enslaved men and women performing different kinds of tasks in urban and rural areas. With no particular physical features, all dolls are similar, and only their stereotyped clothes allow for identifying them as figures of men or women. In one display, the dolls rendering black women carry baskets with fruits on their heads with their children attached to their backs. Another display shows a doll indicative of an enslaved woman preparing *doce de araçá* (guava jam). The caption accompanying the display portrays enslaved women in an offensive way by associating the sensuality of its body with the sweets produced by her labor:

> Stirring mangaba sweet: . . . The leafy mango trees exalted by poets of the last century, were not just the setting of romantic scenes, parties in *terreiros* or meetings of missies. Under a pleasant shadow, a black slave, fat and sluggish, would set a tripod over the wood logs, make a good fire, and patiently begin to make guava sweet. [. . .] The sweet syrup made by black slave women still has a special place in Bahian cuisine, as the most delicious of desserts.[74]

Also part of the exhibition, a glass display shows an enslaved woman grinding flour in a large pestle and mortar and a group of four dolls representing enslaved men and women working in a sugar mill, supervised by another doll signifying a white overseer. Another glass case shows fabric dolls representing three enslaved men carrying a sedan chair occupied by a dark-skinned woman in a long white dress, carrying a white baby in her arms. However, the caption does not indicate the status of this woman but rather emphasizes that "the sedan chair was for very long the only means of transport in which the 'masters' were carried by the slaves."[75]

In addition to these derogatory representations of enslaved individuals in popular forms of art, two central rooms of the museum show sculptures portraying physical punishments inflicted on slaves. The rooms of the first floor of Museu da Cidade pay homage to the various deities of Candomblé religion, depicted by several large-scale statues made in papier maché and clay. However, in the corner of one of the rooms lies a large statue exemplifying an enslaved man sitting enchained at his wrists and ankles with his head on his knees. Curiously, according to the caption, the sculpture, dated 1975, was made by Alecy Azevedo, the same artist who created the large Candomblé deities displayed in the museum's first floor. For the visitors familiar with the Candomblé religion, the statue can suggest that despite dominating the bodies of enslaved individuals, masters were not able to control the spirituality of enslaved men and women. Yet the relation between the numerous huge statues of powerful deities dressed in their typical ceremonial costumes and the enchained enslaved man remains unclear for the ordinary visitors to the museum.

In the museum's second floor, a room is designed to honor the white abolitionist poet Castro Alves (1847–1871). Around the room, large modern panels feature texts and pictures of the poet, his parents, the house he was born in, and the monuments constructed to pay homage to him. But in the middle of the room, an ensemble of two five-feet sculptures (probably executed by the same artist who authored the statues of Candomblé deities) represent an overseer whipping an enslaved man attached to a *pelourinho*, barefoot and with naked buttocks. Although the connection between Castro Alves and the set of sculptures remains unexplained, the caption not only describes what a *pelourinho* is and who the *feitor* (overseer) is but also defines the word "slave" as a "person without power and rights, who is under the absolute dependence of a master." According to this definition, which contradicts the very extensive recent historiography on Brazilian slavery, enslaved men and women did not lead revolts, run away, or fight for freedom. As in other Brazilian museums, the prevailing image of the enslaved reflects the 1960s and 1970s historiography that equated the image of the slave with that of the victimized individual who lived in a state of total submission or "anomie."[76]

A similar victimizing image of the enslaved population is also presented in the only Brazilian museum whose name refers to slavery, the Museu do Escravo (Slave's Museum), in Belo Vale (Minas Gerais), a city of about 10,000 inhabitants, 50 miles from the state capital, Belo Horizonte.[77] The museum, created by the priest Luciano Jacques Penido in 1977 and based on his collections, was originally housed in a rural state, the Fazenda da Boa Esperança. On May 13 1988, the 100th anniversary of the abolition of slavery in Brazil, the museum was relocated in a new building in the downtown section of Belo Vale, behind the eighteenth-century Church of São Gonçalo da Ponte. Especially constructed to house the museum, the new building reproduces an eighteenth-century colonial house.

The Museu do Escravo is composed of six large rooms, housing its various collections that include more than 4,000 artifacts from several regions and donated by different donors. The museum's rooms do not carry the names of enslaved individuals but are named after the sponsors who made contributions to aid in its creation. The collections are displayed in five different rooms. The first room focuses on the indigenous populations who were enslaved in Brazil; the second room displays objects of sacred art; the third room is dedicated to the big house and exhibits various luxury objects of daily use; nineteenth-century images of European travelogues hang in the fourth room and include reproductions of Debret's and Rugendas's lithographs portraying Brazilian slave life, images of the popular slave saint Anastácia, a reproduction of the text of the Golden Law that abolished slavery in Brazil, as well as slave sale and runaway slave notices published in Brazilian newspapers. This room, as well as the open hallways facing the internal backyard, exhibit other numerous objects used to torture and punish enslaved men and women, such as iron necklaces, balls, shackles, masks, and chains, accompanied by illustrations representing how these instruments were employed.⁷⁸

Apart from including a variety of artifacts, the exhibition is not well organized. Very often there are no labels with references to the objects displayed, and there are no panels explaining their context and use. In addition to the instruments of punishment that impress visitors, including members of the local community, tourists, and students, the museum's central backyard recreates a slave quarters.⁷⁹ In this area, physical punishment is spectacularized by a full-body life-size statue embodying a standing enslaved man with his wrists and ankles attached to a *pelourinho* (Figure 4.10). As in Museu da Cidade and the Charqueada São João, the Museu do Escravo equates the life of enslaved men and women with physical punishment. This image is probably associated with the long-lasting military dictatorship (1964–1985), a period of extensive repression of civil rights that corresponds to the period in which the museum was created. But despite this emphasis, which is like any other museum addressing the issue of slavery, sexual violence against enslaved women is never mentioned. Even though there is a project to reformulate the museum, its current organization reflects the dominant trend in

Figure 4.10 Courtyard of Museu do Escravo. Belo Vale, Minas Gerais, Brazil (photograph by Glauco Umbelino, 2007).

Brazilian museums and heritage sites that overemphasize victimization and omits any mention of resistance and the contribution of the enslaved population to the construction of Brazilian society.[80] Both the Museu da Cidade and the Museu do Escravo reproduce the image of African and Afro-Brazilian men and women as mere objects, and there is no mention of agency.[81]

Dedicated in December 2005 and opened to the public in January 2006, the Museu de Artes e Ofícios (Museum of Arts and Crafts) in Belo Horizonte, Minas Gerais, provides a different perspective on how slave labor is memorialized in Brazilian museums. The museum does not have a particular exhibition or room focusing on slavery, but it has gathered 2,500 pieces telling the history of preindustrial labor in Brazil. As a result, its focus is not on enslaved and free workers or their experiences but on the work instruments they employed and the objects they produced. For example, the museum displays a *monjolo*, a kind of mill powered by water and used to grind corn. In one of the museum's catalogues, it is explained that the mill's name, *monjolo*, derives from the Quimbundu language, which is also "the denomination of one of the numerous groups of Africans enslaved in Brazil."[82] Although Brazil imported the largest number of Africans in the Americas and heavily relied on slave labor until 1888, except in the passages focusing on the street vendors and barbers and in the catalog examining the mining industry, the words "slavery" and "slave" are rarely mentioned in the museum's permanent exhibition and its various catalogues, including the texts commenting on images in which enslaved men and women are clearly depicted.[83]

Certainly, the most important slavery artifact displayed in the Museu de Artes e Ofícios is a large scale that served to weigh enslaved individuals. According to the descriptive label, the 1767 scale belonged to a royal plantation and was purchased in Bahia in the 1980s. But even though mentioning that the practice of weighing slaves was not common in Brazil, there is no additional panel explaining the use of the scale in the context of the Atlantic slave trade. Thus, despite the sophisticated museological approach developed in the Museu de Artes e Ofícios, by focusing only on work instruments and neglecting the enslaved men and women and their descendants who used these tools, the museum conceals the crucial role that slave labor and enslaved workers played in Brazil.

FROM INVISIBILITY TO VICTIMIZATION

Despite the differences between the slave system in Brazil and the United States, this chapter showed similar patterns in the ways slave labor is memorialized and forgotten in the public spaces of the two countries. In Brazil, even though enslaved workers constructed most public and private buildings, their contributions are rarely officially acknowledged. This context is not very different in the United States. Indeed, despite the important financial means of many US private and public institutions, most initiatives aiming at recognizing the use of slave labor in the construction of public buildings emerged only in the last ten years. Projects like the so-called Emancipation Hall in the Capitol Visitor Center received great public visibility, even though the new facility has only recently started paying homage to former enslaved individuals like Sojourner Truth and Frederick Douglass. Moreover, even though the use of slave labor is mentioned in the Capitol's official guides, folders, and orientation film, the guided tours do not highlight the contribution of enslaved African Americans to the construction of the buildings.

Whereas in the United States most written narratives by former enslaved individuals like Frederick Douglass have underlined the cruel treatment inflicted on enslaved men and women, most important and visible US slavery heritage sites omit this important aspect of slave life, instead underscoring the luxurious lifestyles of slave owners. In contrast, despite the scarce number of projects aiming at promoting the heritage of slave labor in Brazil and the absence of a developed plantation tourism industry, most slavery heritage sites and museum exhibitions tend to equate the history of slavery with victimization. This approach—stressing the cruelty of slavery—is not aimed at denouncing the violation of human rights but rather at impressing visitors without raising any issues regarding the history of slavery and its present legacies of racial and social exclusion. In the face of all the suffering endured by the enslaved men and women who labored in these sites, visitors are invited to have a meal and spend the night in rooms displaying instruments of torture and reproducing whipping posts where slaves were beaten to death. Although intended to memorialize slavery, by excluding any references to slaves' daily lives and African heritage, most initiatives presenting slavery in Brazil portray enslaved individuals as passive victims and rather endeavor to mask the country's slave past.

Unlike Brazil, in the United States the contribution of the African American enslaved population, especially enslaved men, is now officially acknowledged in most public projects. This new visibility can be associated with two main factors. Historical and contemporary slavery are gaining growing attention in the works of scholars and international organizations like UNESCO. More importantly, the election of Barack Obama as the first black president of the United States in 2008, as well as the fact that First Lady Michelle Obama's ancestors were enslaved, are elements that certainly contribute to give more visibility to African American historical actors, including enslaved men and women. Even if this new attention is the result of a particular and transitory context, the recent initiatives developed in Washington, DC, are permanent markers that will survive the Obamas' years.

Exhibiting slavery in museums and memorializing it in public monuments are still very recent trends, making it difficult to measure its extent and evaluate its impacts on the understanding of slavery and its legacies. The various museum exhibitions and slavery heritage sites examined in this chapter suggest instead that even in the initiatives that are intended to memorialize slavery, acknowledging the contributions of Afro-Brazilians and African Americans to the construction of Brazil and the United States is still a problematic task because the slave past and its legacies of racism and social inequalities are still very present in these two societies.

NOTES

1. See Eichstedt and Small, 2002.
2. Douglass, 1845: 8–9.
3. Douglass, 1845: 12.
4. Douglass, 1845: 18.
5. Douglass, 1845: 19.
6. Douglass, 1845: 19.
7. Douglass, 1845: 12.
8. Douglass, 1845: 20.
9. Douglass, 1845: 20.
10. Douglass, 1845: 14.
11. See Preston, 1980: 184–186; 190–192; 231n, 232n. See Douglass, n.d.
12. I am grateful to Professor Diane Barnes for clarifying several issues regarding Douglass's visit to the Eastern Shore and the Wye House plantation, including providing me with information on Samuel E. Chamberlaine. See Preston, 1980: 192–193.
13. Douglass, 1881: 452. See also the revised edition, Douglass, 1892: 540–542.
14. Douglass, 1881: 453.
15. See Henderson, 2011: 69–70.
16. Tickner, 2006.
17. "Mrs. Mary D. Tilghman," 2012: B01.
18. Williamson, 2006: B01.
19. See Douglass, 1845: 22–23; Williamson, 2006: B01; Ydstie, 2007.
20. Williamson, 2006: B01.
21. Ydstie, 2007.
22. Williamson, 2006: B01.
23. See Alderman and Campbell, 2008: 340.
24. See Rarey, 2013; Rarey, forthcoming.
25. Its official name is the Venerável Ordem Terceira do Rosário de Nossa Senhora às Portas do Carmo.
26. Igreja do Rosário dos Pretos, no. do processo 0122-T-38, Livro Belas Artes no. de inscrição 129, vol. 1, F. 023, June 17, 1938. See Lima, Melhem, and Pope, 2009: 17.
27. Vargas became president of Brazil in 1930, following a coup d'état. In 1934, he led a new constitutional government that was ended in 1937, when he established a dictatorship led by him that lasted until 1945. On these heritage policies, see Williams, 2001: Chap. 4; Instituto do Patrimônio Histórico e Artístico Nacional, 1980: 12–19.
28. See Araujo, 2010a: 259–261.
29. An article of Porto Alegre's newspaper *Correio do Povo* of December 22, 1900, referred to the legend when the construction of the building was finished. Also, the legend was the object of the novel by Afonso Morais, *As torres malditas* (1931). See Franco, 1988: 140.
30. Lima, 1997.
31. See Mello, 2010: 67, and Lima, 1997: 168.

32. Isabelle, 1835: 502–503.
33. Igreja Nossa Senhora das Dores, Processo no. 0096-T-38, Livro Belas Artes no. de inscrição 065, vol. 1, F. 032, July 20, 1938. See Lima, Melhem, and Pope, 2009: 101.
34. See Igreja Nossa Senhora das Dores (website); Bicca, 2010: 46.
35. See Holland, 2007; Bell, 2009; Kapsch, 1993.
36. Allen, 2005: 8.
37. See Committee Reports (2009–2010), acnowledging the role that slave labor played in the construction of the United States Capitol, and for other purposes.
38. The resolution to place a bust of Dr. King in the National Statuary Hall passed in Congress on December 21, 1982.
39. United States Capitol Historical Society and National Geography Society, 2011: 135.
40. In 1994, Wallenberg's bust was donated by Lilian Hoffman, organizer of the Colorado Committee of Concern for Soviet Jewry and chairperson of the Raoul Wallenberg National Commission to the US Congress, to be placed in the Capitol building. The bust was dedicated in the Capitol's rotunda on November 2, 1995 and placed in the Emancipation Hall in April 2009.
41. See "Sojourner Truth Bust Unveiling" (website).
42. These observations are based on four visits to the Emancipation Hall and the Capitol made by me and my research assistant, Erica Metcalfe, a PhD student in the US history at the Department of History at Howard University, during the fall 2012 and spring of 2013.
43. "Pelosi Remarks at Capitol Slave Labor Commemorative Stone Marker Unveiling" (website).
44. Southall, 2013: A18.
45. See Architect of the Capitol, "Rosa Parks," (website).
46. See Statue Dedication Ceremony for Frederick Douglass, 2013 (website).
47. Southall, 2013.
48. "In Berlin, Michelle Obama and daughters visit Holocaust Memorial," 2013.
49. Auslander, 2012.
50. Lovejoy and Law, 2003: 159.
51. Lovejoy and Law, 2003: 160.
52. Lovejoy and Law, 2003: 162.
53. Freyre, 2003 [1933]. The first English translation was published in the United States in 1946. See Freyre, 1986.
54. The opening of the *telenovela A escrava Isaura* (1976, URL) is available on YouTube. The soap opera is based on the novel *A escrava Isaura* by Bernardo Guimarães (1875).
55. See, for example, the enslaved men who were punished after the Malê rebellion in 1835, see Reis, 1993: 219.
56. Debret, 1834–1839: vol. 2, 139.
57. On the images and narratives that emphasize the suffering of the Brazilian black population, see Santos, 2008: 157–175.
58. See Menegat, 2008: 1; Fundação de Economia e Estatística, 1981: 50.
59. Saint-Hilaire, 1939: 138.
60. Saint-Hilaire, 1939: 138.
61. Saint-Hilaire, 1939: 138.
62. Wierzchowski, 2002.
63. Santini, 2011: 17.
64. The film *Concerto campestre*, directed by Henrique de Freitas Lima (2005) is based on an homonymous novel by Luiz Antônio de Assis Brasil (1997).
65. See Charqueada São João (website).

66. Santini, 2011: 30.
67. See Charqueada São João (website).
68. See Charqueada Santa Rita Pousada de Charme (website).
69. See Charqueada Santa Rita Pousada de Charme (website).
70. Guiterrez, 2002.
71. Eichstedt and Small, 2002: 134–137.
72. See IPHAN, Process no. 1069-T-82, Livro de Belas Artes, Inscription 288-A, September 16, 1943; Livro Histórico, Inscription 220, September 16, 1943.
73. On *capoeira*, see Assunção, 2002.
74. The Portuguese caption reads: "Mexendo Doce de Araçá: As frondosas mangueiras [sic] cantadas pelos poetas do século passada não eram apenas cenário de cenas românticas, de festas nos terrais ou reuniões de sinhazinhas. À sombra amena, uma negra escrava gorda e pachorrenta, armava um tripé sobre as achas de lenha, fazia um bom fogo e pacientemente começava a fazer o doce de araçá. A calda em ponto de fio, as cumbuquinhas cortas à espera da fervura. O doce de clada das negras escravas, ainda hoje tem lugar especial na culinária baiana, como as mais deliciosas sobremesas." Probably the author of this caption meant *mangabeira* (mangaba tree) instead of *mangueira* (mango tree). Museu da Cidade da Bahia, Salvador, Bahia, Brazil.
75. Museu da Cidade da Bahia, Salvador, Bahia, Brazil.
76. Whereas scholars like Florestan Fernandes, Octavio Ianni, and José de Souza Martins referred to a state of "anomie," Celso Furtado stated that Brazilian enslaved individuals lived in a state close to "mental retardation." See Araujo, 2010a, 36–37.
77. Museu do Escravo (website).
78. See the museum's filmed visit, along with an interview with the museum's director Antônio Rezende, on the website, Brasil Raça Mundi (November 9, 2012).
79. For a study of the student visitors to the Museu do Escravo, see Seabra, 2012.
80. See Letícia Julião (website).
81. This element was also mentioned by the students who visited the museum. See Seabra, 2012: 89.
82. Guimarães, 2008: vol. 3, 12.
83. In 2008, the museum published six catalogues corresponding to its various areas. For the passages mentioning slave labor, see Fukelman and Lima, 2008: vol. 2, 43–45, 51–54; Libby, 2008: vol. 4, 11–23.

5 Great Emancipators

The Emancipation Proclamation (January 1, 1863) in the United States and the Golden Law (May 13, 1888) abolishing slavery in Brazil were soon incorporated into the public memory of the two nations. This memorialization occurred on three different levels. The first level was through the transmission to their descendants of freedpeople's experience of enslavement. The second level was through historical memory. In the United States and Brazil, commemorative images, posters, bills, stamps, as well as public festivals and official monuments, celebrated not the former enslaved men and women but the white emancipators President Abraham Lincoln (1809–1865) and Princess Isabel Cristina of Bragança and Bourbon (1846–1921). The third level is through the writing of history by historians, journalists, and writers in both Brazil and the United States, which also greatly contributed to presenting these two historical figures as the Great Emancipators who granted freedom to the slaves.[1]

By exploring the second level of memorialization, this chapter examines various initiatives celebrating the Emancipation Proclamation and the abolition of slavery in Brazil, with a particular focus on permanent markers built in Washington, DC, and Rio de Janeiro. Both Lincoln and Isabel disappeared from the public scene just after the end of slavery in the two countries. Whereas the US president was assassinated in 1865, the Brazilian princess went into exile in 1889, following the military coup that ended the monarchy and proclaimed the Republic in Brazil, facts that certainly favored their sanctification in the public memory of these two major former slave societies. In the United States and Brazil, monuments and museum exhibitions usually celebrate Lincoln and Isabel as the Great Emancipators. Yet enslaved, freed, and free black social actors who fought against slavery are often excluded from these public representations, and when they are represented, they are portrayed in submissive roles and in positions of gratitude toward the white emancipators. The comparison between the memorialization of Lincoln and Isabel as the individuals who freed the slaves reveals similar paternalistic figures. They both embody emancipation not as a long and difficult process but rather as a concession that has nothing to do with the struggle of those who resisted slavery but was possible only through their generosity.² Ultimately, this chapter argues that both in Brazil and in the United States the commemoration of Great Emancipators contributed to construct a paternalistic vision of emancipation, eventually hindering or at least delaying the emergence of black emancipators in public memory.

TWO GREAT EMANCIPATORS

Both in the United States and Brazil, the abolition of slavery resulted from a long and slow process that started with the end of the slave trade and continued over the ensuing decades. The abolitionist movement contributed not only to the self-emancipation of many slaves but also to the approval of various laws or emancipation decrees. Still, the pace of the end of slavery in both countries greatly differed. In the United States, the abolition of slavery started by the end of the eighteenth century in the Northern states, soon creating a division between free states and Southern slave states. The disunion that provoked the Civil War eventually led to the end of slavery in 1865, but the scars of this division remain present in the US collective memory.³ Unlike the United States, slavery remained alive in Brazil until 1888. By this time, the country had already a large free and freed black population. The first prohibition of the slave trade in 1831 and its final ban in 1850, largely influenced by British pressures, importantly affected the Brazilian slave system, as the number of available enslaved workers dramatically decreased.⁴ With the late emergence of an abolitionist movement led by white and black intellectuals and urban professionals, slavery was gradually abolished through various national laws granting freedom to the newborn children of enslaved mothers (1871) and sexagenarians (1885). During this period, Brazil and Cuba were the only two countries in the Americas to maintain slavery. Brazil was in pace of modernizing itself. Urbanization and the growth of the coffee industry in the southeast had led to the weakening of the northeast planter class, the monarchy's main supporter. The introduction of thousands of European immigrant workers on the southeastern coffee plantations, accompanied by massive slave flights and movements demanding rights, deteriorated the Brazilian slave system by eventually causing the abolition of slavery in 1888 and the end of the monarchy in 1889.

When Lincoln was elected president of the United States in 1860, the abolitionist movement had been established in the country for almost a century, and the number of free states exceeded the number of slave states. Lincoln was not an abolitionist, and his visions of slavery and race, very often contradictory, changed over time. Early in his career as a politician, he demonstrated being morally opposed to slavery, even though not proposing any clear measure to end it.⁵ Before becoming president, in occasional statements, Lincoln associated slavery with many evils, including the lack of freedom, geographic mobility, and family separation.⁶ During the election campaign of 1848, he started voicing more explicitly his opposition to the institution of slavery, but his opposition to slavery became visible during the public debates regarding the Kansas-Nebraska Act of 1854, which gave the settlers the possibility of allowing slavery in the newly created territories, thereby *de facto* reversing the Missouri Compromise of 1820. In the context of these debates, which eventually would lead the United States into the Civil War, Lincoln became the first presidential candidate of the recently created Republican Party in 1860. However, in his first inaugural address of March 4, 1861, Lincoln repeated his intention to not "interfere with the institution of slavery in the States where it exists," clearly showing that his stance was to prevent the expansion of the institution of slavery and not to abolish it.[7] Yet, the imminent Civil War changed the course of events, and slavery became a central issue during Lincoln's presidency. On September 22, 1862 (effective on January 1, 1863), Lincoln issued the Emancipation Proclamation of the Confederate states of the south. The decree was followed by the Thirteenth Amendment to the US Constitution of December 1865 that finally abolished slavery in the United States.

On May 13, 1888, 33 years later than in the United States, Brazilian slavery was abolished. By this time, Dom Pedro II (1825–1891) ruled the country. Crowned as Emperor of Brazil in 1840, he had expressed very cautious opposition to slavery. After he attained majority, he freed the slaves whom he had inherited. Still, as several historians have explained, the emperor did not have Constitutional power to abolish slavery. This decision had to be passed by the Parliament, whose slavocratic majority, whether liberal or conservative, was the main supporter of the Brazilian monarchy.[8] Slavery being an essential pillar of Brazilian monarchy, abolishing it could ruin the monarchical system. Thus, it is not difficult to understand why the emperor did not take any effective measures to abolish slavery.[9]

In the 1870s, the movement for the abolition of slavery intensified in Brazil. By this time, Dom Pedro II's daughter and royal heiress, Princess Isabel, had acquired popularity among the freed and enslaved black population. Already in 1871, in the absence of her father and as princess regent of Brazil, she signed the Free Womb Law. This law freed the children of enslaved women born after September 28, 1871, when the law was promulgated. However, one article of the law determined that freed children should remain under the custody of the mother's master until attaining majority (21 years of age). Masters who did not wish to keep the newly freed children would receive an indemnity from the government, and the Brazilian state would take charge of the children.

As part of the gradual abolition process in Brazil, in 1884 slavery was outlawed in the provinces of Ceará and Amazonas. Moreover, in the years preceding the end of slavery, enslaved men, women, and children organized massive escapes in the southeast coffee plantation areas, in a clear movement of self-emancipation. As international pressure claiming the end of slavery was added to this social dynamic, the abolition of slavery in Brazil became an unavoidable issue. On the eve of abolition, Princess Isabel acquired the reputation of protecting fugitive slaves. Some days before the signature of the Golden Law, Afro-Brazilian abolitionist André Rebouças recorded in his notebook that "fourteen fugitive Africans" from the neighboring plantations had lunch in Petropólis Imperial Palace, suggesting that Isabel was responsible for promoting the scheme of slave escapes.[10] Isabel became particularly popular among the members of the Quilombo of Leblon in Rio de Janeiro. The members of this *quilombo* produced camellias and made this flower an important symbol of the abolitionist movement. Abolitionists proudly wore camellias in their lapels, and even Isabel made public appearances wearing one in the lapel of her dress.[11]

After the Emancipation Proclamation and the abolition of slavery in the United States and Brazil, Lincoln and Isabel were neither perceived nor immediately represented as the Great Emancipators. In the United States, although the Emancipation Proclamation did not abolish slavery, it had a great symbolic dimension.[12] The text of Lincoln's decree was widely disseminated in newspapers and read by the Union soldiers to hundreds of slaves who lived in the Confederate states. Soon after being issued, the emancipation decree was popularized through visual representations. As Harold Holzer explains, the Emancipation Proclamation "became the dominant theme of Lincoln art and iconography for the rest of the nineteenth century."[13] However, these images of Lincoln as the Great Emancipator emerged only after his assassination.[14] Likewise, regardless of Isabel's proximity with the abolitionist movement in the months preceding the abolition, as Lilia Moritz Schwarcz points out, it was not until May 13, the same day of the signature of the Golden Law, that Afro-Brazilian abolitionist José do Patrocínio introduced the image of Isabel as the Redeemer.[15] This idea gave birth to *Isabelismo,* a movement venerating Isabel; according to this vision, the abolition of Brazilian slavery was the result of the princess's individual and heroic act. As part of this movement, the Guarda Negra (Black Guard), a guard loyal to Isabel and composed of free blacks including numerous fighters of *capoeira*, was created to protect the monarchy. Between the abolition of slavery in May 1888 and the military coup that proclaimed the Republic in November 1889, the Guarda Negra was engaged in protecting Isabel and fighting the Republicans.[16]

Among the first public images associated with the US Emancipation Proclamation is the oil painting *First Reading of the Emancipation Proclamation of President Lincoln* (1864) by the artist Francis Bicknell Carpenter (1830–1900), portraying Lincoln reading the decree to his cabinet of ministers for the first time in 1862.[17] The painting was first exhibited for a restricted number of guests in the east ballroom of the White House, but soon it was reproduced in a lithograph by Alexander Hay Ritchie (1822–1895) and widely disseminated (Figure 5.1). Despite its success, the painting remained in the possession of the artist, who, after a long a campaign, finally sold it to a benefactor who then donated it to the National Congress in 1877. A stamp reproducing Carpenter's painting was issued by

Figure 5.1 The First Reading of the Emancipation Proclamation before the Cabinet (lithograph by Alexander Hay Ritchie, based on the painting by Francis Bicknell Carpenter, 1866).

the United States Postal Office to commemorate the 100th anniversary of the Emancipation Proclamation in 1963.[18]

In 1864, a lithograph titled *Reading the Emancipation Proclamation* (Figure 5.2) became very popular. Its central character is not Lincoln or an enslaved person, but a Union soldier, who reads the Emancipation Proclamation to a family of slaves in the interior of their modest home.[19] The image portrays various generations of men, women, and children receiving the news and expressing joy, surprise, and gratitude. One of the female characters, with two children on her knees, holds her hands together in thankfulness to the soldier who brought the good news.[20] Although Lincoln does not appear in the scene, his face is represented in the white inferior border of the original lithograph displaying the title of the engraving.

In addition to visual images, various written narratives describe how the Emancipation Proclamation marked the memory of enslaved men, women, and children. However, unlike the visual representations, these written accounts suggest that the proclamation was not a surprise but rather the confirmation of long awaited news. Booker T. Washington, explains it was "a momentous and eventful day to all upon our plantation" because the news had been in the air for several months.[21] The night before the

Figure 5.2 Reading the Emancipation Proclamation (lithograph by J.W. Watte, based on a drawing by H.W. Herrick, 1864).

announcement, slaves were informed that a gathering would take place in the big house in the next morning. The enslaved were excited about the possible news and could barely sleep during the night. According to his recollections, the master's family demonstrated interest in the news but not sadness or bitterness: "As I now recall the impression they made upon me, they did not at the moment seem to be sad because of the loss of property, but rather because of parting with those whom they had reared and who were in many ways very close to them."[22] In addition, he also remembers that a US officer read the Emancipation Proclamation and declared they were free and could go anywhere they wish. Washington also describes this moment as being one of great emotion: "My mother, who was standing by my side, leaned over and kissed her children, while tears of joy ran down her cheeks. She explained to us what it all meant, that this was the day for which she had been so long praying, but fearing that she would never live to see."[23]

152 *Shadows of the Slave Past*

Following the abolition, the image of Princess Isabel as the Redeemer became well established in the public memory and a very popular figure among blacks and whites in Brazil. Complementing the image of the Redeemer, the symbol of the collective grateful former slaves started occupying Brazilian shared memory and popular imagination. This combination of the figures of the Redeemer and grateful former slave is visible in the drawing by Angelo Agostini (1843–1910) illustrating the cover of *Revista Illustrada* of July 29, 1888 (Figure 5.3), a satiric abolitionist and Republican

Figure 5.3 *Freedom's Memorial* (lithograph by Currier & Ives, c. 1876).

weekly magazine. The image portrays a black man, a black woman, and a black boy (probably former enslaved individuals), in the interior of a home or a church, dropping off a bunch of camellias before a framed portrait of the princess. The inferior margin of the portrait reads: "Her Imperial Highness Dona Isabel: The Redeemer."[24] The couple and the child are not alone. At the door of the room where the picture is exhibited, a line of other black individuals carrying bunches of flowers is visible. The image successfully portrays Rio de Janeiro's black individuals expressing gratitude by paying homage to Isabel the day of her birthday by offering her bouquets of camellias, the symbol of the abolitionist movement.

COMMEMORATING EMANCIPATION AND ABOLITION

The Emancipation Proclamation was celebrated with parades in various regions from the North to the South of the United States by African Americans and even by the enslaved individuals who were not affected by the decree. Still, in the first years after the proclamation, many African Americans did not have the opportunity to publicly commemorate the date because the Civil War continued in several parts of the country, whereas in other regions of the South, where the date was celebrated, several African Americans were aware of the limitations of Lincoln's decree.[25] As time passed, the date started acquiring importance among African Americans, even though other dates associated with the abolition of slavery, including April 16 in Washington, DC, and Juneteenth (June 19) in Texas, also continued to be celebrated in different places.[26] As Edna G. Medford notes, the "proclamation engendered Lincoln's veneration in the African American community and encouraged the belief that he was the premier white friend of the race."[27] Though this sentiment gradually faded among the next generations of African Americans who did not live the experience of liberation from slavery but who lived the daily violence of racial segregation.

Likewise, in the years that followed the abolition of slavery in Brazil, squares, streets, avenues, and schools were named after Princess Isabel and other abolitionists, including José do Patrocínio (1854–1905) and Joaquim Nabuco (1849–1910). Although in a recent book, Marcus Wood mistakenly states that Nabuco is still the face of abolition of slavery in Brazil, indeed he never occupied a central place in the official history and the collective memory of the abolition of slavery in Brazil.[28] It is Princess Isabel who is celebrated in festivals, masses, school textbooks, and popular iconography, including stamps, coins, and bills, as the great Redeemer. Indeed, the only expressive monument paying homage to Nabuco, unveiled in 1915, is located in his hometown of Recife, far from Rio de Janeiro, São Paulo, and Brasília, Brazil's important urban centers that are still today the country's main spheres of political power.

The first anniversary of the signature of the Golden Law of May 13 was celebrated from the north to the south of Brazil with festivals, parades, balls, Catholic masses, and other festivities with Afro-Brazilian dance and music, like *maculêlê* and *samba de roda*.[29] Also, during the three decades that followed the abolition of slavery, dozens of black societies and clubs were created and named Treze de Maio (May Thirteenth), celebrating the date that marked the abolition of slavery in Brazil. But despite Isabel's official recognition as the public figure who signed the Golden Law, very few permanent markers honoring the princess were created. This paucity can be explained by the rejection of public references associated with the monarchy just after the Republic proclamation in 1889. Hence by the end of the nineteenth century, although Isabel was publicly recognized as the one who freed the slaves, the Republic's government did not develop official initiatives commemorating a princess who was living in exile in France.

Public view started changing after the death of Princess Isabel on November 14, 1921, more than 30 years after the abolition of slavery. The news of her death had great repercussion in Brazil's printed press. All over the country, various kinds of public homages were organized to honor Isabel, and public requests to transfer her remains to Brazil started immediately.[30] To mark the one-month anniversary of the princess's death, the Church of Our Lady of Rosary and Saint Benedict of Black Men celebrated a mass in homage to the Redeemer.[31] This church, opened to the public in Rio de Janeiro in 1725, had housed the homonymous Catholic lay brotherhood gathering enslaved, freed, and free black individuals. The church and the brotherhood had a particular connection with the princess, who used to attend its Sunday masses. During the princess's death anniversary mass, the priest evoked her as "Isabel, the Redeemer" and reminded the audience "she knew to do justice for the slaves of Brazil."[32] In the following years in the commemoration activities of the anniversary of the Golden Law, as well on Isabel's anniversaries of birth and death, she continued to be publicly remembered as the Redeemer.[33]

As in Brazil, after the Emancipation Proclamation in 1863, African Americans started celebrating January 1 with masses, balls, festivals, and parades.[34] Yet it was also following Lincoln's death that the memory of emancipation took more permanent forms in the public space, either through the dissemination of images published in newspapers and illustrated magazines, or through the creation of monuments and memorials. Among the second kind of public initiatives, three were developed in the national capital. These initiatives were not primarily intended to celebrate emancipation, but rather to commemorate Lincoln as the Great Emancipator. As Christopher A. Thomas argues, these projects were part of the process that launched Lincoln's canonization, which started just after his death in 1865.[35] On April 14, 1866, one year after his assassination, the US Post Office created a stamp to pay homage to Lincoln. Since then, dozens of postcards and stamps are periodically created commemorating the president, whose image has appeared the most on US postage, only behind that of George Washington.

ERECTING MEMORIALS TO LINCOLN

The first public monument memorializing the Emancipation Proclamation in Washington, DC, is a full-length statue representing Lincoln, dedicated in 1868 and placed in the south façade of the District of Columbia City Hall. The second initiative is the *Freedom's Memorial*, also known as *Freedmen's Memorial* or *Emancipation Memorial*, which started being planned just after the death of Lincoln in 1865. The monument was erected after a long campaign whose original goal was to build a memorial to the freed population. According to Kirk Savage, the construction's campaign "was the most conspicuous attempt in public sculpture to capture the spirit of Reconstruction, to translate into the sculptural language of the human body principles of freedom that remained abstract and barely imaginable."[36] If the thought of Lincoln as the Great Emancipator would gradually fade among the next generations of African Americans, for those who were freed by the Emancipation Proclamation, the president still occupied an important place. Not surprisingly, the funding campaign to construct the monument was initiated by Charlotte Scott, a freedwoman who just after Lincoln's death donated $5 to her master for a project to pay homage to the president who signed the Emancipation Proclamation. Scott was deeply saddened when she learned about Lincoln's death, and according to a contemporary publication, she stated that "the colored people have lost their best friend on earth! Mr. Lincoln was our best friend, and I will give you five dollars of my wages towards erecting a monument to his memory."[37]

Although financed mostly by freed African Americans, especially Civil War veterans, very soon the Western Sanitary Commission, a private agency run by white citizens, appropriated the project of the Emancipation Memorial, taking control of the campaign and managing the donations received. After a contest, the artist Thomas Ball (1819–1911) was chosen to construct the memorial because of a marble sculpture he had made representing Lincoln just after his assassination. Archer Alexander (1828–1880?), a former runaway enslaved man emancipated in 1863, served as a model for the figure of the freedman represented in the memorial. According to William Greenleaf Eliot, Alexander's boss and biographer, his "freedom came directly from the hand of President Lincoln."[38]

In 1875, after the project was concluded, the memorial consisting of a bronze statue representing the white male emancipator and the freed black man was cast in Munich and sent to the United States. The text at the base of the statue underscores the allegiance of freed individuals to Abraham Lincoln by stating that "the first contribution of five dollars was made

156 *Shadows of the Slave Past*

by Charlotte Scott. A freedwoman of Virginia being her first earnings in freedom and consecrated by her suggestion and request on the day she heard of President Lincoln's death to build a monument to his memory." As in some previous visual representations and monument projects commemorating US emancipation, Lincoln is depicted as the benefactor who grants freedom to the black man (Figure 5.4). The kneeling black man,

Figure 5.4   *Revista Illustrada,* July 9 (drawing by Angelo Agostini, 1888).

a motif that had appeared in the British abolitionist campaign since the eighteenth century, is portrayed in the memorial in a position of gratitude and submission.[39] Kneeling at the president's feet, the statue made permanent the image of the almost naked freedman revering the great white emancipator.[40] But the official document reporting the inauguration ceremony curiously explains that, whereas in the original marble statue the "kneeling slave is represented as perfectly passive, receiving the boon of freedom from the hand of the great liberator," this attribute was changed in the bronze sculpture "to bring the presentation nearer to the historical fact, by making the emancipated slave an agent of his own deliverance."[41] Indeed, the marble sculpture and the bronze statue differ only in one element: in the original sculpture, the freedman's right arm was folded across his chest, whereas in the bronze version the same arm is extended. In addition, in the marble's sculpture, the freedman was wearing a cap, which is absent from the bronze rendering. Still, as Kirk Savage recalls, despite the submissive position of the freedman in both versions of the project, the *Freedom's Memorial* was the only US public monument representing a black individual.[42]

On April 14, 1876, one day prior to the 11th anniversary of Lincoln's death and two days before the 14th anniversary of the emancipation in the national capital, the *Freedom's Memorial* was eventually unveiled in Lincoln Park, in Washington, DC. The day was declared a public holiday, and "every one was free to participate in the exercises or to witness the spectacle of a grateful race doing homage to a cherished name."[43] In the printed program of the ceremony, African American poet Henrietta Cordelia Ray (1852–1915) appears as the author of the poem "Lincoln," written for the occasion, which was read by William E. Matthews (1843–1894), a prominent African American lawyer, investment banker, and orator, who was very close to Frederick Douglass.[44] The poem concluded with the following words:

> Emancipation, hero, martyr, friend!
> While Freedom may her holy scepter claim,
> The world shall echo with "Our Lincoln's" name.[45]

Among the honorable guests who attended the memorial's inauguration was Frederick Douglass. According to John Cromwell, a historian and then professor at Howard University, who was also present at the ceremony, Douglass mentioned the figure of the black man depicted in the memorial only once in his speech, cleverly observing that the statue "showed the negro on his knees when a more manly attitude would have been indicative of freedom."[46] Even though the written version of Douglass's speech does not include this statement, the text is totally opposed to the image conveyed in the statue, which clearly reinforced the idea that freedom was a gift granted by Lincoln to enslaved African Americans. Instead, Douglass's speech emphasized that:

> Lincoln was not, in the fullest sense of the word, either our man or our model. In his interests, in his associations, in his habits of thought, and in his prejudices, he was a white man. He was pre-eminently the white man's President, entirely devoted to the welfare of white men. He was ready and willing at any time during the first years of his administration to deny, postpone and sacrifice the rights of humanity in the colored people, to promote the welfare of the white people of this country. [. . .] Knowing this, I concede to you, my white fellow-citizens, a pre-eminence in this worship at once full and supreme.[47]

Douglass's statement is probably one of the only existing written records by a former slave about a monument commemorating emancipation. Unlike other prominent African American citizens, Douglass refuses to venerate the president and rejected the paternalistic image of the Great Emancipator. In his prophetic speech, he foresees the construction of Lincoln's myth by insisting that it belonged to the whites to commemorate him: "to sound his praises, to preserve and perpetuate his memory, to multiply his statues, to hang his pictures on your walls and commend his example."[48] In addition, in his predictive words, Douglass ably recognizes that the construction of Lincoln's public memory deeply depended on the creation of permanent markers:

> Instead of supplanting you at this altar, we would exhort you to build high his monuments; let them be of the most costly material, of the most costly workmanship; let their forms be symmetrical, beautiful and perfect; let their bases be upon solid rocks, and their summits lean against the unchanging blue overhanging sky, and let them endure forever![49]

In the decades following the *Freedom's Memorial*'s inauguration, its image was disseminated beyond the borders of the national capital through commemorative postcards and stamps illustrated with the picture of the statue. In 1940, a picture of the memorial illustrated a commemorative stamp of the 75th anniversary of 13th amendment abolishing slavery. Therefore, the image of the *Freedom's Memorial* became one of the most popular depictions commemorating emancipation. Yet it was not enough. The construction of a great memorial paying homage to President Abraham Lincoln had been in study since 1901, when the McMillan Plan established the national capital's monumental center and parks. However, its construction started only in 1914. On May 30, 1922, the impressive memorial in Doric style was disclosed, definitely inscribing Lincoln in American memory as the Great Emancipator. The architect Henry Bacon (1866–1924), who had an extensive curriculum of projects for public monuments, signed on to the project.⁵⁰ Jules Guérin (1866–1946) executed the memorial's internal mural paintings. But the memorial's central element was a monumental 19-foot sculpture of the president placed in the central chamber. Titled *Abraham Lincoln* (1920), the marble sculpture was conceived by Daniel Chester French (1850–1931) and sculpted by the Piccirillis, a family of stone carvers of Tuscanian origin.⁵¹ The sculpture represents Lincoln sitting on a square throne facing the memorial's entrance. Positioned across from the reflecting pool, Lincoln oversees the Washington Monument and the millions of individuals who visit the memorial each year, as well as the other monuments located in the National Mall. As if the figure of the president and Great Emancipator were not powerful enough, on the wall above the colossal sculpture the following words are carved: "In this temple, as in the hearts of the people for whom he saved the Union, the memory of Abraham Lincoln is enshrined forever."⁵²

Since the memorial's unveiling, Lincoln's statue has witnessed numerous public events and demonstrations on the memorial's stairs and around the reflecting pool. On August 28, 1963, standing on the stairs of the Lincoln Memorial, Martin Luther King Jr. gave his seminal speech "I Have a Dream." At the feet of the Great Emancipator, the words of King's speech clearly states that 100 years after Lincoln's Emancipation Proclamation, African Americans were still excluded by means of racial segregation and discrimination.⁵³ The seminal event was underscored on the pages of the newspaper *Chicago Defender*:

> Rarely has history witnessed a more moving, dramatic or eloquent moment than the hour when America's foremost civil rights leader, Rev. Dr. Martin Luther King, Jr., delivered his brilliant address on the steps of the Lincoln Memorial with the brooding countenance of the Great Emancipator looking down on the 300,000 people assembled.⁵⁴

Yet as a counterpoint to the figure of the Great Emancipator, Martin Luther King evoked the US slave past not as a witness of the experience of enslavement like Douglass but as an African American man who inherited racial inequalities and segregation that derived from slavery and who gave voice to the descendants of the victims of slavery. That this speech was pronounced at the foot of Lincoln's shrine 41 years after its dedication is an indication that the construction of a memorial honoring the man who abolished slavery contributed neither to erase the legacy of slavery nor to heal its deep wounds.

Since Lincoln's death, many African Americans have celebrated him as the Great Emancipator, even though dissident discourses, like Douglass's 1868 speech, continued to circulate. Still, the scars of slavery, segregation, and racial hatred prevented most African Americans to celebrate Lincoln as the president who freed the nation from slavery. Two months before the assassination of Martin Luther King Jr., Lerone Bennett Jr. published a controversial article in *Ebony* magazine, titled "Was Abe Lincoln a White Supremacist?" in which once again he questioned the image of Lincoln as "the Great Emancipator who freed the Negroes with a stroke of the pen out of the goodness and compassion of his heart," eventually stating that he "was not the Great Emancipator."[55] Yet despite the Civil Rights Movement and black protests that marked the following decades, no other public figure in the official narrative of the abolition of slavery in the United States was able to rise above Lincoln.

The Lincoln Memorial in Washington, DC, is one of the main US national touristic landmarks that attract millions of tourists every year. Although the memorial's visit is free, tourists purchase numerous souvenirs, including T-shirts, mugs, pens, and dolls. Moreover, every year scholars produce numerous articles, monographs, and edited books exploring various aspects of Lincoln's legacy. Equally huge is the number of academic conferences, public lectures, and museum exhibitions focusing on Lincoln that are held each year. The television and film industries also collect the fruits of Lincoln's popularity by annually releasing documentary films and movies exploring various aspects of his life and career. In 2012, the release of the movie *Lincoln* by Steven Spielberg and the numerous popular and academic books published at the approach of the commemoration activities celebrating the sesquicentennial of the Emancipation Proclamation in 2013, clearly confirm the central place occupied by Lincoln in the official public memory of emancipation in the United States.[56]

MONUMENTS TO ISABEL, THE REDEEMER

Unlike African Americans, Afro-Brazilians who celebrated the memory of Princess Isabel were probably not in position to collect funds to honor the Redeemer. In 1933, a group of local elite men and women started working on a project to create a monument to the princess in the city of Juiz de Fora, Minas Gerais. In 1934, after organizing a number of activities to gather the necessary funds, the monument was unveiled in the gardens of the Mariano Procópio Park. The park occupies the area of an estate owned by the rich politician and engineer, Mariano Procópio Ferreira Lage (1821–1872), who in the past was the owner not only of a large coffee plantation but also of numerous slaves. In 1861, he built a villa in his Juiz de Fora's state aimed at hosting the royal family for the inauguration of the Estrada de Rodagem União e Indústria (Union and Industry Highway), a project led by him.[57] In 1921, his son Alfredo Ferreira Lage (1865–1944) unveiled the Mariano Procópio Museum, housed in the villa built by his father. The museum's collections include historical artifacts, artworks, and specimens of Brazilian fauna and flora that he had gathered. The park and the museum were closely associated with Princess Isabel and the royal family because they used to sojourn to the villa. Hence, before the creation of a monument honoring

Isabel, the villa's museum already had a room named after her. The room exhibits artifacts owned by the princess or associated with her, including her official costume and a drawing she executed. It also displays a reproduction of her bedroom and artworks representing the princess, including the oil study *A Princesa Isabel Entrega Cartas de Liberdade* (Princess Isabel Delivers Letters of Manumission) painted by Pedro Peres (1850–1923), depicting a ceremony in which the princess distributes letters of manumission to the slaves.[58] This same room contains a silver statue commemorating the abolition of slavery, portraying a kneeling slave. It also includes various instruments of torture, which are the only references to the enslaved population.[59] Thus, by combining the traditional image of the princess as the Redeemer associated with the representation of the slaves as victimized individuals to whom any agency is denied, the museum conveys the values of Brazilian white slave society.[60]

Placed in the gardens of the Mariano Procópio Park, the monument to Princess Isabel followed the same vision that represented her as the Redeemer observed in the exhibition of the Museum Mariano Procópio. Created by the sculptor Humberto Cozzo (1900–1981), the monument is located close to the "princesses' cave," the name of Isabel's favorite spot in the property's garden.[61] The 11.5-foot monument is composed of a rectangular white granite block, on which are applied two bronze bas-reliefs. At the base of the monument, the date of the signature of the Golden Law abolishing slavery in Brazil is engraved: "May 13, 1888." The top bas-relief is a profile portrait of the princess. Beneath the portrait a bronze plaque simply states, "Princess Isabel, The People of Juiz de Fora." Yet at the lower level, close to the ground, a bigger bronze bas-relief renders an almost naked kneeling slave, an iconic feminized image that emerged in the early nineteenth-century abolitionist campaigns in Europe and the United States. But here the kneeling slave image is emptied of its original abolitionist meaning. With the still visible broken chains on his wrists, the emancipated slave is raising his arms up high, in a position of gratitude to Princess Isabel, whose bas-relief portrait is located at the top of the monument in a separate bronze bas-relief. The image conveyed in the bas-relief, commissioned by the members of the white elite of Minas Gerais, not only reinforces the idea of freedom as a gift but also perpetuates the submissive position of former enslaved Afro-Brazilians and their descendants. The representation of the kneeling slave orients the spectator's gaze toward the portrait of the princess, reinforcing the image of Isabel as the Redeemer.

Regardless of this first initiative in Minas Gerais, the construction of a monument honoring Princess Isabel in Brazil's capital proved to be a much longer and more complicated task than the erection of a memorial to Lincoln in Washington, DC. After becoming president of Brazil in 1930, Getúlio Vargas put an end to the national holiday of May 13, in existence since 1890, a decision justified by the need to encourage work and reduce the number of holidays in the country.[62] However, especially during the Estado Novo regime, Vargas launched new policies of cultural and heritage management that brought Princess Isabel to light in the public space through permanent official initiatives.[63] With the approach of the 50th anniversary of the Golden Law in 1938, elite individuals of Minas Gerais made a public request "in favor of the construction of a monument to the redeemer."[64] Eventually, Vargas issued the law decree no. 427 of May 13, 1938, confirming that the 50th anniversary would be celebrated all over the country. In addition, the decree established that the government would repatriate the remains of Princess Isabel and Count d'Eu from Europe to Brazil. Finally, it also commissioned the construction in the country's capital of a public monument to Isabel "remembering the glorious accomplishment to which her name is associated."[65] Yet these homages were intended not only to celebrate Isabel as the great Redeemer but also to promote the image of Vargas as the father of the poor. As the president who established the system of social welfare, he was considered by many Afro-Brazilians as the one who actually liberated Brazilian workers and peasants from slavery.[66] As a result, the memory of Vargas as the true emancipator of Afro-Brazilians is also a construction related to the public projects developed during his government that eventually associated his image with that of Princess Isabel.

On the eve of the 1938 commemoration activities, Rio de Janeiro's *interventor* Henrique Dodsworth (1895–1975) authorized the construction of a granite marker to be placed in the location where a monument to Isabel, which had been in the planning stages for some time.[67] Also, the Centro Carioca (Carioca Center), a civil association aimed at influencing the activities of Rio de Janeiro's councilmen, obtained permission from the minister of transportation to create a plaque marking the 50th anniversary of the abolition of slavery. Still, these initiatives were greatly influenced by another event that occurred two days prior to the commemorations. On May 11, 1938, the protofascist group Ação Integralista Brasileira (Brazilian Integralist Action) led a coup against the Estado Novo regime. The rebels tried to invade Vargas's official residence, the Palace of Guanabara, in an attempt to kill him, but the operation failed. From that point on, Vargas used the public celebrations of the 50th anniversary of the abolition of slavery as a privileged stage to commemorate his victory over the regime's opponents and to reinforce his prestige among his supporters. Official ceremonies, Catholic masses, labor union parades, balls, concerts, and processions to the tombs of the main abolitionist leaders were among the various events that gathered thousands of people to mark the festivities in Rio de Janeiro. Furthermore, a lunch was offered in the Palace of Catete, the headquarters of the Brazilian federal government, for the 100 former slaves and 100 children who were participating in the literacy program Cruzada Nacional da Educação (National Education Crusade).[68] On May 13, 1938, a ceremony organized by a committee of elite women, presided over by the writer and journalist Maria Eugênia Celso (1886–1963), inaugurated a marble plaque with a bronze bas-relief with the effigy of Princess Isabel, "remembering the unforgettable work bequeathed by the Princess—the redemption of the black race."[69] The plaque was placed on the façade of the city's Post Office building, the former Paço Imperial (Imperial Palace) where the princess had signed the Golden Law. The Brazilian First Lady Darcy Vargas (1895–1968) and the federal district's First Lady Ceci Dodsworth, inaugurated the plaque in an official ceremony presided over by President Vargas.[70] However, in the early 1980s, the Imperial Palace was restored, and Isabel's plaque was removed from its façade. Perhaps to preserve the building's original characteristics and also as an indication of the new democratic wave that marked the end of the military dictatorship, the plaque honoring Isabel as the Redeemer was never put back on the building's façade.[71]

In the afternoon of the same day, a crowd of 100,000 people, including workers, men, women, and children, gathered in front of the Palace of Catete. In his speech, the president of the União Geral dos Sindicatos dos Empregados do Distrito Federal (General Union of Labor Unions of Federal District Employees) stated: "the workers did not want today's date to be like ordinary commemorations of our history. At the moment, the May 13 has a new meaning that should be considered as an homage to the Great Brazilian who centralizes our people's hope."[72] Unlike the previous anniversaries of the Golden Law in which Princess Isabel was the most important figure celebrated, Vargas was the central figure in the festivities of the 50th anniversary of the abolition of slavery in Brazil. The process associating the memory of the Brazilian empire, the abolition of slavery, and Vargas's image as a great statesman continued during the next year. On December 5, 1939, the remains of Dom Pedro II and the Empress Teresa Cristina (1822–1889) were placed in the newly built royal mausoleum in the Cathedral São Pedro de Alcântara, in Petrópolis.[73] Vargas unveiled the mausoleum adorned with full-body sculptures representing the monarchs resting.[74]

The 100th anniversary of Princess Isabel's birth was commemorated in 1946, after the end of the Estado Novo, and the day of her birth, July 29, was declared a national holiday.[75] In addition to ceremonies and the traditional mass celebrated in the Church of Our Lady of Rosary of Saint Benedict and Black Men, Brazil's Post Office created a stamp in honor of the princess, who was illustrated by her profile portrait. However, the stamp did not contain any reference to Isabel as an emancipator.[76] Ten years later, to commemorate Princess Isabel's 110th anniversary, a banknote of 50 *cruzeiros* was released into circulation. A picture of Isabel appears on the recto side, and a reproduction of the painting *Golden Law* by Brazilian academic painter Cadmo Fausto de Souza (1901–1983), whose several paintings on historical events were used to decorate the reverse sides of banknotes, is on the verso side. The image is a classic allegory of a white woman, symbolizing freedom, and holding a stone plaque. In the background, Rio de Janeiro's mountainous landscape is visible. At the woman's feet, broken chains and shackles are the only references to men and women who were freed in 1888.

Following the public initiatives commemorating the memory of Princess Isabel in the early 1950s, during Getúlio Vargas's last term as president of Brazil, concrete measures were eventually taken to bring the remains of Princess Isabel and her husband, the Count d'Eu, from France to Brazil. On March 16, 1951, UDN Congressman Aureliano Leite presented to the National Congress a project proposing the opening of a credit line of 1 million *cruzeiros* to pay for transportation expenses to bring the couple's remains from France to Brazil and for the construction of their tombs in the royal mausoleum in Petrópolis. The project eventually passed, and in that same year, Vargas sanctioned law no. 1403 of August 6, 1951.

On June 22, 1953, a procession headed by Brazilian and French officers and member of the Brazilian royal family led the remains of the royal couple from Paris to Le Havre.[77] After a ceremony and a mass, the coffins, covered with the Brazilian flag, were transported to Rio de Janeiro on the cruiser *Almirante Barroso*. On July 6, 1953, the remains eventually arrived in Rio de Janeiro. The main Brazilian newspapers covered in detail the transfer of the remains from France to Brazil. The newspaper *Diário da noite* fully describes the ceremonies: "An incalculable crowd accompanied the trucks that transported the coffins from the Mauá Square to the Metropolitan Cathedral. The parade presented pathetic moments with the presence of elements of the black race, survivors from the time of slavery that yielded homage to the emancipator."[78] Illustrating the notice, several pictures showed numerous moved Afro-Brazilian men and women who attended the ceremony, suggesting that the princess was still an important figure at least to the older generation of Afro-Brazilians.

Even though President Vargas did not attend the ceremonies to receive Princess Isabel's remains, he certainly obtained political gains from this important event. At the time, another Rio de Janeiro newspaper stated that, although not present, the president followed, with emotion and interest, the ceremonies held all over the city. Therefore, after his death in August 1954, the image of Vargas, who was constantly evoked as the one who truly emancipated the slaves in Brazil, continued to be associated with the image of Princess Isabel, who according to one newspaper:

> destroyed with the stroke of a pen the odious institute servile. [. . .]. But for many years the free worker, who was slowly replacing the former slave, did not have anybody to protect him, support him on the basis of law, and advocate improvements in his living conditions. Vargas was the author of this work, whose meaning makes his popularity. The Brazilian masses will never forget.[79]

The remains of Isabel and her husband, the Count d'Eu, were placed in the Metropolitan Cathedral of Rio de Janeiro, awaiting relocation to the royal mausoleum in Petrópolis. However, ten years later, citizens complained that the remains continued to be stored in the "basement of the temporary headquarters of the Metropolitan Cathedral."[80] In a public speech in the Chamber of the Deputies, Rio de Janeiro's UDN congressman, Arnaldo Nogueira (1920–2006), called for "all men of color to pay contributions of 5 *cruzeiros* to promote the construction of a mausoleum to shelter the remains of the Princess Isabel, the redeemer."[81]

In 1953, following repatriation of the royal couple's remains to Rio de Janeiro, the demands for a monument honoring the princess became more visible in Brazil's printed media. On July 2, 1953, a short notice in Rio de Janeiro's newspaper *A Noite,* reported that the Congressman Oswaldo Orico proposed a project to build a monument to Princess Isabel, opening a credit line of 6 million *cruzeiros*.[82] In 1955, Rio de Janeiro's city council members initiated a campaign to build a monument to pay homage to the princess to be placed at the corner of the Nossa Senhora de Copacabana Avenue and the Princesa Isabel Avenue in Copacabana, Rio de Janeiro. Although barely visible, the initiative did gain space in the city's newspapers. That same year, Maria Eugênia Celso, published a column in *Jornal do Brasil* evoking the words of Magalhães Junior, a member of the city council. According to her, "during a session of the city council, he was the only one to recall the date of May 13, and to celebrate the glory of the abolition, embodied in the most important *carioca* of all times who was Dona Isabel, the Redeemer."[83] At the end of the notice, the author reiterated the need for "a project providing special funding for the monument to Princess Isabel, which is missing in our Rio."[84] Notwithstanding these scarce and isolated elite voices, the memory of Princess Isabel was increasingly forgotten in the public sphere. In 1956, in another article, Celso undercores that on July 29, few newspapers remembered the anniversary of Princess Isabel, "the old presumptive heiress of the Brazilian Crown, which the History consecrated with the blessed name of Redeemer," who in the past was so celebrated. The columnist also reminds the reader that a monument to the princess still did not exist in Rio de Janeiro, her hometown.[85] She insists that educated foreigners who visit Rio de Janeiro, especially North Americans, "soon ask about the monument to Princess Isabel, the emancipator of a race, who thus cannot fail to have immortalized in bronze the gratitude of the people and the memory of the greatest female figure on the continent."[86] Eventually, in a parternalistic tone, the columnist, a member of the Rio de Janeiro's white upper class whose parents had noble titles, concludes the article by calling all black Brazilians to take it upon themselves to support the initiative to construct a tomb to Isabel in order to pay tribute to the princess:

> It would come to the men rescued by her, to all blacks of Brazil, directed and guided by the Association of Men of Color of the Church of Saint Benedict, to take upon themselves the erection of this tomb. For the blacks of Brazil, this public settlement of a debt, would be a dignified gesture, whose gratitude whites equally share. All united in the worship of that illustrious *carioca*, whose glory, transcending her homeland,

brightly radiating throughout the world, as the great benefactor of humanity, let give as soon as possible to Dona Isabel, the Redeemer, the mausoleum she deserves.[87]

Yet even though during this period Brazil's black population highly esteemed the princess and attended public ceremonies honoring her, unlike African Americans who financed the construction of the *Freedmen's Memorial* commemorating Lincoln in Washington, DC, Afro-Brazilians never organized any local or national campaign to collect funds to finance the princess's mausoleum. Indeed, modest Afro-Brazilian individuals did not have the financial means to contribute to a fund-raising campaign. Moreover, Brazil had no tradition of private individuals financing public monuments, and very few memorials paid homage to female figures. But more importantly, during the 1950s, when most former slaves were deceased, the figure of Princess Isabel was no longer popular enough among the Afro-Brazilian population to justify an operation to collect funds to build a permanent monument honoring her. In fact, the idea of the abolition of slavery as a gift given by Princess Isabel was in clear contradiction with the daily racial and social inequalities faced by Afro-Brazilians. Nonetheless, by the end of the 1950s, although regularly denouncing acts of racism in the press, black activists still formulated contradictory interpretations of the Brazilian abolition of slavery. This ambiguity is visible in two articles published in the newspaper *Diário carioca* in June 1959. The first article honored João Profeta Jeremias, the sacristan of the Church of Saint Efigênia and Saint Elesbão and a son of former enslaved parents, who was turning 105 years old on June 20, 1959.[88] Two days later, in response to the article, the president of the União dos Homens de Côr (Union of Men of Color), Joviano Severino de Melo, declared his decision to offer as a birthday gift to Jeremias 20 bank notes of 50,000 *réis* (certainly referring to the bank notes of 50 *cruzeiros*) illustrated with Isabel's effigy. In the same article, Melo also asserts that "the slavocratic mentality continues oppressing the Brazilian blacks, as much as that 71 years after the abolition of slavery, blacks did not receive one meter of land to cultivate."[89] Thus, despite recognizing the limits of the abolition of slavery on the living and working conditions of later generations of Afro-Brazilians, the black activist continued to cherish Isabel as a symbol of redemption.

In spite of the absence of public markers paying homage to Princess Isabel in Rio de Janeiro, at the end of the 1950s some monuments commemorating the abolition of slavery were eventually unveiled in the city's west zone, far from the city's main landmarks. The artist Miguel Pastor designed two public monuments, commissioned by the engineer Elza Pinho Osborne, in charge of the urban development of Rio de Janeiro's west zone.[90] The first was a monument celebrating the former slave Joaquim Manuel da Silva (1854–1963), known as Tio Quincas (Uncle Quincas) or Paizinho Preto (Black Papa). A practitioner of the Afro-Brazilian religion Umbanda that also includes elements of Catholicism and Spiritism, Silva incorporated the spirit of a *preto velho* (old black), a deity associated with old enslaved men. The monument is composed of a 29-foot concrete obelisk, a mural covered with glass tiles and Yoruba inscriptions evoking various *orixás*, and a pedestal on which is placed a bronze statue honoring Paizinho Preto, for which Silva himself served as a model.[91] According to the engineer Elza Pinho Esborne, the statue paid homage not only to Silva but also to "all those who were slaves in Brazil."[92] On May 13, 1958, as part of the commemorative activities of the 70th anniversary of the abolition of slavery, the statue was unveiled in the Square Adolfo Lemos, also known as Praça do Preto Velho (Old Black's Square) and Praça das Camélias (Camellias Square) in Inhoaíba, a poor neighborhood, in the west zone of Rio de Janeiro. Silva attended the ceremony that inaugurated the statue. On that occasion, he offered a bouquet of camellias, the symbol of the abolitionist movement, to the mayor's wife.

In 1960, Pastor created another monument commemorating the abolition of slavery, this time in the square of the Arthur Azevedo Theatre, in Campo Grande, a large neighborhood, located about 28 miles from Rio de Janeiro's downtown. The monument is composed of two 23-foot obelisks of concrete and marble. The first obelisk displays a bas-relief depicting a full-body vertical schematic figure of an enslaved man raising his arms up high. Despite the shackles on the man's wrists, his body expresses the idea of triumph instead of the traditional representation of the victimized and grateful slave. This monument breaks with traditional representations of the black body inasmuch as the white marble bas-relief depicts a white enslaved body, which contrasts with the dark background. On the second obelisk, a white marble bas-relief, a similar figure of an emancipated woman is depicted in a triumphant position carrying a baby in her arms. About 15 feet from to this second obelisk, almost unnoticed, is an additional bas-relief applied to a wall marking the limits of the square. The bas-relief denotes five white and black Brazilian abolitionists, Princess Isabel, Joaquim Nabuco, André Rebouças, Luis Gama, and José do Patrocínio. The ensemble of monuments to the abolition of slavery created by Miguel Antônio Pastor are the first public monuments to give agency to emancipated men and women by signifying freedom as a conquest, not as a gift received from Isabel and other abolitionists. During a period when the issue of Brazilian slave past was hardly addressed in public monuments, this different perspective of the abolition of slavery could be conveyed in the public space only by targeting a very particular population in a peripheral neighborhood. Yet the creation of these monuments was not related to the particular public demands of Afro-Brazilian social actors but was rather associated with local politics. Constructing monuments honoring enslaved individuals in modest and distant black neighborhoods could certainly bring dividends to Rio de Janeiro's politicians.

But following these peripheral initiatives, in 1959, after a long campaign mainly led by Rio de Janeiro's elite women, a project was approved by the city to commission Pastor to construct a monument in homage to Princess Isabel.[93] After a long delay, in November 1959, the three female members of the city council, Velinda Maurício da Fonseca (PTB, Partido Trabalhista Brasileiro; Brazilian Labour Party), Dulce Pinto Ferreira Magalhães (PDC, Partido Democrata Cristão; Democrat Christian Party), and Lygia Maria Lessa Bastos (UDN, União Democrática Nacional; National Democratic Union), signed a request to the city's mayor asking him to allow the construction of a monument to Isabel to be installed at the corner of the Atlântica Avenue and the Princesa Isabel Street. In the written request, the council members, "proud of their sex, show solidarity in appealing to the local legislative and executive powers to no longer delay the public tribute long overdue, not only by the people of Rio, but by all Brazilians to the exalted princess Isabel."[94] On May 19, 1960, the newspaper *Última hora* announced that the construction of the monument was started at the corner of the Princesa Isabel Avenue and Gustavo Sampaio Street, in the white middle- and upper middle-class neighborhood of Copacabana.[95] Following a modernist style, the monument was composed of a 49-foot concrete obelisk to which was added a full-body profile image of Princess Isabel. The imposing monument was considered among the greatest public memorials built in the state of Guanabara (the present-day city of Rio de Janeiro).[96] According to the newspaper *Diario de notícias,* its construction was estimated at 8 million *cruzeiros*.[97] The monument was part of a broader plan of public works that included new tunnels, the expansion of avenues, and the paving of numerous streets.[98]

On December 3, 1960, the monument was eventually unveiled in the presence of the interim governor of the newly created state of Guanabara, José Sette Câmara Filho (1920–2002).[99] Although Rio de Janeiro's newspapers did not provide details about the ceremony, an article published in the newspaper *Diário de notícias* indicated that on December 2, starting at midnight, until December 5, followers of Umbanda, an Afro-Brazilian religion, would perform a ceremony including dances, drumming, and chants of praise to "their Redeemer, the Princess Isabel." Flávio Urumila, a priest of one of the most important Rio de Janeiro's Umbanda temples, invited all Umbanda priests and followers to attend the ceremony to "honor the black race in this homage to the emancipator of slavery in Brazil."[100]

It is difficult to precisely evaluate the monument's reception among Rio de Janeiro's population. In an article in the feminine magazine *Jornal das moças*, Dauny Fritsch, a spiritist author, asked whether Princess Isabel would like to stay petrified in a monument. From a spiritual perspective, she questioned the value of spending millions to build a monument to Isabel while the spirits of the old blacks (*preto velhos*) remained forgotten and the black youth remained socially and economically excluded: "What is the worth of the image in stone, retaining millions, if at the feet of this remembrance the soul of an old black man sobs the lack of prayer? If an abandoned child, cries over the misery of hunger, the lack of affection, and human misunderstanding?"[101] Such interrogation already reflected the decreasing importance of the image of Princess Isabel as the Redeemer of Brazil's enslaved population, in clear contrast with the living conditions of Afro-Brazilians.

The years following the inauguration of Princess Isabel's monument in Rio de Janeiro were marked by social changes and political instability. In 1960, the journalist and conservative politician Carlos Lacerda (UDN) was elected governor of the new state of Guanabara. After the resignation of President Jânio Quadros (1917–1992) in 1961, a military coup deposed President João Goulart (1919–1976) in 1964, inaugurating a dictatorship that lasted until 1985. In January 1965, beginning his last year in office, Lacerda ordered the destruction of the monument to Princess Isabel, which only four years earlier had cost 8 million *cruzeiros*. Why the expensive monument paying homage to Isabel was removed remains unclear. A short notice published in the newspaper *Jornal Brasil* reported that, according to the Regional Administration of Copacabana, the monument would be demolished because Larcerda considered it was in bad taste and anti-aesthetic.[102] A garden, planned with a view of the sea by the landscape architect Napoleão Muniz Freire, would replace the monument.[103] Some days later, another revealing and ironic notice published in the newspaper *Última hora* confirmed the monument's removal within a week.[104] The notice, mocking Carlos Lacerda's *favelas*' removal measures that were in progress at the time, also indicated that the new location of the statue was not disclosed but that "the news that it will be removed to Villa Alliança, like the *favelados*, is only an intrigue of the opposition."[105] This association could suggest that the image of Princess Isabel was closely related to the residents of *favelas*; more likely, the decision of supressing the monument was due to political disputes between the politicians of the new and old administrations. During a period of dictatorship, even though the demolition of the monument was slightly criticized in Rio de Janeiro's newspapers, apparently the event did not have great popular repercussions.[106] At the same time, the lack of public reaction perhaps indicated that the image of Princess Isabel as the Redeemer was losing its importance.

In 1971, also during the military regime, two new marble tombs were added to the royal mausoleum in Petrópolis's cathedral to receive the remains of Princess Isabel and Count d'Eu. On May 9, 1971, the remains were transferred from Metropolitan Cathedral of Rio de Janeiro to be open to the public for three days in the Church of Our Lady of the Rosary and Saint Benedict of the Black Men.[107] Exposing the remains in the traditional black church was an important symbolic gesture connecting the princess and Rio de Janeiro's black population who could pay a last homage to the Redeemer.[108] According to *Jornal do Brasil*, about 30,000 people, most of them people of modest means who sometimes had difficulty writing their names in the attendance book, waited in long lines to see the remains. "It is our color that brings us here for someone who made so much for our ancestors," said two black women, Eunice Lima and her mother Maria Luísa Lima, after signing the attendance book.[109] Both women were deeply moved when revering the remains of the Princess and the Count, after spreading petals of red roses over the coffins.

On May 12, 1971, one day prior to the anniversary of the abolition of slavery, the remains were finally transferred to the royal mausoleum in Petrópolis's cathedral, in the latest massive event celebrating the memory of the Redeemer princess. In Rio de Janeiro, hundreds of people followed the procession that left the church. Among those at the church to attend the ceremony, was Isaura Maria Gonçalves, a 96-year-old daughter of enslaved parents. After not leaving her house for almost six months, Isaura ventured outside "to say farewell forever to the princess and her husband" and to wish that "God bless her and always protect her as she protected us in life."[110] Mr. Abdical Bahia, the judge of the Rosary brotherhood, stated in his farewell speech that "there was nobody else more Brazilian than the princess and the prince honored."[111] According to him, their passage through the Church of Saint Benedict and Our Lady of Rosary of Black Men "was an imposition of justice, in a necessary reverence to those who did so much for the race."[112] Intended to gather the population, the ceremony also had military pomp with the addition of military police and firefighters overseeing the celebration. The Rio de Janeiro commemoration was closed with a presentation by the Esquadrilha da Fumaça (Smoke Squadron), the Brazilian Air Force's air demonstration squadron, which flew three times over the church. According to the newspaper *Jornal do Brasil*:

> Hundreds of white agitated handkerchiefs and tears in many eyes of people of color marked Rio's farewell yesterday to the remains of Princess Isabel and the Count d'Eu, taken in procession to Petropolis, where they will be deposited today in the cathedral's mausoleum, in a ceremony which will be attended by the President of the Republic. At the Church of Our Lady of the Rosary in Rio, at the procession's departure announced by ringing of the bells, and in the streets of Petropolis, modest people and the princes of the Brazilian imperial family remained side by side during the tributes.[113]

In Petrópolis, a crowd of 5,000 men, women, and children awaited the remains of Princess Isabel. The procession carrying the remains was led by the captain of the Brazilian army, Manuel Anselmo, 39 years old, and *preto* (black), who "asked this distinction due to his color, because he 'felt that was bringing something that was linked to his body, as the Princess Isabel's act freeing the slaves was the beginning of the formation of a people without barriers.'"[114] In Petrópolis, the two coffins containing the sets of remains were on display in the courtyard of Princess Isabel's palace, which was one of the official residences of the couple until the proclamation of the Republic in 1889, when the royal family went into exile to Europe. Then the coffins were displayed in the palace's noble ballroom, decorated with black drapes, the imperial arms, and paintings depicting the various members of the royal family, including the Empress Teresa Cristina, the Emperors Dom Pedro I and Dom Pedro II, as well as Dom João VI. In addition, across from Isabel's casket, the gold pen with which she signed the Golden Law was placed on a black cushion. Moreover, the marble table where the princess signed the law abolishing slavery and the text of the law were also exhibited in the salon. The visitors who came to pay tribute to the princess would be once again reminded that she was the great Redeemer who freed the slaves in Brazil. A group of schoolgirls were in charge of the vigil. The celebration ended with a mass in the Petrópolis cathedral, where the coffins were placed in the royal mausoleum. The ceremony certainly brought political gains to the Brazilian government. During the hardest years of the military regime, when public political demonstrations were forbidden, President Emílio Garrastazu Médici (1905–1985) cleverly connected with the population in an official and popular ceremony. He closed the service by signing the act delivering the remains to the Petrópolis Diocese and depositing flowers on the tombs of the emperor, the empress, the princess, and her husband. The couple's remains were placed in two marble tombs that, like those of Dom Pedro II and Dona Leopoldina, were adorned with sculptures representing Isabel and Count d'Eu lying in rest.

In 1973, the painted plaster reproductions of the tombs of Isabel and her husband were placed in one of the rooms of Museu do Negro (Black Museum) in Rio de Janeiro. Created in 1967, the museum is housed in a building adjacent to the Church of Our Lady of Saint Benedict and Rosary of Black Men, where the remains were opened to the public in 1971. By including the reproduction of the tombs in a traditional black institution created by enslaved and freed individuals to memorialize the history of the Catholic black lay brotherhood, the image of the Redeemer princess was again reinforced. The two huge plaster molds replicating the deceased bodies of the royal couple are on display in the museum and share the space with a portrait of black abolitionist André Rebouças, pictures of the princess at different ages, and images of other members of the royal family.

Over the years, representations of Princess Isabel gradually changed. Unlike Lincoln, she was never directly depicted granting freedom to the slaves or placed in any kind of interaction with freed men and women. For example, in a banknote of 1981, Isabel's face is featured on the front side, whereas the reverse side shows the image of two enslaved women extracted from a photograph by the French photographer Jean-Victor Frond (1821–1881). Transformed into a photolithograph, titled *Escravas cozinhando na roça* (Slaves Cooking in the Garden), the picture illustrated the book *Brazil Pittoresco*, published in 1859, almost 30 years prior to the abolition of slavery in Brazil.[115] The image of the banknote, intended to commemorate the memory of Princess Isabel, is rather ambiguous because, instead of celebrating emancipation and freedom, it rather depicts an illustration based on a photograph of women living under slavery. With a rural setting in the background, one woman is sitting on the ground. She holds her head with one hand, in an expression of deep fatigue. The other woman is standing and placing an iron cauldron on a pile of rocks and branches to start a fire and cook.

Princess Isabel was also celebrated in popular culture. As Matthias Röhrig Assunção explains, she "has for a long time been praised in *capoeira* circles as the philanthropic emancipator."[116] Still, starting in the 1970s, in a period of reorganization for the black movement during the dictatorship, and especially after its end in 1985, the narrative of the abolition of slavery in Brazil as a gift from the princess started being questioned by Afro-Brazilian activists. In this new narrative, the abolition never occurred because after May 13, 1888, the Afro-Brazilian population continued to be socially and economically excluded.[117] If in the past *capoeira* songs exalted the princess as the Redeemer, she gradually became the object of criticism.[118] By this time, the commemoration of May 13 was replaced by November 20, the date of the death of Zumbi, the leader of Palmares Quilombo. In 1988, the centennial of the signature of the Golden Law, this change in the public narrative of the abolition of slavery became even more visible. That year during Rio de Janeiro's carnival parade, the school of samba Mangueira presented the theme "One Hundred Years of Freedom, Reality and Illusion," a samba signed by Hélio Turco, Jurandir, and Alvinho, stating that "the long awaited Golden Law, so long ago signed, It was not the end of slavery." During the 1990s, in the public discourses developed by social actors, these samba lyrics also exalted Zumbi as the actual emancipator, who redeemed Brazilian black population from slavery. This same tendency was also present in *capoeira* songs, in which the warrior Zumbi replaced Isabel as the Great Emancipator.[119] Moreover, during the 2000s, the role of the princess as the Great Emancipator was also reassessed in scholarly works.[120]

In 2003, during the celebrations of the 115th anniversary of the signature of the Golden Law, a bronze sculpture representing Princess Isabel was placed on the Princesa Isabel Avenue in Copacabana, in Rio de Janeiro. The statue occupied the same location where the obelisk designed by Miguel Pastor existed between 1960 and 1965, when it was demolished. Unlike 1960, Afro-Brazilian activists did not celebrate the initiative but rather protested. The construction of the monument was a project led by Rio de Janeiro Mayor César Maia (Democratas). Much smaller than the previous monument, the 8.2-foot statue, signed by the sculptor Edgar Duvivier, was a last attempt to give visibility to the Redeemer. As in the traditional representations, the sculpture characterizes the princess as the Redeemer. She is depicted holding the pen with which she signed the Golden Law of 1888, reinforcing the old and official account that the abolition of slavery in Brazil was a gift given to the black population. Yet unlike the Lincoln Memorial or the *Freedom's Memorial*, which are placed in prominent, reflective, and accessible spaces, Isabel's statue is placed at an intersection between two avenues. As a result, it can easily go unnoticed by passersby and does not constitute a place of meditation.

CONTESTED EMANCIPATORS

Various Brazilian governments, especially during the period of the Estado Novo and the military dictatorship, were instrumental in memorializing Princess Isabel, who for several decades remained the face of the abolition of slavery in Brazil. Despite the weakness of the Afro-Brazilian civil rights movement in comparison to the African American Civil Rights movement, over the last two decades, the paternalistic vision of the Brazilian abolition of slavery as a gift from the great Redeemer was seriously questioned and deeply revised in the public sphere, whereas in the United States, Lincoln is still the central figure in the narrative of emancipation.

In the United States, following his death, Lincoln started being identified as the Great Emancipator, a shift that occurred about two years after the signature was placed on the Emancipation Proclamation and the adoption of the 13th amendment that outlawed slavery. The first initiative to construct a permanent monument honoring Lincoln in the national capital was led by African American freed men and women. However, even by this time, African American activists and intellectuals like Frederick Douglass greatly questioned the image of Lincoln as the Great Emancipator. Gradually, whereas Lincoln's sanctification was embraced by US white elites, African Americans who did not live the experience of emancipation had no reason to celebrate the white emancipator in a country where racial hatred and racial inequalities clearly persisted. But despite losing importance among African Americans, in US public memory Lincoln is still represented as the Great Emancipator. His crucial role in unifying the nation divided by the Civil War and his tragic and premature death are important factors that did not allow any other alternative figure to emerge in the narrative of the abolition of slavery in the United States. The industry constructed around Lincoln's memory is a lucrative one.

The construction of Princess Isabel's image as the Redeemer started just after her signing of the Golden Law in 1888, but her memorialization was interrupted with the end of the monarchy in 1889. The princess went into exile and died in France more than 30 years after the abolition of slavery. In spite of being celebrated in the commemorations of the abolition of slavery in Brazil, the first public monument honoring Isabel was not unveiled until long after her death, in the 1930s, far from Rio de Janeiro, then Brazil's national capital. In the first and almost unknown monument constructed by the endeavors of a group of white elite men and women in the city of Juiz de Fora, Isabel's effigy is associated with the representation of a grateful slave, reinforcing her traditional image of Redeemer. Although older generations of Afro-Brazilians certainly esteemed Princess Isabel, the construction of a monument paying homage to her in Rio de Janeiro was far more complicated than the construction of the Freedom's Memorial in Washington, DC. Following the 1930s, despite the various requests of white elite male and female politicians and journalists, Afro-Brazilians did not lead any initiative to collect the funds to create a monument to Princess Isabel. The Estado Novo regime and the military dictatorship, as well as the district and municipal governments of Rio de Janeiro, manipulated Isabel's public memory with the goal of fulfilling particular political agendas and gaining the support of the Afro-Brazilian population.

In both the United States and Brazil, the memorialization of the emancipation focused on the figures of two white Great Emancipators, preventing the emergence of the public memory of black emancipators. Notwithstanding the significance of the Civil Rights Movement and Lincoln's decreasing popularity among African Americans, the United States did not witness the emergence of an alternative figure to replace the Great Emancipator. In contrast, over the last 30 years, and despite the long periods of dictatorial regimes, Afro-Brazilians deconstructed the image of Princess Isabel as the Redeemer, gradually replacing her with the image of Zumbi. Today, even though the media and some elite groups continue sparsely contesting the existence of racism and racial inequalities in Brazil, the country now officially celebrates the several forms of emancipation by focusing on how enslaved men and women fought the institution of slavery as historical agents.

NOTES

1. On Lincoln, see Rice, 1907; Baldwin, 1909; Ulm, 1922; Hertz, 1926. On Princess Isabel, see Calmon, 1941; Lacombe, 1989.
2. See Holzer, Boritt, and Neely, 1984; Peterson, 1994; Thomas, 2002; Holzer, 2012.
3. See Blight, 2001.
4. Bethell, 1970: 69, 340.
5. Tackach, 2002: 5.
6. Tackach, 2002: 8.
7. "First Inagural Address of Abraham Lincoln," 1861.
8. See Beattie, 2011: 175.
9. Schwarcz, 1998: 315.
10. On Princess Isabel's involvement in the abolitionist movement, see Daibert, 2004: Silva, 2003.
11. See Silva, 2003; Machado, 2007: 267.
12. The states affected were Arkansas, Texas, Alabama, South Carolina, North Carolina, Florida, Georgia, Mississippi, Louisiana, and Virginia, the last two with some exceptions.
13. Holzer, 2006: 87.
14. Holzer, 2006: 89; Holzer, 2012: 133.
15. Schwarcz, 1998: 438; Schwartz, 2007: 25–26.

16. On the Guarda Negra (Black Guard), see Trochim, 1988: 285–300. On the participation of *capoeiras* in the Guarda Negra, see Talmon-Chvaicer, 2008: 84–85.
17. The painting(oil on canvas, 274.32 cm × 457.2 cm) hangs in the Capitol building of the United States, Washington, D.C. About the painting, see Masur, 2012b.
18. See Wood, 2010: 219–220.
19. The lithograph is by J. W. Watte, based on a drawing by H. W. Herrick (Hartford, CT: Lucio Stebbins, 1864).
20. On images of kneeling slaves, see Kerr-Ritchie, 2011: 327–358; Hamilton, 2012: 1–22.
21. Washington, 2003: 48.
22. Washington, 2003: 49.
23. Washington, 2003: 50.
24. "S. A. I. D. [Sua Alteza Imperial Dona] Isabel: A Redemptora," 1888: 1.
25. Katchun, 2003: 118–119.
26. Katchun, 2003: 117. The DC Compensated Emancipation Act ended slavery in Washington, D.C. The act was signed by Lincoln on April 16.
27. Medford, 2006: 2.
28. See Wood, 2010: 17.
29. See Assunção, 2002: 102; Moraes, 2012.
30. "Isabel, a Redemptora: Mais demonstrações de pezar pela sua morte nesta capital, no exterior e nos estados," 1921: 9.
31. See "Princeza Isabel: Solemnes exequias," 1921: 10. Still today the church celebrates an annual mass to commemorate the memory of the princess.
32. "Princeza Isabel: Solemnes exequias": 10.
33. "Uma das maiores figuras da história brasileira . . .," 1933: 2.
34. Blair, 2004: 26.
35. Thomas, 2002: 3.
36. Savage, 1997: 89.
37. "Inaugural Ceremonies of the Freedmen's Memorial Monument . . .," 1876: 6.
38. See Eliot, 1885: 88.
39. For a genealogy of images and sculptures representing Lincoln as the benefactor who grants freedom to the kneeling slave, see Savage, 1997: Chap. 3.
40. See Wood, 2010: 17; Savage, 1997: Chap. 4.
41. "Inaugural Ceremonies of the Freedmen's Memorial Monument . . .," 1876: 8.
42. An exception was a discrete bas-relief representing black individuals that is featured at the base of the monument to the philanthropist Charles Avery in the Allegheny Cemetery in Pittsburgh (Philadelphia). See Savage, 1997: 82.
43. "Inaugural Ceremonies of the Freedmen's Memorial Monument . . .," 1876: 3.
44. On Matthews, see Bragg, 1925: 99–102; Simmons, 1887: 246–250; Graham, 1983: 133; 164; 212–213; 272.
45. "Inaugural Ceremonies of the Freedmen's Memorial Monument . . .," 1876: 16.
46. See Murray, 1916: 198–199, quoted in Savage: 1997, 117.
47. "Inaugural Ceremonies of the Freedmen's Memorial Monument . . .," 1876: 19.
48. "Inaugural Ceremonies of the Freedmen's Memorial Monument . . .," 1876: 19.
49. "Inaugural Ceremonies of the Freedmen's Memorial Monument . . .," 1876: 19.
50. On the Lincoln Memorial, see Thomas, 2002.
51. Thomas, 2002: 122.
52. Epigraph inscribed on Abraham Lincoln's sculpture, Lincoln Memorial, Washington, DC.
53. King Jr., 1963.
54. "Rev. Martin Luther King's Speech Was History Talking," 1963: 4.
55. Bennett, 1968: 35.

56. Among the numerous books on Lincoln published in 2012 and 2013 are Masur, 2012; Drehle, 2012; Reilly and Zimmerman, 2011; Mansfield, 2012; Holzer; 2012; Holzer, 2013; and DeRose, 2013.
57. Costa, 2005: 16.
58. This painting was unveiled in a later ceremony held at Rio de Janeiro City Hall, in which Princess Isabel distributed 40 letters of manumission. See Azevedo, 1886: 75.
59. Costa, 2011: 230.
60. Costa, 2011: 23.
61. See Neves and Silva, 2011.
62. The decree no. 155 B of January 1890 established May 13 as a national holiday. The national holiday was extinguished by the decree no. 19.488 of December 15, 1930. See Moraes, 2012: 14.
63. See Williams, 2001: Chap. 3.
64. "Para que seja erguido um monumento à princesa Isabel," 1938: 2.
65. Artigo 2o, Decreto-Lei no. 427 de 13 de maio de 1938.
66. An idea that remains alive today among elder black individuals. According to Cornélio Cancino, a descendant of slaves, "Princess Isabel only signed ; it was Getúlio who freed us from slavery": Mattos and Rios, 2005: 56.
67. From 1937 to 1945, during the Estado Novo regime, Vargas dismissed the elected governors in the states and the federal district (Rio de Janeiro) and replaced them with *interventores* (intervenors). Nominated by Vargas, Dodsworth was the *interventor* of the federal district of Rio de Janeiro.
68. "O cincoentenário da abolição . . .," 1938a: 5.
69. "O cincoentenário da abolição . . .," 1938b: 2.
70. "Cincoentenário da abolição . . .," 1938b: 7; "Cincoentenário da abolição . . .," 1938a: 8; "O cincoentenário da abolição," 1938a: 5.
71. A 1983 picture published in the newspaper *Última hora* shows the plaque on the building's façade. See "MEC reforma prédios históricos . . .," 1983: 7.
72. "A Memorável manifestação trabalhista ao chefe do governo . . .": 1938: 7.
73. The couple died in exile, and their remains were repatriated from Portugal to Brazil in 1925.
74. See Williams, 2001: 151–152.
75. Law decree no. 9488 of July 19, 1946, declaring the July 29, 1946 a national holiday to celebrate the 100th anniversary of Princess Isabel.
76. "Primeiro centenário do nascimento da Princesa Isabel . . .": 1946: 3.
77. The ceremonies are described in detail in an article of Rio de Janeiro's newspaper. See "Marinha," 1953: 9. The Brazilian cruiser *Barroso* was sent to Europe to participate in the crowning ceremonies of the Queen Elizabeth II of England. See "Vêm para o Brasil os restos mortais da Princesa Isabel e do Conde d'Eu," 1953: 1.
78. "A chegada dos despojos da Princesa Isabel e do Conde d'Eu," 1953: 3.
79. "Gustavo Barroso Sôbre o Maior Estadista Brasileiro . . .," 1955: 8.
80. "Campanha por túmulo de Isabel," 1963: 12.
81. "Campanha por túmulo de Isabel," 1963: 12.
82. "Monumento à Princesa Isabel," 1953: 7.
83. Celso, 1955: 8.
84. Celso, 1955: 8.
85. Celso, 1956: 8.
86. Celso, 1956: 8.
87. Celso, 1956: 8.
88. "Profeta faz 105 anos," 1959: 1; 11–12.
89. "Cédulas com Isabel a prêto de 105 anos," 1959: 11.

90. Today Campo Grande is the largest district of Rio de Janeiro. According to Census 2010 conducted by the IBGE (Instituto Brasileiro de Geografia e Estatística), the majority of the population of both Campo Grande and Inhoaíba is either black or brown. See "Diálogo com o Leitor . . .": 1958, 5; Teixeira, 1960: 5.
91. Today for security reasons, the bronze statue representing Paizinho Preto is kept in the office of Campo Grande regional administration and placed on the pedestal for public view once a year on May 13.
92. "Engenheira em Campo Grande, a autora de 'Zé do Pato', a melhor peça do Festival," 1958: 13.
93. Teixeira, 1960: 4.
94. "Apêlo das mulheres: estátua à Redentora," 1959: 3.
95. "Viação: Monumento à Princesa Isabel," 1960: 4. There are no scholarly works about this monument, but the architect Vera Dias wrote an informative blog entry showing pictures of this monument: see Vera Dias, "Princesa Isabel, por duas vezes monumento," 2010.
96. Teixeira, 1960: 4.
97. "Monumento à princesa," 1960: 9.
98. "Remodelação total do Rio em 20 dias," 1960: 22.
99. With the proclamation of the Brazilian Republic in 1889, the city of Rio de Janeiro continued to be the capital of Brazil and became a federal district, whereas the region surrounding the city became the state of Rio de Janeiro, with Niterói as its capital. On April 21, 1960, when the federal district moved to the newly built capital Brasília, the city of Rio de Janeiro became the state of Guanabara from 1960 to 1975. "Construção da 2ª. etapa da adutora do Guandu e melhoramentos de Copacabana," 1960: 1; "Auxiliares de Sette fizeram fila para lhe dar bandeja de adeus," 1960: 7.
100. "Ao pé do monumento à redentora . . .," 1960: 9.
101. Fritsch, 1961: 53.
102. "Monumento à Isabel vai cair," 1965: 12.
103. "Monumento à Isabel vai cair," 1965: 12.
104. Created by the journalist Samuel Wainer (1910–1980) in 1951, the newspaper *Última hora* supported Getúlio Vargas and therefore became the target of his enemy Carlos Lacerda (UDN).
105. "No listão do destêrro," 1965: 3. On Lacerda's "favela razings," see Fischer, 2008: 60; 76; 79–80.
106. The criticism appears in a letter by Hamilton Monteiro de Freitas, published in "Cartas dos leitores," 1965: 6.
107. "Cabido entrega amanhã com ata despojos dos Príncipes sob as bênçãos do Cardeal," 1971: 4; "Trasladação da Princesa começa hoje," 1971: 1; "Restos mortais da Princesa e Conde deixam a Catedral," 1971: 34.
108. Based on conversations with old guards of the Museu do Negro, Marcus Wood wrongly assumed that the remains of Isabel and Conde d'Eu were exposed during two weeks in a room of Museu do Negro. Indeed, the remains were exposed for only three days in the Church of Saint Benedict and Our Lady of the Rosary of Black Men, an event that was widely covered by the local newspapers, which the author certainly did not consult. See Wood, 2011: 126–127; Wood, 2013: 451.
109. "Gente humilde vê o ataúde da Princesa Isabel e faz questão de deixar seu nome," 1971: 19.
110. "Rio dá adeus com lenços e sinos,"1971: 7.
111. "Rio dá adeus com lenços e sinos," 1971: 7.
112. "Rio dá adeus com lenços e sinos," 1971: 7.

113. "Lenços deram adeus do Rio a D. Isabel," 1971: 1.
114. "Lenços deram adeus do Rio a D. Isabel," 1971: 7.
115. The book is a bilingual edition in Portuguese and French. See Ribeyrolles and Frond, 1859. The original photograph shows four enslaved women and one enslaved baby.
116. Assunção, 2002: 3.
117. Araujo and Saillant, 2007: 463; Mattos and Rios, 2005: 290.
118. Assunção, 2002: 3.
119. Downey, 1998: 131.
120. Among the scholarly works that revised the image of Isabel as the great emancipator, see Barman, 2002: Daibert, 2004; Daibert, 2006; Daibert, 2010: 93–124; Mesquita, 2009.

6 Iconic Rebels

After the 1960s, the old representations of Great Emancipators and enslaved men and women as passive victims who submissively accepted their status were gradually replaced by a new image of slaves as freedom fighters. This new trend, I argue, follows a transformation that is much like the various manifestations visible in the public memory of the Holocaust, which, since the end of the Second World War, started featuring a growing number of monuments paying homage to men and women who organized resistance movements in the ghettos and Nazi camps. Moreover, the emergence of slave rebels in public memory is associated with three changes that occurred during the second half of the twentieth century: first, the transnational movements for civil rights led by populations of African descent in Europe, Africa, and the Americas; second, the independence and creation of new nations, especially in the Caribbean, whose new national identities were closely connected to the image of freedom fighters; third, the growing number of scholarly studies focusing on slave resistance and agency. To underscore the elements that led to the growing visibility of slave rebels, this chapter explores public representations of loyal and submissive slaves, both in Brazil and the United States, by paying particular attention to the representations of Nanny, Uncle Tom, *Pai* João, and Slave Isaura, who despite their subservient attitudes were not totally submissive to the slave system. Further, I show how the images of these enslaved men and women were gradually replaced by the images of slave and freed black fighters. Especially starting in the 1960s, several monuments and activities commemorating slave rebels or maroons were developed in different countries of Latin America and the Caribbean, including Haiti, Mexico, Jamaica, Guyana, Colombia, Cuba, and Venezuela. I argue that these initiatives associated resistance against slavery with the fight against European colonialism and US imperialism. Finally, I examine the memorialization of Zumbi, by showing how today he is represented as a national hero in Brazil.

SUBMISSIVE AND LOYAL SLAVES

Until the middle of the twentieth century, public representations of enslaved men and women in the United States and Brazil greatly emphasized submission and victimhood. In the popular novels *Uncle Tom's Cabin* by Harriet Beecher Stowe and *Gone with the Wind* by Margaret Mitchell and their various adaptations to the cinema, slaves are depicted as cheerful, loyal, and submissive.[1] These images of enslaved men and women became popular in Brazil not only through the Portuguese translations of the US novels but also because of their numerous theatrical, cinematic, and television adaptations.

As early as 1853, the novel *Uncle Tom's Cabin* was translated into Portuguese and published in Brazil as *A cabana do pai Thomaz*.[2] Although promoting the image of the faithful slave represented by Uncle Tom, the novel also inspired Brazilian abolitionists like Joaquim Nabuco, who read it "thousands of times."[3] However, during the 1870s, when the abolitionist movement acquired more visibility in the various major Brazilian cities, the novel became more popular among Brazilian literate elites who were sympathetic to the abolitionist cause. In 1872, an article published in São Paulo's newspaper *Correio paulistano*, Harriet Beecher Stowe's novel is highly praised. The anonymous author of the article states that the novel "has some scenes of horror and cruelty. But when there are evil men who practice them, there must be others to reveal them, to revolt, to rise up against them."[4] In addition, the author, who considered the novel the best he has read, recommends all Brazilian men and especially women read it.

In July 1876, following the popularity of the novel, the play *A cabana do pai Thomaz* was performed 12 times in Rio de Janeiro's São Pedro de Alcantara Theater, whose company was led by Guilherme da Silveira.[5] The play was based on *La case de l'oncle Tom: Drame en huit actes*, the French theatrical adaptation of the US novel.[6] The newspaper's article explains that the play not only successfully conveyed the suffering of enslaved individuals but would also spark revolt among Brazilians:

> In a country like ours, where the human body is subjected to the whip, where the slave is freely traded, where it is well possible that several hundreds of individuals die by excess of punishment annually, no other drama than *A cabana do pai Thomaz* is better to move men of good will to revolt, in whose hearts pulses Calvary's sane doctrine against this institution which will be always the black part of the memory of our grandparents.[7]

The article also points out that, although the story is set in the South of the United States, the main elements of the drama could easily take place in Brazil. However, the author remains silent about the cast, which was composed of only white actors, including Antonina Marquelou and Guilherme da Silveira, who played the roles of the enslaved woman Eliza Harris and her son Harry Harris. Regardless of the warm reception in Rio de Janeiro, the play featuring the victimization of enslaved men and women was perceived as a threat to the slave system. Although scheduled to have its premiere in São Paulo on December 15, 1877, the police banned the company's performance with the justification that the "topic of the play hurt slavery, a legal institution."[8] Yet over the years that followed, with the growing importance of the Brazilian abolitionist movement, the play continued to be performed in Rio de Janeiro and eventually in São Paulo as well, promoting abolitionist ideas but at the same time consolidating the subservient image of Uncle Tom in both the United States and Brazil.

After the abolition of slavery in Brazil, *A cabana do pai Thomaz* remained popular and was staged on various occasions, especially during the commemoration activities of the abolition of slavery on May 13. In 1909, the novel eventually received its first Brazilian silent movie adaptation by Antônio Serra, but, as in other theatrical and movie productions of the time, the cast was entirely white. In June 1928, the film adaptation of *Uncle Tom's Cabin*, directed by Harry A. Pollard and released in the United States in 1927, premiered in Brazil. The film was very well received and, according to a newspaper, was "one of the biggest season's success of the year and also one of the safer bet for the box office."[9] Notwithstanding its use to denounce the institution of slavery by conveying the image of submissive slaves, the success of the novel and its adaptations in film and theater in Brazil neither opposed the long-standing presence of slavery in the country nor rejected the traditional representations of slaves as passive victims. In other words, even though slavery was now abolished, the repeated depictions of submissive slaves only reinforced the maintenance of the old slavocratic mentality.

Other US novels and films portraying slavery became very popular in Brazil as well. In 1940, four years after its publication in English, the novel *Gone with the Wind* by Margaret Mitchell was translated into Portuguese as *E o vento levou* and was well received in Brazil.[10] In an article published in the newspaper *Gazeta de notícias*, the poetess and writer Haydée Nicolussi (1905–1970) praises the book:

> However, I do not mean that Margaret Mitchell's book is good because it depicts some dozens of slaves exceptionally happy during the time of slavery, and that the American industrialism, progressing with the victory of the emancipators, to some extent asphyxiated the country's aristocratic life before the Secession War, because the truth is that the problem of race continues to this day and is only now that the US policy is trying to willingly and harmonically solve this question.[11]

By comparing the novel and the film, Nicolussi regrets that the character of the enslaved woman Dilcey, "the mother of the little black girl Prissy," does not appear in the movie. Furthermore, she also explains that the "black nanny" is wonderful not only in the screen but also in the novel: she has "attitudes and words that make the work remarkable, providing a psychological idea of an era and a caste."[12] Thus, both in the book and in the movie, Mammy successfully embodied the role of the loyal enslaved woman who was ready to spend her whole life, even during the most difficult times, with the family who owned her.

The movie adaptation of *Gone with the Wind* premiered in a gala session held on September 12, 1940 in the Metro Theater, Rio de Janeiro.[13] Sponsored by the US embassy, the film's premiere was an official event, gathering important authorities, members of the local elite, as well as US diplomatic guests. Hosted by the First Lady Darcy Vargas, the revenue of the opening night was to be used to construct the Cidade das Meninas (City of Girls), a charity initiative led by her, intended to house and educate 6,000 poor orphaned young girls.[14] On that occasion, Rio de Janeiro's press published the first lady's compliments to the United States: "I don't have words to translate my gratitude to the ambassador of the United States, for his gesture, so spontaneous, sympathetic, and generous. This attitude did not surprise me. By knowing the United States, I know how this great friendly people cultivates the sentiment of gallantry and human solidarity."[15] Additionally, a message from film stars Clark Gable and Vivien Leigh, greeting the first lady, preceded the première movie screening. Like the commemoration activities honoring Princess Isabel, this event contributed to promote Vargas's government. It also helped to improve relations between Brazil and the United States, inasmuch as, during the first stages of the Second World War, the Vargas regime still showed some sympathy toward the Nazi and fascist regimes of Germany and Italy.

The various Rio de Janeiro's newspapers commented on the success of the movie's opening night, and during the following weeks, crowds continued to fill the theater. As in Rio de Janeiro, the São Paulo's avant-première of *E o vento levou*, held on September 19, 1940, was also a great event. Hosted by the state's First Lady Leonor Mendes de Barros (1905–1992), the wife of the *interventor* Adhemar de Barros (1901–1969), the revenue of the opening night was dedicated to a charity initiative, the Casa Maternal e da Infância (Nursery and Childhood House).[16] Although it is hard to determine the impact of *E o vento levou* among Brazilian high- and middle-class audiences, who could afford to attend theaters, numerous cinemas around the country continued to screen the movie during the rest of the decade, suggesting its very positive reception.

Brazilian literature and cinema also disseminated representations of the obedient and loyal slave. One of the most popular slave characters in nineteenth-century Brazilian literature was the Slave Isaura, the submissive heroine of the abolitionist novel *A escrava Isaura* by Bernardo Guimarães.[17] The novel is set on a coffee plantation on the banks of the Paraíba River, in the northern area of the then province of Rio de Janeiro, during the second half of the nineteenth century. Isaura, an enslaved woman servant who lived in the big house was the daughter of an enslaved mulatto woman and a benevolent Portuguese overseer, who despite several attempts was not able to buy his daughter's freedom. In the novel, Isaura is described as a beautiful young woman who had such a lovely color that nobody would be able to say that there was African blood in her veins.[18] Unlike other slaves who lived in Brazil during the nineteenth century, especially in the rural areas, she learned how to read and write. Whereas Isaura's mistress protected her, her privileges made the other enslaved women jealous. Still, after the decease of her mistress, her mistress's son, who sexually harassed her, inherited Isaura. Because she refused her master's sexual advances and was constantly victimized by him, she eventually ran away from the plantation and settled in another province, with the help of her father. After taking another name, Isaura attempted to rebuild her life as a free woman. Because of her beauty and elegant manners, she gained the protection of a white elite man who fell in love with her. However, her true identity was soon discovered. With resignation, she accepted her return to captivity. Regardless of these hardships and her unsuccessful escape, Isaura remained loyal to her master and mistress until the end of the novel, when her white lover eventually took over her master's plantation and freed all the slaves, including her.

During the 1960s and the 1970s, the novels *Uncle Tom's Cabin* and *A escrava Isaura* were also adapted as *telenovelas*. In *A cabana do pai Tomás,* although several black actors and actresses were available to play the leads, the main character Uncle Tom was played by the Brazilian actor Sérgio Cardoso who used blackface to become "black." In 1976, *A escrava Isaura* was adapted as a *telenovela* produced by Globo television network. One year before the broadcasting of the North American television series *Roots*, based on the homonymous novel by Alex Haley, *A escrava Isaura* was Brazil's first own television production focusing on slavery. The *telenovela* had a great impact on the construction of the public memory of slavery in Brazil, greatly emphasizing Isaura's victimization. However, unlike the United States miniseries that featured Kunta Kinte's enslaved African character on national television, Brazil's most important television network was not willing to spotlight an Afro-Brazilian actress playing the role of an enslaved woman. The actress chosen to play the role of Isaura was Lucélia Santos, a white actress whose physical features were clearly distinct from the other black slave characters featured in the *telenovela*. By presenting the enslaved heroine as a white woman, Globo television network not only refused to give a central role to an Afro-Brazilian actress but also led the audience to mistakenly assume that there were enslaved whites in Brazil. Moreover, the contrast between Isaura and the other slave characters was not only due to physical features. In the *telenovela*, whereas the other black slave characters were represented as rude, malicious, and stupid, Isaura was represented as a docile, enduring, and righteous slave, characteristics that helped the audience to sympathize with her. Yet Isaura's submissive nature did not prevent her from running away with her father to escape the sexual harassment and physical punishment inflicted by her master.

Over the following decades, *A escrava Isaura* aired several times in Brazil and was also broadcast in another 80 countries. In 2004, Record Television Network produced a second version of the *telenovela*, once again with a white actress, Bianca Rinaldi, in the protagonist's role. In both versions, the opening credits consisted of an animation conceived with Jean-Baptiste Debret's lithographs portraying urban slavery in nineteenth-century Rio de Janeiro.[19] By watching *A escrava Isaura*, national and international audiences became familiar with Debret's images of slavery, especially the ones depicting physical punishments, reinforcing the representations of victimization conveyed in the *telenovela*.[20]

In Brazil, the male representation of the submissive slave is embodied in the figure of *Pai* João (Father João). Portrayed in Brazilian popular culture as the peaceful, submissive, and victimized enslaved man, *Pai* João can also be associated with the spirit of *preto velho* (old black man) in Afro-Brazilian religions, such as Candomblé and Umbanda.[21] Yet by examining several songs and stories featuring *Pai* João, Brazilian historian Martha Abreu shows he was rather an ambiguous figure. Despite being at times naïve, lazy, and dull, as previous scholars have claimed, he could also be astute and smart.[22] Abreu's interpretation of *Pai* João as a dubious figure sheds light on the understanding of other docile slave characters. Although the representations of faithful slaves such as Mammy and Uncle Tom were disseminated in Brazil through US novels and films, a closer examination of Brazilian docile slave characters like Isaura and *Pai* João shows that they were not completely obedient, but what made them submissive was how they were appropriated in the public sphere.

HEROES AND FIGHTERS

Notwithstanding the continuous dissemination of representations of passive and obedient slaves, over time these images were contested in the international arena. Indeed, since the end of the 1940s, the emphasis on fighters and heroes was already embedded in the various initiatives commemorating the memory of the Holocaust, whose monuments and memorials promoted the heroic actions of men and women who were engaged in resisting the Nazi regime in the ghettos and concentration camps. In addition, in the early 1950s, black intellectuals like Aimé Césaire clearly associated Nazism and European colonialism in his *Discours sur le colonialisme*. Also, in his seminal book *Peau noir, masques blancs*, Franz Fanon extensively compared the derogatory images of blacks and Jews.[23] These associations paved the path for the development of later connections between the image of Jewish and black fighters. Starting in the 1960s, the image of slave rebels as heroes increasingly gained popularity, especially in Latin America and the Caribbean. This focus on black resistance was closely related to the complex context that emerged with the rise of the Cold War. Black and white internationalist activists and intellectuals engaged themselves in anti-imperialist and anticolonial actions in various parts of the so-called Third World, including Africa, Latin America, and the Caribbean. At the international level, the response to the anticolonial struggles was the containment of Communism and anticolonial movements, whereas in the United States the reaction was the repression of Civil Rights and Black Power movements. As a result, the monuments commemorating Jewish and slave resistance are not isolated initiatives. Conveying similar representations of fighters rising up, bearing arms, and breaking chains, they are consonant with the struggles that reverberated in various areas of the public sphere, including diplomacy and mass cultural industry.

Even during the Second World War, Jewish resistance against the Nazi regime, especially in Poland, was officially recognized in the public sphere. In 1944, the Central Committee of Polish Jews in Lublin decided to build a monument to pay tribute to the Jewish fighters who organized the Warsaw Ghetto uprising. On April 19, 1946, the first step for the monument's construction was made with the addition of a circle stone plaque paying homage to "those who died in an exceptionally heroic struggle for dignity and freedom of the Jewish people, a free Poland, for the liberation of men: Polish Jews."[24] In 1948, the Monument to the Ghetto Heroes was unveiled in Warsaw, near the circle plaque, where the Judenrat headquarters were located and close to the place where the first armed confrontation with the Nazis occurred. The monument, conceived by the Jewish sculptor Natan Rapoport (1911–1987), was placed on a large granite base originally planned by survivor and architect Mark Leon Suzin (Figure 6.1). Consisting of a granite wall, the monument has two sides. The western side of the monument features a massive bronze sculpture representing Jewish fighters, whereas the eastern part shows a long line of men, women, and children marching in distress, evoking the iconic image of the Jewish diaspora. Combining the two crucial themes of exile and resistance, as James E. Young points out, Rapoport's monument "was the first memorial after the war to mark both the heroism of Jewish resistance to the Nazis and the complete annihilation of the Jews in Warsaw."[25] Although it received criticism because of its social realist features, the monument became an important site of memory of the Holocaust. The image of the Monument to the Ghetto Heroes was largely disseminated in

186 *Shadows of the Slave Past*

Figure 6.1 Monument to the Ghetto Heroes, Warsaw, Poland (2013. © User: Bosyantek/Wikimedia Commons/CC-BY-SA-3.0).

postcards and stamps.²⁶ Moreover, during the last decades, distinguished visitors and tourists paid homage to the ghetto heroes by visiting the monument. As mentioned in Chapter 2, W. E. B. Du Bois is probably the first African American to have visited the monument during a trip to Poland in September 1949. Du Bois narrated this visit to the Warsaw Ghetto and his impressions about the Monument to the Ghetto Heroes in a talk held at the headquarters of the Communist journal *Jewish Life* on April 15, 1952, published in the journal the next month.²⁷ As Rothberg argues, Du Bois was particularly intrigued by the monument because its form evoked some kind of double consciousness, combining the representation of Jewish motifs with a Socialist realist treatment, offering "a stark opposition between the heroism and suffering of the Jews."[28] Du Bois' account shows that the monument was effective in making the connection between the past and the present because according to him it "brought back again the problem of race and religion [. . .]. Gradually [. . .] I rebuilt the story of this extraordinary resistance to oppression."[29] In a time of ongoing racial segregation in the United States, when there were no monuments paying homage to slave rebels in the Americas, the Monument to the Ghetto Heroes led Du Bois to replace the iconic representation of victims with the image of the fighters.

Over the decades that followed, the Monument to the Ghetto Heroes continued to attract international attention. In 1970, Willy Brandt, leader of the Social Democratic Party of Germany and chancellor of the then Federal Republic of Germany, kneeled at the foot of the monument, a gesture that resulted in one of the most iconic images of repentance for the Holocaust. In 1977, US President Jimmy Carter also visited the monument, and in June 1983, Pope John Paul II kneeled at the monument as well. In 2011, President Barack Obama traveled to Poland and visited the Monument to the Ghetto Heroes. During his visit, he left a wreath at the monument's foot and met with Jewish leaders and Holocaust survivors. On this occasion, Obama did not make a public speech. Yet he conjured Warsaw's visit during a speech delivered at the United States Holocaust Memorial Museum on April 23, 2012. First, the US president referred to his visit to Buchenwald, repeating Elie Wiesel's words: "memory has become a sacred duty of all people of goodwill." In addition, the president also mentioned his visit to the Monument to the Ghetto Heroes: "I've stood with survivors, in the old Warsaw ghettos, where a monument honors the heroes who said 'we will not go quietly; we will stand up, we will fight back.'"[30] Apart from frequently mentioning his visits to international Holocaust sites like Buchenwald and the Warsaw Ghetto and his excursion to West African slave trade sites such as the Cape Coast Castle after taking office, Obama neither referred to US slavery in his public speeches nor visited any US slavery site. Apparently, it is much easier to acknowledge the atrocities committed by other nations in other places, whereas addressing the crimes against humanity committed at the domestic level is a much more complicated task, to be avoided especially in the year of presidential elections. Indeed, as discussed in Chapter 4, when the bust paying homage to Sojourner Truth was inaugurated in the US Capitol's Emancipation Hall, it was the First Lady Michelle Obama who gave public remarks. On that occasion, the first lady referred again to her slave ancestry and described Truth not only as a victim of slavery but as a woman who fought for freedom and civil rights. According to the first lady, therefore, the visitors to the US Capitol would be exposed to "the story of brave women who endured the greatest of humanity's indignities. They'll hear the story of Sojourner Truth who didn't allow those indignities to destroy her spirit, who fought for her own freedom, and then used her powers [. . .] to help others; who fought for the right to vote and for the rights of all women."[31] Yet, as explained in Chapter 4, despite the importance of placing for the first time the statue of an African American woman in the US Capitol's Emancipation Hall, unlike Michelle Obama's prediction, Sojourner Truth's bust is not highlighted during the tours, and most visitors do not even notice that it is there.

During the 1950s, other important monuments paying homage to the prisoners of concentration camps who bravely resisted the Nazis were created as well. In 1958, after the demolition of most of the buildings at Buchenwald, a large memorial with a permanent museum exhibition was unveiled at the site of the former concentration camp, near Weimar, situated in then East Germany. The vast area that composes the memorial includes a large monument commemorating the resistance against the Nazi regime, conceived by the sculptor Fritz Cremer (1906–1993). As in the Monument to the Ghetto Heroes in Warsaw, the monument *Revolt of the Prisoners* follows a typical socialist aesthetic, underscoring triumphant resistance rather than victimhood. It features a group of 11 bronze male figures, adults and children. Whereas the victims who perished in the camp are represented in small-scale stones spread along the camp, the monument symbolizes the resistance against the Nazi regime, portraying the various large-scale standing figures, raising their hands and holding weapons, as heroic fighters.[32] Like many other public initiatives of the same kind associated with Soviet aesthetics, this monument does not highlight individual heroes but rather groups of nameless individuals. Although celebrating heroes and fighters, the monuments and memorials commemorating maroons in the Americas mainly focus on individual characters, most of them male.

MAROONS AND SLAVE FIGHTERS

Starting in the 1960s and earlier, before the launching of UNESCO's Slave Route Project, the commemoration of men and women who led slave rebellions and formed runaway slave communities became visible in public monuments in Latin America and the Caribbean. As Catherine Reinhardt suggests, especially in the Caribbean, the maroon was transformed into a hero, symbolizing the ancestors' resistance to slavery.[33] At the summit of the Cold War and during the process of decolonization and anti-imperialist struggles, these monuments were consonant with the emerging production of historians, some of them Marxist, focusing on slave resistance.[34] Moreover, the growing number of public representations of slave rebels was connected to the actions and achievements of the US Civil Rights Movement and to the movements of self-assertion of populations of African descent in

Europe, Africa, and the rest of the Americas. Like the figures represented in the monuments honoring the heroes of the ghettos and Nazi camps, maroons and slave fighters are depicted in triumphant attitudes, with hands raised, holding weapons, and breaking chains.

Elected president of Haiti in 1957, François Duvalier (1907–1971), alias Papa Doc, commissioned a public monument commemorating slave fighters. The statue, originally conceived by the Haitian artist Albert Mangonès (1917–2002) in 1945, was unveiled in 1967, when Duvalier was ruling the country as President for Life. The sculpture *Le Marron inconnu* (before Unknown Maroon) was placed in front of the National Palace in the Place au Marron Inconnu (Unknown Maroon's Square) in Haiti's capital, Port-au-Prince. The statue symbolizes resistance against slavery by depicting the maroon with his left leg extended with a broken chain attached. With his left hand, he blows a conch shell that was used as a trumpet to call out other slaves, and with his right hand he holds a machete.

According to Duvalier, the statue *Le marron inconnu* "is the highest expression of the heroism of our Race and we must perpetuate his imperishable glory in bronze and stone." The day of the monument's unveiling ceremony, December 6, 1968, was declared a holiday in all schools and universities.[35] The ceremony included presentations by two choirs and speeches by various national authorities, including the monument's creator, Albert Mangonès. In his speech, the sculptor explained that when the president commissioned the work, he wanted it "to erect in the heart of the city, a center of national piety to the memory of the unknown, who was the First, in the territory, who was able too chose 'the total risk of Freedom.'"[36] Ironically, Mangonès presented to the Haitians a monument celebrating freedom commissioned by a dictator who took civil liberties from the people and who tortured and killed thousands of his opponents. In his own speech, however, Duvalier explains that when the statesman decides to create a monument commemorating an event of the past:

> he wants to exalt the national sentiment, offering to the future generations the example of those who seeded in the native land, their moral courage, their political genius, their superhuman abnegations and often their blood. Finally, he wants to make a pious tribute to those who overcame their ordinary human condition, who stood up to the epic, to give birth and develop a Nation in its full sovereignty, independence, and pride. That is why We, Negroes of Haiti, We are for the black African masses of the universe the highest exponent or a kind of common denominator of all national and racial consciousness.[37]

In a period of bloody dictatorship, the statue celebrating freedom and underscoring the rebellious spirit of a country that was born from a slave rebellion contributed to promote Duvalier's broader Black Nationalist political project.[38] By unveiling a statue intended to commemorate the unknown and unnamed maroon, the President for Life successfully perpetuated his own memory.

190 *Shadows of the Slave Past*

During the 1970s, other monuments commemorating maroons were dedicated in Caribbean and Latin American countries. In 1976, a bronze statue in honor of the maroon Gaspar Yanga (Figure 6.2) was unveiled by the municipality of Yanga (state of Veracruz, Mexico). The city of Yanga has

Figure 6.2 Gaspar Yanga, Yanga, Mexico (2008. Photograph © Erasmo Vazquez Lendechy/CC-BY-SA-3.0).

about 16,000 inhabitants and is not far from Veracruz, one of the largest slave ports in colonial Mexico. Even though the African presence in Mexico has been rarely acknowledged in public initiatives, the Afro-Mexican population of the state of Veracruz is visible and even today preserves elements of African cultural traditions.

In 1609, Yanga escaped from slavery and, along with other maroons, formed a *palenque* in a mountain close to the banks of Rio Blanco in Veracruz. In 1631, after years of armed conflict with the Spaniards, the maroons obtained freedom and were granted land to establish an independent territory.[39] Yanga is acknowledged as the founder of San Lorenzo de los Negros (renamed Yanga in 1932), the first settlement of freedmen and freedwomen in the Americas.[40] Over time, Yanga was perceived not only as a maroon who fought against slavery but also as a freedom fighter, a hero who organized resistance against the Spanish colonizers.[41]

In the statue, Yanga is represented wearing short pants, bare chested, and barefoot. Depicted as a strong African man, his posture is that of a fighter, his muscles are well defined, and his legs are separated. He is holding a wooden machete with his right hand and a long stick with his right hand, and a broken shackle and chain dangle from his right wrist. Like the monument *Le marron inconnu* in Haiti and the statues that were later installed in Baillif, Gorée, and Drancy, the motif of the broken chains appears again to evoke freedom. The plaque at the basis of the monument describes Yanga "as a black African, precursor of black slaves' freedom." Although Yanga's monument marked the emergence of Afro-Mexican assertion in Veracruz, the reception of the statue among the local population revealed the ambiguities of how Afro-Mexicans conceive the representation of black heroes. Some social actors criticized the fact that, unlike official Mexican male heroes who are always represented as "illustrious, serious, and well-dressed men," Yanga is dressed in tatters and barefoot.[42] Still, Yanga's image, as conveyed in the statue and probably endorsed by the community leaders at the time of the monument's creation, is similar to older official representations, like the mural *Canto a los heroes* (Chant to the Heroes) of 1952. Painted by the muralist painter José Gordillo, the mural is located in the main stairwell of the building that houses the Museo de la Secretaria de Hacienda y Crédito Publico (Museum of the Ministry of Finance and Public Credit) in Mexico. Like other mural paintings, Gordillo's work celebrates the Mexican nation's opposition to the imperialist powers. At the upper portion of the painting, there is an enormous figure of a worker, surrounded by engines that evoke the power of the United States. In the lower part of the mural are important Mexican national heroes who were officially recognized after the Mexican Revolution of 1910, including Emiliano Zapata and Pancho Villa, the independence leader Miguel Hidalgo, and President Lázaro Cárdenas. Yanga is placed in the left side of the mural painting, behind the writer and nun Sor Juana de la Cruz, and is depicted bare chested in a feminized attitude. Appropriated in the official iconography that emerged during the second phase of the revolution, Yanga is perceived as a liberator who played the role of precursor of Mexico's independence.

The unveiling of Yanga's statue in 1976 was not an isolated event and coincided with the first edition of Yanga's Carnival, a festival organized by the municipality to commemorate the creation of the first black township of the Americas.[43] During the festival held every year, participants use blackface to celebrate the maroons' victory over the Spaniards.[44] More recently, in a process that Odile Hoffman called invention of tradition, the festival was renamed *Carnaval de la negritud* (Negritude Carnival). By establishing connections with Africa and the African diaspora, especially African Americans, the festival is helping to reconstruct and reinforce black and "African" identities in Yanga and the state of Vera Cruz.[45]

Among the most important heroes commemorated in Jamaica's public arena is Sam Sharpe (1801–1832), the enslaved man who led the Christmas Rebellion, or Baptist War. Born in Jamaica, Sharpe was an educated enslaved domestic worker, a position that allowed him to become a lay deacon. In December 1831, Sharpe called a general strike that was soon transformed into the largest slave rebellion in the history of the island, gathering thousands of enslaved individuals who resisted for two months.[46] The rebellion was violently repressed, and at least 530 participants died in battle or were executed by the British.[47] On April 19, 1832, Sharpe was tried, and on May 23, 1832, he was hanged in Charles Square across from the courthouse at Montego Bay. The carnage of hundreds of enslaved individuals that followed the slave rebellion had a great repercussion in Britain and played a crucial role in the abolition of slavery throughout the British Empire and British West Indies.[48]

Following Jamaica's independence in 1962, slave rebels, along with other national heroes, started being honored in the country's public space, as part of a broader project of self-assertion that emerged with the creation of the new nation. In 1964, Marcus Garvey's remains were repatriated from London to Kingston and reinterred in King George VI Park. A few days later, he was declared Jamaica's first national hero. Starting in 1968, the National Heroes Day was observed in the third week of October in Jamaica. The holiday commemorates those who fought for freedom from slavery and colonization. But the commemoration of national heroes became more visible during the two consecutive terms (1972–1980) of Prime Minister Michael Norman Manley (1924–1997) of the progressive People's National Party (PNP).[49] The renewed emphasis on slave fighters was in accordance with Manley's project of democratic socialism that heavily relied on the support of the working class and the redistribution of wealth. During his government, Manley promoted social programs at the domestic level, whereas in international affairs, he developed closer ties with neighboring Cuba and kept a nonaligned position. As part of this context, the King George VI Park in Kingston was renamed National Heroes Park in 1973. Maintained by the federal government, the park is located in a site that for more than a century was used for different purposes and was the stage for the August 1838 festivities celebrating the end of apprenticeship and effective freedom for former slaves in British West Indies. In the years that followed the change of name, several monuments commemorating Jamaican national heroes were added to the site.

In 1976, Charles Square, the very site where Sam Sharpe was hanged in Montego Bay, was renamed to pay tribute to him. In the same year, because of the escalating violence between Manley's supporters and his opponents of the conservative Jamaica Labour Party (JLP), a state of emergency was declared in the country, which continued until December, when the elections were held and Manley reelected. Yet, although in the 1980 elections Manley was defeated by his JLP opponent Edward Seaga (1930–), the celebration of black national heroes was not interrupted. Appropriated by the new regime, which collaborated extensively with the United States, it gained even more importance. On March 31, 1982, Sharpe received Jamaica's Order of National Hero, and a monument honoring him was unveiled in National Heroes Park. Nevertheless, by that time, Jamaican authorities were concerned about how well Sharpe was known to a contemporary public and about his actual role in the rebellion because of a lack of scholarly studies on the rebellion.[50] The plaque accompanying the bust underscores his heroic role with a statement attributed to him: "I'd rather die on yonder gallows than live in slavery." Sharpe's nomination as national hero and the addition of his bust to National Heroes Park certainly contributed to disseminate the history of the rebellion and awareness of one of its leaders.

On October 16, 1983, a monument with five bronze statues paying homage to Sharpe was placed in Sharpe Square in Montego Bay. Unlike the bust displayed in National Heroes Park, in this monument Sharpe's leading role is emphasized. He is depicted with one hand raised, preaching to an audience composed of a black woman and a boy, as well as two bare chested men, possibly enslaved. The monument was conceived by Jamaican sculptor Kay Sullivan, whose sculptures are displayed in various public venues around the country and were given as gifts to presidents of several foreign nations, including Nelson Mandela, Bill Clinton, Carlos Menem, and Fidel Castro. But the bronze statues are not displayed alone in the square. The site also includes two slavery heritage structures constructed in the early nineteenth century: the Cage, used as a prison for enslaved Africans, seamen, and vagrants, and the Court House, where trials of enslaved men and women were held, including Sharpe's trial. Today, the old building of the Court House became the Civic Centre, a facility containing a museum, art gallery, and conference rooms. Moreover, on August 1, 2007 (Emancipation Day), as part of the commemoration activities of the bicentennial of the British abolition of the slave trade, a pyramidal structure named Freedom Monument was unveiled in the square. Thus Sharpe Square, the original site where hundreds of enslaved men were killed following the Baptist War, became an important landmark memorializing slavery that is visited by locals and international tourists.

As in Jamaica, similar initiatives honoring slave rebels were developed in Guyana. On May 23, 1976, coinciding with the tenth anniversary of Guyana's independence, a monument to commemorate the 1763 Berbice Uprising, a slave rebellion against the then Dutch colonizers, was dedicated in Georgetown, the country's capital.[51] Commissioned by the federal government, the monument was created by the Guyanese sculptor Philip Moore (1921–2012), and the plinth was designed by Albert Rodrigues. The 15-foot bronze statue of a monumental male figure lies on a high cylindrical concrete pedestal. The male figure was immediately associated with Cuffy (or Coffij), the leader of the 1763 uprising, organized by African-born and creole enslaved individuals of Amina, or Akan, origin. The figure's gigantesque body, whose legs and arms indicate movement, is covered with bas-reliefs depicting geometric patterns and faces. Moreover, with either hand, the figure is choking a pig, signifying ignorance, and a dog, symbolizing covetousness, lust, and greed. The voluminous head, with a circular-shaped opened mouth, a large nose, and prominent eyes, can be associated with West African *bocio* sculptures. As Suzanne Preston Blier notes, the "prominence given to the head within these sculptures both in terms of surface elaboration and with respect to proportional size underscores its centrality in body perception, specifically notions of success, power, and individuation."[52] How the public received the monument also seems to confirm this association because, since its unveiling, rumors started that the faces of Prime Minister and later President Linden Forbes Sampson Burham (1923–1985) were carved on the back of Cuffy's head, conferring the monument special powers.[53] During the official ceremony that inaugurated the statue in 1976, Burham explained that the 1763 uprising "was not a rebellion; it was the beginning of a revolution which ultimately terminated so far as political independence is concerned on the 26th of May 1966, in our time and age."[54] Combining the representation of a slave fighter with the Guyanese people's struggle for liberation from colonial rule, the monument helped to reinforce Burnham's political agenda by crystalizing in the public space a connection between slavery and European colonial rule in West Indies and his role as the country's liberator. At the same time, by evoking a West African aesthetic, the sculpture also contributed to promote a political dialogue with African nations, an aspect also emphasized in Burnham's speech when he associated the Dutch colonizers against whom Berbice's slaves revolted with the whites who oppressed the population of color in South Africa.⁵⁵ Cuffy's image, which had already illustrated a commemorative $1 coin released in 1970, became even more popular after the sculpture's unveiling and today is displayed in colorful postcards sold to tourists. As 2013 marked the 250th anniversary of the rebellion, numerous commemorative activities were held in Guyana, including lecture series, exhibitions, a musical production titled *Berbice Uprising 1763–2013*, and the release of another coin. The new coin portrays a naked enslaved man in profile, raising one hand with a broken chain dangling from his wrist. In the background, the sun, representing freedom, is shining. According to the coin's official description released by the Bank of Guyana, the image "depicts a slave who is rescued from his owner by Cuffy and other liberation fighters. This revolt was the prelude to the freedom from bondage and extreme cruelties that was subsequently won, and is symbolized by the broken shackles."⁵⁶

In March 1985, a monument similar to the one representing Cuffy was dedicated in Bridgetown, the capital of Barbados. Created by Guaynese-Barbadian sculptor Karl Broodhagen (1909–2002), the *Emancipation Monument* pays homage to Bussa, an allegedly African-born enslaved man who is said to have led the 1816 Rebellion in Barbados.⁵⁷ The statue, commemorating the 150th anniversary of the abolition of slavery in the British Caribbean, is based on a previous small-scale bronze sculpture named *Slave in Revolt*, conceived by Broodhagen in 1973. Like Yanga's statue, the monument imparts a similar representation of a slave fighter. Almost naked, he is shown with his legs separated, raising his arms, from which the broken shackles and chains are hanging. Even before the monument was made public, the figure depicted was identified as being Bussa, the leader of the 1816 slave revolt.⁵⁸ Starting in 1997, the recognition of the figure represented in the statue as being Bussa gained force when the monument became one of the main sites of the commemoration activities of Emancipation Day in Barbados. Eventually, in 1998, Bussa was added to the official list of national heroes of Barbados.⁵⁹ Regardless of the controversies about Bussa's actual role in the rebellion, the *Emancipation Monument* can be seen as a form of symbolical reparation to those who lived in enslavement and their descendants in Barbados. It became an efficient way to reconnect the country's black population with Africa.⁶⁰ Moreover, as in other monuments commemorating slave fighters in the Americas, for the first time resistance against slavery was brought to light in the country.

During the 1990s, Colombia started honoring its slave fighters as well. The initiative, which was similar to that of the Jamaica's National Heroes Park program, was developed in Cartagena. A coastal city in the Bolívar Department, Cartagena was one of the largest slave ports of the Spanish Americas during the period of the Atlantic slave trade. The city, listed in the UNESCO World Heritage List since 1984, is the first tourist destination in Colombia, welcoming about 200,000 tourists every year. On September 18, 1994, the Parque Apolo (Apolo Park) was expanded, and a memorial was unveiled in the site. The project, led by the Fundación Casa Museo de El Cabrero (Foundation House Museum of El Cabrero) commemorates the 100th anniversary of Colombian President Rafael Nuñez (1825–1894), who was born in the city and lived in the house museum established in the same location. The memorial consists of a circular structure with Greco-Roman columns where three sets of three bronze busts are displayed on marble pedestals. Among the national heroes honored is the legendary character Domingos Bioho (also known as Benkos Bioho, Dionísio Biohó, Rey Benkos, Rey de la Matuna, and Biohó Rey), whose bust is exhibited along with eight other national heroes, including Cacique Carex, a sixteenth-century native chief, and the Spanish governor of Cartagena, Pedro Zapata de Mendoza. Despite the scarcity of historical evidence about Bioho, he is described as an African-born enslaved man who escaped slavery with his family in 1599 and who, during the early seventeenth century, allegedly created the *palenque* San Basilio.[61] After several years of fighting the Spanish, the maroons negotiated the *palenque*'s autonomy, which lasted between 1605 and 1619, when eventually Bioho was captured. In 1621, Bioho was hanged and quartered. In popular memory, he became the legendary founder of San Basilio and over the years was transformed into a black hero.

The large Bioho bust displayed in Parque Apolo depicts a man of African descent described as a "black leader, [who] defended his freedom until losing his life."[62] The insertion of Bioho among other white and native national heroes in Parque Apolo shows a shift in Colombia's official public memory that now also acknowledges the role of black and native historical actors in constructing the new nation. Notwithstanding this new recognition, the memorial rather promotes a narrative that emphasizes the harmonious relations among black, whites, and natives, placing side by side the bust of an enslaved man and the bust of the governor of Cartagena in the middle of the seventeenth century, when the province became the largest port of entry for enslaved Africans. Although the bust's plaque mentions freedom, it does not make any reference to slavery or specify that Bioho was a slave fugitive.

Yet in October 1997, another monument (Figure 6.3) paying homage to Bioho was created in San Basilio de Palenque, the village of which he is the mythical founder. Situated some 35 miles from Cartagena, today the village is inhabited mostly by Afro-Colombians. Contrasting with Cartagena, San Basilio de Palenque is a very modest town and not an important tourist destination, even though the statue became a landmark visited by few tourists interested in Afro-Colombian heritage. Unlike the bust exposed in Parque Apolo, the monument displayed in the village does not present Bioho as an official national hero but rather as a slave fighter. The sculpture, conceived by the artists Luis Guillermo Vallejo and Óscar

Figure 6.3 Monument to Benkos Bioho, San Basilio de Palenque, Colombia (2009. Photograph © User:Wehwalt/Wikimedia Commons/CC-BY-SA-3.0).

Salazar G., depicts a black man's torso. With his mouth opened, he is raising one arm from which broken shackles and chains are dangling. In 2005, because of its African-rooted cultural, religious, and artistic traditions, San Basilio de Palenque was added to UNESCO's list of intangible heritages of humanity. Hence, Bioho's monument helps to reinforce the growing assertion of Afro-Colombian traditions that are preserved and promoted in San Basilio.

The large majority of monuments honoring maroons in the Americas feature male figures. Yet during the 1990s, two public sculptures unveiled in Cuba and Jamaica paid homage to female enslaved women who resisted slavery by violent means. In Cuba, unlike Mexico, Jamaica, and Barbados, the fight against slavery was closely associated with the struggle for independence from Spain. On July 25, 1991, one day prior to the 38th anniversary of the Moncada Barracks attack that launched the movement led by Fidel Castro and Che Guevara, who eventually overthrew the dictator Fulgêncio Batista, a commemorative monument of the Escalera rebellions that swept the island in 1843 was unveiled. The monument, composed of three sculptures depicting enslaved individuals, was placed at Triunvirato sugar plantation, one of the various sites where slaves revolted in Matanzas, which since 1978 was declared Cuba's national monument.[63] Like other sculptures representing slave fighters, their bodies are depicted in motion, not in a static and passive position. Of particular interest is the sculpture rendering of the enslaved woman named Carlota, who led the insurgence. Like Yanga and Cuffy, Carlota is identified in the primary sources as an African-born woman, more precisely as a Lucumí, a name usually assigned to Yoruba-speaking individuals in Cuba.[64] According to the account provided by the official Cuban newspaper *Grandma*, when the rebellion was dismantled, Carlota "was captured, and alive was tied to horses that pulled in the opposite direction to dismember her body."[65] One day after the monument was dedicated, during a speech to commemorate the 38th anniversary of the Moncada Barracks attack, Castro, in the presence of Nelson Mandela and like Burnham in Guyana, established a connection between slavery and apartheid by stating: "[a]nd how does the apartheid differ from that practice developed for centuries to drag tens of millions of Africans from their land and bring them to this hemisphere to enslave, to exploit them to the last drop of sweat and blood?"[66] In the Triunvirato's monument, Carlota is represented like her male slave rebel counterparts. Her body is in movement, and her arms are opened. A broken shackle is visible on her left wrist, and she holds a machete with her right hand. Projecting her torso forward, the female slave fighter is depicted as a strong black woman with defined muscles. Still, although suggesting resistance through her gestures and the dynamic position of her body, the sculpture conveys a traditional representation of the female enslaved body. With a cloth barely covering her sex, Carlota's huge breasts are totally exposed, as in many nineteenth-century visual depictions of enslaved women found in European travel accounts.

In spite of the pertinence of the monument's location at the actual sugar plantation heritage site where the slave insurgence took place, about 77 miles from Havana, the monument is not very visible to most of the population and the thousands of tourists who visit Cuba every year. However, the maroon's presence in Cuban's public memory of slavery continued to grow in the ensuing years. On July 7, 1997, a monument *"al Cimarron, a la memoria de la rebeldia esclava"* (to the maroon, to the memory of slave revolt) was dedicated in the copper mining village of El Cobre in the province of Santiago de Cuba. During the colonial period, the village had a significant enslaved, freed, and free black population.[67] Conceived by the Afro-Cuban sculptor Alberto Lescay, the 314-foot monument in iron and bronze represents a standing maroon raising one hand to the sky. The statue was placed on the top of a hill in a town listed as a site of memory of the Latin American and Caribbean section of UNESCO's Slave Route Project. Although described in UNESCO's official documents as not being very accessible, since its unveiling, the monument has been a focal point for ceremonies and various manifestations of cultural assertion of Afro-Cuban populations.[68] Unlike the other monuments honoring maroons in the Caribbean region, the sculpture does not denote in detail the maroon's physical traits but evokes only a human figure. According to Lescay, he attempted to convey the idea of freedom, and because everyone conceives the idea of freedom in different ways, he created a dynamic image, suggesting transformation, leaving to the spectators the task of discovering what their imagination registers.[69]

Like Carlota in Cuba, another female slave fighter, known as "Nanny of the maroons," is commemorated with a monument in the National Heroes Park in Kingston, Jamaica. Nanny was an early eighteenth-century maroon who became known as the leader of the Windward Maroons and was also described as an *obeah* woman (religious specialist). In October 1975, during Manley's government, Nanny was the first woman to be added to the list of Jamaica's national heroes. The monument's creation was part of the context that would inscribe the names of other slave fighters like Bussa and Sharpe in the official lists of national heroes of Barbados and Jamaica. Despite scarce documentary evidence about her, Nanny is a legendary figure in Jamaica's oral tradition, popular culture, and collective memory.[70] As Werner Zips explains, her image, indeed like the image of other maroons, was reconstructed in different ways in a work of memory intended to fulfill interests of present-day social actors.[71] In the plaque that accompanies the monument paying homage to Nanny, she is described as "an outstanding military leader, skilled in guerrilla warfare [. . .] She led with courage and inspired her warriors to maintain that special spirit of freedom and independence." In addition, the text also refers to Nanny's allegedly supernatural powers, an idea that is referenced in the monument as well. Unlike other statues representing maroons breaking chains, the monument is constituted of three abstract vertical metallic structures. The central structure represents Nanny, and through the action of the wind, it reproduces the sound of an *abeng*, an animal horn that was used to call other slaves and that, like the conch shell, became a symbolic instrument suggestive of the maroons. The other two sculptures represent the maroons who followed Nanny.

In Venezuela, the most important maroon commemorated in the public space is José Leonardo Chirino (or Chirinos), the leader of the Coro Revolt, the slave rebellion that erupted in the region of Coro in the late eighteenth century. He was the son of a native woman with an enslaved African man; his wife was enslaved, as well as his four children.[72] Chirino worked for a merchant named José Tellería with whom he traveled to Saint-Domingue and became aware of the struggle for freedom led by the slaves on the island. Back in Coro, Chirino led the rebellion, gathering enslaved and free black individuals on May 10, 1795, during the Haitian Revolution. The rebels occupied plantations and abolished slavery. Eventually, the insurrection was dismantled by the Spanish forces, who killed most of the rebels. Chirino was hanged, and the members of his family were sold separately in other cities.

Chirino's name remained alive in Venezuela's history and popular memory, a country whose population of African descent is unofficially estimated at 14 percent.[73] His popularity increased since the 1980s, when numerous Afro-Venezuelan groups started developing activities denouncing racism and highlighting Venezuela's African heritage.[74] This visibility increased when President Hugo Chávez (1954–2013) took office in 1999, and several initiatives to officially commemorate Chirino as a slave fighter were established in the country's public space. By this time, Chávez began developing his program of socialist reforms intended to fight social inequalities and liberate the country from the influence of the United States. Promoting his own image as the leader of the Bolivarian Revolution, Chávez associated his name with the name of Simon Bolivar (1783–1830), who led the fight for independence in the Spanish colonies of South America in the early nineteenth century. Moreover, whereas Chavez asserted that Bolivar was not white but *zambo*, in various public speeches he also identified himself as *mestizo*, *zambo*, *indio*, and *negro*, attracting the support of Venezuelan lower classes of color.[75]

Mirroring Bolivar and Chávez, Chirino's image is promoted in the public sphere as the first leader who fought against Spanish domination and for the independence of Venezuela. As a result of this political dynamic, Chirino was gradually included in the official history of Venezuela. In 1995, to commemorate the bicentennial of the Coro Revolt, several publications about the rebellion and its leader were released in Venezuela by promoting Chirino's role not only as a rebel but also, like Yanga in Mexico, as Venezuela's first emancipator.[76] As part of the commemorations, with

Figure 6.4 Bust Honoring José Leonardo Chirino, Macanillas, Venezuela (2010. Photograph © User: ArwinJ/Wikimedia Commons/CC-BY-SA-3.0).

the support of Venezuela's federal government, the National Congress, and other institutions, a plaque paying homage to Chirino was inaugurated in the National Pantheon on May 10, 1995. Moreover, during the bicentennial festivities, a bust honoring Chirino was also exhibited in a square named after him, in Macanillas, his hometown (Figure 6.4). One plaque accompanying the monument illustrates Chirino's role as Venezuela's emancipator: "José Leonard Chirino, 1795–1995. Two hundred years of the first Venezuela movement for independence."[77] Another plaque stresses the importance of the site that "was the stage of the beginning of Venezuela's independence" and refers to Chirino as the "first martyr of Venezuelan emancipation."[78] Since the bicentennial commemoration, a growing number of textbooks make references to Chirino's role as the leader of the Coro Revolt. On May 10, 2003, another monument paying tribute to him was unveiled at the site of Coro's airport, named after him as well. The full-body statue shows him bare chested and barefoot. He is pointing his right arm forward in a leader's gesture, whereas with his left hand he is holding a machete. The plaque accompanying the monument does not refer to Chirino as Venezuela's first emancipator; instead describing him as "the expression of rebellion and the struggle against social inequality."[79] Despite the unveiling of these statues, the presence of

Chirino in Venezuelan public space has been circumscribed to the region of Coro. More recently, this situation started changing. In 2005, May 10 was established as the "Day of Afrovenezolidad and José Leonardo Chirino," connecting his name to all Afro-Venezuelans and asserting him as a national figure.

ZUMBI

As in other countries in Latin America and the Caribbean, the emphasis on slave rebels also became visible in Brazil over the last 40 years. Although *quilombos* were widespread all over the country, until the abolition of slavery in 1888, the most famous Brazilian runaway slave community was the seventeenth-century Palmares Quilombo, situated in the present-day region of the state of Alagoas. Considered a state within the state that gathered thousands of men, women, and children, Palmares survived the attacks of Portuguese and Dutch military campaigns for almost one century. The name of its last leader, Zumbi, has always been a part of Brazilian oral tradition and popular memory.

Despite Zumbi's growing presence in popular memory and the public sphere during the twentieth century, this process was interrupted by the military coup of 1964 that plunged the country into a dictatorship that lasted until 1985.[80] During this period, however, activists and Marxist historians often evoked Zumbi's name as the symbol of the fight against oppression. In 1969, one of the organizations that called for armed resistance against the Brazilian military regime named itself Vanguarda Armada Revolucionária Palmares (Palmares Armed Revolutionary Vanguard) in homage to Palmares Quilombo. But during the 1970s, Zumbi's name started appearing again in the public initiatives. In 1974, the Brazilian composer and singer Jorge Ben composed the song *Zumbi*. The song's video clip was shown on *Fantástico*, Brazil's most popular television show, broadcast on Sundays. The clip mixed images of nineteenth-century European travel accounts rendering slave markets and physical punishments inflicted on enslaved men and women in Brazil with images of a performance by black actors and actresses dressed in white and breaking their chains. Even with the chaos depicted in the play, the image of black individuals breaking chains, symbolizing liberation from slavery, was powerful and also representative of a period when the opposition to the Brazilian military dictatorship was growing. In this context, the image of the breaking chains also evokes the possible end of the then 10-year dictatorship established in the country, the end of censorship, and the liberation of political prisoners incarcerated by the dictatorial regime. The song's refrain, "I want to see what will happen/ When Zumbi arrives/ Zumbi is the Lord of war/ Zumbi is the lord of demands/ When

Zumbi arrives/ It is he who commands," reinforced the image of Zumbi as a black warrior.[81] At the same time, the song and its video clip connected the image of the Brazilian maroon to the fight against the military rule. What would happen when Zumbi, the warrior and liberator, would arrive? More than a symbol of the fight against social and racial inequalities led by Afro-Brazilians, Zumbi is presented as a national hero, the one who could liberate the country from dictatorship.[82]

Ben's song reflected Zumbi's forthcoming popularity. Especially after 1978, when the Movimento Negro Unificado (Unified Black Movement) was created in São Paulo, the date of Zumbi's alleged death, November 20, started being commemorated in Brazil's main capitals. In the ensuing years, the new generation of black activists gradually replaced the old commemoration of the abolition of slavery on May 13, centered around the figure of Princess Isabel, to celebrate Zumbi on November 20. After more than two decades of dictatorship, the idea of the abolition of slavery as a gift given by Princess Isabel was clearly rejected. By celebrating Zumbi, Afro-Brazilian activists emphasized the agency of the enslaved population and its descendants who no longer accepted the image of passive victims propagated in the images of Uncle Tom, Slave Isaura, and *Pai* João.

In 1984, the Brazilian filmmaker Carlos Diegues, a participant of the Cinema Novo (New Cinema) movement that created films featuring Brazilian social problems, brought slavery and slave resistance to the big screen with his film *Quilombo*.[83] The film gave continuity to his *Ganga Zumba: Rei dos Palmares*, completed in 1963.[84] In *Quilombo*, Zumbi is seen as a warrior and a hero. Unlike Ganga Zumba, who capitulated to the Portuguese forces, Zumbi fought his enemies to defend the *quilombo*. Even though Zumbi was actually beheaded by the Portuguese army in their last incursion in Palmares, in the film, the maroon leader commits suicide by jumping off the mountain. Diegues's film greatly contributed to disseminate the image of Zumbi as a hero who sacrificed his life to fight for freedom.

Until a few years ago, Brazil had very few public monuments commemorating slavery, but today the country has numerous monuments memorializing Zumbi of Palmares. Zumbi became the quintessential symbol of the fight against slavery and racism. The decline of the military regime and the first democratic elections for governor, senator, and deputies at the federal and state levels in 1982 allowed black Brazilian activists, such as Abdias Nascimento (1914–2011) to be elected to the National Congress.[85] As a deputy between 1983 and 1987, Nascimento was a pioneer not only in proposing a law to make the anniversary of Zumbi's death a national holiday but also in submitting a second project to create a memorial to the unknown slave at Praça dos Três Poderes (Square of Three Powers) in Brasília, even though neither of these two projects was ever approved by the National Congress.

The first monument commemorating a slave rebel in Brazil was unveiled in 1986, one year after the end of the military dictatorship. The monument honoring Zumbi is a replica of a brass head from the Kingdom of Ife (in present-day Nigeria). Today, the Ife head, which epitomizes an individual in a position of authority, is one of the most famous objects in the ethnographic collections of the British Museum in London. Intentionally or not, because Zumbi was beheaded, the sculpture points to his own head and death, at the same time representing him as an African warrior, even though he was born in Brazil.[86] The monument was placed in the central square of Presidente Vargas Avenue in Rio de Janeiro. Starting in 1995, when the 300th anniversary of Zumbi's death was commemorated, the activities held on November 20 gained increasing visibility. Despite the heavy traffic that makes it difficult to stop to observe the statue, the monument became a site of Afro-Brazilian memory for black activists and Afro-Brazilian religious groups, who celebrate November 20 every year. During the wave of demonstrations that took place in Brazil in 2013, protesters often appropriated the monument (Figure 6.5), expanding its significance.

Like its maroon counterparts in Barbados, Jamaica, and Venezuela, on March 21, 1997, the name of Zumbi was added to the *Book of National Heroes*, a steel book containing the names of several Brazilian male historical figures located at the Praça dos Três Poderes (Square of Three Powers) in Brasília.[87] Eventually, in 2003 federal law number 10,639 established

Figure 6.5 Monument to Zumbi, Rio de Janeiro, Brazil (2013. Photograph © Halley Pacheco/CC-BY-SA-3.0).

November 20 as the National Black Consciousness Day, making the date an official holiday in dozens of Brazilian cities. In the following years, all over Brazil, squares, schools, and even ships were named after Zumbi. On May 30, 2008, the city of Salvador inaugurated its first monument commemorating Zumbi, more than 20 years later than Rio de Janeiro. Notwithstanding its large population of African descent (80 percent), this delay can be explained in two ways. First, Bahia's black movement was not as well organized as in Rio de Janeiro, where it had support from the Democratic Labor Party. Second, as a result, despite the presence of Afro-Brazilian groups in the public scene since the 1970s, especially during the Carnival, the local authorities did not necessarily support the official inscription of slave resistance as the main narrative to be presented in the public space of the capital city, which is still perceived as the site of the joyful celebration of African roots. Indeed, the statue commemorating Zumbi was the fruit of a joint initiative of the Palmares Cultural Foundation, the nongovernmental organization *A Mulherada* (an organization promoting black women's rights), the Ministry of Culture, and the municipality of Salvador. Contrasting with the statues of other maroons unveiled in other Latin American and Caribbean countries, the monument to Zumbi was placed in a highly visible place in the Praça da Sé, in Salvador's historic center, a site visited by millions of tourists from around the world every year. The full-body bronze statue on a granite square base represents Zumbi as a warrior holding a spear. On the base of the sculpture, the text inscribed on two plaques not only recalls the struggle for civil rights led by Afro-Brazilians but also proclaims that Zumbi was the "leader of the country's first democratic experience" and that the monument "is the symbol of the resistance of Brazilian black people and the materialization of the memory of fights and conquests by the exercise of freedom and the strengthening of black consciousness." The monument and the two texts accompanying it show an important shift in the narrative of Brazilian slavery. The emphasis and the popularization of the image of Zumbi, a warrior who fought against slavery, helped to transform the image of the enslaved in Brazil. Presented in the past as passive victims, enslaved men and women are now displayed as powerful fighters.

Another initiative also highlighted the importance of Zumbi in Brazilian public memory as a warrior who fought against slavery. On November 15, 2007, Minister of Culture Gilberto Gil opened the Memorial Park of Palmares Quilombo, the most important initiative promoting an historical site associated with the resistance against slavery.[88] The process that resulted in the creation of this park started in the 1980s, during the military dictatorship. In 1986, the IPHAN recognized the Serra da Barriga as national heritage by inscribing the site in the list of archaeological, ethnographic, and landscape sites.[89] On March 21, 1988, during the centennial celebrations of the abolition of slavery in Brazil, a federal decree officially established the site as a national monument. The park is located near the city of União dos Palmares, at Serra da Barriga, in the state of Alagoas, situated in a region close to the *quilombo*'s original location. The construction of the country's first Afro-Brazilian cultural theme park received the support of the Palmares Foundation, the Ministry of Culture, the Ministry of Tourism, and several other government agencies. The site comprises a complete structure to receive tourists, including a visitors' center, various belvederes, a replica of Zumbi's house, and indigenous huts. Even though its location remains far from the most important of Brazilian tourist destinations, every year on November 20, several ceremonies are held in Memorial Park. In November 2011, according to his will, the ashes of the activist Abdias Nascimento were buried in the park during a ceremony in the presence of several world-renowned African diaspora activists and scholars.

Numerous monuments celebrating Zumbi were erected across a number of Brazilian cities during the last decade, especially in the state of Rio de Janeiro. These various initiatives memorializing Zumbi made him a national hero in Brazil. Although the first public initiatives commemorating Zumbi started in the 1970s, the growing number of monuments made public in the 1990s celebrating him indicates that this phenomenon is not simply related to the necessity of making the history of black historical actors known to wider audiences. This huge popularity also relates to the emergence of the public memory of other maroons in the Caribbean and Latin America and is the result of the demands of Afro-Brazilian social actors to end social and racial inequalities. Despite the fact that more than 50 percent of Brazil's present-day population is of African descent, only recently has the country started facing its slave past and officially recognizing the crucial role played by its enslaved black population in the construction of the nation. The increasing importance of Zumbi as a national hero and the symbol of resistance against oppression is helping to promote a new image of the populations of African descent not only in Brazil but also across the diaspora.

PUBLIC RECOGNITION

Starting in the 1960s, both in the United States and Brazil, the old representations of submissive enslaved individuals embodied in the characters of novels, films, and popular culture, like Nanny, Uncle Tom, and *Pai* João, were gradually replaced by a new image of slave fighters. This transformation was not exclusive to the realms of slavery. Indeed, following the end of the Second World War, memorials honoring Jewish fighters who fought the Nazi regime were unveiled in Poland and the former East Germany. The analysis of monuments honoring slave fighters unveiled in Haiti, Mexico, Barbados, Jamaica, Cuba, Venezuela, and Brazil indicates that local and international political contexts greatly contributed to the emergence of slave rebels in the public place. The creation of these initiatives paying homage to slave rebels and maroons was a direct consequence of the fights for recognition led by organized groups in the Caribbean and Latin America. It was also associated with the emergence of new nations and the development of national identities. At the same time, despite public speeches by national leaders, the memorialization of maroons as symbols of the struggle against oppression were not always intended to empower the populations of African descent. In several cases, the creation of monuments and the inscription of these maroons' names in the list of National Heroes served to reinforce the political agendas of governments who were seeking to assert their political, economic, and cultural independence vis-à-vis the former European colonial powers and the United States. Although the visibility of maroons in the public space is closely associated with the growing interest that slavery is receiving at the international level, in most Caribbean and Latin American countries, the memorialization of maroons is circumscribed to a particular region. Except for Brazil, where Zumbi became a national hero honored in monuments in important urban centers and in some Caribbean nations, in most countries examined in this chapter, the statues paying homage to the maroons were unveiled in the former maroon settlements, far from the gaze of the majority of the population and international tourists.

NOTES

1. See Stowe, 1852; Mitchell, 1936. In 1903, a first silent film version of *Uncle Tom's Cabin*, directed by Edwin S. Porter, was released. Harry A. Pollard directed a later silent version in 1927. Adapted to the cinema in 1939, *Gone with the Wind*, was directed by Victor Fleming.
2. Stowe, 1853.
3. Nabuco, 1900: 215.
4. "Um passeio às Caldas," 1872: 3.
5. In its first season in Rio de Janeiro, the play was performed 12 times. See "Chronica: Theatros," 1876: 95; "Theatro São Pedro de Alcantara," 1876: 2.
6. Dumanoir and d'Ennery, 1853.
7. Del Marco, 1876: 6.
8. See Magaldi and Vargas, 2000: 14. The news was dissiminated in various newspapers of São Paulo and Rio de Janeiro; see "Companhia dramatica," 1877: 3; *Correio paulistano*, 1877: 4.
9. "'A Cabana do Pae Thomaz' em sessão especial, hontem no Pathé Palace," 1928: 10.
10. Mitchell, 1936; Mitchell, 1940.
11. Nicolussi, 1940: 6.
12. Nicolussi, 1940: 6.
13. "Em benefício da 'Cidade das Meninas' . . .," 1940: 3.
14. An area of 5,000 acres to construct the Cidade das Meninas was donated to the Foundation Darcy Vargas through the decree-law no. 5441 of April 30, 1943. On the role of First Lady Darcy Vargas in charity activities among local communities during the government of her husband Getúlio Vargas, see Fischer, 2008: 235–236.

15. Jefferson Caffery was the Ambassador of the United States in Brazil from 1937 to 1949. See "Elegâncias," 1940: 10.
16. "Todo São Paulo aguarda com incontida curiosidade o deslumbramento de 'E o vento levou . . .,'" 1940: 6.
17. Guimarães, 1875.
18. Guimarães, 1875: 2.
19. The scenes depicted in the watercolors were also reproduced in the lithographs published in his album. Debret, 1834–1839.
20. See Opening of the *telenovela A Escrava Isaura*, (1976, URL) is available on YouTube. The soap opera is based on the novel *A escrava Isaura* by Bernardo Guimarães (1875).
21. Ramos, 1935.
22. More recently, Martha Abreu explored the various representations of *Pai* João as well. See Abreu, 2004: 247.
23. Césaire, 1950; Fanon, 1952.
24. According to the plaque's Hebrew and Polish inscription.
25. Young, 1989: 69.
26. Young, 1989: 70.
27. See Du Bois, 1952: 14–15. Michael Rothberg dedicates a whole chapter to Du Bois's impressions of his visit to the Warsaw Ghetto in 1949. See Rothberg, 2010: Chap. 4.
28. Rothberg, 2010: 128.
29. Du Bois, 1952: 15.
30. "Remarks by the President at the United States Holocaust Memorial Museum . . .," 2012.
31. "Sojourner Truth Bust Unveiling," 2009.
32. Young, 1989: 78.
33. See Reinhardt, 2006: 59. In the United States, several monuments and memorials portray slave fugitives, who certainly played a role in destroying slavery in the country. However, this chapter is intended to examine the memorialization of men and women who led rebellions and formed runaway slave communities.
34. Among the pioneer works focusing on slave resistance in the United States are Aptheker, 1963, 1966; Starobin, 1970; Mullin, 1972; Genovese, 1974, 1979. In Brazil, despite some problematic interpretations, the works of scholars of the São Paulo school of sociology contributed to review the position of Brazilian slaves as passive victims. On this issue, see Lara, 1995: 53–68; Araujo, 2010a: 36, 216.
35. Duvalier, 1969: 24.
36. Duvalier, 1969: 40.
37. Duvalier, 1969: 56.
38. See Brown, 2002: 108; Béchacq, 2006: 203–240.
39. See Landers, 2006: 124.
40. Sue, 2013: 118; Eltis, Bradley, Engerman, and Cartledge, 2011: 345.
41. Carretero, Maranto, and Silva, 1990: 27–28.
42. Githiora, 2008: 209.
43. See Herrera, 2006: 30–33.
44. Carretero, Maranto, and Silva, 1990: 26–27.
45. See Hoffmann, 2006: 121.
46. Heuman, 1981: 86; Brown, 2008: 232.
47. See Craton, 1982: 314–315; Brown, 2008: 233.
48. Besson, 2011: 324.
49. Michael Norman Manley was the son of Norman Manley (1893–1969), who founded the People's National Party and led Jamaica's movement for independence.
50. See Lambert, 2007: 355. See also Brathwaite, 1977.

51. Letters exchanged between the rebels and the Dutch indicate that the rebellion was motivated by the mistreatment of the slaves. See Kars, 2009: 191–217.
52. Blier, 1995: 155.
53. Vidal and Whitehead, 2004: 73.
54. Burnham, 1976: 16.
55. Burnham, 1976.
56. Bank of Guyana, 2013, 3.
57. According to Barbadian historian Hilary Beckles, Bussa was born in Africa and was the leader of the 1816 Rebellion. See Beckles, 1998. However, these two elements have been contested. Jerome Handler, for example, argues that there is no evidence that "Busso or Bussoe," as he is named in the primary sources, was born in Africa or that he was the main leader of the rebellion. See Handler, 2000: 22–23. On the debate between the two scholars, see Lambert, 2007: 345–370.
58. Brown, 2002: 107.
59. Lambert, 2007: 350.
60. Lambert uses the notion of "surrogation" to explain this process, see Lambert, 2007: 364.
61. His name, Biohon, corresponds to the name of a region in Guinea-Bissau, where he was probably sent into slavery in the Americas. See Olsen, 2002: 61. See also Escalante, 1996: 77–79; Rout, 1976: 110. See also García, 2007: 368.
62. In the original Spanish, the inscription is, "Caudillo negro, defendio su libertad hasta perder la vida."
63. Resolution no. 003, October 10, 1978.
64. See Finch, 2007: 193, 262; Reid-Vazquez, 2011: 47–48.
65. Rojas, n.d.
66. In the original in Spanish: "Y en qué se diferencia el apartheid de aquella práctica aplicada durante siglos de arrancar decenas de millones de africanos del seno de su tierra y traerlos a este hemisferio para esclavizarlos, para explotarles hasta la última gota de sudor y de sangre?" See Castro, 1991. On the political uses of Carlota's memory by Castro's regime, see Houser, 2013.
67. See Díaz, 2000.
68. See Díaz, n.d.
69. See Ferrer, n.d.
70. Gottlieb, 2000: 23.
71. Zips, 1998: 192.
72. See Geggus, 1997: 42, n145.
73. Despite these estimates, Venezuela's census does not include questions regarding the population of African descent. Moreover, Afro-Venezuelans are not recognized in the country's Constitution. See García, 2007: 223–225.
74. Salas, 2005: 79.
75. Gottberg, 2011: 291; 293.
76. There is a vast bibliography in Spanish on the revolt. See Nectario, 1994; Márquez, 1995: Ramos, 1996; Rodríguez, 1996; Gil, Dovale, and Lusmila, 1996. In English, see Rivera, 2013.
77. In Spanish: "José Leonardo Chirino, 1795–1995. Doscientos años del primer movimiento independentista de Venezuela."
78. In Spanish: "Este sitio fue el escenario de ese germen de la independencia de Venezuela: 10-5-1795. Su cabecilla: José Leonardo Chirino. Primer mártir de la emancipación venezolana."
79. In Spanish: "Un homage del pueblo coriano a la expression de la rebeldia y la lucha por la igualdad social encarnada en el zambo." The word "*zambo*," which often appears in the texts describing Chirino, was used during the colonial period to identify the offspring of a native person and a black individual.
80. See Araujo, 2012: 95–111.

81. The lyrics read: "Eu quero ver/ Eu quero ver/ Eu quero ver/ Quando Zumbi chegar/ O que vai acontecer/ Zumbi é senhor das guerras/ È senhor das demandas/ Quando Zumbi chega é Zumbi/ É quem manda." See Ben, 1974.
82. See Andrews, 1991: 217; Fryer, 2000: 71; Dunn, 2000: 178.
83. See Diegues, 2005 (DVD).
84. The film was not released until 1972 because of the military dictatorship. See Diegues, 1963.
85. On the role of Abdias Nascimento in authoring projects to bring slavery to the public space in Brazil, see Araujo, 2010a: 226–228.
86. For more details on the controversies related to the construction of the monument, see Soares, 1999: 129.
87. Tancredo Neves (1910–1985) was a Brazilian politician. In 1984, he was one of the leaders of the movement Diretas Já, which called for the direct election of the president. Eventually, Neves was elected indirectly as president of Brazil in 1985. However, one day prior to taking the oath of office, Neves was sent to the hospital with diverticulitis and died some weeks later, thus never taking office.
88. Parque Memorial Quilombo dos Palmares (website).
89. See Livro Arqueológico, Etnográfico e Paisagístico, Inscription 090, of February 19, 1986, process no. 1069-T-82.

Conclusion

This book looked at the processes through which various social actors and groups articulate the slave past in the public space by exploring the transfers and exchanges that flow in various places and times during the process of remembrance. In its previous chapters, I explored how postslave societies remember, display, reenact, conceal, and forget the unpleasant stages of their involvement in the Atlantic slave trade and slavery. I also discussed how these societies are gradually incorporating these uncomfortable pasts into their national histories and identities by displaying these old scars in the public urban spaces of their main cities. Moreover, relying on the transnational and comparative analysis of monuments, memorials, museum exhibitions, and heritage sites, located in various regions of the Americas, Europe, and Africa, I examined the different ways sites of memory of slavery and the Atlantic slave trade are promoted and commemorated. Also, I showed how these different initiatives have sometimes associated the experience of the victims of slavery with the suffering of the survivors of other atrocities, especially the Holocaust.

I followed the different phases of the Atlantic slave trade in order to show how visual images and written accounts representing the enslavement of men, women, and children were appropriated in present-day museum exhibitions and how they oriented the ways in which slave trade heritage sites are interpreted for the general public and tourist audiences. These written, visual, and oral narratives describing enslavement were produced in the context of British abolitionist propaganda. They often suppressed warfare, focusing instead on hazardous abductions. Moreover, written accounts and visual images intriguingly depict white enslavers and slave traders. Not only were these depictions forged to promote abolitionist propaganda by underscoring the nefarious effects of European slavers in Africa, but they were also determined by the technical restrictions of black-and-white engraving. Strangely, none of these images depict enslavement in West Central Africa, the region that provided the largest number of enslaved Africans to the Atlantic slave trade and where Luso-Brazilian men actively participated in slave raids. My analysis showed that these early images continue to influence the ways enslavement in Africa is portrayed in monuments, museum exhibitions, and even in films. Indeed, monuments recently built in West Africa rarely evoke the role of African slaver elites in the Atlantic slave trade. Likewise, several movies and television series depict white enslaver men kidnapping individuals in the coastal areas or the interior of the African continent. Also, most museum exhibitions barely explain the context of enslavement in Africa, presenting instead an idyllic representation of African societies that contrasts with the image that follows after the arrival of Europeans. These simplified representations, intended to respond to the demands of local and international black audiences, avoid portraying the complex and sensitive aspects of the history of the Atlantic slave trade in societies where the populations of African descent continue to experience the consequences of racism and racial inequalities.

Following the enslavement in Africa's hinterland, captive men, women, and children were brought to slave depots in the coastal areas of West Africa and West Central Africa. Once again, despite the crucial role of West Central African slave ports during the Atlantic slave trade, the most important preserved slave trade building structures that became tourist landmarks are located on the West African coast. Over the twentieth century, several slave castles were officially included in UNESCO's World Heritage List and officially recognized as slave trade heritage sites. However, sites like the House of Slaves on Gorée Island acquired national and international notoriety even though scholars around the world seriously questioned its authenticity as a slave depot. Moreover, the promotion of slave trade sites, such as the Elmina and Cape Coast castles and the House of Slaves, has relied on accounts of individuals and groups of social actors who oftentimes associated these slave trade sites with the heritage sites of the Holocaust, especially Dachau, Buchenwald, Auschwitz, and Drancy. More than presenting the political dimension of memories in competition, these intriguing dialogues and unexpected connections have also contributed to legitimize the memorialization of slavery among Western audiences.

Like the experiences of enslavement and confinement in slave depots, the Middle Passage and the arrival of enslaved Africans in the Americas were memorialized in Brazil and the United States. The analysis of museum exhibitions shows that the reconstitution of the slave ship remains a central element in symbolizing the horrors that marked the Atlantic slave trade. Yet these representations of experiences of deportation, extreme suffering, and death continue to be highly contested. Many museum exhibitions depict Africans as mere commodities, denying agency to these enslaved men, women, and children. At the same time, until two decades ago, the sites of the arrival of Africans remained concealed in the urban areas of former Brazilian and US slave trade ports. However, my research shows that in some of these ports, like Salvador in Bahia, the erasure of the marks of the slave past gave origin to a process that I call memory replacement. Through this process, the local populations have created stories to reconstruct the slave past of the Atlantic slave trade in order to deal with the inexistence of officially recognized heritage sites. But in former slave ports like Rio de Janeiro and New York, the unearthing of slave wharfs and slave cemeteries over the last 20 years is finally leading public authorities to formally establish permanent markers to commemorate the Atlantic slave trade. Certainly, the safeguarding and the development of these slave heritage sites still encounter obstacles. Still, the black populations of the two countries are occupying these spaces and converting them into sacred spaces to commemorate African ancestors. Through this process, both Brazil and the United States are gradually recognizing the Atlantic slave trade and its painful legacies as a central element of their national histories.

In Brazil and the United States, slave labor has been memorialized and forgotten in similar ways. In both countries, the use of enslaved workers to construct public and private buildings is hardly officially acknowledged. Although many slave narratives written by men and women enslaved in the United States underscore the suffering caused by physical punishments, slavery heritage sites like former plantations often omit this dimension of slave life, emphasizing instead the luxurious lifestyles of the masters and mistresses. In Brazil, the incipient projects promoting former plantations and jerked beef factories as tourist and heritage sites often overemphasize victimization, displaying images of physical punishments and instruments of torture. Transforming violence into a spectacle, these depictions fail to inform and raise awareness about the complex mechanisms of the Brazilian slave system and its present legacies. This insensitive approach is also visible in several former slavery sites transformed into small hostels and restaurants. These venues exhibit instruments of torture, and whipping posts that were used to punish slaves are highlighted, neither providing any references about the daily lives of enslaved individuals nor underscoring any elements of African heritage. Likewise, in the United States, the memorialization of slavery met similar hindrances, but during the last decade and particularly after the election of President Barack Obama, several initiatives were developed to celebrate the contribution of enslaved African Americans, especially in Washington, DC. Yet because these projects remain recent, their impact is still difficult to measure. Indeed, recognizing the contribution of enslaved men and women to the construction of Brazil and the United States is still challenging if this recognition is not followed by sustained policies because in both countries the legacies of slavery, including racism as well as racial and social inequalities, have not yet been overcome.

In the United States and Brazil, white emancipators embody the memory of the abolition of slavery. Whereas in the United States, President Lincoln became the Great Emancipator, in Brazil Princess Isabel represented the figure of the Redeemer for a very long time. The first public monument paying homage to Lincoln in Washington, DC, was a project led by former enslaved African Americans. Although over the years, his image as the Great Emancipator gradually lost importance among the next generations of African Americans, today Lincoln is still a central figure in the US narrative of the abolition of slavery. His assassination and his leading role in unifying the United States overshadowed the emergence of any other figure representing the abolition of slavery in the United States. Like Lincoln, Princess Isabel's image as the Redeemer emerged immediately after the signature of the Golden Law in 1888. But because of the military coup that ended the monarchy in 1889, the memorialization of Isabel as the great Redeemer was suddenly interrupted. Although celebrated in the commemoration activities of the abolition of slavery in Brazil, only several years after her death, Isabel gained her first public monument located far from Brazil's national capital. As in the first memorial honoring Lincoln in Washington, DC, the first monument paying homage to the princess associated her image with the representation of a grateful slave. Still, unlike African Americans, Afro-Brazilians did not lead any campaign to raise funds to erect a statue to the Redeemer. In the following years, Isabel's public memory was greatly manipulated by political authorities in order to obtain Afro-Brazilians' support. Also, similarly to what happened with Lincoln, older generations of Afro-Brazilians highly regarded Princess Isabel. However, over time both Lincoln and Isabel lost importance among those African Americans and Afro-Brazilians who did not experience life under slavery. Despite these similarities and differences, in Brazil the image of Isabel as the Redeemer was gradually replaced by the figure of Zumbi, the leader of Palmares Quilombo. In the United States, because no powerful slave rebel figure emerged, Lincoln remains the Great Emancipator and the central figure in the narrative of the abolition of slavery.

Over the 1960s, at the height of the Civil Rights Movement in the United States and when a growing number of activists started questioning the role of Isabel as the Brazil's Redeemer, in both countries the old representations of submissive slaves were slowly replaced with images of slave rebels. The creation of public monuments and memorials honoring slave fighters was a direct consequence of the movements of cultural assertion organized by black groups in Caribbean and Latin American countries. Yet the analysis of the local and international contexts showed that the creation of monuments honoring maroons and the inscription of their names in the list of National Heroes were also intended to promote the political agendas of several national governments. The visibility of slave fighters in the public arena is related to increasing international interest in slavery and its legacies. Likewise, in Brazil, Zumbi became a national hero honored in monuments in important urban centers, whereas in most Caribbean and Latin American countries, the monuments to slave rebels were placed in former maroon settlements and remain invisible for most locals and international tourists.

The traumatic experiences lived by enslaved Africans and their descendants during the era of the Atlantic slave trade were transmitted to subsequent generations and remain alive today, especially in Western societies like Brazil and the United States, where populations of African descent continue to be excluded and marginalized. Over the last two decades, slavery and the Atlantic slave trade have received increased visibility in the Americas, Europe, and Africa. This book aims to contribute to understanding this dynamic phenomenon by shedding light on the various dimensions of the rise of the public memory of slavery. Through the analysis of public initiatives in the urban spaces, I showed that the memorialization of slavery is a complex and transnational process that has resulted from the political struggle of social actors fighting for social justice led by public authorities who incorporate the demands of these social actors, seeking to obtain political gains. Most initiatives examined in this book are not successful in depicting the complex processes of slavery and the Atlantic slave trade because the several social actors that lead these initiatives have conflictual perspectives regarding this past. When one group succeeds in occupying the public space with its own particular viewpoint, the other groups' perspectives are excluded. This dynamic creates obstacles for the emergence of possible projects that could successfully deal with and perhaps heal the wounds of the traumatic past. More importantly, it also suggests that the deep scars of slavery remain very much alive in most former slave societies.

Bibliography

ARCHIVES AND MUSEUMS

African Burial Ground, New York City, New York, United States
Biblioteca Nacional, Rio de Janeiro, Rio de Janeiro, Brazil
Museu AfroBrasil, São Paulo, São Paulo, Brazil
Destrehan Plantation, New Orleans, Louisiana, United States
Holocaust Memorial Museum, Washington, DC, United States
Le Musée d'histoire de Ouidah, Ouidah, Republic of Benin
Library of Congress, Washington, DC, United States
Moorland Spingarn Research Center, Howard University, Washington, DC, United States
Museu da Cidade, Salvador, Bahia, Brazil
Museu Histórico Nacional, Rio de Janeiro, Rio de Janeiro, Brazil
Museu Náutico da Bahia, Salvador, Bahia, Brazil
Museu do Negro, Rio de Janeiro, Rio de Janeiro, Brazil
Museu do Escravo, Belo Vale, Mina Gerais, Brazil
Museu Júlio de Castilhos, Porto Alegre, Rio Grande do Sul, Brazil
Museum of London Docklands, London, United Kingdom
Museu de Artes e Ofícios, Belo Horizonte, Minas Gerais, Brazil
National Museum of American History, Washington, DC, United States
Oliveira Lima Library, Washington, DC, United States

PERIODICALS CONSULTED

A Batalha (Brazil)
A Noite (Brazil)
A Reforma (Brazil)
Correio da manhã (Brazil)
Correio paulistano (Brazil)
Diário carioca (Brazil)
Diário de notícias (Brazil)
Diário da noite (Brazil)
Ebony (United States)
Gazeta de notícias (Brazil)
Jornal do Brasil (Brazil)
Jornal das moças (Brazil)
La Nation (Republic of Benin)

Michigan Chronicle (United States)
New Pittsburgh Courier (United States)
New York Amsterdam News (United States)
New York Times (United States)
New York Voice (United States)
O Globo (Brazil)
O Mequetrefe (Brazil)
The Chicago Defender (United States)
The Culvert Chronicles (United States)
The Jacksonville Free Press (United States)
The Liberator (United States)
Última hora (Brazil)

TRAVELOGUES

Atkins, John. *A Voyage to Guinea, Brazil and the West Indies*. London: C. Ward and R. Chandler, 1735.
D'Almada, André Alvares. *Tratado breve dos rios de Guiné do Cabo-Verde desde o rio do Sanaga até aos Baixos de Sant'Anna*. Porto, Portugal: Typographia Comercial Portuense, 1841.
Dalzel, Archibald. *The History of Dahomy: An Inland Kingdom of Africa* [facsimile of the 1793 edition published by T. Spilbury and Son, London]. New York: Elibron Classics, 2005.
Debret, Jean-Baptiste. *Voyage pittoresque et historique au Brésil ou séjour d'un artiste français au Brésil depuis 1816 jusqu'en 1831 inclusivement*. Paris: Firmin Didot Frères, 1834–1839.
Forbes, Frederick Edwin. *Dahomey and the Dahomans: Being the Journals of Two Missions to the King of Dahomey and Residence at his Capital in the Years 1849 and 1850*, vol. 1. London: Longman, Brown, Green, and Longmans, 1851.
Frézier, Amédée François. *Relation du voyage de la mer du Sud aux côtes du Chili et du Pérou fait pendant les années 1712, 1713, et 1714*, vol. 2. Paris: J-G. Nyon, E. Ganeau, J. Quillau, 1716.
Graham, Maria. *Journal of a Voyage to Brazil and Residence There, During Part of the Years 1821, 1822, and 1823*. London: Longman, Hurst, Rees, Orme, Brown, and Green, 1824.
Hugo, Abel Jospeh. *France pittoresque ou description pittoresque, topographique et statistique des départments et colonies de la France*, vol. 3. Paris: Delloye, 1835.
Isabelle, Arsène. *Voyage à Buenos-Ayres et a Porto Alègre, par la Banda-Oriental, les Missions d'Uruguay et la Province de Rio-Grande-do-Sul (de 1830 à 1834)*. Havre, France: Imprimerie de J. Morlent, 1835.
Rugendas, Johann Moritz. *Voyage pittoresque dans le Brésil*. Paris: Engelmann, 1835.
Lindley, Thomas. *Narrative of a Voyage to Brazil: Terminating in the Seizure of a British Vessel; with General Sketches of the Country, its Natural Productions, Colonial Inhabitants*. London: J. Jonhson, 1805.
Livingstone, David, and Charles Livingstone. *Narrative of an Expedition to the Zambesi and Its Tributaries: And of the Discovery of the Lakes Shirwa and Nyassa, 1858–1864*. New York: Harper & Bros., 1893.
Livingstone, David, and Horace Waller. *The Last Journals of David Livingstone in Central Africa, from 1865 to His Death: Continued by a Narrative of His Last*

Moments and Sufferings, Obtained from His Faithful Servants, Chuma and Susi. London: J. Murray, 1874.

Norris, Robert. *Memoirs of the Reign of Bossa Ahadee, King of Dahomy, An Inland Country of Guiney, to which are added the Author's Journey to Abomey, the Capital, and A Short Account of the African Slave Trade.* London, 1789.

Ribeyrolles, Charles, and Victor Frond. *Brazil pittoresco: historia-descripções-viagens-instutuicções-colonisação.* Rio de Janeiro: Typhographia Nacional, 1859.

Raynal, Guillaume-Thomas. *Histoire philosophique et politique des établissements et du commerce des Européens dans les deux Indes.* Genève: Jean-Léonard Pellet, 1780.

Saint-Hilaire, Augusto de. *Viagem ao Rio Grande do Sul (1820–1821).* São Paulo: Companhia Editora Nacional, 1939.

Schlappriz, Luis, and Franz Heinrich Carls. *Memória de Pernambuco. Álbum para os amigos das artes.* Recife: Lithografia F. H. Carls, Rua de Cadeia, 1860.

Snelgrave, William. *A New Account of Some Parts of Guinea and the Slave-Trade.* London: P. Knapton, 1734.

SLAVE NARRATIVES

Cugoano, Ottobah. *Thoughts and Sentiments on the Evil of Slavery, or, The Nature of Servitude As Admitted by the Law of God, Compared to the Modern Slavery of the Africans in the West Indies In an Answer to the Advocates for Slavery and Oppression: Addressed to the Sons of Africa.* London: Printed for and sold by the author, 1791.

Cugoano, Quobna Ottobah. *Thoughts and Sentiments on the Evil of Slavery and Other Writings.* New York: Penguin, 1999.

Douglass, Frederick. *Life and Times of Frederick Douglass, His Early Life as a Slave, His Escape from Bondage, and His Complete History to the Present Time.* Hartford, CT: Park Publishing Co, 1881.

Douglass, Frederick. *Life and Times of Frederick Douglass, His Early Life as a Slave, His Escape from Bondage, and His Complete History to the Present Time.* Boston: De Wolfe & Fiske, 1892.

Douglass, Frederick. *Narrative of the Life of Frederick Douglas, an American Slave. Written by Himself.* Boston: Anti-Slavery Office, 1845.

Eliot, William G. *The Story of Archer Alexander: From Slavery to Freedom, March 30, 1863.* Boston: Cupples, Upham and Company, 1885.

Equiano, Olaudah, and Vincent Carretta. *The Interesting Narrative and Other Writings.* New York: Penguin, 2003.

Gronniosaw, James Albert Ukawsaw. *Narrative of the Most Remarkable Particulars in the Life of James Albert Ukawsaw Gronniosaw, an African Prince, as Related by Himself.* Bath, United Kingdom: W. Gye, 1770.

Lovejoy, Paul E., and Robin Law. *The Biography of Mahommah Gardo Baquaqua: His Passage from Slavery to Freedom in Africa and America.* Princeton: Markus Wiener Publishers, 2003.

Slavery Illustrated: In the Histories of Zangara and Maquama, Two Negros Stolen from Africa and Sold into Slavery Related by Themselves. Manchester and London: W. Irwin and Simpkin, Marshall, and Co., 1849.

Smith, Venture. *A Narrative of the Life and Adventures of Venture Smith, A Native of Africa: but Resident about Sixty Years in the United States of America. Related by Himself.* New London, CT: Holt, 1798.

Taylor, Isaac. *Scenes in Africa, for the Amusement and Instruction of Little Tarry-at-Home Travellers.* London: Harris and Son, 1820.
Walsh, Robert. *Notices of Brazil in 1828 and 1829*, vol. 1. London: F. Westley and A. H. Davis, 1830.
Washington, Booker T. *Up from Slavery: With Related Documents.* Boston: Bedford/St. Martin's, 2003.

NOVELS AND PLAYS

Delany, Martin Robinson. *Blake; or, The Huts of America, A Novel.* Boston: Beacon Press, 1970.
Del Marco. "Theatros." *O Mequetrefe* July 18 (1876): 6.
Dumanoir, Philippe François Pinel, and Alphonse d'Ennery. *La case de l'oncle Tom: Drame en huit actes.* Paris: Michel Lévy Frères, 1853.
Gonçalves, Ana Maria. *Um defeito de cor.* Rio de Janeiro: Record, 2006.
Guimarães, Bernardo. *A escrava Isaura.* Rio de Janeiro: Casa Garnier, 1875.
Guimarães, Carlos Magno. "Água: Força, Equipamentos, Artes e Ofícios." in Museu de Artes e Ofícios, *Jardim das energias, Ofícios de madeira.* Belo Horizonte, Minas Gerais: Museu de Artes e Ofícios, 2008.
Haley, Alex. *Roots: The Saga of an American Family.* New York: Vanguarda Books, 2007.
Hill, Lawrence. *Someone Knows My Name.* New York: W. W. Norton, 2007a.
Hill, Lawrence. *The Book of Negroes.* Toronto: Harper Collins, 2007b.
Mitchell, Margaret. *Gone with the Wind.* New York: Macmillan, 1936.
Mitchell, Margaret (trans. Francisca de Basto Cordeiro). *E o Vento Levou.* Rio de Janeiro: Irmãos Pongetti Editores, 1940.
Morais, Afonso. *As Torres Malditas.* Porto Alegre: Globo, 1931.
Morrison, Toni. *Beloved.* New York: Alfred Knopf, 1987.
Stowe, Harriet Beecher. *Uncle Tom's Cabin.* Boston and Cleveland, OH: John P. Jewett & Company and Jewett, Proctor & Worthington, 1852.
Stowe, Harriet Beecher (trans. Francisco Ladislau Alvares d'Andrada). *A cabana do pai Thomaz ou, A vida dos pretos na América.* Paris: Rey & Belhatte, 1853.
Wiesel, Elie, and Marion Wiesel, *Night.* New York: Hill and Wang, 2006.
Wiesel, Elie. *La Nuit.* Paris: Éditions de Minuit, 1958, 2007.
Wiesel, Elie. *Night.* New York: Hill and Wang, 1960.

OTHER PRIMARY AND SECONDARY SOURCES

Abreu, Martha. "Outras histórias de Pai João: Conflitos raciais, protesto escravo e irreverência sexual na poesia popular, 1880–1950." *Afro-Ásia* (2004): 235–276.
"'A cabana do pae Thomaz' em sessão especial, hontem no Pathé Palace." *Correio da manhã* June 3 (1928): 10.
"A chegada dos despojos da Princesa Isabel e do Conde d'Eu." *Diário da noite* July 7 (1953): 3.
Alderman, Derek H., and Rachel M. Campbell. "Symbolic Excavation and the Artifact Politics of Remembering Slavery in the American South Observations from Walterboro, South Carolina." *Southeastern Geographer* 48, no. 3 (2008): 338–355.

Allen, William C. "History of Slave Laborers in the Counstruction of the United States Capitol." Washington, DC: The Architect of the Capitol, June 2005.
"A Memorável manifestação trabalhista ao chefe do governo: Há muitos anos a cidade não assiste a espetáculo de tão impressionante beleza cívica como o que hotem a empolgou ao cair da tarde." *Jornal do Brasil* May 14 (1938): 7.
Andrews, George Reid. *Blacks & Whites in São Paulo, Brazil, 1888–1988*. Madison: University of Wisconsin Press, 1991.
"Ao pé do monumento à redentora: Negros homenagearão Princesa Isabel com ritual de Umbanda." *Diário de notícias* November 27 (1960): 9.
"Apêlo das mulheres: Estátua à Redentora." *Diário carioca* November 17 (1959): 3.
Aptheker, Herbert. *American Negro Slave Revolts*. New York: International Publishers, 1963.
Aptheker, Herbert. *Nat Turner's Slave Rebellion: Together with the Full Text of the So-Called "Confessions" of Nat Turner Made in Prison in 1831*. New York: Humanities Press, 1966.
Araujo, Ana Lucia. *Public Memory of Slavery: Victims and Perpetrators in the South Atlantic*. Amherst, NY: Cambria Press, 2010a.
Araujo, Ana Lucia. "Slavery, Royalty and Racism: Representations of Africa in Brazilian Carnaval." *Ethnologies* 31, no. 2 (2010b): 131–167.
Araujo, Ana Lucia. "History, Memory and Imagination: Na Agontimé, a Dahomean Queen in Brazil." In *Beyond Tradition: African Women and their Cultural Spaces*, edited by Toyin Falola and Sati U. Fwatshak, 45–68. Trenton, NJ: Africa World Press, 2011.
Araujo, Ana Lucia. "Dahomey, Portugal, and Bahia: King Adandozan and the Atlantic Slave Trade." *Slavery and Abolition* 3, no. 1 (2012a): 1–19.
Araujo, Ana Lucia. "Zumbi and the Voices of the Emergent Public Memory of Slavery and Resistance in Brazil." *Comparativ. Zeitschrift für Globalgeschichte und vergleichende Gesellschaftsforschung* 22, no. 2. "Memories of Slavery," special issue edited by Michael Zeuske and Ulrike Schmieder (2012b): 95–111.
Araujo, Ana Lucia, and Francine Saillant. "L'esclavage au Brésil: Le travail du mouvement noir." *Ethnologie Française* XXXVII, no. 3 (2007): 457–466.
Araújo, Marta, and Silvia Rodríguez Maeso. "Slavery and Racism as the 'Wrongs' of (European) History: Reflections from a Study of Textbooks." In *Slavery, Memory, and Identity*, edited by Douglas Hamilton, Kate Hodgson, and Joel Quirk, 151–166. London: Pickering and Chatto, 2012.
"The Arrival, Jamestown 1619: From African to African-American: Aug. 20 Event Will Commemorate 375 Years of African-American Heritage." *New Pittsburgh Courier* July (1994): B-1.
Assunção, Matthias Röhrig. *Capoeira: The History of an Afro-Brazilian Martial Art*. London and New York: Routledge, 2002.
Auslander, Mark. "Enslaved Labor and Building the Smithsonian: Reading the Stones." *Southern Spaces*, December (2012), www.southernspaces.org/2012/enslaved-labor-and-building-smithsonian-reading-stones.
"Auxiliares de Sette fizeram fila para lhe dar bandeja de adeus." *Jornal do Brasil* December 4 (1960): 7.
Ayad, Christophe. "Gardien de fers." *Libération* August 31 (2001), www.liberation.fr/portrait/0101384926-gardien-de-fers.
Azevedo, Arthur de. "Chronica Fluminense." *A Vida Moderna* no. 10–11, September 11 (1886): 75.
Azevedo, Paulo Ormindo de. *Alfândega e o Mercado: Memória e Restauração*. Salvador: Secretaria de Planejamento, Ciência e Tecnologia do Estado da Bahia, 1985.
Bako-Arifari, Nassirou. "La mémoire de la traite négrière dans le débat politique au Bénin dans les années 1990." *Journal des Africanistes* 70, no. 1–2 (2000): 221–231.

Baldwin, William R. *Abraham Lincoln: Tribute to the Memory of the Great Emancipator on the One Hundredth Anniversary of His Birth.* New York, 1909.
Ball, Edward. *Slaves in the Family.* New York: Ballatine Books, 1998.
Bank of Guyana. "250th Anniversary: 1763 Berbice Slave Rebellion, 2013," brochure.
Banner-Haley, Charles Pete. "The Necessity of Remembrance: A Review of the Museum of African American History." *American Quarterly* 51, no. 2 (1999): 420–425.
Barker, Cyril Josh, "Respect Due: African Burial Ground Memorial Opened." *New York Amsterdam News* October 11 (2007): 1.
Barman, Roderick. *Princess Isabel of Brazil: Gender and Power in the Nineteenth Century.* Wilmington, DE: SR Books, 2002.
Basséne, Pape Chérif Bertrand. "Mémoire de l'esclavage et de la traite négrière en Sénégambie (1965–2007): Dialectique de la diversité mémorielle." PhD diss., 3 vols., Université Laval, 2011.
Beattie, Peter. "Common Bedfellows? Brazilian Antislavery and Anti–Capital Punishment Efforts in Comparative Perspective." In *Paths of the Atlantic Slave Trade: Interactions, Identities, and Images,* edited by Ana Lucia Araujo, 161–202. Amherst, NY: Cambria Press, 2011.
Béchacq, Dimitri, "Le parcours du marronage dans l'histoire haïtienne: Entre instrumentalisation politique et réinterprétation sociale, Haïti face au passé." *Ethnologies* 28 (2006): 203–240.
Beckles, Hilary. *Bussa: The 1816 Revolution in Barbados.* Cave Hill, Barbados: Department of History, University of the West Indies, Cave Hill, 1998.
Bellagamba, Alice, "Tracing the Legacy of Internal Slavery and Slave Trade in Contemporary Gambia." In *Politics of Memory: Making Slavery Visible in the Public Space,* edited by Ana Lucia Araujo, 35–53 (New York: Routledge, 2012).
Bell, Felicia. "'The Negroes Alone Work': Enslaved Craftsmen, the Building Trades, and the Construction of the United States Capitol, 1790–1800." PhD diss., Howard University, 2009.
Benjamin, Richard. "Museums and Sensitive Histories: The International Slavery Museum." In *Politics of Memory: Making Slavery Visible in the Public Space,* edited by Ana Lucia Araujo, 178–196. New York: Routledge, 2012.
Bennett Jr., Lerone. "Was Abe Lincoln a White Supremacist?" *Ebony* February (1968): 35.
Bergad, Laird W. *The Comparative Histories of Slavery in Brazil, Cuba, and the United States.* New York: Cambridge University Press, 2007.
Berlin, Ira, and Leslie Harris. "Uncovering, Discovering, and Recovering: Digging in New York's Slave Past Before the African Burial Ground." *The New-York Journal of American History,* 66, no. 2 (2005): 23–34.
Bernardes, Tavares Reinaldo. "Cemitério dos Pretos Novos, Rio de Janeiro, século XIX: Uma tentativa de delimitação espacial." MA thesis, Universidade Federal do Rio de Janeiro, Museu Nacional, 2012.
Besson, Jean. "Missionaries, Planters, and Slaves in the Age of Abolition." In *The Caribbean: A History of the Region and Its Peoples,* edited by Stephan Palmié and Francisco A. Scarano, 317–330. Chicago: University of Chicago Press, 2011.
Bethell, Leslie. *The Abolition of the Brazilian Slave Trade: Britain, Brazil and the Slave Trade Question: 1807–1869.* New York: Cambridge University Press, 1970.
Bicca, Briane, ed. *Programa Monumenta: Porto Alegre.* Brasília: Instituto do Patrimônio Histórico e Artístico Nacional, 2010.
Blair, William A. *Cities of the Dead: Contesting the Memory of the Civil War in the South, 1865–1914.* Chapel Hill: University of North Carolina Press, 2004.
Blakey, Michael L., and Lesley M. Rankin-Hill. *The Skeletal Biology of the New York African Burial Ground,* vol. 1. Washington, DC: Howard University Press, 2009.

Blier, Suzanne Preston. *African Vodun: Art, Psychology, and Power*. Chicago: University of Chicago Press, 1995.
Blight, David. *Race and Reunion: The Civil War in American Memory*. Cambridge, MA: Belknap Press of Harvard University Press, 2001.
Boletín Oficial de las Cortes Generales (Congreso de los Diputados), IX Legislatura, Serie D (General). February 26 (2010), no. 343.
Bragg, George F. *Men of Maryland*. Baltimore, MD: Church Advocate Press, 1925.
Brathwaite, Edward Kamau. *Nanny, Sam Sharpe and the Struggle for People's Liberation*. Kingston, Jamaica: Agency for Public Information, 1977.
Brasil, Luiz Antônio de Assis. *Concerto campestre*. Porto Alegre: LP&M, 1997.
Brown, Laurence, "Monuments to Freedom, Monuments to Nation: The Politics of Emancipation and Remembrance in the Eastern Caribbean." *Slavery and Abolition* 23, no. 3 (2002): 93–116.
Brown, Vincent. *The Reaper's Garden: Death and Power in the World of Atlantic Slavery*. Cambridge, MA: Harvard University Press, 2008.
Browning, Christopher R. *Remembering Survival: Inside a Nazi Slave-Labor Camp*. New York: W. W. Norton & Co., 2010.
Brundage, W. Fitzhugh. "Meta Warrick's 1907 'Negro Tableaux' and (Re)Presenting African American Historical Memory." *The Journal of American History* 89, no. 4 (2003): 1368–1400.
Bruner, Edward M. "Tourism in Ghana: The Representation of Slavery and the Return of the Black Diaspora." *American Anthropologist* 98, no. 2 (1996): 290–304.
Burnham, Forbes. "Symbol of Freedom; Address by the Leader of the People's National Congress, Prime Minister, Comrade Forbes Burnham, at the Unveiling of the '1763 Monument' on May 23, 1976." Georgetown, Jamaica: Office of the Prime Minister, 1976.
"Cabido entrega amanhã com ata despojos dos Príncipes sob as bênçãos do Cardeal." *Jornal do Brasil* May 8 (1971): 4.
Calmon, Pedro. *A Princesa Isabel: A "Redentora."* São Paulo: Companhia Editora Nacional, 1941.
"Campanha por túmulo de Isabel." *Jornal do Brasil* 1. Caderno, September 19 (1963): 12.
Campbell, James T. *Middle Passages: African American Journeys to Africa, 1787–2005*. New York: Penguin, 2006.
Cancel, Robert. "Whose Africa Is It Anyway, Or, What Exactly Is Skip Gates Signifyin'?" *African Arts* 33, no. 2 (2000): 1, 4, 6, 8, 10, 86–88.
Candida, Simone. "Achados arqueológicos do Cais do Valongo estão abandonados em terreno no Porto." *O Globo* January 31 (2013), http://oglobo.globo.com/rio/achados-arqueologicos-do-cais-do-valongo-estao-abandonados-em-terreno-no-porto-7450049#ixzz2YsVw96sF.
Candido, Mariana P. *Fronteras de esclavización: Esclavitud, Comercio e Identidad en Benguela, 1780–1850*. Mexico City El Colegio de Mexico, 2010.
Candido, Mariana P. *An African Slaving Port and the Atlantic World: Benguela and Its Hinterland*. New York: Cambridge University Press, 2013.
Carretero, Sagrario Cruz, Alfredo Martínez Maranto, and Angélica Santiago Silva. *El Carnaval en Yanga: Notas y comentarios sobre una fiesta de la negritud*. San Angel, Mexico: Consejo Nacional para la Cultura y las Artes, Dirección General de Culturas Populares, Unidad Regional Centro de Veracruz, 1990.
Carrillo, Karen Juanita. "Burial Ground Upheaval." *New York Amsterdam News* June 17 (2004a): 1.
Carrillo, Karen Juanita. "Controversies Continue over African Burial Ground Memorial." *New York Amsterdam News* June 10 (2004b): 4.

"Carta Aberta, Open Letter, Lettre Ouverte." *Lusotopie* 16, no. 2 (2009): xiii–xvii.
"Cartas dos leitores." *Jornal do Brasil* July 24 (1965): 6.
Carvalho, Marcus J. M. de. "A repressão do tráfico atlântico de escravos e a disputa partidária nas províncias: Os ataques aos desembarques em Pernambuco durante o governo praieiro, 1845–1848." *Tempo* 14, no. 27 (2009): 133–149.
Carvalho, Marcus J. M. de. "O desembarque nas praias: O funcionamento do tráfico de escravos depois de 1831." *Revista de História* no. 167 (2012): 223–260.
Castro, Fidel. "Discurso pronunciado por el comandante en jefe Fidel Castro Ruz, Primero Secretario del Comité Central del Partido Comunista de Cuba y Presidente de los Consejos de Estado y de Ministros, en el Acto Central por el XXXVIII aniversario del as alto al cuartel Moncada, efectuado en la Plaza Victoria de Girón, en la Provincia de Matanzas, el 26 e julio de 1991," www.cuba.cu/gobierno/discursos/1991/esp/f260791e.html.
"Cédulas com Isabel a prêto de 105 anos." *Diário Carioca* June 12 (1959): 11.
Célius, Carlo. "L'esclavage au musée: Récit d'un refoulement." *L'Homme* 38, no. 145 (1998): 249–261.
Celso, Maria Eugenia, "Coquetel." Notas Sociais, *Jornal do Brasil* May 31 (1955): 8.
Celso, Maria Eugenia, "Coquetel." Notas Sociais, *Jornal do Brasil* August 3 (1956): 8.
Césaire, Aimé. *Discours sur le colonialisme*. Paris: Réclame, 1950.
Chivallon, Christine. "Bristol and the Eruption of Memory: Making the Slave-Trading Past Visible." *Social & Cultural Geography* 2, no. 3 (2001): 347–363.
Chivallon, Christine. "Resurgence of the Memory of Slavery in France: Issues and Significations of a Public and Academic Debate." In *Living History: Encountering the Memory of the Heirs of Slavery*, edited by Ana Lucia Araujo, 83–97. Newcastle, United Kingdom: Cambridge Scholars Publishing, 2009.
Chivallon, Christine. *L'Esclavage du souvenir à la mémoire: Contribution à une anthropologie de la Caraïbe*. Paris: Karthala, 2012.
"Chronica: Theatros." *Revista do Rio de Janeiro* 3, no. 1 (1876): 95;
Ciarcia, Gaetano. "Restaurer le futur. Sur la Route de l'Esclave à Ouidah (Bénin)." *Cahiers d'etudes africaines* 192, no. 4 (2008): 687–706.
Cicalo, André. "From Public Amnesia to Public Memory: Re-Discovering Slavery Heritage in Rio de Janeiro." In *African Heritage and Memory of Slavery in Brazil and the South Atlantic World*, edited by Ana Lucia Araujo. Amherst, NY: Cambria Press, forthcoming.
"Cincoentenário da abolição: O Centro Carioca convidou as senhoras Getulio Vargas e Henrique Dodsworth para Inaugurar a Placa da Redemptora." *Diario carioca*, May 5 (1938a): 8.
"Cincoentenário da abolição: O ministro da viação autorizou o Centro Carioca a colocar uma placa no edifício dos Correios e Telégrafos." *Diário carioca* May 3 (1938b): 7.
Cleveland, Kimberly. "The Art of Memory: São Paulo's AfroBrazil Museum." in *Politics of Memory: Making Slavery Visible in the Public Space*, edited by Ana Lucia Araujo, 197–212. New York: Routledge, 2012.
Colin-Thébaudeau, Katell. "Les Lumières et l'esclavage: Variation sur Le Traité des Deux Indes, de l'Abbé Raynal." *Francophonie en Amérique*, edited by Justin K. Bisanswa and Michel Tétu, 104–113. Québec, CIDEF-AFI, 2005.
Committee Reports, 111th Congress, 1st Session, House Report 111–153, "Directing the Architect of the Capitol to place a marker in Emancipation Hall in the Capitol Visitor Center which acknowledges the role that slave labor played in the construction of the United States Capitol, and for other purposes" (2009–2010), http://thomas.loc.gov/cgi-bin/cpquery/R?cp111:FLD010:@1(hr153).
"Companhia dramatica." *A Reforma*, December 15 (1877): 3.
Connerton, Paul. *How Societies Remember*. New York: Cambridge University Press, 1989.

"Construção da 2ª. etapa da adutora do Guandu e melhoramentos de Copacabana." *Correio da manhã*, December 3 (1960): 1.

Correio paulistano December 14 (1877): 4.

Costa, Carina Martins. "Uma casa e seus segredos: a formação de olhares o Museu Mariano Procópio." MA diss., Fundação Getúlio Vargas, 2005.

Costa, Carina Martins. "Uma arca de tradições: Educar e comemorar no Museu Mariano Procópio." PhD diss., Fundação Getúlio Vargas, 2011.

Costa, Gilberto. "Fundação Palmares quer que Cais do Valongo, no Rio, vire patrimônio da humanidade." *Agência Brasil: Empresa Brasil de Comunicação* August 22 (2012), http://agenciabrasil.ebc.com.br/noticia/2012-08-22/fundacao-palmares-quer-que-cais-do-valongo-no-rio-vire-patrimonio-da-humanidade.

Cottias, Myriam. *La question noire: Histoire d'une construction colonial.* Paris: Bayard, 2007.

Craton, Michael. *Testing the Chains: Resistance to Slavery in the British West Indies.* Ithaca, NY: Cornell University Press, 1982.

Curtin, Philip D. *The Atlantic Slave Trade: A Census.* Madison: Wisconsin University Press, 1969.

Curtin, Philip D. *Africa Remembered: Narratives by West Africans from the Era of the Slave Trade.* Prospect Heights, IL: Waveland Press, 1997.

Daflon, Rogério. "Ruínas nos Subterrâneos do Porto Maravilha: Escavações de obra de drenagem da Zona Portuária encontram restos do cais da Imperatriz e do Valongo." *O Globo*, online edition, March 1 (2011), http://oglobo.globo.com/rio/mat/2011/03/01/escavacoes-de-obra-de-drenagem-da-zona-portuaria-encontram-restos-dos-cais-da-imperatriz-do-valongo-923909746.asp.

Daibert, Robert Jr. *Isabel, a "redentora" dos escravos: uma história da princesa entre olhares negros e brancos, 1846–1988.* Florianópolis: Editora da Universidade Federal de Santa Catarina, 2004.

Daibert, Robert Jr. "Princesa Isabel (1846–1921): A 'política do coração' entre o trono e o altar." PhD diss., Universidade Federal do Rio de Janeiro, 2006.

Daibert, Robert Jr. "A Princesa Isabel no cenário imperial: A Lei Áurea e o abolicionismo católico." *Revista do Instituto Histórico e Geográfico Brasileiro* 171, no. 446 (2010): 93–124.

DeCoste, F. C., and Bernard Schwartz, eds. *The Holocaust's Ghost: Writings on Art, Politics, Law, and Education.* Edmonton: University of Alberta Press, 2000.

De Jong, Ferdinand. "Shining Lights: Self-Fashioning in the Lantern Festival of Saint Louis, Senegal." *African Arts* 42, no. 4 (2009): 38–53.

DeRose, Chris. *Congressman Lincoln.* New York: Threshold Editions, 2013.

"Diálogo com o Leitor: Sra. Elza Pinho Osborne diz o que fês (e por que o fêz) no 14. Distrito de Obras." *Jornal do Brasil* 2 Caderno, December 5 (1958): 5.

Dias, Vera. "Princesa Isabel, por duas vezes monumento." April 3 (2010), http://ashistoriasdosmonumentosdorio.blogspot.com/2010/04/princesa-isabel-por-duas-vezes-monumento.html

Díaz, María Elena. *El Cobre, Cuba: Images, Voices, Histories, Archival Materials*, n.d. Santa Cruz: History Department, University of California, http://humweb.ucsc.edu/elcobre/images_commemoration.html.

Díaz, María Elena. *The Virgin, the King, and the Royal Slaves of El Cobre: Negotiating Freedom in Colonial Cuba, 1670–1780.* Stanford, CA: Stanford University Press, 2000.

Didi-Huberman, Georges. *Quand les images prennent position: L'oeil de l'histoire, 1.* Paris: Les Éditions de Minuit, 2009.

Dores, Igreja Nossa Senhora das. "Processo no. 0096-T-38, Livro Belas Artes no. de inscrição 065, vol. 1, F. 032, July 20, 1938." In *Bens Móveis e Imóveis Inscritos nos Livros do Tombo do Instituto do Patrimônio Histórico e Artístico Nacional, 1938–2009*, edited by Francisca Helena Barbosa Lima, Mônica Muniz Melhem,

and Zulmira Caário Pope. Rio de Janeiro: Instituto do Patrimônio Histórico e Artístico Nacional and Coordenação-Geral de Documentação e Pesquisa, 2009.
Doss, Erika. *Memorial Mania: Public Feeling in America*. Chicago: University of Chicago Press, 2010.
Douglas, Lawrence. "Wartime Lies: Securing the Holocaust in Law and Literature." In *The Holocaust's Ghost: Writings on Art, Politics, Law, and Education*, edited by F.C. DeCoste and Bernard Schwartz, 16–36. Edmonton: University of Alberta Press, 2000.
Downey, Gregory J. "Incorporating Capoeira: Phenomenology of a Movement Discipline." PhD diss., University of Chicago, 1998.
Dresser, Madge. "Remembering Slavery and Abolition in Bristol." *Slavery and Abolition* 30, no. 2 (2009): 223–246.
Dreyfus, Jean-Marc, and Sarah Gensburger. *Nazi Labour Camps in Paris: Austerlitz, Lévitan, Bassano, July 1943–August 1944*. New York and Oxford: Berghahn Books, 2011.
Du Bois, W.E.B. "The Negro and the Warsaw Ghetto." *Jewish Life* (May 1952): 14–15.
Dunn, Cristopher. *Brutality Garden: Tropicália and the Emergence of a Brazilian Counterculture*. Chapel Hill: University of North Carolina Press, 2000.
Duvalier, François. *Hommage au marron inconnu*. Port-au Prince: Presses Nationales d'Haiti, 1969.
Ebron, Paulla A. "Tourists as Pilgrims: Commercial Fashioning of Transatlantic Politics." *American Ethnologist: The Journal of the American Ethnological Society* 26, no. 4 (1999): 910–932.
Eckstein, Lars. "The Pitfalls of Picturing Atlantic Slavery: Steven Spielberg's *Amistad* vs Guy Deslauriers's *The Middle Passage*." *Cultural Studies Review* 14, no. 1 (2008): 72–84.
Eichstedt, Jennifer L., and Stephen Small. *Representations of Slavery: Race and Ideology in Southern Plantation Museums*. Washington, DC: Smithsonian Institution Press, 2002.
"Elegâncias." *Jornal do Brasil* September 8 (1940): 10.
"Elmina 2015 Strategy: 'Building on the Past to Create a Better Future.'" Elmina: KEEA and Elmina Cultural Heritage and Management Programme, 2003.
Eltis, David, and David Richardson. *Atlas of the Transatlantic Slave Trade*. New Haven: Yale University Press, 2010.
Eltis, David, Keith R. Bradley, Stanley L. Engerman, and Paul Cartledge, eds. *The Cambridge World History of Slavery: Vol. 3, AD 1420–AD 1804*. New York: Cambridge University Press, 2011.
"Em benefício da 'Cidade das Meninas': A primeira apresentação do filme 'E o vento levou'." *A Batalha*, August 21 (1940): 3.
"Engenheira em Campo Grande, a autora de 'Zé do Pato', a melhor peça do Festival." *Jornal do Brasil* 1 caderno, August 5 (1958), 13.
Escalante, Aquiles. "Palenques in Colombia." In *Maroon Societies: Rebel Slave Communities in the Americas*, edited by Richard Price, 74–81. Baltimore, MD: Johns Hopkins University Press, 1996.
"Establishment of the African Burial Ground National Monument: A Proclamation by the President of the United States of America, February 27 (2006)," http://georgewbush-whitehouse.archives.gov/news/releases/2006/02/20060227-6.html.
"Extract of a Letter dated Rio de Janeiro." *The Liberator* II, no. 1, January 7 (1832): 2.
Fanon, Franz. *Peau noire, masques blancs*. Paris: Seuil, 1952.
Ferrer, Maria Fernanda. "Alberto Lezcay: Espíritu vivo." *La Jiribilla: Revista digital de cultura cubana*, n.d., www.lajiribilla.co.cu/2005/n233_10/233_15.html.
Finch, Aisha. "Insurgency at the Crossroads: Cuban Slaves and the Conspiracy of La Escalera, 1841–44." PhD diss., New York University, 2007.
Finley, Cheryl. "Committed to Memory: The Slave Ship Icon in the Black Atlantic Imagination." PhD diss., Yale University, 2002.

"First Inaugural Address of Abraham Lincoln." *The Avalon Project: Documents in Law, History, and Diplomacy.* Yale Law School, Lillian Goldman Law Library, March 4, 1861, http://avalon.law.yale.edu/19th_century/lincoln1.asp.

Fischer, Brodwyn. *A Poverty of Rights: Citizenship and Inequality in Twentieth-Century Rio de Janeiro.* Stanford, CA: Stanford University Press, 2008.

Forsdick, Charles. "The Panthéon's Empty Plinth: Commemorating Slavery in Contemporary France." *Atlantic Studies* 9, no. 3 (2012): 279–297.

Francis, Jacqueline. "To Be Real: Figuring Blackness in Modern and Contemporary African Diaspora Visual Cultures." *Radical History Review*, no. 103 (2009): 188–202.

Franco, Sérgio da Costa. *Porto Alegre: Guia histórico.* Porto Alegre: Editora da Universidade Federal do Rio Grande do Sul, 1988.

Frederick Douglass Papers. "Self-Made Men." Address before the Students of the Indian Industrial School at Carlisle, PA, Folder 1 of 16 (Series: Speech, Article, and Book File–B: Frederick Douglass). Library of Congress: n.d.

French, Howard W. "Goree Island Journal; The Evil That Was Done Senegal: A Guided Tour." *New York Times* March 6 (1998), www.nytimes.com/1998/03/06/world/goree-island-journal-the-evil-that-was-done-senegal-a-guided-tour.html?src=pm.

Freyre, Gilberto. *The Masters and the Slaves: A Study in the Development of Brazilian Civilization.* New York: Knopf, 1986.

Freyre, Gilberto. *Casa-grande e senzala.* São Paulo: Global, [1933] 2003.

Fritsch, Dauny. "Monumento à Princêsa Isabel." *Jornal das moças* January 19 (1961): 53.

Fryer, Peter. *Rhythms of Resistance: African Musical Heritage in Brazil.* Middletown, CT: Wesleyan University Press, 2000.

Fukelman, Clarisse, and Patrícia Souza Lima, "Ofícios Ambulantes." In *Museu de Artes e Ofícios: A proteção do viajante, Ofícios do comércio, Ofícios ambulantes*, vol. 2, 35–57. Belo Horizonte, Minas Gerais: Museu de Artes e Ofícios, 2008.

Fundação de Economia e Estatística. *De Província de São Pedro a Estado do Rio Grande do Sul: Censos do RS, 1803–1950.* Porto Alegre: Fundação de Economia e Estatística, Museu de Comunicação Hipólito José da Costa, 1981.

García, Clara Inés Guerrero. "Memorias palenqueras de la libertad." In *Afroreparaciones: Memorias de la esclavitud y justicia reparativa para negros, afrocolombianos y raizales,* edited by Claudia Mosquera Rosero-Labbé and Luiz Claudio Barcelos, 363–388. Bogotá: Universidad Nacional de Colombia, Facultad de Ciencias Humanas, Departamento de Trabajo Social y Centro de Estudios Sociales, Grupo de Estudios Afrocolombianos, 2007.

García, Jesús Chucho. "La deuda del Estado venezolano y los Afrodescendientes." *Journal of Latin American and Caribbean Anthropology* 12, no. 1 (2007): 223–232.

Geggus, David Patrick. "Slavery, War, and Revolution in the Greater Caribbean, 1789–1815." In *A Turbulent Time: The French Revolution and the Greater Caribbean,* edited by David Barry Gaspar and David Patrick Geggus, 1–50. Bloomington: Indiana University Press, 1997.

Genovese, Eugene D. *Roll, Jordan, Roll: The World the Slaves Made.* New York: Pantheon Books, 1974.

Genovese, Eugene D. *From Rebellion to Revolution: Afro-American Slave Revolts in the Making of the Modern World.* Baton Rouge: Louisiana State University Press, 1979.

"Gente humilde vê o ataúde da Princesa Isabel e faz questão de deixar seu nome." *Jornal do Brasil* May 11 (1971): 19.

Githiora, Chege. *Discourse of Race and Identity in the African Diaspora.* Trenton, NJ: Africa World Press, 2008.

Gottberg, Luis Duno. "The Color of Mobs: Racial Politics, Ethnopopulism, and Representation in the Chávez Era." In *Venezuela's Bolivarian Democracy: Participation, Politics, and Culture Under Chávez*, edited by David by Smilde and Daniel Hellinger, 271–297. Durham, NC: Duke University Press, 2011.

Gottlieb, Karla. *The Mother of Us All: A History of Queen Nanny, Leader of the Windward Jamaican Maroons*. Trenton, NJ: Africa World Press, 2000.

Graham, Leroy. *Baltimore: The Nineteenth Century Black Capital*. Washington, DC: University Press of America, 1983.

Greene, Meg. *Henry Louis Gates, Jr.: A Biography*. Santa Barbara, CA: Greenwood, an imprint of ABC-CLIO, LLC, 2012.

"Guide du Musée historique de l'A.O.F. à Gorée." Dakar: Institut de l'Afrique Noire, 1955.

Guimarães, Carlos Magno. "Água: Força, equipamentos, artes e ofícios." In *Museu de Artes e Ofícios: Jardim das energias, Ofícios de madeira*, vol. 3, 10–31. Belo Horizonte: Museu de Artes e Ofícios, 2008.

Guran, Milton. *Agudás: Os "Brasileiros" do Benim*. Rio de Janeiro: Editora Nova Fronteira, 1999.

"Gustavo Barroso Sôbre o Maior Estadista Brasileiro: As Massas Brasileiras Jamais Esquecerão Vargas." *Última hora* August 30 (1955): 8.

Haas, Robert L. "Musée historique de Ouidah: Centre international d'études et de recherches sur la traite et la diaspora noire." Paris: UNESCO, 1984.

Halbwachs, Maurice. *Les cadres sociaux de la mémoire*. Paris: F. Alcan, 1925.

Halbwachs, Maurice. *La mémoire collective*. Paris: Presses Universitaires de France, 1950.

Hamilton, Cynthia S. "Hercules Subdued: The Visual Rhetoric of the Kneeling Slave." *Slavery and Abolition* (2012): 1–22.

Handler, Jerome. "The Barbados Slave Insurrection of 1816: Can It Be Properly Called Bussa's Rebellion ?." *Sunday Advocate* March 26 (2000): 22–23.

Handler, Jerome S., and Annis Steiner. "Identifying Pictorial Images of Atlantic Slavery: Three Case Studies." *Slavery and Abolition* 27, no. 1 (2006): 51–71.

Hartman, Saidiya. *Lose Your Mother: A Journey Along the Slave Route*. New York, Farrar, Straus and Giroux, 2008.

Hawthorne, Walther. *From Africa to Brazil: Culture, Identity, and Atlantic Slave Trade, 1600–1830*. New York: Cambridge University Press, 2010.

Heilprin, John, "Island's Painful Past May Be Marked for Future." *The Post and Courier,* June 4 (1997): 1.

Henderson, Désirée. *Grief and Genre in American Literature, 1790–1870*. Burlington: Ashgate, United Kingdom: 2011.

Herrera, Claudia. *The African Presence in México: From Yanga to the Present*. Chicago: Mexican Fine Arts Center Museum, 2006.

Hertz, Emanuel. *Great Emancipator, a Politician and Proud of It: Abraham Lincoln Was One of the Ablest Party Organizers and Keenest Directors Ever Seen in American Affairs*. New York: Political News, 1926.

Heuman, Gad. *Between Black and White: Race, Politics, and the Free Coloreds in Jamaica, 1792–1865*. Westport, CT: Greenwood Press, 1981.

Heywood, Linda M., and John K. Thornton. *Central Africans, Atlantic Creoles, and the Foundation of the Americas, 1585–1660*. New York: Cambridge University Press, 2007.

Hinchman, Mark. "African Rococo: House and Portrait in Eighteenth-Century Senegal." PhD diss., University of Chicago, 2000.

Hoffmann, Odile. "Negros y afromestizos en México: Viejas y nuevas lecturas de un mundo olvidado." *Revista Mexicana de Sociología* 68, no. 1 (2006): 103–135.

Holland, Jesse J. *Black Men Built the Capitol: Discovering African-American History in and Around Washington DC*. Guilford, CT: Globe Pequot Press, 2007.

Holsey, Bayo. *Routes of Remembrance: Refashioning the Slave Trade in Ghana.* Chicago: University of Chicago Press, 2008.

Holzer, Harold. "Picturing Freedom: The Emancipation Proclamation in Art, Iconography, and Memory." In *The Emancipation Proclamation: Three Views (Social, Political, Iconographic),* edited by Harold Holzer, Edna Greene Medford, and Frank J. Williams, 83–136. Baton Rouge: Louisiana State University Press, 2006.

Holzer, Harold. *Emancipating Lincoln: The Proclamation in Text, Context, and Memory.* Cambridge: Harvard University Press, 2012.

Holzer, Harold. *Lincoln: How Abraham Lincoln Ended Slavery in America: A Companion Book for Young Readers to the Steven Spielberg Film.* New York: Newmarket Press, 2013.

Holzer, Harold, G.S. Boritt, and Mark E. Neely. *The Lincoln Image: Abraham Lincoln and the Popular Print.* New York: Scribner Press, 1984.

Honorato, Cláudo de Paula. "Valongo: O mercado de escravos do Rio de Janeiro, 1758–1831." MA thesis, Universidade Federal Fluminense, 2008.

Honorato, Cláudio de Paula. "O mercado do Valongo e comércio de escravos africanos—RJ (1758-1831)." In *Escravidão africana no Recôncavo da Guanabara,* edited by Mariza de Carvalho Soares and Nielson Rosa Bezerra, 147–174. Niterói, Rio de Janeiro: Editora da Universidade Federal Fluminense, 2011.

Horton, James Oliver, and Lois E. Horton, eds. *Slavery and Public History: The Tough Stuff of American Memory.* New York: The New Press, 2006.

Hourcade, Renaud. "Commemorating a Guilty Past: The Politics of Memory in the French Former Slave Trade Cities." In *Politics of Memory: Making Slavery Visible in the Public Space,* edited by Ana Lucia Araujo, 124–140. New York: Routledge, 2012.

Houser, Myra Ann. "Avenging Carlota in Africa: Angola and the Memory of Cuban Slavery." Paper presented in the 24th Biennial Conference of the Southern African Historical Society, University of Botswana, Gaborone, Botswana, June 27–29 (2013).

Hulser, Kathleen. "Exhibiting Slavery at the New-York Historical Society." in Politics of Memory: Making Slavery Visible in the Public Space, 232–251. New York: Routledge, 2012.

"Inaugural Ceremonies of the Freedmen's Memorial Monument to Abraham Lincoln, Washington City, April 14th, 1876." Saint-Louis, MO: Levison & Blythe, 1876.

"In Berlin, Michelle Obama and daughters visit Holocaust Memorial." June 19 (2013), www.jta.org/2013/06/19/news-opinion/israel-middle-east/in-berlin-michelle-obama-daughters-visit-holocaust-memorial.

Instituto do Patrimônio Histórico e Artístico Nacional. *Proteção e Revitalização do Patrimônio Cultural no Brazil: Uma Trajetória.* Brasília: Ministério da Educação e Cultura, Secretaria do Patrimônio Histórico e Artístico Nacional, Fundação Pró-Memória, 1980.

Instituto do Patrimônio Histórico e Artístico Nacional. *Bens Móveis e Imóveis Inscritos nos Livros do Tombo do Instituto do Patrimônio Histórico e Artístico Nacional, 1938–2009.* Brasília: Ministério da Cultura e Instituto do Patrimônio Histórico e Artístico Nacional, 2009.

"Interview with President Obama by Anderson Cooper, Cape Coast, Ghana," CNN, July 14 (2009), http://ac360.blogs.cnn.com/category/pres-obama-african-journey/.

"Isabel, a Redemptora: Mais demonstrações de pezar pela sua morte nesta capital, no exterior e nos estados." *Jornal do Brasil* November 18 (1921): 9.

Jamestown Settlement. *Dispatch: A Newsletter of the Jamestown-Yorktown Foundation* 20, no. 2 (2006a).

Jamestown Settlement, *Permanent Exhibition, Three Cultures, One Century: America's Story.* Williamsburg, VA: Jamestown-Yorktown Foundation, 2006b.

"Jamestown to Commemorate 1619 Arrival of Africans." *Michigan Chronicle*, July 20 (1994): 4-B.
Jones, Hilary. *The Métis of Senegal: Urban Life and Politics in French West Africa*. Bloomington: Indiana University Press, 2013.
Kapsch, Robert James. "The Labor History of the Constitution and Reconstruction of the White House, 1793–1817." PhD diss., University of Maryland, 1993.
Kardux, Johanna C. "Slavery, Memory, and Citizenship in Transatlantic Perspective." In *American Multiculturalism After 9/11: Transatlantic Perspectives*, edited by Derek Rubin and Jaap Verheul, 165–180. Amsterdam: Amsterdam University Press, 2009.
Kars, Marjoleine. "Policing and Transgressing Borders: Soldiers, Slave Rebels, and the Early Modern Atlantic." *New West Indian Guide* 83, nos. 3–4 (2009): 191–217.
Katchka, Kinsey A. "Re-siting Slavery at the Gorée-Almadies Memorial and Museum." *Museum Anthropology* 27, nos. 1–2 (2008): 3–12.
Katchun, Mitch. *Festivals of Freedom: Meaning and Memory in African American Emancipation Celebrations, 1808–1915*. Amherst: University of Massachusetts Press, 2003.
Keaton, Trica Danielle, T. Denean Sharpley-Whiting, and Tyler Edward Stovall. *Black France/France Noire: The History and Politics of Blackness*. Durham, NC: Duke University Press, 2012.
Kerr-Ritchie, Jeffrey. "Slaves Supplicant and Slaves Triumphant: The Middle Passage of an Abolitionist Icon." In *Paths of the Atlantic Slave Trade: Interactions, Identities, and Images*, edited by Ana Lucia Araujo, 327–358. Amherst, NY: Cambria Press, 2011.
Lacombe, Lourenço Luís. *Isabel: A princesa redentora. Biografia baseada em documentos inéditos*. Petrópolis, Rio de Janeiro: Instituto Histórico de Petrópolis, 1989.
Lambert, David. "'Part of the Blood and Dream': Surrogation, Memory and the National Hero in the Postcolonial Caribbean." *Patterns of Prejudice* 41, nos. 3–4 (2007): 345–371.
Landers, Jane. "Transforming Bondsmen into Vassals: Arming Slaves in Colonial Spanish America." In *Arming Slaves: From Classical Times to the Modern Age*, edited by Christopher Leslie Brown and Philip D. Morgan, 120–145. New Haven, CT, and London: Yale University Press, 2006.
Lao, Nondoté Anicet. "Le Festival du Danxomè: Enjeux et défis pour la Commune d'Abomey dans le context de la decentralisation." MA diss., Université d'Abomey-Calavi, 2008.
Lara, Silvia Hunold. "No fio da navalha: As lutas escravas na histéria e na política." *Idéias* 2, no. 2 (1995): 53–68.
Law, Robin. "A Neglected Account of the Dahomian Conquest of Whydah (1727): The 'Relation de la Guerre de Juda' of the Sieur Ringard of Nantes." *History in Africa* 5 (1988): 321–338.
Law, Robin. "'My Head Belongs to the King': On the Political and Ritual Significance of Decapitation in Pre-Colonial Dahomey." *The Journal of African History* 30, no. 3 (1989): 399–415.
Law, Robin. "The Slave-Trader as Historian: Robert Norris and the History of Dahomey." *History in Africa* 16 (1989): 219–235.
Law, Robin. "Ethnicity and the Slave Trade: 'Lucumi' and 'Nago' as Ethnonyms in West Africa." *History in Africa* 24 (1997): 205–219.
Law, Robin. "Commemoration of the Atlantic Slave Trade in Ouidah." *Gradhiva*, no. 8 (2008): 11–27.
Lee, Felicia R, "Bench of Memory at Slavery's Gateway." *New York Times* July 2008: E1.

"Lenços deram adeus do Rio a D. Isabel." *Jornal do Brasil* May 13 (1971: 1.
Les Guides Bleus: Afrique Occidentale Française, Togo. Paris: Hachette, 1958.
Levi, Primo. *The Drowned and the Saved*. New York: Vintage International, 1989.
Lewis, Simon. "Slavery, Memory, and the History of the 'Atlantic Now': Charleston, South Carolina and Global Racial/Economic Hierarcy." *Journal of Postcolonial Writing* 45, no. 2 (2009): 125–135.
Libby, Douglas Cole. "Metalurgia." In *Museu de Artes e Ofícios, A proteção do viajante, Ofícios do comércio, Ofícios ambulantes*, vol. 4, 11–23. Belo Horizonte, Minas Gerais: Museu de Artes e Ofícios, 2008.
The Liberator II, no. 1, January 7 (1832): 2.
Lima, Francisca, Helena Barbosa, Mônica Muniz Melhem, and Zulmira Caário Pope. *Bens móveis e imóveis inscritos nos Livros do Tombo do Instituto do Patrimônio Histórico e Artístico Nacional, 1938–2009*. Rio de Janeiro: Instituto do Patrimônio Histórico e Artístico Nacional and Coordenação-Geral de Documentação e Pesquisa, 2009.
Lima, Solimar Oliveira de. *Triste pampa: Resistência e punição de escravos em fontes judiciárias no RS, 1818–1833*. Porto Alegre: Editora da Pontifícia Universidade Católica do Rio Grande do Sul, 1997.
Lima, Vivaldo da Costa. "Nações-de-candomblé." In *Encontro de nações de candomblé*, 11–28. Salvador, Ianamá: Centro de Estudos Afro-Orientais, 1984.
Lovejoy, Paul E. *Transformations in Slavery: A History of Slavery in Africa*. New York: Cambridge University Press, 2000.
Lovejoy, Paul E. "'Freedom Narrative' of Transatlantic Slavery." *Slavery and Abolition* 32, no. 1 (2011): 91–107.
Lowenthal, David. "On Arraigning Ancestors: A Critique of Historical Contrition." *North Carolina Law Review* 87, no. 3 (2009): 901–966.
Lugan, Bernard. "François Hollande et la légende 'Gorée,'" October 14 (2012), http://bernardlugan.blogspot.com/2012/10/francois-hollande-et-la-legende-goree.html.
MacGonagle, Elizabeth. "From Dungeons to Dance Parties: Contested Histories of Ghana's Slave Forts." *Journal of Contemporary African Studies* 24 no. 2 (2006): 249–260.
Machado, Maria Helena Pereira Toledo. "De rebeldes a fura-greves: As duas faces da experiência da liberdade dos quilombolas do Jabaquara na Santos da pós-emancipação." In *Quase-cidadão: Histórias e antropologias da pós-emancipação no Brasil*, edited by Olívia Maria Gomes da Cunha and Flávio dos Santos Gomes, 241–282. Rio de Janeiro: Editora da Fundação Getúlio Vargas, 2007.
Magaldi, Sábato, and Maria Thereza Vargas. *Cem Anos de Teatro em São Paulo*. São Paulo: Editora do Senac, 2000.
Mansfield, Stephen. *Lincoln's Battle with God: A President's Struggle with Faith and What It Meant for America*. Nashville, TN: Thomas Nelson, 2012.
"Marinha." *Correio da manhã*, 1 caderno, June 24 (1953): 9.
Mark, Peter. *"Portuguese" Style and Luso-African Identity: Precolonial Senegambia, Sixteenth-Nineteenth Centuries*. Bloomington: Indiana University Press, 2002.
Márquez, Pompeyo. *El gesto emancipador de José' Leonardo Chirinos*. Caracas: Epsilon Livros, 1995.
Martin Luther King Jr., "I Have a Dream." Speech, August 28, 1963. In *The Avalon Project: Documents in Law, History and Diplomacy*, Yale Law School, Lillian Goldman Law Library, http://avalon.law.yale.edu/20th_century/mlk01.asp.
Masur, Louis P. *Lincoln's Hundred Days: The Emancipation Proclamation and the War of the Union*. New York: Belknap Press, 2012a.
Masur, Louis P. "The Painter and the President." Opinionator, *New York Times*, July 25 (2012b), electronic edition, http://opinionator.blogs.nytimes.com/2012/07/25/the-painter-and-the-president/.

Mathy, Jean-Philippe. *Melancholoy Politics: Loss, Mourning, and Memory in Late Modern France*. University Park: Pennsylvania State Press, 2011.
Mattos, Hebe, Martha Abreu, and Milton Guran. "Inventário dos lugares de memória do tráfico atlântico de escravos e da história dos africanos escravizados no Brasil." Rio de Janeiro: Laboratório de História Oral e Imagem Universidade Federal Fluminense, 2013.
Mattos, Hebe, and Ana Maria Lugão Rios. *Memórias do cativeiro: Família, trabalho e cidadania no pós-abolição*. Rio de Janeiro: Civilização Brasileira, 2005.
Mattoso, Katia M. de Queirós. *Être esclave au Brésil, XVI–XIXe siècles*. Paris: Harmattan, 1979.
Mauny, Raymond. *Guide de Gorée*. Dakar: Institut Français d'Afrique Noire: 1951.
"Mayor Announces Acceleration of Construction Schedule of City's Third Water Tunnel." *New York Voice*, March 14 (1992): 3.
McCandless, Peter. *Slavery, Disease, and Suffering in the Southern Lowcountry*. New York: Cambridge University Press, 2011.
"MEC reforma prédios históricos: No Rio, 5 museus terão obras reiniciadas." *Ultima hora* May 26 (1983): 7.
Medford, Edna G, ed. *Historical Perspectives of the African Burial Ground: New York Blacks and the Diaspora*. Washington, DC: Howard University Press, 2009.
Medford, Edna Greene. "Imagined Promises, Bitter Realities: African Americans and the Meaning of the Emancipation Proclamation." In *The Emancipation Proclamation: Three Views (Social, Political, Iconographic)*, edited by Harold Holzer, Edna Greene Medford, and Frank J. Williams, 1–47. Baton Rouge: Louisiana State University Press, 2006.
Meggett, Linda. "New Monument Honors Slaves." *The Post and Courier*, July 3 (1999): A1.
Mello, Bruno Cesar Euphrasio de. "A cidade de Porto Alegre entre 1820 e 1890: As transformações físicas da capital a partir das impressões dos viajantes estrangeiros." MA thesis, Universidade Federal do Rio Grande do Sul, 2010.
Menegat, Carla. "Considerações acerca da análise de rede social de um casal da elite do charque: Vila de São Francisco de Paula de Pelotas, 1824–1835." Paper presented in *Vestígios do passado: A história e suas fontes, IX Encontro Estadual de História, Associação Nacional de História, Seção Rio Grande do Sul, ANPUH, RS*. Porto Alegre, July 14–18 (2008).
Mesquita, Maria Luiza de Carvalho. "O 'Terceiro Reinado': Isabel de Bragança, a imperatriz que não foi." MA thesis, Universidade Severino Sombra, 2009.
"Monumento à Isabel vai cair." *Jornal do Brasil* January 13 (1965): 12.
"Monumento à princesa." *Diário de notícias* October 9, (1960): 9.
"Monumento à Princesa Isabel." *A noite* July 2 (1953): 7.
Moorer, Talise D. "African Burial Ground Becomes National Landmark." *New York Amsterdam News* March 2 (2006): 4.
Moraes, Renata Figueiredo. "As festas da abolição: O 13 de maio e seus significados no Rio de Janeiro (1888–1908)." PhD diss., Pontifícia Universidade Católica do Rio de Janeiro, 2012.
Morgan, Philip. "Introduction." In *African American Life in the Georgia Lowcountry: The Atlantic World and the Gulla Geechee*, edited by Philip Morgan, 1–12. Atlanta: University of Georgia Press, 2010.
"Mrs. Mary D. Tilghman." *State of Maryland Obituaries* July 28 (2012), http://maryland.obituaries.funeral.com/2012/07/28/mrs-mary-d-tilghman/.
Mullin, Gerald W. *Flight and Rebellion: Slave Resistance in Eighteenth-Century Virginia*. New York: Oxford University Press, 1972.
Murray, Freeman H.M. *Emancipation and the Freed in American Sculpture*. Washington, DC: Murray Brothers, 1916.
Nabuco, Joaquim. *Minha formação*. Rio de Janeiro: Garnier, 1900.

"National Museum of American History's New Exhibition Goes 'On the Water,'" May 19 (2009), http://ahm.si.edu/press/releases/national-museum-american-history%E2%80%99s-new-exhibition-goes-%E2%80%9C-water%E2%80%9D.

Nectario, María. *Documentos de la insurrección de José Leonardo Chirinos.* Caracas: Fundación Historia y Comunicación, 1994.

Neves, Julliana Garcia, and Marcela Franca e Gomes Silva. "'A Princesa Isabel, o Povo de Juiz de Fora': Monumento à Princesa Isabel no Parque do Museu Mariano Procópio." In *Anais da XXVIII Semana de História da Universidade Federal de Juiz de Fora, "Genocídios, Massacres e Nacionalismos."* 199–210. Juiz de Fora: Universidade Federal de Juiz de Fora, Centro Acadêmico de História, 2011.

Nicolussi, Haydée. "E o vento levou: O romance que supera a expectativa." *Gazeta de notícias* Supplemento, November 10 (1940): 6.

"No listão do destêrro." *Última hora* January 15 (1965): 3.

Obama, Barack. "A More Perfect Union," Philadelphia, March 18, 2008." In *The Speech Race and Barack Obama's 'A More Perfect Union,'* edited by T. Denean Sharpley-Whiting, 237–252. New York: Bloombury, 2009.

Obama, Barack. "A World That Stands as One." Berlin, July 24 (2008), *Barack Obama, Change We Need,* http://my.barackobama.com/page/content/berlinvideo/.

O'Reilly, Bill, and Dwight Jon Zimmerman. *Lincoln's Last Days: The Schocking Assassination That Changed America Forever.* New York: Henry Holt and Company, 2011.

"O cincoentenário da abolição: As grandes comemorações cívicas que se realizarão nesta capital." *Diário carioca* May 13 (1938a): 5.

"O cincoentenário da abolição: foram brilhantes as comemorações de hontem—O Discurso do Sr. Costa Rego proferido no Theatro Municipal." *Diário carioca* May 14 (1938b): 2.

Olsen, Margaret M. "African Reinscription of Body and Space in New Granada." In *Mapping Colonial Spanish America Places and Commonplaces of Identity, Culture, and Experience,* edited by Santa Arias and Mariselle Meléndez, 51–67. Lewisburg, PA: Bucknell University Press: London: Associated University Press, 2002.

"Ouidah 92: Appel du Président Soglo aux peuples noirs." *La Nation* November 26 (1992): 3.

"Ouidah 92 est avant tout une manifestation du souvenir: Discours d'ouverture du Président Soglo," *La Nation* February 10 (1993).

Pace, Julie. "Obama Visits Slave Site of Disputed Importance." *New York Times* June 27 (2013), www.nytimes.com/aponline/2013/06/27/world/africa/ap-af-obama-slavery-goree-island.html.

"Para que seja erguido um monumento à princesa Isabel." *Diário carioca,* "Noticiário." January 15 (1938): 2.

Parés, Luis Nicolau. "The Jeje in the Tambor de Mina of Maranhão and in the Candomblé of Bahia." *Slavery and Abolition* 22, no. 1 (2001): 91–115.

Parés, Luis Nicolau. "Cartas do Daomé." *Afro-Ásia* 47 (2013): 295–395.

"Pelosi Remarks at Capitol Slave Labor Commemorative Stone Marker Unveiling." February 28 (2012), http://pelosi.house.gov/news/press-releases/2012/02/pelosi-remarks-at-capitol-slave-labor-commemorative-stone-marker-unveiling.shtml.

Pereira, Júlio César Medeiros da Silva. *À flor da terra: O cemitério dos pretos novos no Rio de Janeiro.* Rio de Janeiro: Garamond, Instituto do Patrimônio Histórico e Artístico Nacional, 2007.

Perry, Warren R., Jean Howson, and Barbara A. Bianco. *The Archaeology of the New York African Burial Ground,* vol. 2. Washington, DC: Howard University Press, 2009.

Peterson, Merrill D. *Lincoln in American Memory.* New York: Oxford University Press, 1994.

Pétré-Grenouilleau, Olivier. *Les traites négrières: Essai d'histoire globale.* Paris: Gallimard, 2004.
Pierre Verger, "Le culte des vodoun d'Abomey aurait-il été apporté à Saint Louis de Maranhão par la mère du roi Ghèzo?" *Études dahoméennes* VIII (1952): 19–24.
Piqué, Francesca, and Leslie Rainer. *Palace Sculptures of Abomey: History Told on Walls.* London: J. Paul Getty Trust, Thames and Hudson, 1999.
Preston, Dickson J. *Young Frederick Douglass: The Maryland Years.* Baltimore, MD: Johns Hopkins University Press, 1980.
"Primeiro centenário do nascimento da Princesa Isabel: As cerimônias realizadas, ontém, nesta capital." *Diario de notícias,* July 30 (1946): 3.
Prince, Howard M. "Slave Rebellion in Bahia, 1807–1835." PhD diss., Columbia University, 1972.
"Princeza Isabel: Solemnes exequias." *Jornal do Brasil* December 23 (1921): 10.
"Profeta faz 105 anos." *Diário carioca* June 10 (1959): 1; 11–12.
"Proposición no de Ley relativa al reconocimiento de la comunidad negra española, presentada por el Grupo Parlamentario Popular en el Congreso" (núm. expte. 161/000944: "BOCG. Congreso de los Diputados," serie D, núm. 181, April 7 (2009).
"Proposición no de Ley sobre memoria de la esclavitud, reconocimiento y apoyo a la comunidad negra, africana y de afrodescendientes en España, presentada por el Grupo Parlamentario Socialista" (núm. expte. 161/001273: "BOCG. Congreso de los Diputados," serie D, núm. 275, October 20 (2009).
Pruitt, Dwain. "Island of Shame Enlightens." *Herald Journal* March 16 (1994): C1.
Ramos, Arthur. *O folclore negro no Brasil: Demopsicologia e psicanálise.* Rio de Janeiro: Livraria Editora da Casa do Estudante do Brasil, 1935.
Ramos, Guédez J.M. *Bibliografía y hemerografía sobre la insurrección de José Leonardo Chirino en la Serranía de Coro, 1795–1995.* Caracas: Universidad Central de Venezuela, 1996.
Rarey, Matthew Francis. "Counter-Witnessing the Visual Culture of Brazilian Slavery." In *African Heritage and Memory of Slavery in Brazil and the South Atlantic World,* edited by Ana Lucia Araujo. Amherst, NY: Cambria Press, forthcoming.
Rarey, Matthew Francis. "Representation, Irrepresentation, and Aesthetic Strategies of Rebellion in Brazil." Paper presented at the 127th Annual Meeting of the American Historical Association, January 3–6 (2013).
Reddiker, Markus. *The Slave Ship: A Human History.* New York: Penguin, 2007.
Reid-Vazquez, Michele. *The Year of the Lash: Free People of Color in Cuba and the Nineteenth-Century Atlantic World.* Atlanta: University of Georgia Press, 2011.
Reinhardt, Catherine A. *Claims to Memory: Beyond Slavery and Emancipation in the French Caribbean.* New York, Oxford: Berghahn Books, 2006.
Reis, João José. *Slave Rebellion in Brazil: The Muslim Uprising of 1835 in Bahia.* Baltimore, MD: Johns Hopkins University Press, 1993.
"Remains of Colonial Era Slaves Buried." *The Jacksonville Free Press* October 15 (2003): 5.
"Remarks by the President at the United States Holocaust Memorial Museum, Washington DC," April 23 (2012), www.whitehouse.gov/the-press-office/2012/04/23/remarks-president-united-states-holocaust-memorial-museum.
"Remodelação total do Rio em 20 dias." *Diário da noite* October 25 (1960): 22.
"Restos mortais da Princesa e Conde deixam a Catedral." *Jornal do Brasil* May 9–10 (1971): 34.
"Rev. Martin Luther King's Speech Was History Talking." *The Chicago Defender* August 31 (1963): 4.
Rhodes, Gary. "'Back of the Big House': Controversial Slavery Exhibit Tells Behind-the-Scenes Plantation Story," *The Free Lance-Star* March 15 (1997): 12.

Ribbe, Claude. *Le crime de Napoléon*. Paris: Éditions Privés, 2005.
Ribbe, Claude. *Napoleon's Crimes: A Blueprint for Hitler*. Oxford: Oneworld, 2008
Rice, Alain. *Creating Memorials, Building Identities: The Politics of Memory in the Black Atlantic*. Liverpool: Liverpool University Press, 2010.
Rice, Wallace de Groot Cecil. *The Lincoln Year Book: Axioms and Aphorisms from the Great Emancipator*. Chicago: AC McClurg & Co, 1907.
Richards, Sandra L. "Landscapes of Memory: Representing the African Diaspora's Return 'Home.'" In *Africa and Trans-Atlantic Memories: Literary and Aesthetic Manifestations of Diaspora and History,* edited by Naana Opoku-Agyemang, Paul E. Lovejoy, and David V. Trotman, 291–301. Trenton, NJ: Africa World Press, 2008.
"Rio dá adeus com lenços e sinos." *Jornal do Brasil* May 13 (1971): 7.
Rivas P. A. Gil, Prado L. Dovale, and Bello L. Lusmila. *La insurrección de los negros de la Sierra Coriana, 10 de Mayo de 1795: Notas para la discusión*. Caracas: Direccio´n de Cultura, Universidad Central de Venezuela, 1996.
Rivera, Enrique Salvador. "Social Control on the Eve of a Slave Revolt: The Case of Coro, 1795." MA thesis, University of Maryland, 2013.
Roberts, Blain, and Ethan Kytle. "Looking the Thing in the Face: Slavery, Race, and the Commemorative Landscape in Charleston, South Carolina, 1865–2010." *The Journal of Southern History* 78, no. 3 (2012): 639–684.
Rodrigues, Jaime. *De costa à costa: Escravos, marinheiros e intermediários do tráfico negreiro de Angola ao Rio de Janeiro (1780–1860)*. São Paulo: Companhia das Letras, 2005.
Rodriguez, Luis C. *José Leonardo Chirino y la Insurrección de la Serranía de Coro de 1795: Insurrección de libertad o rebelión de independencia: Memoria del simposio realizado en Mérida los días 16 y 17 de noviembre de 1995*. Mérida, Venezuela: Universidad de Los Andes, 1996.
Rodrigues, Raimundo Nina. *Os africanos no Brasil*. São Paulo: Companhia Editora Nacional, 1935.
Rojas, Marta. "Carlota, la rebelde." *Diario Granma: Órgano Oficial del Comité Central del Partido Comunista de Cuba,* May (2005), www.granma.cubaweb.cu/secciones/30_angola/artic04.html.
Rothberg, Michael. "After Adorno: Culture in the Wake of Catastrophe." *New German Critique* 72 (1997): 45–81.
Rothberg, Michael. *Multidirectional Memory: Remembering the Holocaust in the Age of Decolonization*. Stanford, CA: Stanford University Press, 2010.
Rousso, Henry. *Le syndrome de Vichy: 1944–198--*. Paris: Seuil, 1987.
Rousso, Henry. *Vichy: L'événement, la mémoire, l'histoire*. Paris: Gallimard, 2001.
Rout, Leslie B. *The African Experience in Spanish America, 1502 to the Present Day*. Cambridge: Cambridge University Press, 1976.
Roux, Emmanuel de. "Le mythe de la Maison des esclaves qui résiste à la réalité." *Le Monde* December 27 (1996).
Rush, Dana. "Vodun Vortex: Accumulative Arts, Histories, and Religious Consciousnesses Along Coastal Bénin." PhD diss., University of Iowa, 1998.
"S. A. I. D. [Sua Alteza Imperial Dona] Isabel: A Redemptora." *Revista Illustrada* 13, no. 507, Rio de Janeiro, July 9 (1888): 1.
Saillant, Francine, and Pedro Simonard. "Afro-Brazilian Heritage and Slavery in Rio de Janeiro Community Museums." In *Politics of Memory: Making Slavery Visible in the Public Space,* edited by Ana Lucia Araujo, 223–225. New York: Routledge, 2012.
Salas, Jesús María Herrera. "Ethnicity and Revolution: The Political Economy of Racism in Venezuela." *Latin American Perspectives* 32, no. 2 (2005): 72–91.
Santini, Valesca Henzel. "Charqueada São João: Um lugar de memória onde os tempos se misturam." BA senior thesis in museology, Universidade Federal do Rio Grande do Sul, 2011.

Santos, Myrian Sepúlveda dos. "The Repressed Memory of Brazilian Slavery." *International Journal of Cultural Studies* 11, no. (2008): 157–175.
Sassi, Jonathan D. "Africans in the Quaker Image: Anthony Benezet, African Travel Narratives, and Revolutionary-Era Anti-Slavery." *Journal of Early Modern History* 10, nos. 1–2 (2006): 95–130.
Savage, Kirk. *Standing Soldiers, Kneeling Slaves: Race, Ward, and Monument in Nineteenth-Century America*. Princeton, NJ: Princeton University Press, 1997.
Schenck, Marcia C., and Mariana P. Candido, "Uncomfortable Pasts: Talking About Slavery in Angola." *African Heritage and Memory of Slavery in Brazil and the South Atlantic World*, edited by Ana Lucia Araujo. Amherst, NY: Cambria Press, forthcoming.
Schlappriz, Luis, and Franz Heinrich Carls. *Memória de Pernambuco. Álbum para os amigos das artes*. Recife, Pernambuco: Lithografia F. H. Carls, Rua de Cadeia, 1860.
Schmidt, Nelly. "Teaching and Commemorating Slavery and Abolition in France: From Organized Forgetfulness to Historical Debates." In *Politics of Memory: Making Slavery Visible in the Public Space*, edited by Ana Lucia Araujo, 106–123. New York: Routledge, 2012.
Schnee, Clara Silverstein. "One Nation, Two Founding Stories: A Study of Public History at Jamestown and Plymouth." MA thesis, University of Massachusetts Boston, 2011.
Schramm, Katharina. *African Homecoming: Pan-African Ideology and Contested Heritage*. Walnut Creek, CA: Left Coast Press, 2010.
Schwarcz, Lilia Moritz. *As barbas do imperador: D. Pedro II, um monarca nos trópicos*. São Paulo: Companhia das Letras, 1998.
Schwartz, Lilia Moritz. "Dos males da dádiva: Sobre as ambiguidades no processo da abolição brasileira." In *Quase-cidadão: Histórias e antropologias da pós-emancipação no Brasil*, edited by Olívia Maria Gomes da Cunha and Flávio dos Santos Gomes, 23–54. Rio de Janeiro: Editora da Fundação Getúlio Vargas, 2007.
Seabra, Elizabeth Aparecida Duque. "Visitas de estudantes a museus: Formação histórica, patrimônio e memória." PhD diss., Universidade Estadual de Campinas, 2012.
Seck, Ibrahima. "Esclavage et traite des esclaves dans les manuels de l'enseignement secondaire au Sénégal." *Afrika Zamani*, nos. 15–16 (2007): 99–124.
Seeman, Erik S. "Sources and Interpretations: Reassessing the '*Sankofa* Symbol' in New York's African Burial Ground." *William and Mary Quarterly* LXVII, no. 1 (2010): 101–122.
Sengstacke, Myiti. "Masses Honor Slave Remains." *Chicago Defender* October 6 (2003): 1.
Shaw, Rosalind. *Memories of the Slave Trade: Ritual and the Historical Imagination in Sierra Leone*. Chicago: University of Chicago Press, 2002.
Silva, Eduardo. *As camélias do Leblon e a abolição da escravatura: Uma investigação de história cultural*. São Paulo: Companhia das Letras, 2003.
Silveira, Renato da. "Sobre a fundação do terreiro do Alaketo." *Afro-Ásia* 29–30 (2003): 345.
Simmons, William J. *Men of Mark: Eminent, Progressive, and Rising*. Cleveland, OH: George M. Rewell and Co., 1887.
Singleton, Theresa A. "The Slave Trade Remembered on the Former Gold and Slave Coasts." *Slavery and Abolition* 20 (1999): 150–169.
Slenes, Robert W. "African Abrahams, Lucretias and Men of Sorrows: Allegory and Allusion in the Brazilian Anti-Slavery Lithographs (1827–1835) of Johann Moritz Rugendas." *Slavery and Abolition* 23, no. 2 (2002): 147–168.
Slenes, Robert W. "Overdrawn from Life: Abolitionist Argument and Ethnographic Authority in the Brazilian 'Artistic Travels' of J. M. Rugendas, 1827–35." *Portuguese Studies* 22, no. 1 (2006): 55–80.

Smith, Bruce. "Fort Moultrie Exhibit Addresses Slave Trade." *Spartanburg Herald* February 27 (2009), www.goupstate.com/article/20090227/ARTICLES/902270952.

Smith, Laurajane. *Uses of Heritage*. London: Routledge, 2006.

Smith, Laurajane, George Cubitt, Geoff Cubitt, Kalioppi Fouseki, and Ross Wilson, eds. *Representing Enslavement and Abolition in Museums: Ambiguous Engagements*. New York: Routledge, 2011.

Soares, Mariza de Carvalho. "Nos Atalhos da memória: monumento a Zumbi." In *Cidade vaidosa: Imagens urbanas do Rio de Janeiro*, edited by Paulo Knauss, 117–135. Rio de Janeiro: Sette Letras, 1999.

Soglo, Nicéphore. "L'allocution du Président Soglo au 28e Sommet de l'OUA à Dakar." *La Nation* Cotonou, July 13 (1992): 5.

Sousa, Gabriel Soares de, and Manoel Augusto Pirajá da Silva. *Notícia do Brasil*. São Paulo: Martins, 1945.

Southall, Ashley. "Statue Unveiled at Capitol in Honor of Rosa Parks." *New York Times*, February 28 (2013): A18.

Sparks, Randy J. *The Two Princes of Calabar: An Eighteenth-Century Atlantic Odyssey*. Cambridge, MA: Harvard University Press, 2004.

Stam, Robert, and Ella Shohat. *Race in Translation: Culture Wars Around the Postcolonial Atlantic*. New York: New York University Press, 2012.

Starobin, Robert S. *Denmark Vesey; The Slave Conspiracy of 1822*. Englewood Cliffs, NJ: Prentice-Hall, 1970.

Sue, Christina A. *Land of the Cosmic Race: Race Mixture, Racism, and Blackness in Mexico*. New York: Oxford University Press, 2013.

Swarns, Rachel L. *American Tapestry: The Story of the Black, White, and Multiracial Ancestors of Michelle Obama*. New York: Amistad, 2012.

Sweet, James H. *Domingos Álvares, African Healing, and the Intellectual History of the Atlantic World*. Chapel Hill: University of North Carolina Press, 2011.

Tackach, James. *Lincoln's Moral Vision: The Second Inaugural Address*. Jackson: University Press of Mississippi, 2002.

Tall, Emanuelle Kadya. "De la démocratie et des cultes voduns au Bénin." *Cahiers d'Études Africaines* 137 (1995): 195–208.

Talmon-Chvaicer, Maya. *The Hidden History of Capoeira: A Collision of Cultures in the Brazilian Battle Dance*. Austin: University of Texas Press, 2008.

Teixeira, Laís. "Carioca pediu e vai ganhar: Obelisco à Princesa Izabel no Rio." *Correio da manhã*, July 29–August 4 (1960): 5.

"Theatro São Pedro de Alcantara." *A Reforma* July 9 (1876): 2.

Thiaw, Ibrahima. "The Archaeology of the Memories of the Atlantic Slave Trade on Gorée Island, Senegal." Paper presented in the Workshop on African and African Diasporic Knowledges, University of Cape Town, October 23–25 (2006).

Thiaw, Ibrahima. "L'Espace entre les mots et les choses: Mémoire historique et culture matérielle à Gorée (Sénégal)." In *Espaces, culture matérielle et identities en Sénégambie*, edited by Ibrahima Thiaw, 17–40. Dakar: Conseil pour le développement de la recherche en sciences sociales en Afrique, 2010.

Thomas, Christopher A. *The Lincoln Memorial and American Life*. Princeton, NJ: Princeton University Press, 2002.

Thomas, Hugh. *The Slave Trade: The Story of the Atlantic Slave Trade: 1440–1870*. New York: Simon & Schuster, 1997.

Thornton, John K. *Africa and Africans in the Making of the Atlantic World, 1400–1800*. New York: Cambridge University Press, 1998.

Thornton, John. "Notes and Documents: The African Experience of the '20. and Odd Negroes' Arriving in Virginia in 1619." *The William and Mary Quarterly* 55, no. 33 (1998): 421–434.

Tickner, Neil. "Frederick Douglass' Early Slave Home Unearthed by UM Archeologists." *University of Maryland Newsdesk*, August 4 (2006), www.newsdesk.umd.edu/sociss/print.cfm?articleID=1305.
Tillet, Salamishah. "In the Shadow of the Castle: (Trans)Nationalism, African American Tourism, and Gorée Island." *Research in African Literatures* 40, no. 4 (2009): 122–141.
Tillet, Salamishah. *Sites of Slavery: Citizenship and Racial Democracy in the Post-Civil Rights Imagination.* Durham, NC: Duke University Press, 2013.
"Todo São Paulo aguarda com incontida curiosidade o deslumbramento de 'E o vento levou.'" *Correio paulistano* September 4 (1940): 6.
"Trasladação da Princesa começa hoje." *Jornal do Brasil* May 9–10 (1971): 1;
Trochim, Michael R. "The Brazilian Black Guard. Racial Conflict in Post-Abolition Brazil." *The Americas* 44, no. 3 (1988): 285–300.
Tshimanga, Charles, Didier Gondola, and Peter J. Bloom, eds. *Frenchness and the African Diaspora: Identity and Uprising in Contemporary France.* Bloomington: Indiana University Press, 2009.
Ulm, Aaron Hardy. *In the House Where Abraham Lincoln Died, and the Sixty-Two Years' Quest for Mementoes of the Great Emancipator.* Moline, IL: Desaulniers & Co, 1922.
"Uma das maiores figuras da história brasileira: Transcorre hoje o 12. Anniversario do fallecimento da Princeza Izabel." *Diário carioca* November 14 (1933): 2.
"Um passeio às Caldas." *Correio paulistano* September 20 (1872), 3.
UNESCO, "Report of the Rapporteur on the Third Session of the World Cultural and Natural Heritage." Paris: UNESCO, 1979.
United States Capitol Historical Society and National Geography Society. *We, The People: The Story of the United States Capitol, Its Past and Promise.* Washington, DC: United States Capitol Historical Society, 2011.
"Vêm para o Brasil os restos mortais da Princesa Isabel e do Conde d'Eu." *Diário de notícias* June 10 (1953): 1.
Verger, Pierre. *Flux et reflux de la traite des nègres entre le Golfe de Bénin et Bahia de Todos os Santos, du XVIIe au XIXe siècle.* Paris: Mouton, 1968.
Vergès, Françoise. *La mémoire enchaînée: questions sur l 'esclavage.* Paris: Albin Michel, 2006.
"Viação: Monumento à Princesa Isabel." *Última hora,* May 19 (1960): 4.
Vidal, Silvia, and Neil L. Whitehead. "Dark Shamans and the Shamanic State: Sorcery and Witchcraft as Political Process in Guyana and the Venezuelan Amazon." In *Darkness and Secrecy: The Anthropology of Assault Sorcery and Witchcraft in Amazonia*, edited by Neil L. Whitehead and Robin Wright, 51–81. Durham: University of North Carolina Press, 2004.
"Visitez Abomey, Bénin: Capitale historique de l'un des plus puissants royaumes d'Afrique." Abomey, 2010.
Vlach, John Michael. *Back of the Big House: The Architecture of Plantation Slavery.* Chapel Hill: University of North Carolina Press, 1993.
Von Drehle, David. *Rise to Greatness: Abraham Lincoln and America's Most Perilous Year.* New York: Henry Holt and Company, 2012.
Wallace, Elizabeth Kowaleski. *The British Slave Trade & Public Memory.* New York: Columbia University Press, 2006.
Walvin, James. *The Zong: A Massacre, the Law, and the End of Slavery.* New Haven, CT: Yale University Press, 2011.
Warfield, Carolyn. "'Slave House' Curator Lectures in Detroit." *Michigan Citizen* XIII, no. 50 November 9 (1991): A-7.
Warren, Kim, and Elizabeth MacGonagle, "'How Much for Kunta Kinte?': Sites of Memory and Diasporan Encounters in West Africa." In *African Hosts & their*

Guests: Cultural Dynamics of Tourism, edited by W. E. A. Beek and Annette Schmidt, 75–102. Woodbridge, Suffolk: James Currey, 2012.

Wemyss, Georgie. *The Invisible Empire: White Discourse, Tolerance and Belonging*. Farham and Burlington: Ashgate, 2009.

Whitaker, Morgan. "Obama Makes 'Powerful' Visit to Goree Slave-Trade House." *Politics Nation*, MSNBC (2013), http://tv.msnbc.com/2013/06/27/obama-makes-powerful-visit-to-goree-slave-trade-house/.

Wiedmer, Caroline. *The Claims of Memory: Representations of the Holocaust in Contemporary Germany and France*. Ithaca, NY: Cornell University Press, 1999.

Wierzchowski, Leticia. *A casa das sete mulheres*. Rio de Janeiro: Editora Record, 2002.

Williams, Daryle. *Culture Wars in Brazil: The First Vargas Regime, 1930–1945*. Durham, NC: Duke University Press, 2001.

Williams, Daryle. "'Peculiar Circumstances of the Land': Artists and Models in Nineteenth-Century Brazilian Slave Society." *Art History* 35, no. 4 (2012): 702–727.

Williamson, Elizabeth. "Unearthing Slavery, Finding Peace: A Dig at an Eastern Shore Plantation Could Help Local Blacks See Their Past." *Washington Post*, July 21 (2006): B01, www.washingtonpost.com/wp-dyn/content/article/2006/07/20/AR2006072002041_pf.html.

Wilson, Dreck Spurlock. *African American Architects: A Biographical Dictionary, 1865–1945*. New York: Routledge, 2004.

Wilson-Fall, Wendy. "Women Merchants and Slave Depots: St. Louis, Senegal and St. Mary's, Madagascar." In *Paths of the Atlantic Slave Trade: Identities, Images and Interactions*, edited by Ana Lucia Araujo, 273–303. Amherst, NY: Cambria Press, 2011.

Wilson, Sherril D. "Rediscovery: The African Burial Ground." *The New-York Journal of American History* 66, no. 2 (2005): 58–61.

Winstone, Martin. *The Holocaust Sites of Europe*. London: I. B. Tauris, 2010.

Wood, Marcus *The Horrible Gift of Freedom: Atlantic Slavery and the Representation of Emancipation*. Atlanta: University of Georgia Press, 2010.

Wood, Marcus. "The Museu do Negro in Rio and the Cult of Anastácia as a New Model for the Memory of Slavery." *Representations* no. 113 (2011): 126–127.

Wood, Marcus. *Black Milk: Imagining Slavery in the Visual Cultures of Brazil and America*. New York: Oxford University Press, 2013.

Wood, Marcus. *Blind Memory: Visual Representations of Slavery in England and America, 1780–1865*. Manchester, IN: Manchester University Press, 2000.

Ydstie, John. "Plantation Dig Reveals Md. Town's Painful Past." *National Public Radio* October 20 (2007), www.npr.org/templates/story/story.php?storyId= 15383164.

Young, James E. "The Biography of a Memorial Icon: Nathan Rapoport's Warsaw Ghetto Monument." *Representations* no. 26, special issue, "Memory and Counter-Memory" (1989): 69–106.

Zips, Werner. "Nanny: Nana of the Maroons? Some Comparative Thoughts on Queen Mothers in Akan and Jamaican Maroon Societies." In *Sovereignty, Legitimacy, and Power in West African Societies: Perspectives from Legal Anthropology*, edited by Emile Adriaan Benvenuto van Rouveroy van Nieuwaall and Werner Zips, 191–227. Hamburg: LIT, 1998.

AUDIOVISUAL SOURCES

Appio, Helena, Henry Louis Gates, Nick Godwin, and Nicola Colton. *Wonders of the African World with Henry Louis Gates*, Jr. Alexandria, VA: Public Broadcasting Service Home Video [1999], 2003. DVD.

Ben, Jorge. "Zumbi." *A Tábua da Esmeralda*. New York: Universal Music [1974], 2004. Audio CD.

Borgeaud, Pierre-Yves. *Youssou N'Dour: Return to Gorée*. New York: Lawrence Douglas, 2006. DVD.
Braga, Gilberto. *A escrava Isaura*. Rede Globo, 1976.
Campanella II, Roy. *Brother Future* [1991] 2009. DVD.
Chomsky, Marvin J. *Roots* [1977] 2007. DVD.
Cicalo, André. *Memories on the Edge of Oblivion*, documentary film. Manchester: University of Manchester, 2010, http://vimeo.com/41609298.
Denmark Vesey's Rebellion. Public Broadcasting Service, 1982.
Deslauriers, Guy. *Middle Passage*, 2009. DVD.
Diegues, Carlos. *Ganga Zumba*. 1963.
Diegues, Carlos. *Quilombo* [1984] 2005. DVD.
Fleming, Victor. *Gone with the Wind* [1929] 2006. DVD.
Guiterrez, Ester J. B. *Museu do Charque*. Pelotas: Estúdio Tríade, 2002. CD-ROM.
Herzog, Werner. *Cobra Verde*. Germany: Werner Herzog Filmproduktion [1987] 2000. DVD.
Kalin, Andrea, and Bill Duke. *Prince Among Slaves*. Alexandria, VA: PBS Home Video, 2007. DVD.
Kalin, Andrea, Bill Duke, John Rhode, David Grossbach, Joseph Vitarelli, Mos Def, and Terry Alford. *Prince Among Slaves*. Alexandria, VA: PBS Home Video, 2007. DVD.
Lima, Henrique de Freitas. *Concerto campestre*. Rio de Janeiro: Labo Cine do Brasil Ltda, 2005. DVD.
Mattos, Hebe, and Martha Abreu. *Jongos, calangos e folias: Música negra, memória e poesia*. Rio de Janeiro, RJ: Universidade Federal Fluminense, 2007. DVD.
Mattos, Hebe, and Martha Abreu. *Passados presentes: Memória negra no sul fluminense*. Rio de Janeiro, RJ: Universidade Federal Fluminense, 2011. DVD.
Porter, Edwin S. *Uncle Tom's Cabin*, 1903.
Pollard, Harry A. *Uncle Tom's Cabin* [1927] 1999. DVD.
Spielberg, Steven. *Amistad* [1997] 1999. DVD.
Spielberg, Steven. *Lincoln* [2012] 2013. DVD.
Wiesel, Elie, and Oprah Winfrey. *Auschwitz Death Camp: Oprah, Elie Wiesel*. Chicago: Harpo, 2006. DVD.

WEBSITES

African Burial Ground, National Monument, New York, www.nps.gov/afbg/index.htm.
Architect of the Capitol, "Rosa Parks," www.aoc.gov/capitol-hill/other-statues/rosa-parks.
Brasil Raça Mundi, www.youtube.com/watch?v=N6xz-QSOQk4
Charles H. Wright Museum of African American History, http://thewright.org.
Charqueada Santa Rita Pousada de Charme, www.charqueadasantarita.com.br/site/museu-do-charque—historico.
Charqueada São João, www.charqueadasaojoao.com.br/historia.htm.
David Eltis et al., *The Transatlantic Slave Trade Database: Voyages*, www.slavevoyages.org.
Igreja Nossa Senhora das Dores, www.igrejadasdores.org.br/sites/igrejadasdores.
"Forced Crossings." *On the Water*, http://amhistory.si.edu/onthewater/exhibition/1_4.html.
H-Africa list-serve, http://h-net.msu.edu/cgi-bin/logbrowse.pl?trx=lx&sort=3&list=h-africa&month=9911&week=&user=&pw.
International African American Museum, www.iaamuseum.org/.
Le Mémorial de la Shoah à Drancy, www.memorialdelashoah.org/b_content/getContentFromNumLinkAction.do?type=1&itemId=1396.

Letícia Julião, "História: Breve Diagnóstico," www.dejore.com.br/museudoescravo/m_historia.htm.
Museu do Escravo, Município de Belo Vale, Minas Gerais, www.dejore.com.br/museudoescravo/m_historia.htm.
Office of the Exhibits Central, http://oecexhibits.si.edu/blog/2009/10/.
Parque Memorial Quilombo dos Palmares, http://serradabarriga.palmares.gov.br/.
Portal Arqueológico dos Pretos Novos, www.pretosnovos.com.br/.
Rio de Janeiro, Porto Maravilha, www.portomaravilhario.com.br/. A video on the project is available at http://vimeo.com/8096894.
Smithsonian National Museum of American History, http://americanhistory.si.edu/about/mission.
"Sojourner Truth Bust Unveiling," 2009, www.youtube.com/watch?v=QtmTEiTDBeg.
Statue Dedication Ceremony for Frederick Douglass, United States Capitol Building, June 19, 2013, www.speaker.gov/frederickdouglass/.
Opening of *telenovela A escrava Isaura* (1976), www.youtube.com/watch?v=4NUhkSzFwJM
Toni Morrison Society, www.tonimorrisonsociety.org/.
Taylor, Jason Decaires. Molinere Underwater Sculpture Park, www.underwatersculpture.com/sculptures/viccisitudes/.
UNESCO, World Heritage List, Island of Gorée, http://whc.unesco.org/en/list/26/.

Index

1816 Rebellion (Barbados) 195, 209n57
2014 FIFA World Cup 99
2016 Olympic Games 99

AARIS Architects 95
abduction(s) 9, 15, 28, 30–2, 41, 211
abeng 200
abolition of slavery 1, 7
abolition of slavery in: Brazil 11–12, 139, 146, 147–9, 152–4, 162, 166–8, 170–3, 176n66, 181, 202–203, 205, 213, 214; British colonies 32, 192, 195; French colonies 4; New York 97; Texas 153; United States 80, 126, 147–9, 153, 158, 160, 163, 213–14; Washington DC 153, 175n2
abolition of the slave trade 19, 41; British 4, 26, 32, 40, 80, 194; US 5
abolitionist movement 147, 149; in Brazil 143, 167, 174n10, 180–1
Abomey xi, 19, 23, 24; royal palaces 18, 19, 23, 25
Abreu, Martha 110 n33, 184, 208 n22
A cabana do pai Thomaz (play) 180–1, 207
A cabana do pai Thomaz (translated novel) 180, 219
A casa das sete mulheres 134, 238
Adandozan, King 19, 30
Adorno, Theodor 46, 53
A escrava Isaura (novel) 183, 219
A escrava Isaura (telenovela) 144n54, 184, 208n20, 239, 240
African Americans 3, 5, 6, 13, 38, 48, 50–3, 63, 79, 90–5, 97, 124–7, 142, 143, 153–5, 158–60, 166, 174, 213, 214

African Burial Ground xii, 27–8, 94–8, 216
"African Holocaust" 49, 95
Afro-Brazilians 11, 82, 99, 100, 133, 143, 160–2, 164, 166, 169, 174, 203
Agaja, King 21, 22, 35
agency 10–12, 42, 77, 113, 141, 161, 167, 179, 203, 212
Agonglo, King 30
Agontimé 30, 44n44
Agostini, Angelo xiii, 152
Akan 96, 194,
Alaketu (Candomblé temple) 36
alcohol 30, 32, 127
alcoholic beverage *see* alcohol
Alderman, Derek H. 117
Alexander, Archer 155
Almada, André Alvares d' 29
Álvares, Domingos 29
Alves, Castro 139
Amazon(s) xi, 18, 22–5
Aminata 36–7
Amistad (film) 34, 44n59, 239
Amistad, La (schooner) 34
amnesia 28, 91
Ancestral Chamber (African Burial Ground Memorial) xii, 96
Angola 14n21, 45, 47, 80
A Noite (newspaper) 165, 216
A Reforma (newspaper) 216, 223, 236
Asante Empire 17
Atlantic Ocean 38, 61
Atlantic slave trade 3, 8, 12–13, 15–16, 19, 27–9, 31–2, 35, 45, 47, 49–56, 58–60, 63, 64, 76–8, 84, 105, 141, 195, 211; apologies for 27, 71; benefit 18, 33; commemoration 2, 4, 8, 16,

24, 69, 92, 211; exhibitions 79; heritage/heritage sites 1, 54, 65, 96, 100, 103; history 6, 11, 26, 70, 109, 212; in public discourses 72; markets 17; memorialization 7, 9, 46, 48; memory 88, 89; museum 80, 81; painful past 108, 213; propaganda againt 23; public memory 10; remembered 38; to Brazil 84, 86, 109; to the United States 84, 90, 91, 109, 127; trauma 38, 214
Auschwitz 10, 49, 54, 66–7
Auslander, Mark 127
authenticity 8, 56, 71, 212
Aux Esclaves (statue) 69
Ayidjoso (square) xi, 23

Back of the Big House (exhibition) 3
Bacon, Henry 158
baianas 136
Ball, Edward 92–3
Ball, Thomas 155
Baptist War (Jamaica) *see* Christmas Rebellion
Baquaqua, Mahommah Gardo 29–32, 87, 127
Barbados 4, 85, 195, 198, 199, 204, 206
Barros, Adhemar de 182
Bay of All Saints 81, 102, 136
Bay of Guanabara 85, 86
Beaudoin, Eugène 66
beheading 19
Beloved 2, 219
Ben, Jorge (Jorge Benjor) 202, 239
Benguela 7, 45
Bioho, Domingos xiii, 196–8, 209n61
Bergad, Laird 89
Bight of Biafra 14n21, 29, 37
Bight of Benin 14n21, 29, 32, 34, 36, 37
Birkenau 54, 66
Blair, Tony 27, 175 n34,
Blier, Suzanne Preston xv, 194, 209n52
Bloomberg, Mike 94
Blount, Jonathan 94
Boehner, John 126
Bragança, Prince Regent Dom João Carlos de 19, 171
Brandt, Willy 187
Brigadeiro Sampaio Square *see* Praça da Forca (Gallows Square)
Britain 2, 5, 9, 27, 54, 80, 192

British: abolitionist movement 2, 157; abolitionist propaganda 15, 28, 77, 109n1, 211; abolitionist ideas 9–10, 41, 42; Bicentennial of the abolition of the British slave trade 4, 5, 26, 27, 91, 194; Broodhagen, Karl 195; *Brooks* (slave ship) 77, 80, 109n1; Brown, James 61; Browning, Christopher R. 46, 54; Buchenwald 10, 50, 117, 187–8, 212; Burham, Linden Forbes Sampson 194; Burton, Richard 19; Bush, George W. 48, 61, 63, 74n72, 95; Bussa 195, 199, 209n57

Calhoun, John C. 91
camellias 149, 153
Campbell, Rachel M. 117
Candomblé 30, 36, 101, 138, 139, 184
Canto a los heroes (mural painting) 191
Cape Coast Castle 47–8, 50, 52, 54, 63, 104, 187, 212
Cape Coast Castle Museum 48
Capitol (US) 5, 124–7, 142, 144 n37, 144n40, 144n42, 175n17, 187, 188
Capitol Visitors Center 125, 142
capoeira 101, 104, 109, 136, 149, 172
Caribbean 1–4, 7, 12, 26–7, 52, 61, 69, 80, 85, 136, 179, 185, 188, 190, 199, 202, 205–7, 214; British 195; French 4, 9
Carlota (slave rebel) 198–9, 209n66
Carnaval de la negritud (Negritude Carnival) 192
Carpenter, Francis Bicknell xiii, 149–50
Cartagena 195–6
Carter, Jimmy 61, 187
Carvalho, Marcus J. M. 88
Casa das Minas (Candomblé temple) 30
Castro, Fidel 193, 198
Celso, Maria Eugênia 162, 165
Cemitério dos Pretos Novos (Cemetery of New Blacks) 98
Center for Contemporary Jewish Documentation 70
Césaire, Aimé 184
Charles H. Wright Museum of African American History 80, 82, 109n4
Charleston 2, 10, 91–3, 108

charqueada(s) (jerked beef factory) 133–5
Charqueada Santa Rita 135, 239
Charqueada São João 134–5, 140, 239
Chávez, Hugo 200
Chirac, Jacques 70
Chirino, José Leonardo xiii, 200–2, 209n77
Christmas Rebellion *see* Baptist War
Church Nossa Senhora das Dores (Our Lady of Sorrows) xii, 119–22, 239
Church of Our Lady of the Rosary and Saint Benedict of the Black Men (Rio de Janeiro) 154, 163, 169–70, 177n108
Church of Our Lady of Rosary of Black Men (Salvador, Bahia) xii, 117–18, 121, 136, 137
Circle of the Diaspora (African Burial Ground Memorial) 95
Circuito Histórico e Arqueológico da Celebração da Herança Africana (Historical and Archaeological Trail of African Heritage Celebration) 99
"Cité de la Muette" (The Silent City) 67
Civil Rights Movement 6, 38, 108, 160, 173–4, 214
Civil War 5, 125, 147–8, 153, 155, 173
Cliff, Jimmy 61
Clinton, Bill 6, 48, 61, 63, 74n72, 193
Cobra Verde (film) 19, 23, 48
Coffij see Cuffy
Cold War 3, 4, 10, 46, 51, 91, 108, 15
Colombia xiii, 179, 195–7
Colonel Lloyd 114–16
Columbus 3, 90, 108
Coly, Eloi 64
commemorations 108, 162–3, 173, 200
Communism 51, 185
Concerto campestre (film) 134, 144n64
Conspiracy of the Tailors (Brazil) 19
Cooper, Anderson 50, 53
Coro Revolt 200–1
Correio da manhã (newspaper) 216, 219, 224, 230
Correio paulistano (newspaper) 180, 207n8, 216, 224, 237
Cristo na coluna xii, 121–2
Cromwell, John 157
Cuba 4, 32, 89, 147, 179, 193, 198–9, 206
Cuffy 194

Cugoano, Quobna Ottobah 28, 30, 36
Curtin, Philip 59–60

Dachau 10, 59, 71, 212
Dalzel, Archibald xi, 21–3
Debret, Jean-Baptiste 81, 85, 106, 184
decapitation *see* beheading
dehumanization 45, 56
Deslauriers, Guy 35
Diário carioca (newspaper) 166, 220, 223, 232, 233, 237
Diário da noite (newspaper) 164
Diário de notícias (newspaper) 168, 220, 231, 232, 233, 237
diaspora: Jewish; African 45, 48, 52–4, 97, 100–1, 192, 206
Didi-Huberman, Georges 41
Diener, Roger 71
Dinkins, David Norman 94
Dix, Eloise 95
Dodson, Howard 94
Dodsworth, Henrique 162
Dom Pedro II 98, 148, 163, 171
Door of No Return (Cape Coast Castle, Ghana) 48, 50, 52
Door of No Return (House of Slaves, Gorée Island) 59, 63
Douglass, Frederick 5, 114–17, 126–7, 142, 157–9, 173
Drancy xii, 10, 46, 57, 65–71, 75n75, 191, 212, 239
Dubois, W.E.B. 48, 51, 90, 186, 187, 208n27
dungeons 48–50, 52, 54, 59, 64, 71
Duvalier, François 189
Duvivier, Edgar 172

Earle, Augustus xii, 105, 106
Ebron, Paulla 63
Edward Lloyd *see* Colonel Lloyd
El Cobre (Santiago de Cuba) 199
Eliot, William Greenleaf 155
Elmina Castle 6, 47–50, 52–4, 59, 71, 212
Emancipation Day: Barbados 195; Ghana 52; Jamaica 194
Emancipation Hall (US Capitol) 5, 124–6, 144n40 and n42, 187–8, 223
Emancipation Memorial see Freedom's Memorial
Emancipation Monument (Barbados) 195
Emancipation Proclamation xiii, 11, 146, 149, 150–5, 159–60, 173

England *see* Britain
enslavement 1–2, 7, 9, 15–18, 26–35, 37–8, 40–2, 45, 47, 49, 51, 58, 65, 76, 79, 91, 146, 159, 195, 211, 212
E o vento levou (film) 182, 208n15, 232, 237, 207n1
E o vento levou (translated novel) 181
Equiano, Olaudah 26, 28, 30, 43n43, 80, 85
Esborne, Elza Pinho 167
Estado Novo 118, 161–3, 173–4, 176n67
Eu, Count d' 162, 164, 169, 170, 171, 177n108

Fanon, Franz 185
Farroupilha Revolution 121
favelados 169
favelas 169
Forbes, Frederick 19, 24, 194
Fort Moultrie (National Monument) 92, 93
France xii, 4, 6, 40, 54, 65–70, 154, 164, 173
François Duvalier 189
Freedmen's Memorial see Freedom's Memorial
Freedom Monument (Jamaica) 194
Freedom's Memorial xiii, 152, 155, 157–8, 166, 173–5
French Revolution 18, 19, 38
Freyre, Gilberto 128
Frézier, Amédée François 102
Frond, Jean-Victor 171
Fuller, Meta Vaux Warrick 90
Fundação Cultural Palmares (Palmares Cultural Foundation) 100, 111 n96, 205
Furro, Broteer 29, 85; *see also* Smith, Venture

Gadsden's Wharf 92, 93
Gambia 14n 21, 29, 31, 32, 37, 71
Gamboa 98, 101
Gargalheira 128, 130, 133
Garvey, Marcus 192
Gate of No Return (Ouidah, Republic of Benin) 45, 56
Gates of Hell 67
Gates, Henry Louis 49, 50–2
Gazeta de notícias (newspaper) 181, 216

General Service Administration (GSA) 94, 95
Gezo, King 18, 24, 30
Ghana 2, 6, 7, 10, 14, 29–30, 45, 47–50, 52, 54, 56, 104
Glele, King xi, 18–20
Glover, Danny 59
Golden Law 139, 146, 149, 154, 161, 163, 171–3, 214
Gonçalves, Ana Maria 36, 219
Gone With the Wind (film) *see E o vento levou* (film)
Gone With the Wind (novel) 180–1
Gordillo, José 191
Gorée Island xi, 7, 10, 47, 57–61, 63, 65, 69, 71, 73n47, 77, 104, 212, 232, 240
Goulart, João 169
Graham, Maria xii, 86, 102, 105, 106
Great Emancipator(s) 8, 11, 146–7, 149, 154–5, 158–60, 172–4, 179, 213–14
Grenada xvi, 83
Gronniosaw, James Albert Ukawsaw 19, 33
Ground Zero 97
Guarda Negra (Black Guard) 149, 175n16
Guérin, Jules 159
Guiltiness 121

Haiti 4, 179, 189, 191, 206
Haitian Revolution 75n89, 200
Haley, Alex 37, 38, 71, 183, 219
Hawthorne, Walter 29
heritage site(s) 8, 64–5, 69, 71, 77, 90, 116–17, 199
Herzog, Werner xi, 19, 21, 43n18, 48
Hill, Lawrence 36, 219
Hollande, François 61, 71, 73n63, 230
Hollant-Denis, Nicole 95
Holocaust 2, 7, 10, 12, 45–7, 49, 50–3, 55, 59–60, 63, 65, 68–72, 75n89, 79, 95, 100, 184–5, 187, 211–12; deniers 64; heritage sites 45–6, 69; memorial(s) 144n48, 228; survivor(s) 32, 46–7, 50, 54–5, 185, 187, 211
Holocaust Memorial (Drancy) 71
Howard University 93, 94, 157
Huber, Victor 86

Index   245

identity 7, 8, 95
Instituto de Pesquisa e Memória Pretos Novos (New Blacks Institute of Research and Memory) 99
International Slavery Museum 4, 11n68, 26–8, 43n32, 82
IPHAN 118, 121, 136, 205
Isabel, Princess 11–12, 146, 148–9, 142, 153–4, 160–74, 175n24, 176n58, 177 n95, 182, 203, 213, 214, 219–21, 223, 226, 228, 230, 234, 237
Isabelismo 149

Jamaica 4, 19, 52, 179, 192–5, 198–9, 204, 206, 208n49
Jamaica Labor Party 193
Jamestown 10, 89–91, 108
Jean, Michäelle 49
jerked beef 113, 133, 135–6, 213
Jewish martyrs 67
Jews 49, 50, 54, 66–7, 69–70, 105, 112n110, 125–6, 185, 187
Jim Crow 79, 90
John Paul II (Pope) 59, 61, 63, 187
John, Ancona Robin Robin 37
John, Little Ephraim Robin 37
Jornal das moças (newspaper) 168, 216, 226
Jornal do Brasil (newspaper) 165, 169, 170, 216, 220, 222–6, 228, 230
Juiz de Fora 160, 161, 173, 232
Juneteenth 153

Kamb, Bulfinch 19
Kehinde 36
kidnapping xi, 15–16, 18, 28–9, 32–8, 212
Kingdom of Dahomey 17–19, 21, 22–4, 30, 33
Kingdom of Ketu 18, 36
King George VI Park (Jamaica) *see* National Heroes Park (Jamaica)
Kingston (Jamaica) 192–3, 199
Kinte, Kunta 37, 183
Kytle, Ethan 91

La case de l'oncle Tom: Drame en huit actes 180, 219
La Nation (newspaper) 216, 232, 236
Lacerda, Carlos 169, 117 n104
Lage, Mariano Procópio Ferreira 160

Landing of First Twenty Slaves at Jamestown 90
Lane, Artis 125
Lantern Festival of Saint-Louis 65
Largo do Paço 97; *see also* Praça XV
Le marron inconnu (The Unknown Maroon) 189, 191
Le Musée d'histoire de Ouidah 54, 55, 216
Leon, Rodney 95
Lescay, Alberto 199
Levi, Primo 32, 64
Lewis, John 124
Lewis, Simon 91
Lincoln, Abraham xiii, 11–12, 146–50, 153–61, 166, 171, 173–4, 175n26, 213–14
Lincoln Memorial 6, 159–60, 172
Lindley, Thomas 102
Liverpool 4, 26, 43n35, 82
Lods, Marcel 66
London, Sugar and Slavery (gallery) 26–7
Lowery, Harriette 116–17
Luanda 6–7, 47, 54
Luso-Brazilian slave merchants 18, 26, 56

MacGonagle, Elizabeth 52
McLean, Ollie 95
maculelê 154
Mahi Kingdom (country) 24, 29, 43n27
Maison des Esclaves (House of Slaves) xi, 10, 45, 47, 57–65, 69, 71, 73n42, 74n72, 77, 104
Malcolm X 48
Malê revolt 118, 144n55
Mandela, Nelson 61, 193, 198
Mangonès, Albert 189
manillas 28
Manley, Michael Norman 192–3, 199, 208n49
Mariano Procópio Museum 160
Mariano Procópio Park 160–1
Marshall Plan for Africa 54
Martin Luther King Jr. 3, 6, 124, 159, 175n54
Matanzas 198
Mattos, Hebe 88
Mauny, Raymond 58
May 13 139, 146, 148–9, 154, 161–3, 165, 167, 172, 177n91, 181, 203
Medford, Edna G. 153

Mémorial national des déportés de France (National Memorial of France's Deportees) 67
Memorial to the Murdered Jews of Europe (Berlin, Germany) 126
Memorial to the Unknown Jewish Martyr 126
memorialization 146; of emancipation 174; of enslavement 45; of maroons 12, 207, 208n33; of Princess Isabel 173, 214; of slavery 2, 3, 5, 7–10, 13, 52, 114, 143, 194, 212–13, 215; of the Atlantic slave trade 7, 53; of the Holocaust 46, 53; of the Second World War 66; of Zumbi 12, 179; projects 8
memory replacement 10, 77, 83–4, 89, 103–4, 108, 212
Mercado Modelo (Salvador, Bahia) xii, 103–4
Mexican Revolution 191–2
Mexico xiii, 179, 190–2, 198, 200, 206
Middle Passage 7, 10, 26, 48–9, 56, 60, 63–4, 76–8, 80–3, 85, 87, 92–3, 96, 107–8, 212
Middle Passage (film) 35, 44n59
military dictatorship: Brazil 3, 5, 108, 131, 140, 169, 173–4, 202–4, 210n84; Republic of Benin 56
Mitchell, Margaret 180, 181, 207n1, 219
Miterrand, Danielle 61
Mixôbiwo, Obokô 36
Moisa, Christian 69
Moisa, Jean 69
Molinere Underwater Sculpture Park 83, 240
montage 41
Montego Bay 192, 193
monument "*al Cimarron, a la memoria de la rebeldia esclava*" 199
Monument to the Ghetto Heroes xiii, 185–8
Moore, Philip 194
Moorland, George 27
Morrison, Toni 2, 13n5, 92, 93, 111n61, 219, 240
Movimento Negro Unificado (Unified Black Movement) 203
Musée de l'Afrique Occidentale (Museum of French West Africa) 60

Musée d'histoire de Ouidah (Ouidah Museum of History) 54–5
Musée historique d'Abomey (Historical Museum of Abomey) 42n6
Musée Historique du Sénégal à Gorée (Historical Museum of Senegal on Gorée) 60
Museu AfroBrasil (AfroBrazil Museum) 79, 82
Museu da Cidade (City's Museum) 137–8, 140–1, 145n74
Museu de Artes e Ofícios (Museum of Arts and Crafts) 137, 141, 216
Museu do Charque 135
Museu do Escravo (Slave's Museum) xiii, 137, 139–41, 145n77, 216
Museu do Percurso do Negro (Black's Route Museum) 122–3
Museu Júlio de Castilhos xii, 128, 132, 137, 216
Museu Nacional da Escravatura 7
Museu Náutico da Bahia (Nautical Museum of Bahia) 81–2, 109n12, 216
Museum of London Docklands 26, 28
Muslim slave trade 1, 15–16, 40, 70

Nabuco, Joaquim 153, 167, 180
Nanny 12, 179, 182, 206
"Nanny of the maroons" 199–200
Nascimento, Abdias 203, 206, 210n85
National Black Consciousness Day (Brazil) 205
National Heroes Day (Jamaica) 192
National Heroes Park (Jamaica) 192–3, 199
National Mall 5, 6, 127, 159
National Museum of American History 79–80, 109n9, 216
National Park Service 93, 95
National September 11 Memorial and Museum 97
National Statuary Hall Collection 124, 126
Nazi: camp(s) 12, 46, 53–4, 64, 67, 69, 74n84, 79, 179, 184, 188–9; Germany 51, 67, 182, 188, 206; regime 49, 69, 70, 71, 74n84, 125, 182, 184, 188, 206
N'Diaye, Joseph xi, 58, 59, 60, 61, 62, 63, 64, 65, 71, 73n47
N'Dour, Youssou 61, 63, 74n66
New York 2, 10–11, 108
New York City 8, 93, 94, 97–9, 109, 216

New York Times 217, 226, 229–30, 232, 236
Nigeria14n21, 30, 32–3, 45, 47, 80, 204
Night (novel) 54, 55, 219;
Norris, Robert 19, 22, 43n23
Nuit, La see Night
Nuñez, Rafael 196

Obama, Barack 5, 11, 50–1, 53, 63, 64, 117, 125–6, 142, 187, 213
Obama, Michelle 5, 11, 63, 125–7, 142, 144n48, 187–8, 228
Offeong, Egboyoung 26
Of the People: The African American Experience (exhibition) 79
O Globo (newspaper) 217, 222, 224
Ojarorô, Otampê 36
On the Water: Stories from Maritime America (exhibition) 80, 109n10, 232
OUA (Organization of African Unity) 55, 236
Ouidah xi, 1, 7, 21, 22, 25, 32, 36, 54, 56, 216
Ouidah Museum of History, The *see* Le Musée d'histoire de Ouidah
Ouidah 92: Retrouvailles Afriques-Amériques 24, 43n31, 47, 55, 73n37, 73n38, 232
Oyo Empire 17

Paes, Eduardo 100
Pai João 12, 179, 184, 203, 206, 208n22
Paizinho Preto 166–7, 177n91
palenque 191
palenque San Basilio 196
Palmares Quilombo 5, 172, 202, 205–6, 210n88, 214, 240
Parque Apolo (Apolo Park) 196
Pastor, Miguel 166–8, 172
Patrocínio, José do 149, 153, 167
pau-de-arara 131, 133
Pedra do Sal (Salt Stone) 100
Pelosi, Nancy 125–6, 144, 232
Pelotas: city 133; Stream 134–5
Pelourinho (Salvador's neighborhood) 118–19, 137
Pelourinho (whipping post) 121, 128, 131, 139–40
People's National Party (Jamaica) 192, 208n49
Pernambuco xii, 29, 87–8, 105–6, 112n110, 127–8

Pétré-Grenouilleau, Olivier 70, 74n88
Petrópolis 163, 164, 169, 170, 171
Pilgrimage 61, 63
Pittman, William Sidney 90
Poland xiii, 51, 185–7, 206
Porto Alegre xii, 119, 121–3, 128, 132, 137, 143n29
Porto de Galinhas (Porto of Chickens) 88–9
Portugal 6–7, 14n18, 19, 54, 121, 134
Praça da Forca (Gallows Square) 121, 123
Praça XV (Square XV) 97
Praia do Chega Nego (Beach where the Black Arrives) 88
preto velho(s) 167, 18
Prince Among Slaves (film) 16, 35, 219
Pruitt, Dwain 59
public guilt 24
public memory 8, 9, 12, 14n18, 65, 69, 76–7, 85, 88, 93–4, 103, 117, 128, 146–7, 152, 173, 174, 183, 196, 199, 205; maroons 206; of Lincoln 158, 160; of Princess Isabel 214; of slave rebels 179; of slavery 14n18, 76, 89, 94, 103, 128, 199, 215; of the Atlantic slave trade 45, 60; of the Holocaust 2, 12, 179

Quadros, Jânio 169
Quilombo (film) 203, 239
Quilombo of Leblon 149

racism 7, 9, 11, 26, 51, 111n61, 143, 166, 174, 200, 203, 212–13
Ralph Appelbaum Associates 79, 109
Rapoport, Natan 185
Ray, Henrietta Cordelia 157
Rebouças, André 98, 149, 167, 171
Recife 10, 81, 85, 88, 105, 108, 153
Rede Globo (television channel) 134, 135
Redeemer *see* Princess Isabel
Republic of Benin xi, 2, 10, 18, 23–5, 29, 45, 47, 65
returnees 32, 56
Revista Illustrada xiii, 152, 234
Revolt of the Prisoners (monument) 188
Rey Benkos *see* Domingos Bioho
Rey de la Matuna *see* Domingos Bioho
Ribbe, Claude 70
Ringard, Captain 21

Rio de Janeiro xi, xii, 5, 10, 11, 32, 77, 85–7, 91, 97–103, 105, 108, 109, 127–8, 133, 146, 149, 153–4, 162–74, 176n67, 177n99, 181–3, 204–7, 213
Rio de Janeiro: Porto Maravilha (Rio de Janeiro: Wonderful Port) 99, 111n95, 224, 240
Rio Grande do Sul xii, 119–23, 128, 132–4, 216
Rios, Ana Lugão 8
Ritchie, Alexander Hay xiii, 149, 150
Rivedoux, Adolphe d'Hastrel xi, 57
robbery 17, 29, 119, 128
Roberts, Blain 91
Rodrigues, Albert 194
Rodrigues, Jaime 98
Roosevelt, Theodore 90
Roots (novel) 37, 219
Roots (television series) 183, 239
Rosa Parks 5, 126, 144 n45, 236, 239
Rothberg, Michael 7, 10, 45, 51, 208n27
Roux, Emmanuel de 60
Rua Bom Jesus (former Rua da Cruz) 105
Rua da Cruz *see* Rua Bom Jesus
Rugendas, Johann Moritz xii, 82, 86, 87, 107, 128, 131, 139
Ryvangen Memorial Grove 79

Saint-Hilaire, Auguste 133–4
Salazar G., Óscar 198
samba 100, 172
samba de roda 154
San Basilio de Palenque (village) xiii, 197–8
Sankofa symbol 96
San Lorenzo de los Negros 191
São Paulo xii, 79, 82–3, 153, 180–2, 203
Savage, Kirk 155, 157
Scenes of Africa (book) 23, 31–3
Schomburg Center for Research in Black Culture 94
Scott, Charlotte 155, 156
Seaga, Edward 193
Seck, Ibrahima 63
Second World War 1, 12, 46, 54, 66, 69, 74n84, 79, 179, 182, 185, 206
Selinger, Shelomo xii, 67, 68
Senegal 2, 7, 10, 14n21, 40, 45, 57, 59, 60, 63–5, 80

senzala xiii, 136, 137
Seven Portuguese Wonders in the World, The (Portuguese contest) 6
Sharpe, Sam 192, 193, 199
Sharpe Square (Jamaica) 193, 194
Sierra Leone 14n21, 45, 47, 93
signare(s) 57, 60, 61, 65, 73n43
Silva, Luiz Inácio Lula da 61, 99, 135
Singleton, Theresa 65
Slave Isaura (character) 12, 179, 182, 183–4, 203
slave market(s) 76, 85–6, 88, 97, 102–3, 105, 107
slave narratives 2, 16, 28, 33, 36–7, 47, 80, 85, 113, 218
slave raids 16, 26, 28–9, 34, 37, 49, 211
slave resistance 12, 179, 185, 203, 205, 208n34
Slave Route Project, The 3, 4, 7, 89, 90, 108, 188, 199
slavery 10, 18, 24, 29–31, 33, 35–8, 41, 50–1, 54, 64–5, 69–70, 72, 87, 95, 104, 125, 136, 137, 174, 206, 209n61, 215; apologies for 71; commemoration 6, 8, 16, 163, 164, 192, 195, 198, 205, 211; contemporary 11; heritage/heritage sites 1, 57, 60, 99, 116, 133, 142, 187, 193, 211, 213; history of 9, 82, 135; images of 40, 128; in Bahia (Salvador)104; in Brazil 11, 29, 105, 118–19, 124, 128, 133, 139, 146–9, 153, 181, 202; in the British colonies 32, 80, 192; in Colombia 196; in the French colonies 4, 78; in Jamestown 90; in Mexico 191; in museums 4, 26–7, 108, 137–42; in New York City 94, 97; in Porto Alegre 121, 122; in Rio de Janeiro 32, 184; in Rio Grande do Sul 135; in the United States 115, 146–8, 159, 181, 187, 208n33; in Venezuela 200; legacies of 9, 11, 14n18, 51, 142–3, 213, 214; memory/memories of 45–7, 49, 70, 92; tourism 53, 89
slave ship xii, xvi, 33, 56, 77–84, 86–9, 96, 102, 108, 212

Slaves' Route (Ouidah) 24, 56
Smith, Venture *see* Broteer Furro
Smithsonian Castle 127
Snelgrave, William 18, 19, 218
Soglo, Nicéphore 54–5
Solar do Unhão xiii, 136–7
Someone Knows My Name (novel) 36
Souza, Francisco Félix de 18–19, 42n11, 56
Spain 6, 7, 198
Spielberg, Steven 34–5, 160, 239
Sullivan's Island 92–3
Suzin, Mark Leon 185
Sweet, James H. 29

Taylor, Isaac xi, 23, 31–4
Taylor, Jason DeCaires 83, 240
Tercentenary Monument 90
Teresa Cristina (Empress) 98, 163, 171
Transatlantic Slave Trade Database: Voyages, The 13n1, 73n54 and n55, 84, 110n51
Thomas, Christopher A. 154
Tilghman, Mary D. 116–17
Tilghman, Richard 116
Tio Quincas *see* Paizinho Preto
Tokoudagba, Cyprien xi, 25
tourism 2–3, 48, 52–3, 63, 103–4, 113, 119, 133–4, 136, 142
Treze de Maio (May Thirteenth) 154
tronco xii, 130–1
Truth, Sojourner 5, 124–6, 142, 144n41, 187–8, 240
Turner, William 78

Última hora (newspaper) 168, 169, 176n71, 177n104, 217, 227, 231, 232, 237
Um defeito de cor (novel) 36
Uncle Tom (character) 12, 179–81, 183–4, 203, 206
Uncle Tom's Cabin (film) 207n1, 239
Uncle Tom's Cabin (novel) 180, 183
UNESCO 1, 3, 4, 7, 11, 26, 47, 48, 55, 56, 60, 64, 73n47, 89, 90, 91, 99, 100, 108, 119, 137, 142, 188, 195, 198, 199, 212
União dos Homens de Côr (Union of Men of Color) 166
Union des Étudiants Juifs de France (Union of Jewish Students of France) 69

United States Holocaust Memorial Museum 16, 79, 187, 216
US Congress 95, 124–6, 144 n38, 149

Vallejo, Luis Guillermo 196
Valongo Wharf 85, 97–101
Vanguarda Armada Revolucionária Palmares (Palmares Armed Revolutionary Vanguard) 202
Vargas, Darcy 163, 182, 207n14
Vargas, Getúlio 18, 161, 164, 176n67, 177n104, 207n14, 223
Venezuela xiii, 4, 179, 200–1, 204, 206, 209n78
Veracruz 190, 191
Verger, Pierre 55, 81
Vesey, Denmark 92–3, 110n55, 239
Vichy 66, 69, 74n86
Vicissitudes xii, xvi, 83–4
victimhood 2, 15, 42, 65, 128, 180, 188
victimization 11, 128, 133, 141–2, 181, 183, 213
Vodun 24, 30, 44n44, 55, 56

Wagener, Zacharias 105
Wallace, Elizabeth Kowaleski 49
Wallenberg, Raoul 125, 144n40
Walsh, Reverend Robert 86, 105, 106
warfare 9, 15–17, 21, 23–4, 28–9, 37–8, 41, 43n36, 199, 211
Warsaw Ghetto 51, 185–7, 208n27
Washington DC 3–5, 11, 79, 124, 127, 142, 146, 153, 155, 157, 160–1, 166, 174, 213–14
Washington, Booker T. 150
Weitzman, Steven 126, 219
West Africa 1–3, 7, 9, 14n21, 15–19, 21, 26, 34–8, 41–2, 45–8, 52–3, 65, 71, 127, 212
West Central Africa 9, 14n21, 15–16, 26, 37, 42, 71, 91, 211–12
West India Docks 26
White House 149
Wiesel, Elie 50, 54–5, 72n29, 117, 187, 219, 239
William Wilberforce House Museum 80
Williams, Daryle 85
Winfrey, Oprah 54, 117, 239
Wonders of the African World (film documentary) 49–50, 238
Wood, Marcus 9, 103, 153, 177 n108

World Heritage List 47, 48, 60, 73n62, 99, 100, 119, 137, 195, 212
Wright, Charles H. 79
written narratives 7, 9, 15–16, 18, 46, 113, 142, 150
Wye House 114–17, 143n12

Yanga (municipality) xiii, 190, 192
Yanga, Gaspar xiii, 190–2, 195, 198, 200
Young, James E. 185
Youssou N'Dour: Return to Gorée (film) 61–2, 74n67, 219, 239

Zangara 35–6
Zips, Werner 199
Zong 77, 109n3
Zoungbodji 56
Zumbi xiii, 5, 12, 172, 174, 179, 202–7, 210n81, 214

CPSIA information can be obtained
at www.ICGtesting.com
Printed in the USA
FSHW011253101019
62892FS